SERIES ENDORSEMENTS

"There are so many fine commentaries available today, but it's great to have a reliable author you can turn to for solid Reformed reflection on Scripture. In this case, there are sixteen of them—friends and fellow shepherds who have given me great insight into God's Word over the years. I'm looking forward eagerly to Fesko's Galatians commentary—and to each one after that!"

Michael S. Horton

J. Gresham Machen Professor of Apologetics and Systematic Theology at Westminster Seminary California

Host of the *White Horse Inn* Talk Show

Editor-in-Chief of *Modern Reformation* magazine

"Those of us who have promoted and practiced *lectio continua* expository preaching through the years eagerly await the volumes Tolle Lege Press has announced in its *Lectio Continua Expository Commentary on the New Testament.* We are equally eager to read such a series written by pastors who have practiced the method in their churches. The international and interdenominational character of the series will only add to the richness of its insights."

T. David Gordon

Professor of Religion and Greek at Grove City College

Author of *Why Johnny Can't Preach* (P&R, 2009)

SERIES ENDORSEMENTS

"As the history of preaching is unfolded, it becomes clear how important the orderly, systematic preaching through the Scriptures has been, and why it has been a favorite homiletic approach over the centuries. One is surprised to discover how many of history's great preachers made a regular practice of preaching through one book of the Bible after another. Origen, the first Christian preacher from whom we have any sizable collection of sermons, preached most of his sermons on the *lectio continua*. We find the same with John Chrysostom who is usually referred to as the greatest Christian preacher. We find the same true of Augustine as well. At the time of the Protestant Reformation, Zwingli, Calvin, Bucer, and Knox followed this system regularly, and they passed it on to the Puritans. Today, we see a real revival of *lectio continua* preaching. *The Lectio Continua Expository Commentary on the New Testament* represents a wonderful opportunity for the Church to recover a truly expository pulpit."

Hughes Oliphant Old

Retired John H. Leith Professor
of Reformed Theology and Worship at
Erskine Theological Seminary
Author of *The Reading and Preaching of the Scriptures in the Worship of the Christian Church* (7 vols., Eerdmans, 2007)

"The concept behind this series is a fascinating one and, given the list of authors, I am confident that the final product will not disappoint. This promises to be a great resource for churches seeking to know the Word of God more fully."

Carl R. Trueman

Professor of Church History at
Westminster Theological Seminary in Philadelphia, PA

THE LECTIO CONTINUA
EXPOSITORY COMMENTARY ON THE NEW TESTAMENT

Hebrews

David B. McWilliams

Series Editor
Jon D. Payne

TOLLE LEGE PRESS
POWDER SPRINGS, GEORGIA

THE LECTIO CONTINUA EXPOSITORY COMMENTARY SERIES

Hebrews

by David B. McWilliams

Series Editor: Jon D. Payne

Produced and Distributed by:

TOLLE LEGE PRESS
147 Ponderosa Trail
Dallas, GA 30132

www.TolleLegePress.com
800–651–0211

Jacket design by Jennifer Tyson

Type design by Luis Lovelace

Photograph of City Cathedral in Basel, Switzerland by Wadyslaw.

ISBN: 978-1-938139-01-7

Printed in the United States of America.

Consulting Editors

DR. JOEL R. BEEKE (Ph.D. Westminster Seminary)
Professor of Systematic Theology and Homiletics and President of
Puritan Reformed Theological Seminary
Pastor of the Heritage Netherlands Reformed Congregation
Editorial Director of Reformation Heritage Books,
Grand Rapids, Michigan

DR. T. DAVID GORDON (Ph.D. Union Theological Seminary)
Professor of Religion and Greek at Grove City College, Pennsylvania
Former Associate Professor of New Testament at
Gordon-Conwell Theological Seminary, Boston, Massachusetts

DR. DAVID W. HALL (Ph.D. Whitefield Seminary)
Pastor of Midway Presbyterian Church (PCA) in
Powder Springs, Georgia
General Editor of and contributor to *The Calvin 500 Series* (P&R)

REV. ERIC LANDRY (M.Div. Westminster Seminary California)
Pastor of Christ Presbyterian Church in Murrieta, California
Executive Editor of *Modern Reformation* magazine

DR. MALCOLM MACLEAN (D.Min. Highland Theological College)
Pastor of Greyfriars Free Church of Scotland in Inverness
Editor of Christian Focus Publication's Mentor imprint

DR. WILLIAM M. SCHWEITZER (Ph.D. University of Edinburgh)
Pastor of Gateshead Presbyterian Church (EPCEW) in
Newcastle/Gateshead, England

DR. GUY P. WATERS (Ph.D. Duke University)
Professor of New Testament at Reformed Theological Seminary
Former Assistant Professor of Biblical Studies at
Belhaven College, Jackson, Mississippi

To My Parents

Contents

Contents

Abbreviations used in the Lectio Continua Series

*	Author's translation
BDAG	Bauer-Danker Greek-English Lexicon
ca.	Circa
CNTC	Calvin's New Testament Commentaries
CTS	Calvin Translation Society
ESV	English Standard Version
KJV	King James Version
LXX	Septuagint
Macc.	Maccabees—Apocryphal Book
NICNT	New International Commentary on the New Testament
NICOT	New International Commentary on the Old Testament
NIV	New International Version
NKJ	New King James
NRSV	New Revised Standard Version
NSBT	New Studies in Biblical Theology
WCF	Westminster Confession of Faith
WSC	Westminster Shorter Catechism
ZECNT	Zondervan Exegetical Commentary on the New Testament

BOOKS OF THE BIBLE

Genesis	**Gen.**	2 Chronicles	**2 Chron.**	Daniel	**Dan.**
Exodus	**Exod.**	Ezra	**Ezra**	Hosea	**Hos.**
Leviticus	**Lev.**	Nehemiah	**Neh.**	Joel	**Joel**
Numbers	**Num.**	Esther	**Esth.**	Amos	**Amos**
Deuteronomy	**Deut.**	Job	**Job**	Obadiah	**Obad.**
Joshua	**Josh.**	Psalms	**Ps.**	Jonah	**Jonah**
Judges	**Judg.**	Proverbs	**Prov.**	Micah	**Mic.**
Ruth	**Ruth**	Ecclesiastes	**Eccl.**	Nahum	**Nah.**
1 Samuel	**1 Sam.**	Song of Solomon	**Song**	Habakkuk	**Hab.**
2 Samuel	**2 Sam.**	Isaiah	**Isa.**	Zephaniah	**Zeph.**
1 Kings	**1 Kings**	Jeremiah	**Jer.**	Haggai	**Hag.**
2 Kings	**2 Kings**	Lamentations	**Lam.**	Zechariah	**Zech.**
1 Chronicles	**1 Chron.**	Ezekiel	**Ezek.**	Malachi	**Mal.**

Matthew	**Matt.**	Ephesians	**Eph.**	Hebrews	**Heb.**
Mark	**Mark**	Philippians	**Phil.**	James	**James**
Luke	**Luke**	Colossians	**Col.**	1 Peter	**1 Pet.**
John	**John**	1 Thessalonians	**1 Thess.**	2 Peter	**2 Pet.**
Acts	**Acts**	2 Thessalonians	**2 Thess.**	1 John	**1 John**
Romans	**Rom.**	1 Timothy	**1 Tim.**	2 John	**2 John**
1 Corinthians	**1 Cor.**	2 Timothy	**2 Tim.**	3 John	**3 John**
2 Corinthians	**2 Cor.**	Titus	**Titus**	Jude	**Jude**
Galatians	**Gal.**	Philemon	**Philem.**	Revelation	**Rev.**

City Cathedral in Basel, Switzerland where Johannes Oecolampadius preached

Series Introduction

The greatest need of the church today is the recovery of sound biblical preaching that faithfully explains and applies the text, courageously confronts sin, and boldly trumpets forth the sovereign majesty, law, and promises of God. This type of powerful preaching has vanished in many quarters of the evangelical church only to be replaced by that which is anemic and man-centered. Instead of doctrinally rich exposition which strengthens faith and fosters Christian maturity, the standard fare has become informal, chatty, anecdote-laden messages, leaving unbelievers confused, and believers in a state of chronic spiritual adolescence.[1]

There is indeed a dire need for the recovery of solid biblical preaching. Not only does reformation of this sort lead Christ's sheep back to the verdant pastures of his soul-nourishing Word, it also provides a good example to future generations of ministers. For this reason, I am pleased to introduce *The Lectio Continua Expository Commentary on the New Testament* (LCECNT), a new series of expository commentaries authored by an array of seasoned pastor-scholars from various Reformed denominations on both sides of the Atlantic.

---

1. A stinging, yet constructive critique of modern-day preaching is found in T. David Gordon's *Why Johnny Can't Preach: The Media Have Shaped the Messengers* (Phillipsburg, NJ: P&R, 2009). "I have come to recognize that many, many individuals today have never been under a steady diet of competent preaching. . . . As starving children in Manila sift through the landfill for food, Christians in many churches today have never experienced genuine soul-nourishing preaching, and so they just pick away at what is available to them, trying to find a morsel of spiritual sustenance or helpful counsel here or there" (Gordon, *Why Johnny Can't Preach*, 17).

What is the *lectio continua* method of preaching? It is simply the uninterrupted, systematic, expository proclamation of God's Word—verse by verse, chapter by chapter, book by book. It is a system, unlike topical or thematic preaching, that endeavors to deliver the whole counsel of God (Acts 20:26–27). Christian discipleship is impoverished when large portions of Scripture are ignored. Carried out faithfully, the *lectio continua* method ensures that every passage is mined for its riches (even those verses which are obscure, controversial, or hard to swallow). Paul states that "all Scripture is breathed out by God and profitable for teaching, for reproof, for correction, and for training in righteousness, that the man of God may be competent, equipped for every good work" (2 Tim. 3:16–17).

Lectio continua preaching has a splendid heritage. It finds its roots in the early church and patristic eras. Its use, however, was revived and greatly expanded during the sixteenth-century Protestant Reformation. When Huldrych Zwingli (d. 1531) arrived at the Zurich Grossmünster in 1519, it was his desire to dispense with the standard lectionary and introduce *lectio continua* preaching to his congregation by moving systematically through the Gospel of Matthew. At first, some members of his church council were suspicious. They were uncomfortable replacing the lectionary with this seemingly new approach. But Zwingli explained that the *lectio continua* method of preaching was not new at all. On the contrary, important figures such as Augustine (d. 430), Chrysostom (d. 407) and Bernard of Clairvaux (d. 1153) all employed this homiletical strategy. Zwingli is quoted by his successor Heinrich Bullinger (d. 1575) as saying that "no friend of evangelical truth could have any reason to complain" about such a method.[2]

---

2. It is interesting to note that, the year before Zwingli began preaching sequentially through books of the Bible, he had received a new edition of Chrysostom's *lectio continua* sermons on Matthew's Gospel. See Hughes Oliphant Old, *The Patristic Roots of Reformed Worship* (Black Mountain, NC: Worship

Series Introduction

Zwingli rightly believed that the quickest way to restore biblical Christianity to the church was to preach the whole counsel of God verse by verse, chapter by chapter, book by book, Lord's Day after Lord's Day, year after year. Other reformers agreed and followed his pattern. In the city of Strasbourg, just ninety miles north of Zurich, men such as Martin Bucer (d. 1551), Wolfgang Capito (d. 1570), and Kaspar Hedio (d. 1552) practiced *lectio continua* preaching. Johannes Oecolampadius (d. 1531) boldly preached the *lectio continua* in Basel. And let us not forget John Calvin (d. 1564); between 1549 and 1564, the Genevan reformer preached sequentially through no fewer than twenty-five books of the Bible (over 2,000 sermons).[3]

The example of these reformers has been emulated by preachers throughout the centuries, from the Post-Reformation age down to the present. In the last half of the twentieth century, Martyn Lloyd-Jones (d. 1981), William Still (d. 1997), James Montgomery Boice (d. 2000), and John MacArthur all boldly marched straight through books of the Bible from their pulpits. But why? Surely we have acquired better, more contemporary methods of preaching? Is the *lectio continua* relevant in our twenty-first century context? In a day when biblical preaching is being increasingly undermined and marginalized by media/story/therapy/personality-driven sermons, even among the avowedly Reformed, these are important questions to consider.

Shortly before the Apostle Paul was martyred in Rome by Emperor Nero, he penned a second epistle to Timothy. In what proved to be some of his final words to his young disciple, he

---

Press, 2004), 195. Cf. Old's *The Reading and Preaching of the Scriptures in the Worship of the Christian Church*, vol. 4: *The Age of the Reformation* (Grand Rapids, MI: Eerdmans, 2002), and Timothy George, *Reading Scripture with the Reformers* (Downers Grove, IL: IVP Academic, 2011), 228–253. Elements of this introduction are adapted from Jon D. Payne, "The Roaring of Christ through *Lectio Continua* Preaching," *Modern Reformation* (Nov./Dec. 2010; Vol. 19, No. 6): 23–24, and are used by permission of the publisher.

3. T. H. L. Parker, *Calvin's Preaching* (Edinburgh: T&T Clark, 1992), 159.

wrote, "I charge you in the presence of God and of Christ Jesus
... *preach the word*; be ready in season and out of season; reprove,
rebuke, and exhort, with complete patience and teaching" (2
Tim. 4:1–2). This directive was not meant for only Timothy. No,
it is the primary duty of every Christian minister (and church)
to carefully heed and obey these timeless words; according to
God's divine blueprint for ministry, it is chiefly through the
faithful proclamation of the Word that Christ saves, sanctifies,
and comforts the beloved Church for which He died.[4] In other
words, the preaching of the Gospel and the right administration
of the sacraments are the divinely sanctioned and efficacious
means by which Christ and all his benefits of redemption are
communicated to the elect. For this reason alone the *lectio continua* method of preaching should be the predominant, regular
practice of our churches, providing a steady diet of Law and
Gospel from the entirety of God's Word.

Some may ask, "Why another expository commentary series?" First, because in every generation it is highly valuable
to provide fresh, doctrinally sound, and reliable expositions
of God's Word. Every age possesses its own set of theological,
ecclesiastical, and cultural challenges. In addition, it is benefi-
cial for both current and rising ministers in every generation to
have trustworthy contemporary models of biblical preaching.
Second, the LCECNT uniquely features the expositions of an
array of pastors from a variety of Reformed and confessional
traditions. Consequently, this series brings a wealth of exegetical, confessional, cultural, and practical insight, and furnishes
the reader with an instructive and stimulating selection of *lectio
continua* sermons.

This series is not meant to be an academic or highly technical
commentary. There are many helpful exegetical commentaries

---

4. See Matthew 28:18–20; Romans 10:14–17; 1 Corinthians 1:18–21; 1 Peter 1:22–25, 2:2–3; Westminster Shorter Catechism Q. 89.

written for that purpose. Rather, the aim is to provide *lectio continua* sermons, originally delivered to Reformed congregations, which clearly and faithfully communicate the context, meaning, gravity, and application of God's inerrant Word. Each volume of expositions aspires to be redemptive-historical, covenantal, Reformed and confessional, trinitarian, person-and-work-of-Christ-centered, and teeming with practical application. Therefore, the series will be a profound blessing to every Christian believer who longs to "grow in the grace and knowledge of our Lord and Savior Jesus Christ" (2 Pet. 3:18).

A project of this magnitude does not happen without the significant contributions of many people. First, I want to thank Raymond, Brandon, and Jared Vallorani of Tolle Lege Press. Their willingness to publish this voluminous set of commentaries is less about their desire to blossom as a Reformed publishing house and more about their sincere love for Christ and the faithful proclamation of the Bible. Also, many thanks to my fellow preachers who graciously agreed to participate in this series. It is a privilege to labor with you for the sake of the Gospel, the health and extension of the church, and the recovery of *lectio continua* preaching. Thanks to the editorial staff of Tolle Lege Press, especially Eric Rauch, Vice President of Publishing and Michael Minkoff, Copy Editor. Thanks are also due to Dr. Brian Cosby, Dr. David Hall, Rev. Ross Hodges, Dr. Gabriel Williams, Dr. Bill Schweitzer, Rev. Eric Landry, and Mrs. Vicky McWilliams for their editorial contributions to this volume.

Thanks also must be given to the congregation of Christ Church Presbyterian, Charleston, South Carolina, for warmly encouraging their minister to work on projects such as this one which impact the wider church. Furthermore, I would like to express the deepest gratitude to my dear wife, Marla, and our two precious children, Mary Hannah and Hans. The peace and joy in our home, nurtured by delightful Lord's Days, regular family worship, and a loving, patient wife, makes editing a series like this one possible.

Finally, and most importantly, sincere thanks and praise must be given to our blessed triune God, the eternal fountain of all grace and truth. By his sovereign love and mercy, through faith in the crucified, resurrected, and ascended Christ, we have been "born again, not of perishable seed but of imperishable, through the living and abiding word of God; for 'All flesh is like grass and all its glory like the flower of grass. The grass withers and the flower falls, but the word of the Lord remains forever.' And this word is the good news *that was preached to you*" (1 Pet. 1:23–25).

Jon D. Payne
Series Editor
Charleston, SC

Preface

Preaching is the chief theological medium. So I have ever believed; so have I taught my students in Systematic Theology, and my congregation. The chief theological medium is not the classroom lecture, a theology book, or the theological journal—important as these are. Preaching the Word of God is the minister's primary calling and task. By preaching, sinners are called to Christ, the church is instructed, and God's people are led to heaven. Nothing can be substituted for preaching; nothing compares with its importance for the soundness and future usefulness of the church. When the Word is preached something supernatural is taking place. How we should long for a revival of preaching.

Therefore, when Jon Payne, editor of *The Lectio Continua Expository Commentary on the New Testament* asked me to prepare a volume on Hebrews, I was happy to comply. Unlike my Mentor commentary on Galatians in which some technical matters show through, the exegetical detail remains for the most part hidden in this volume on Hebrews. This is not a technical commentary but, rather, an exposition that expands on my sermons on Hebrews. The references to other works on Hebrews are intentionally kept at a minimum and much of the vast literature that I have been privileged to study is not even mentioned.

I sincerely hope that this will not be off-putting to those who desire to think seriously about this portion of God's Word. After all, since preaching is the chief theological medium, the sort of exposition required by the *Lectio Continua* series should benefit Christians at all levels of preparation, just as the Sunday sermons should bless the mature, the less mature, those long in the faith, those new to the faith, the very learned and those just beginning to learn. Indeed, Jon Payne specified that the authors of the series produce expositions that are exegetical, God-centered, applicatory, and with quotes and illustrations; in brief, expositions that are sermonic in nature. This I have attempted to do, reflecting my own sermons on Hebrews.

I have noted often in my reading how many of the sound, old preachers of Scotland were also Biblical commentators. It seems to me still that those best able to produce commentaries are those called of the Lord to weekly exposition of the Word on the Sabbath. David Dickson (1583–1663), the first to write a commentary on the *Westminster Confession,* was also a noted Biblical commentator who was the motivating force behind a notable series of commentaries from that era. "From these volumes," writes the venerable John Macleod, "men may see what good work was the outcome of the old Scottish habit of lecturing in order through the books of Scriptures. This method of pulpit instruction was based on a careful exegesis of the text and it interwove into its fabric the doctrine and the connections of doctrine that were brought to light by the exposition of the passage." Macleod's conclusion represents the same design as *The Lectio Continua* series, for he adds:

> The Church is debtor to David Dickson for initiating and giving an impetus to this exegetical and expository movement which was meant to bring to the common man in the pew and at the hearth the ripe fruit of academic work so that in the best sense the learning of the study might be made popular.[1]

Should the Spirit of God so bless our feeble efforts to revive exposition through books of the Bible where it has been ne-

1. John Macleod, *Scottish Theology In Relation to Church History* (Edinburgh: Banner of Truth, 1974), 85–86.

glected and to feed the flock of God thereby, would we not be humbly and immensely grateful?

This exposition of Hebrews is sent out with prayer for such blessing and with the earnest desire of bringing glory to the great High Priest of his people, Jesus Christ the sovereign Head and King of the church. My gratitude is boundless toward my wife who already sees me turning to another writing project subordinate to my preaching ministry and supports my endeavor. I am grateful to the Session of Covenant Presbyterian Church in Lakeland, Florida for encouraging me to work at odd moments on projects such as this one and to eager listeners and doers of the Word to whom I preach, as a norm, three times per week. Thanks go to Jon Payne and all who have helped make it possible to send forth this exposition of sacred Scripture and to *Tolle Lege Press* for desiring to publish the series and to do so in such an attractive and useful format.

Although I have benefited from innumerable writers on Hebrews, the commentaries of Philip E. Hughes and of F. F. Bruce still appeal to me as among the best, as well as the older work of John Brown of Edinburgh. Their finger prints will be found throughout my sermons on the marvelous book of Hebrews.

Praise to the Lamb that was slain who now as High Priest intercedes for his people. *Soli Deo Gloria!*

David B. McWilliams, Ph.D.
The Minister's Study
February, 2015

Introduction

Christ who redeemed us from our sins is firmly secured in his exalted, heavenly glory at the Father's right hand. No matter what discouragements come to believers in Jesus, this incontestable fact, once we find the truth of it lodged deeply within our hearts, wins out over all troubles and hindrances to our progress in Christian living. No other New Testament book sets forth the present work of Christ for us as does Hebrews. The sustained emphasis of this hybrid sermon-epistle is what Christ is doing right now for the people he redeemed once for all. Therefore, it is sad that Hebrews is so little known, read, or understood by many professing Christians.

Let us grant from the start that understanding Hebrews presents challenges. The constant references to Old Testament revelation,[1] our limited knowledge of its setting and authorship, and its complex inner logic, sustained by many subthemes, makes Hebrews a difficult book. Yet, when we begin to see Christ's achievement and glory and his present intercessory reign, as well as the implications for our daily struggles, who can doubt that learning Hebrews and meditating on the truth revealed in its pages is worth the effort?

It is, after all, a part of God's Word, and one that stresses from start to finish the continuing ministry of Jesus for us. A number of considerations encourage our pursuit of Hebrews as this brief

---

1. George Guthrie has counted "roughly thirty-seven quotations, forty allusions, nineteen cases where OT material is summarized, and thirteen where an OT name or topic is referred to without reference to specific context." *Hebrews*, in *Commentary on the New Testament Use of the Old Testament*, ed. G. K. Beale, D. A. Carson (Grand Rapids: Baker, 2007), 919.

introduction will indicate. This introduction is not a comprehensive restatement of what will be found in the exposition. My purpose here is first to commend the book of Hebrews to the reader as a vital exhortation for Christians today, and then to suggest the central themes and main lines of reasoning that should be held in mind as we study Hebrews.

Why Should Christians Today Study Hebrews?

First, Hebrews was written to people like us, to Christians who neared exhaustion in their trials and struggles to live according to the gospel. Like us, some of these Christians were tempted to forget the gospel and felt like going back. The writer of Hebrews, whoever he may have been, is addressing Jewish Christians who having believed in Christ were now being persecuted for their faith. While they have not yet suffered martyrdom their property has been despoiled (10:32–34; 12:4) and the hardships of Christian discipleship were apparent. The pressures of living for Christ required the writer of Hebrews to exhort these Jewish Christians to faithfully persevere in their profession of Christ (e.g. 3:6, 14; 10:23).

The Christology of Hebrews is never abstracted from the everyday reality of Christian living and faithful perseverance. Has the need for encouragement in faithful perseverance changed? Do we have less need for encouragement and exhortation than the original readers of this book? We may need this encouragement for different reasons and in different historical and geographical settings than those to whom Hebrews was originally written. We may not be tempted away from Christ by the same external and internal pressures. Nonetheless, Christians today in lands where persecution is rife or in places where affluence tempts to draw the heart from the Lord need Christ-centered exhortations to stand firm in the faith just as did the original readers of Hebrews.

Introduction

A second related reason for seriously pursuing Hebrews is that here we find exhortation of a special sort; specifically, exhortation that lifts the believer's thoughts and heart to the present rule and reign of Christ our ascended Lord. The exhortation to believe, follow and obey in Hebrews is no bland moralism but is pointedly Christ-centered with a special reference to the intercessory ministry of Christ for his people. This is clear on the face of the book and is demonstrable when two key passages are compared.

The first passage in the comparison is Hebrews 13:22: "I appeal to you, brothers, bear with my word of exhortation, for I have written to you briefly." The point to be seen from this passage is that the entire book of Hebrews is a word of exhortation. The second passage relating to the comparison is Hebrew 8:1–2: "Now the point in what we are saying is this: we have such a high priest, one who is seated at the right hand of the throne of the Majesty in heaven, a minister in the holy places, in the true tent that the Lord set up, not man." This passage shows that a central purpose of Hebrews is to showcase the heavenly, high priestly ministry of Jesus. Therefore, when we take the two passages together, we must conclude that *Hebrews is an exhortation in which the heavenly high priestly ministry of Jesus is the main point.*[2] This confirms our contention that Hebrews should commend itself to us in our need of divine exhortation and the encouragement of Christ's heavenly, intercessory work for us.

The third incentive for seriously pursuing Hebrews is the book's emphasis on the newness that has come as a result of Jesus' work and that his work is "superior" and "better" than everything that has preceded it. Hebrews pulsates with a sense of this newness and superiority of the work of Christ over the old. Christ is superior to the prophets, to angels and to the old

---

2. Dr. Richard Gaffin first made this connection for me when I sat under him as a student. We will look at this more when we reach 8:1ff.

priesthood of Aaron. His sacrifice is better than the sacrifices of the Levitical law, his intercession exceeds that of the old priesthood, and the new covenant that has arrived in Jesus is superior to the old. The writer of Hebrews exhorted the halting, exhausted Jewish Christians to press on rather than return to the passing and provisional. Today, Christians need these reminders. Do not return to the old; rather, grasp the glory of the new in Christ. Let your hearts be swamped and swayed by the wondrous things that Christ has done and is now doing.

Christian, do you feel like turning back? Have you never known this temptation? Do you need strengthening in your faith? Who of us does not?

Who Wrote Hebrews and to Whom?

Before summarizing the main theme, it will be helpful to mention a few typical introductory matters. We do not know who wrote Hebrews. It was once almost universally thought that Paul wrote it, but a few considerations cast Paul's authorship in doubt. The reference to hearing the gospel "by [or from] those who heard" (2:3) may be a reference to the original twelve apostles, and if this is so, it rules Paul out as the author, since he received the gospel by revelation (Gal. 1:11–12). There is also the Greek style of Hebrews, uncommon to Paul. In addition, there is no salutation nor reference to the author in the concluding remarks, as was customary with Paul. Many staples of Paul's epistles are absent such as his use of "Christ Jesus," "in Christ," references to the moral law (the emphasis in Hebrews is on the ceremonial law), and emphasis on the resurrection.

A long list of suggestions has come down to us and much ink has been spilled on the subject, but in reality we simply do not know who wrote the book. In God's providence we have the letter as it stands and are called to read it in canonical perspective deriving benefit from the book with scanty knowledge of its background. After all, we do not know the specific geographical provenance of Hebrews or the location of the readers either. Though we read in 13:24 "those who come from Italy send you greetings" that is no help in determining either question conclusively. The recipients of the letter, however, were Jewish Christians and possibly were unfamiliar with Semitic languages (none of the Old Testament references seems to depend upon the Hebrew text but upon Greek translation). While the emphasis on the sacrificial system might indicate that the Jewish Christians who received the letter were Palestinian, the emphasis on Greek may indicate that the book was written to Hellenistic Jewish Christians of the Diaspora. We simply do not know.

There is a constant emphasis in Hebrews on maintaining a confession of faith in Christ, and the additional sustained emphasis on detailed Old Testament themes undoubtedly means that the recipients were Hebrew Christians. The writer's warnings against apostasy are taken from Old Testament sources and the "elementary teachings" (6:1) indicate an adherence to Judaism or to a Jewish background. As these believers begin to come under persecution (10:34) they are tempted to turn back to their former Judaism, probably failing to understand how such severe treatment is consistent with the rule of Christ as high priest of his people. However, the issue of relating providence and promise is universal for believers and very applicable in our own day and to our circumstances.

Hebrews is preoccupied with the theme of perseverance in the faith and warning against apostasy. The Hebrew Christians tempted to turn back to the old system needed to understand that all things are now "better," by which the author means that the very best has arrived in Christ and is seen in his mediatorial triumph. The temptation to return to Judaism was strong, since the evidence indicates that the Temple was still standing when the writer addressed his theme (Heb. 9:8–9; 10:2–3). The testing of the believer during this time does not in the least alter this reality. B. F. Westcott underscores the stark trial of these Hebrew Christians:

> The student of that epistle [Hebrews] cannot but observe that no men were ever called upon to endure greater sacrifices, to surrender more precious hopes, to bear deeper disappointments, than those to whom it was first addressed. Men who had lived in the light of the Old Testament, men who had known the joy of a noble ritual, men who had habitually drawn near to God in intelligible ways, men who had but lately welcomed Him in Whom they believed that the glory of Israel should be consummated, were most unexpectedly required to face what seemed to them to be the forfeiture of all that they held dearest.[3]

The writer of Hebrews, therefore, is compelled to demonstrate the superiority of the new that has come in Christ.

The Main Themes and Reasoning of Hebrews

There are a variety of themes in the book that can best be seen by observing the flow of the epistle. The epistle is sermonic, that is, filled with exhortation, encouragement, and a constant pressing of the claims of Christ on these believers. Hebrews begins by exalting Christ in his preeminence over prophets and angels (1:1–14) and then underscores in chapters 2–10 the heavenly high priestly ministry of Christ. The Son assumed human nature (2:16–17), enabling him as the God-man to be tempted as the one who cares for the tempted (2:18). The Son's preeminence over Moses is asserted (2:2–6). Israel's failure to enter into Sabbath rest constitutes a warning for God's people today (chapters 3 and 4) but the author stresses the almighty sympathy of the Son, our priest, for his people (4:14–16). Chap-

---

3. Brooke Foss Westcott, *Christus Consummator* (Eugene, OR: Wipf and Stock, 2004), 4.

ter 5 unpacks for us the divine choice of the Son as high priest, with a rebuke and warning for spiritual dullness. The warning against apostasy at the end of the chapter leads to the warning against falling away in chapter 6 along with a promise that true believers will continue faithful (6:9–12).

The great theme of Christ as fulfiller of the priesthood of Melchizedek constitutes the concern of Hebrews 7 in which we learn that Jesus is "the guarantor of a better covenant" who "holds his priesthood permanently, because he continues forever"; consequently, "he is able to save to the uttermost those who draw near to God through him, since he always lives to make intercession for them" (7:22, 24–25). Hebrews 8 defines for us how Christ's mediation is applied in the heavenly sanctuary and provocatively states the newness of the new covenant in Christ. Chapter 9 focuses on Christ's fulfilling and exceeding the types of Old Testament ritual. Chapter 10 stresses that the Jewish sacrifices were inadequate to take away sin, but that Jesus offered a "once for all sacrifice" that is effectual for his people. This chapter contains one of the greatest encouragements in the New Testament to full assurance of faith and drawing near to God's gracious throne (10:19–25) right alongside additional warnings and exhortations to faithfulness.

The eleventh chapter of Hebrews, known universally as the "roll call of faith," unfolds God's promise keeping grace throughout redemptive history. Then, in chapter 12, additional exhortations and warnings are placed in the context of the greater weight of reverence for God demanded by our knowledge of the gospel. Though Mount Sinai was filled with terrible manifestations of God's power and justice, Mount Zion brings with it a new depth of seriousness demanding that God's people live in the reality that "our God is a consuming fire" (12:28). In the final chapter of Hebrews, the duties of believers one to another, including to the church leadership, are underscored along with the call to separation (13:10–14). The epistle is concluded with "one of the noblest doxologies in the N.T."[4]

As you read and study the content of Hebrews, remember that "the progressiveness of divine revelation, then, is the master thought of the Epistle. Christ is the culmination of the long succession of lawgiver and prophets. They existed for his sake; they were a preparation for him."[5]

From this brief survey, the applicability of Hebrews should be clear. Hebrews was written to people like us, to Christians who were nearing exhaustion in their trials and struggles to live gratefully and obediently in response to the gospel. Like us, some of these Christians were tempted to forget and felt like going back. It is sad but true that most Christians have wanted at one time or another to leave it all, forsake Christian profession and return to a life without all the struggles that come to followers of Christ.

The writer of Hebrews, whoever he may have been, is addressing Jewish Christians who, having believed in Christ, were now being persecuted for their faith. While they had not yet suffered martyrdom, their property had been despoiled (12:4). The writer's great concern is to encourage, pastorally and strongly, the perseverance demanded in such circumstances. The writer produced an epistle, more like a sermon, a sermon-epistle, the whole of which was an exhortation. The exhortation, however, was far from mere moralism. It was based on the finished work and heavenly high priestly role of Christ (Heb. 13:22; 8:1).

Though a great variety of themes pervade Hebrews, such as the church as new wilderness community, the Sabbath rest of the people of God, the relationship between eschatology and ethics, the issue of apostasy, and much more, let us focus brief-

4. A. T. Robertson, *Word Pictures In The New Testament* (Grand Rapids: Baker, 1932), 5.451.

5. J. Gresham Machen, *The New Testament: An Introduction to its Literature and History* (Edinburgh: Banner of Truth, 1976), 248.

ly on a few points best kept in mind about the heavenly high priestly work of Christ. The epistle stresses the superiority of Christ throughout. Christ is superior to angels, to Moses and Joshua, but particularly to Aaron. Here we find the pervading theme of Hebrews. The Son died once for all, established the new and better covenant, and in his exalted state intercedes for his people.

The book's stress on the heavenly, high priestly ministry of Christ is the main incentive for perseverance and the chief enticement for Christians to indwell the words, content, and pages of Hebrews. While there are many theological themes in Hebrews, the chief and foremost concern of Hebrews is to set forth for the weak and feeble Christian the encouragement of the heavenly, high priestly ministry of Christ. Indeed, this is the writer's main point (8:1). The writer emphasizes that, in Christ our priest, things are "better." The best has arrived in Christ, superior to the old, leading on to our eternal rest.

At the forefront of our study of Hebrews, these are some thoughts to keep in mind regarding the priestly work of Christ:

First, *the priestly work of Christ is inseparable from his person.* Hebrews is dominated by the magnificence of Christ's person. The Deity of Christ is stressed in a number of ways in the first chapter. The one ascended is the Son of God who assumed human nature and died for sinners. The new phase of his Messianic rule in the ascension is founded in the author's recognition of Christ's deity.

Second, *the finished work of Christ is foundational to his heavenly ministry.* Unlike the Socinian view that ascribes Christ's priesthood solely to his ascension life, Hebrews (along with other texts in the New Testament) makes it plain that the sacrifice of Christ is part of his priestly work (9:11–12; 24–25; 10:11–12; 13:11–12). This sacrifice is "once for all." The old writers were wise in speaking of "the finished work of Christ," drawing from Hebrews and other passages. Hebrews stresses the accomplishment of redemption through the shed blood of our high priest. This sacrifice is done—finished. It is not continued in his heavenly ministry. His heavenly ministry is the fruit of this once for all accomplishment.

> The heavenly high priesthood of Christ means, therefore, that Christ appears in the presence of God at the right hand of the throne of the Majesty in the heavens to present himself as the perfected high priest to plead, on the basis of what he has accomplished, the fulfillment of all the promises, the bestowment of all the benefits, and the enduement with all the graces secured and ratified by his own high priestly offering. This is a ministry directed to the Father. This is it pre-eminently. The Godward reference is primary here as it is also in the once-for-all priestly offering. But it is also a ministry on behalf of men.[6]

Moreover, it is important to remember, in the words of A. A. Hodge:

> His work of propitiation, therefore, must have been real and not metaphorical, because it is declared to be the substance of which the services of the Levitical priests were the "shadows," "figures," or "types." But shadows are cast by literal substances, not by metaphors; and a type or image necessarily implies real characters and attributes which it represents.[7]

Third, *the sympathy of our high priest finds a specific point of contact with the tempted and tried people of God* (Heb. 2:17–18; 4:14–15). It is for the tried and tempted that the Savior minis-

6. John Murray, *The Heavenly, Priestly Activity of Christ,* in *Collected Writings of John Murray* (Edinburgh: Banner of Truth, 1976), 1.48.

7. A. A. Hodge, *The Atonement* (Philadelphia: Presbyterian Board of Publication, 1867), 157.

ters in his heavenly ministry. Murray's words are overflowing with comfort:

> To view the heavenly sympathy of our Lord from the aspect of our existential need, how indispensable to comfort and to perseverance in faith, to know that in all the temptations of this life we have a sympathizer, and helper, and comforter in the person of him from whom we must conceal nothing, who feels with us in every weakness and temptation, and knows exactly what our situation physical, psychological, moral and spiritual is! And this he knows because he himself was tempted, like as we are, without sin. That he who has this feeling with us in temptation appears in the presence of God for us and is our advocate with the Father invests his sympathy and help with an efficacy that is nothing less than *omnipotent compassion.*[8]

The exalted Savior has not forgotten the power of temptation sufferings and is not indifferent to our predicament as we struggle to please him. Because he carried with him into the heavens the memory of temptation, we can be exhorted to hold firmly to the faith we possess (Heb. 4:14). "For we do not have a high priest who is unable to sympathize with our weaknesses, but one who in every respect has been tempted as we are, yet without sin." Our Savior has truly experienced the weaknesses we believers face so we may "come boldly unto the throne of grace, that we may obtain mercy, and find grace to help in time of need" (Heb. 4:16). The Greek text indicates "timely help"— our text points to the *present* ministry of Christ on our behalf!

Fourth, *the intercession of our high priest is the great theme of Hebrews*, an intercession founded on the once for all, finished atonement of Christ. The atonement of Christ and the intercession of Christ are distinguishable, but are not separable.

8. Murray, *Heavenly, Priestly Activity of Christ*, 50.

The atonement is past—an accomplishment once for all, never again to be repeated. Let us stress, the atonement is finished, complete. There could be no intercessory work of Christ except on the basis of a "once for all" atonement. The intercession of Christ is based upon the finished work of Christ and its efficacy is eternal; it is the constant and ongoing presentation of the fruit of the atonement, the righteousness and merit of Christ on behalf of those for whom Christ died. The intercession of our high priest is the presentation of his merits on the behalf of his people in the presence of God upon his throne where now Christ sits regnant with the Father.

The intercession of Christ is, first of all, *entreaty.* Christ "by his own blood" has "entered in once into the holy place, having obtained eternal redemption for us" (Heb. 9:12). There, in the Most Holy Place, in the very presence of God the Father, Christ the believer's High Priest exercises a ministry of advocacy (1 John 2:1–2).

The intercession of Christ on behalf of his needy people is *effectual intercession.* He is glorified in heaven and his merit is received on our behalf by the Father. His prayer for resurrection was heard by the Father.[9] His greatness and glory are seen in his sitting on God's right hand (Heb. 1:3). His work is accepted and his sitting displays his triumph. His *completed atonement* is accepted and he is conquering this world, making his enemies his footstool (Heb. 10: 11–13).

The point of the book of Hebrews is to encourage the believer in the knowledge that "we have such a high priest, one who is seated on the right hand of the throne of the Majesty in heaven..." (Heb. 8:1). The word of exhortation (13:22) is an invigorating word because our high priest is exalted to God's right hand.

---

9. It seems best to think that *ek thanatou* in Heb. 5:7 means "out of death" and not simply "from death."

Keeping these truths in mind will make our reading of Hebrews most profitable. Let us with joyful anticipation now turn to the text itself. May the Lord bless this exposition to his own glory and to your good as your great high priest supplies grace upon grace for your perseverance in the midst of the trials and triumphs of Christian living.

Hebrews

1

The Glory of Christ

HEBREWS 1:1–3

Long ago, at many times and in many ways, God spoke to our fathers by the prophets, but in these last days he has spoken to us by his Son, whom he appointed the heir of all things, through whom also he created the world. He is the radiance of the glory of God and the exact imprint of his nature, and he upholds the universe by the word of his power. After making purification for sins, he sat down at the right hand of the Majesty on high . . .

Now, the writer addresses the fainting Christian right from the start in the first few verses. How does he do that? The writer encourages believers in faithful perseverance, not by first addressing us, not by beginning overtly with exhortation, but by pointing to Christ and his glory. An essential point for Christian growth is found here. The needs of our feeble hearts are not first to be addressed by immediate, overt exhortation. Rather, the greatest essential of exhortation is that we first dwell upon Christ and not upon ourselves. Refreshment and renewal come to the hearts of Christians when a fresh view of Christ in his glory captivates the mind and affections. Only in the context of this focus on Christ and his work, will overt exhortation impact

1

us; apart from this Christ-centeredness, appeals to the affections are ineffectual. This is what the writer of Hebrews is up to and in this he shows himself to be a wise and skillful pastor of souls. Look now at how he begins.

Christ: More Glorious Than the Prophets

First, the author by divine inspiration wants his readers to see that, *Jesus is more glorious than the prophets.* "Long ago, at many times and in many ways, God spoke to our fathers by the prophets, but in these last days he has spoken to us by his Son." The writer affirms that God is the author of Old Testament revelation. He rejects "limited inspiration," the idea that one part of Scripture is more divinely inspired than another or that some parts of the Bible may be discarded. Rather, the writer of Hebrews understands the progressive unfolding of God's unified plan of redemption and that the coming of Jesus is a matter of fulfillment—indeed, *ultimate* fulfillment.

God spoke to our fathers by the prophets, from Genesis to Revelation, God spoke. God is a speaking God, and his word is verbally inspired. The author of Hebrews says literally that God spoke "in" (not "by") the prophets. Vos rightly points out that this little preposition demonstrates that the prophets were not simply mechanical instruments of revelation but that, the delivery of the prophecy was under God's control.[1] This theme meshes with what the Bible tells us about its inspiration and the unfolding plan of redemption in revelation. Consider: we know God only because God has chosen to reveal himself. Prior to the Fall, God spoke directly to Adam, the representative of humanity. Man was never intended to be without a Word from God. God spoke to Adam, explaining his role and the use of the trees in the garden (Gen. 1:28–29; 2:15–16). God interpreted man's world for him by means of his Word. Two issues are ap-

---

1. Geerhardus Vos, *The Teaching of the Epistle to the Hebrews*, 72.

parent: (a) it is *normal* (recall we are speaking of the pre-Fall setting) for God to communicate with man; (b) that communication from the beginning was *verbal*. The broken relationship between God and man after the fall is discernible in the fact that God no longer spoke to man without intermediaries, that is, without his servants the prophets. However, the fact that he spoke even through the prophets demonstrates God's gracious desire to continue communications with man even after the Fall.

The Lord revealed himself to the prophets *at many times and in many ways*. The prophets spoke God's Word and not their own (2 Pet. 1:21) and the wonder of the revelation often eluded them (1 Pet. 1:10). In the unfolding of the redemptive drama the Lord revealed himself through dreams, voices, angels, visions, divine promptings, and miracles. Indeed, the writer of Hebrews is likely reflecting upon Numbers 12:6–7 which tells us some of the ways that God would reveal his will to prophets other than Moses with whom the Lord spoke "mouth to mouth." Though there was a variety in the manner of revelation, yet the revelation was in essence unified. Though there is variety in Scripture, it is fundamentally single-minded. There is one grand theme and that is the person and work of Christ. All that went before finds its ultimate fulfillment and final revelation in Christ: "Long ago, at many times and in many ways, God spoke to our fathers by the prophets, but in these last days he has spoken to us by his Son."

The coming of the Son brings to completion the revelation of the gospel and the fulfillment of the old. God has now given to us a complete revelation of his saving purpose in the coming of Christ. "This is the real theme of the whole letter: the past has given way to better things."[2] Those of us to whom the revelation has come are pointedly living in *these last days*. The prophets

---

2. Donald Guthrie, *Hebrews* in *The Tyndale New Testament Commentaries* (Grand Rapids: Erdmans, 1983), 62.

spoke God's Word but now the Word has been made flesh. What a privileged people we are. God has spoken; spoken in his Son; spoken with finality. There will be no additional revelation. God "has spoken"; this implies a contrast with what has gone before: the old in his prophets; the new in his Son. Christ was manifested "once for all, at the end of the ages" and in that appearing brings to fruition the original goal of creation with this new beginning achieved in his perfect work. Believers living now, in the last days, the time between the ascension and the return of Christ, live in the days of fulfillment, of the brilliance of the finished work of Christ and in the hope of Christ's coming. These are the days of the new, better, and eternal covenant (Heb. 8:8, 6; 13:20); the forgiveness of sins has arrived through the death of Christ (8:17). As Vos points out, the writer literally says God has spoken "in the latter part of these days" indicating that "we are now living in the age of consummation and attainment."[3]

The Westminster divines were right to apply Hebrews 1:2 as a supporting text to the matter of the sufficiency of Scripture.[4] The coming of Christ not only brings to fulfillment the promise of salvation wrought in the cross and resurrection, but also provides the context in which the Lord has providentially brought the canon of Scripture to a close. Luther was right to find immediate application to us: "If the Word of the prophets has been received, the Gospel of Christ should be received all

---

3. Geerhardus Vos, *The Teaching of the Epistle to the Hebrews*, 53, 55.

4. *Confession of Faith,* 1.1: "Although the light of nature, and the works of creation and providence do so far manifest the goodness, wisdom, and power of God, as to leave men inexcusable; yet they are not sufficient to give that knowledge of God, and of his will, which is necessary unto salvation. Therefore it pleased the Lord, at sundry times, and in divers manners, to reveal Himself, and to declare that His will unto His Church [here the *Confession* cites Hebrews 1:1]; and afterwards, for the better preserving and propagating of the truth, and for the more sure establishment and comfort of the Church against the corruption of the flesh, and the malice of Satan and of the world, to commit the same wholly unto writing: which maketh the Holy Scripture to be most necessary; those former ways of God's revealing His will unto His people being now ceased [again the *Confession* cites Hebrews 1:1].

the more, since it is not a prophet who is speaking but the Lord of the prophets, not a slave but a son, not an angel but God, not to the fathers but to us."[5] Hebrews' reflection upon Num. 12:6–7 reminds us that Old Testament revelation was through dreams and visions, it was piecemeal contrasting the finality and clarity of God's once for all speaking in his Son. Just as Hebrews will argue that the sacrificial system of the Old Testament required a plurality now fulfilled and done away with by Christ's once-for-all sacrifice for sins, so the plurality of revelation in the Old Testament has given way to fulfillment in a completed, sufficient canon and does not remain open-ended. For this reason also, we may be assured that there will be no additional revelation since "those former ways of God's revealing His will unto His people [are] now ceased."[6] How wonderfully Christ exceeds the incompleteness of what has gone before.

Christ: Glorious As the Son

The author of Hebrews is not content to show us that Christ is more glorious than the prophets as essential as that is. The second truth about which he writes is that Christ is glorious as God's Son: "in these last days he has spoken to us by his Son." Literally, the Greek text reads "a son" (1:2, 5, 8; 3:6; 4:14; 5:5, 8; 6:6; 7:3, 28; 10:29) with no possessive pronoun (his), nor with a definite article (the) in order to express the quality of God's Son, that is, stressing his being, who he eternally is. Famed nineteenth century New Testament scholar B. F. Westcott points out that this emphasis is arresting since the article does appear with prophets referencing the prophets as a group, but without the article with relation to God's Son emphasizing his eternal nature and relation to the Father.[7]

---

5. Martin Luther, *Hebrews,* in *Luther's Works,* 109.

6. *Confession of Faith,* 1.1.

7. Brooke Foss Westcott, *The Epistle to the Hebrews,* 6.

This stress, of course, does not negate function but simply reminds us that the Son's Messianic function could only have achieved its purpose because of who Christ is eternally. These references to Christ as Son demonstrate who he is; "Before Abraham was, I am" (John 8:58). Any references to function, to the Son's Messianic role, are founded upon the confession of who the Son eternally is. God has spoken with finality in his Son. Would you know the heart of the Father? Would you know what God has revealed about himself? This you find by looking to the Son whose self-disclosure reveals the Father's heart and is the interpretative key to the whole of Scripture. "This is my Son, my Chosen One, listen to him!" (Luke 9:35).

About the Son the writer tells us five truths:

First, the Son is the appointed heir: "in these last days he has spoken to us by his Son, whom he appointed the heir of all things." Christ as heir is possessor, proprietor of *all things,* the universe, that which is material and spiritual, animate and inanimate—all things are under his sovereign management. The writer possibly has Psalm 2 in the back of his mind, to which he specifically refers in verse 8. In that Psalm, the Lord places his anointed on the messianic throne and promises to give to him the earth and the nations for his inheritance. Of course, the writer of Hebrews has in mind the Son's incarnation, humiliation, and exaltation through which he became, as mediator, proprietor of all things, not only the nations, but all things extensively including the angelic realm as well. As the God-man Christ is heir of all things without exception. "The word *heir,"* remarks Westcott, "marks the original purpose of Creation. The dominion originally promised to Adam (Gen. 1:28; compare Ps. 8) was gained by Christ."[8] This is so; but, what is gained by Christ far exceeds what was promised to Adam. The heirship of Christ the Mediator was determined in the eternal, Trinitarian

---

8. Westcott, *Hebrews,* 8.

counsel; but, was obtained by utter condescension even to the point of the cross (Philippians 2:1–11). Therefore, the Son, as God-man, inherits all things. All things, all people, must submit to the one the Father has appointed heir of all things. You, child of God, are in sovereign hands.

Second, the Son is the Creator: "through whom also he created the world." The heir of all things is the Creator of all things. Literally, the Greek text says that the Son is the one through whom God "made the ages." The writer uses the same language in 11:3 to mean "the universe." The writer clearly means that, through the Son, God has created all that is—all that has come to exist in time and space. No mere creature could create or receive the dominion of the universe. Only a man who was God incarnate can exercise universal sway over the world that he has made. Paul's exalted words in Colossians 1:16–17 correspond to this: "For by him all things were created, in heaven and on earth, visible and invisible, whether thrones or dominions or rulers or authorities—all things were created through him and for him. And he is before all things, and in him all things hold together." John, in the lofty prologue to his Gospel, also focused on this point: "In the beginning was the Word, and the Word was with God, and the Word was God. He was in the beginning with God. All things were made through him, and without him was not any thing made that was made" (John 1:1–3).[9] The Christians of the New Testament era "were convinced that the same person who had lived among

---

9. William Lane, *Hebrews*, 12: "As a hellenistic Jew, the writer was thoroughly familiar with the teaching concerning the Wisdom of God now preserved in the OT and in such later documents as the Wisdom of Solomon. . . . Reflection on the Wisdom of God in Alexandrian theology provided him with categories and vocabulary with which to interpret the person and work of Christ. Although Jesus is introduced as the divine Son (v. 2a), the functions attributed to him are those of the Wisdom of God: he is the mediator of revelation, the agent and sustainer of creation, and the reconciler of others to God. . . . Once the categories of divine Wisdom were applied to Jesus, his associations with the creative activity of God was strengthened" (cf. Prov. 8:22–31; Wis. 7:22; 9:2, 9).

men was the one who created men"[10] and the same reality must determine our thinking, living, and sense of amazement.

Third, the Son is the radiance of God's glory; verse 3: "He is the radiance of the glory of God." Literally, the text reads "who being the radiance," etc. The participle indicates *being* not *becoming* (*hos ōn aupaugasma tēs doxēs*), timeless existence. The writer is referencing who the Son is essentially, in his very nature. God's glory is the beauty of his perfections, his excellencies, his moral purity, the effulgence of the divine attributes. The word *aupaugasma,* used only here in the New Testament, can mean refulgence, that is, that the Son reflects God's brightness or effulgence—meaning a ray from an original light. The latter is evidently the meaning here since the relation between the Father and the Son is being underscored. The language stresses the oneness of the Son with the Father consistent with which is the exalted language of the Nicene Creed: "God of God, light of light, very God of very God, begotten not made; being of one substance with the Father." Gouge, the Puritan divine put it well: "Thus the Son is no whit inferior to the Father, but every way his equal. He was brightness, the brightness of His Father, yea, also the brightness of His Father's glory. Whatever excellency soever was in the Father, the same likewise was in the Son, and that in the most transplendent manner. Glory sets out excellency; brightness of glory, the excellency of excellency."[11]

Fourth, the Son is the exact imprint of God's image: "He is the radiance of the glory of God and the exact imprint of his nature." The Son is the *charactēr* (exact representation, such as an image made by a seal or the imprint of a die) of God's nature (*tes hupostaseōs autou*). For this reason, the Son is the manifestation of God's nature (John 1:1, 14; 14:9). As Paul wrote in Colossians 1:15 and 2:9: "He is the image of the invisible God, the

---

10. Donald Guthrie, *Hebrews,* 65.

11. Cited in A. W. Pink, *An Exposition of Hebrews,* 34.

firstborn of all creation"; "in (Christ) all the fullness of the deity dwells bodily." The language of Hebrews expresses the truth of precise correspondence. If *the radiance of the glory of God* expresses Christ's oneness with the Father, *the exact imprint of his nature* expresses oneness but also distinction. Yet, this is the Son *who became incarnate.* John Murray commented: "The infinite became finite, the eternal and supratemporal entered time and became subject to its conditions, the immutable became the mutable, the invisible became the visible, the Creator became the created, the sustainer of all became dependent, the Almighty infirm."[12] The writer takes us into the very mystery of the Trinity and the incarnation of our Lord. As if this were not enough description of Christ's grandeur, the writer adds:

Fifth, the Son is the cosmic sustainer: "he upholds the universe by the word of his power." The Son upholds, that is, preserves, sustains, and governs the universe as only God can do. Without Christ's sustenance the universe would fall into chaos, indeed, the world would not be. As an older commentator, John Brown beautifully wrote:

> [The materials of the universe were called into being by Christ and arranged in comely order] and by Him, too, they are prevented from running into confusion, or reverting to nothing. The whole universe hangs on His arm; His unsearchable wisdom and boundless power are manifested in governing and directing the complicated movements of animate and inanimate, rational and irrational beings, to the attainment of His own great and holy purposes; and He does all this by the word of His power, or by His powerful word. All this is done without effort or difficulty. He speaks and it is done; He commands, and it stands fast.[13]

---

12. John Murray, *The Person of Christ,* in *Collected Writings,* 2.132.
13. John Brown, *Hebrews,* 32.

Since the Son is one with the Father's essence, the word of the Son is precisely one with the Father's. In the exercise of this sovereign word, not only does the Son sustain the universe (Col. 1:17), but the language employed in Hebrews implies even more. The Son is moving the universe to its appointed goal. The writer uses the verb, *pherein*, meaning "to carry." The Son, therefore, is moving, carrying history and God's entire plan to its predestined goal. He is seeing to it that the purpose for which God created the universe is carried to its completion. The Son sets the stars in their courses, fills the barns with grain, brings rain upon the earth, and guides the destinies of men and things. If he upholds and directs all things then, you believer, are safe in his hands.We may trust him in hardship and should be determined to ascribe to him the preeminence that is his by nature.

In referencing a parallel text, Colossians 1:18, the biographer of Charles Simeon records that "the soul-moving power of his prime of life was with him to the last." One who heard Simeon preach on "that in all things He might have the preeminence" recorded that the passage "was written forever on the listener's heart by the prophetic fire of the utterance, as the old man seemed to rise and dilate under the impression of his Master's glory:—'That He might have the pre-eminence! And He *will* have it!—And He *must* have it!—And He *shall* have it!'"[14] This is the attitude that should impel our lives in view of Christ's supernatural, providential direction of the universe which includes our everyday living. This control and guidance he accomplishes *by the word of his power*, by his utterance (*rhēmati*), his sovereign word. The Son is God.

In verse 10, the writer of Hebrews applies Psalm 102:24ff to Jesus: "You, Lord, laid the foundation of the earth in the beginning, and the heavens are the work of your hands; they will perish, but you remain; they will all wear out like a garment, like a

---

14. H. C. G. Moule, *Charles Simeon* (London: Inter-Varsity, 1948), 75.

robe you will roll them up, like a garment they will be changed. But you are the same, and your years will have no end." Right from the start the writer of Hebrews leads us to worship along with the angelic beings (v. 6, citing Ps. 97:7): "Let all God's angels worship him."

The author of Hebrews takes us to the vertiginous heights. The Son, we have learned, is more glorious than the prophets, the fulfiller of God's sovereign, redemptive purpose. We have also seen that Christ is more glorious as the Son: appointed heir, the Creator, radiance of God's glory, the exact imprint of God's nature and the cosmic sustainer. This is not all. The Son is also glorious in his work of atonement.

The Son is Glorious in His Work of Atonement

Recall the Son's glory! "The remoteness and awesomeness of the former [the Father] is offset by the amazing intimacy of the latter [the Son]."[15] One with the Father, creator, and sustainer of all—this is the one who became flesh and suffered for our sins. "After making purification for sins, he sat down at the right hand of the Majesty on high." By *making purification for sins*, the writer means that the Son made atonement for our sins (compare 2 Peter 1:9). Sin is defilement needing removal. "There is perhaps a reference to the imperfection of the Aaronic purifications (compare Lev. 16:30) which is dwelt upon afterwards."[16]

Here we see the glory of the Son most brightly. Where did the divine nature shine more brightly for us sinners than when in union with human nature the Son suffered and bled to save sinners from sin? There is no place for self-atonement; all works are excluded. He alone could do this for us. Moreover, there is no place for an incomplete atonement, one needing repetition, as did the sacrifices under the law. The Son's infinite nature gave

---

15. Donald Guthrie, *Hebrews*, 68.

16. Westcott, *Hebrews*, 15.

to his finite sufferings infinite value so that our guilt might be removed, our sins forgiven, and our consciences purged—and that once for all. The value of that marvelous atonement is efficacious for God's people forever.

Making purification, or as it can be translated, *having purged*—the Son has done his work; the work of atonement is complete (as is indicated by the aorist middle participle). Nothing need be added. Consider: this is the work of the eternal Son, One with the Father, infinite in majesty, the effulgence of God's very essence; this great Second Person of the Trinity took flesh. The sinless Son purged our sin, even the sin we had not yet committed. Is this not more than wonderful? And why did he accomplish this work? To purge our sins, make atonement, satisfy divine wrath, to remove our guilt. What wonder, what glory, what love is here!

And what dignity is attached to our salvation due to the dignity of the one who offered himself up for us, "the just for the unjust" (1 Pet. 3:18). Who could have met the demands of God's perfect law but the perfect Son of God? Who but the eternal Son of God, "very God of very God," could satisfy the law that demanded our condemnation? Who but God could turn justice, our former enemy, into our friend? When the Son of God condescended to suffer for us, the thunder of Sinai was silenced and his perfect righteousness met every demand of justice. The words of an eighteenth century Calvinistic hymn writer, Augustus Toplady, are truly glorious:

> From whence this fear and unbelief?
> Hath not the Father put to grief
> His spotless Son for me?
> And will the righteous Judge of men
> Condemn me for that debt of sin,
> Which, Lord, was charged on Thee?
>
> Complete atonement Thou hast made,

The Glory of Christ

And to the utmost farthing paid
Whate'er Thy people owed;
Nor can His wrath on me take place,
If sheltered in Thy righteousness,
And sprinkled with Thy blood.

If Thou hast my discharge procured,
And freely in my room endured
The whole of wrath divine;
Payment God cannot twice demand,
First at my bleeding Surety's hand,
And then again at mine.

Turn then, my soul, unto thy rest;
The merits of thy great High Priest
Have bought thy liberty:
Trust in His efficacious blood,
Nor fear thy banishment from God,
Since Jesus died for thee.[17]

Already in this verse, there is anticipation of the contrast with the Aaronic priesthood and the regular, ongoing sacrifices required in that system. These sacrifices were mere types and shadows of the work of Christ for us. There was Aaron; but now the Son. In conjunction with the previous references to the Son's deity, the writer is enabling us to understand that "the efficacy of Christ's sacrifice is traced to the dignity of his person."[18] Here is the superiority of Jesus to the old order. The one who offers himself is better than the sacrifices of the old. His sacrifice is better; his sacrifice is complete and efficacious.

Hebrews places the emphasis upon the sacrifice of Jesus which is "better" because it does not just cleanse the flesh but cleanses the conscience (9:14) and Jesus' sacrifice is "better" because offered once for all, never to be repeated (Hebrews 10:10).

17. Augustus Toplady, "From whence this fear and unbelief?" in *Songs for the Service of Prayer*, compiled by R. S. Thain (Chicago: F. H. Revell, 1880), 91.

18. Brown, *Hebrews*, 34.

The once for all character of Christ's atonement is already indicated by the aorist participle *"making* purification for" sins. "The middle voice indicates that the Son made purification for sins *in himself,* clearly relating the act of purification to his sacrifice."[19] The Son accomplished redemption, really and effectually purged our sins. Therefore, the Father sees no sin in his people to condemn: "As far as the east is from the west, so far does he remove our transgressions from us" (Ps. 103:12).

Now notice, that "after making purification for sins, he sat down at the right hand of the Majesty on high." Why does the writer of Hebrews stress that the Son sat down at the right hand of the Majesty on high, a clear allusion to Psalm 110:1? After the High Priest had served God on the Day of Atonement he presented himself before the Lord. The writer here wants us to grasp that the mission of the Son, or Great High Priest, has been accomplished. The Son sat down on the right hand of God on his glorious throne.

The right hand is the place of power (1 Kings 2:19). *Majesty on high* refers to God the Father and the heavenly enthronement (8:1). Once humbled, now the Son is exalted above measure (Eph. 4:10; Phil. 2:9). Christ resumed as God-man the original dignity and glory that he had with the Father before ever the world was, and he rules with the glory, authority, and power of God (John 17:5). The Son is our prophet—God's final word to us; the Son is our priest—he made purification for sins; and, the Son is our King who rules and reigns on the throne of God.

Having suffered, the Son is now elevated to the highest seat of honor and dignity as we are told in 2:9: "clothed with glory and honor because of the suffering of death"! When the Jewish high priest entered the Holy of Holies, sprinkled with the blood on the mercy seat, he was not allowed to sit down in the presence of Divine majesty. The Son, our great high priest, finished his work

---

19. Lane, *Hebrews,* 15.

of atonement and then in exaltation sat down—not only in the Divine presence but on the divine throne, holding sway over the universe. His work is now finished, completed, done.

It is impossible that Christ be robbed of those purchased with his own shed blood. Jesus now sits on the right hand of the majesty on high which, in sum, is:

- The place of power from which he reigns;
- The place of reward from which position no one and nothing can take from him his purchased people;
- The place of completion demonstrating that the atonement is completed once for all;
- And, as Hebrews will emphasize, the place of intercession for his own.

Christ's atonement was once-for-all, final, and sufficient, as evidenced by his current presence *seated* at God's right hand. At the same time, Christ's current presence in heavenly majesty has profound implications for his *continuing* mediatorial work on our behalf. The writer will stress this in subsequent chapters using the model of the Old Testament day of atonement ritual; the sacrificial blood that was shed outside the Tabernacle is efficacious as it is brought beyond the veil, into the Holy of Holies, and sprinkled around the Mercy Seat, so that blood *continues* to plead for his people.

How did this apply to the needs of the original readers of Hebrews and how does it apply to us today? The writer is saying to those who were tired, worn out, and tempted to turn back, "get your eyes off yourself and on your Savior." The Son is:

- Superior to the prophets
- The appointed heir
- The Creator

- The radiance of God's glory
- The exact imprint of God's nature
- The cosmic sustainer
- The atonement for sin
- The exalted high priest
- The exalted priest who also is King having "sat down at the right hand of the majesty on high."

See him! Don't waver. Be constant in faith and hope; persevere, run the race. Keep moving toward your heavenly home, no matter the opponents or the obstacles.

Will you note as we start our study of Hebrews, having looked at three verses only, that these three verses are rich in theological content? The writer is addressing a most pressing practical need, that of perseverance in the midst of trouble and strife. How does he start? To what themes does he turn? Obviously, the most practical thing to do is to teach theology. Do you need to stay the course? Then deepen your understanding of who Christ is. Do you need strength to make it in life? Then, you need theology way down deep in the marrow of your bones.

That is the divinely inspired prescription of the writer of Hebrews; and, his exhortations will—all of them—be drawn from theology. Philip Hughes rightly said: "many adherents of the church have settled for an undemanding and superficial association with the Christian faith."[20] True; but, that will not do. Mile wide and inch deep thinking will not prepare you for trouble in the Christian life. That's what the writer is saying.

Hear the doctrine and with it the warnings, and appeals; they are of eternal weight. Get out of yourself and into Christ. Be absorbed with his love, his grace, his person, his work. Your hope is not in self but in him. Therefore, let each Sunday

---

20. Philip Edgcumbe Hughes, *A Commentary on the Epistle to the Hebrews*, 1.

through to next Sunday be about him. Apply these realities to marriage, family, work, temptation and comprehensively to all of life. Worship and adore him; live for him; draw your sustenance from him. Live out of his fullness because of who he is, what he has done and what he will do.

The old hymn-writer well summarized this portion of Hebrews:

> Majestic sweetness sits enthroned
> upon the Savior's brow.
> His head with radiant glories crowned,
> his lips with grace o'er flow . . .
>
> No mortal can with him compare
> among the sons of men.
> Fairer is he than all the fair
> that fill the heavenly train.[21]

Hebrews is about the supremacy of Christ; let's continue to study its rich content together seeking from the text a much needed, enlarged vision of who our Savior is. Your exalted High Priest upon whom you depend for persevering grace is able to bring you to your appointed end. He is the inheritor of all things, indeed of the entire universe. Seventeenth century writer John Trapp rightly said: "Be married to this heir and have all."

---

21. Samuel Stennet, "Majestic sweetness sits enthroned (1787)," from *The People's Hymnal for Public and Social Worship*, prepared by Edmund S. Lorenz (Dayton, OH: W. J. Shuey, 1890), 152.

2

Superior to Angels

HEBREWS 1:4–14

And to which of the angels has he ever said, "Sit at my right hand until I make your enemies a footstool for your feet"? Are they not all ministering spirits sent out to serve for the sake of those who are to inherit salvation?

Every day we should compare our own lack of majesty with the majesty of Christ. Humbling ours hearts under the Lord's hand and recognizing his greatness is a sure way to begin our day with God's glory uppermost in our minds and filling our hearts. Surely the text before us helps us to recognize the unsurpassed greatness of our Lord Jesus as we see him who is superior even to holy angels which are his creatures. The value of this is to raise Christ to his rightful place in our thoughts and affections and to keep us from sin. Where do we put the Son in our thinking and in our hearts? Do we see him as the One around whom the universe revolves—the One around whom our *personal* universe must revolve? Is he our *all* or do we compromise his majesty in all sorts of practical ways? As H. C. G. Moule put the question in his exposition of Colossians, is Christ "at best a sort of

Ptolemaic sun, rolling together with other luminaries around an earthly centre?"[1]

This passage presents a powerful challenge to our self-centered view of life. In the first three verses of Hebrews, the author has shown that Christ is glorious. Christ is more glorious than the prophets, fulfilling the Word delivered through them and the works performed by them; he is glorious as the Son (the appointed heir, the Creator, the effulgence of God's glory, the exact imprint of God's nature, the cosmic sustainer); Christ is glorious in his work of atonement and glorious in his exaltation to the right hand of God. Next, the author of Hebrews makes clear that Christ is even more glorious than the angels who surround God's throne. The writer does this by looking at seven Old Testament passages that help his readers contrast Christ and the angels, showing that the Son is infinitely superior.

The Point of the Contrast

Why does the writer of Hebrews draw out this contrast between the Son of God and angels? Why stress his superiority? Should this not be obvious? Many suggestions have been given by students of Hebrews. For example, it has been suggested that these Hebrew Christians favored viewpoints held by the Dead Sea Sect holding to a kingly Messiah subordinate to a priestly Messiah, both subordinate to the archangel Michael. In this context, it became necessary to stress that Christ has become "as superior to angels as the name he has inherited is more excellent than theirs" (v. 4). Hebrews gives no evidence that the author is combating such error, however. Others have posited that the writer opposed Gnosticism with its hierarchy of angelic beings and angel worship. This is also unlikely, since there is no evidence for this in the remainder of the book, and Gnostic angel wor-

---

1. H. C. G. Moule, *Colossians Studies* (New York: A. C. Armstrong and Son, 1898), 15.

ship would not have been the peculiar temptation of Hebrew Christians. This cannot be ruled out absolutely, however, since we do have evidence of Jewish ceremonies, mingled with proto-Gnosticism, and angel worship in the book of Colossians (Col. 2:16-19). Others speculate that Hebrews is battling an Ebionite Christology that views Jesus as an angel.

A view of older commentators still vies for my allegiance. On this view, when we take into account that angels were involved in the giving of the law (Deut. 33:2; Psalm 68:17; Hebrews 2:2; Acts 7:53) and, further, when we remember that the theme of Hebrews thus far has been the final revelation of the gospel in God's Son, the author proclaims that this final revelation is not inferior to the giving of the law because the Son is superior to angelic beings. Indeed, the superiority of the Son over angels is not only a matter of revelation but of the glory of his person essentially and of his mediatorial glory as well. As Brown says: "His place is on the throne,—their [the angels'] place is before it."[2]

How can the revelation that has come through Christ be inferior to the old, how can the Son as revealer be inferior to the angels, since the Son sits on God's right hand? Angels are august beings; in the Apocalypse, John was tempted to worship an angel and received the angel's rebuke for it (Rev. 19:9–10). Christ, the exalted *theanthropos*, must receive our worship. We must bow before Christ as do the angels themselves. I find this older view compatible with the findings of Randall C. Gleason, who has argued that the denial of angelic rule in the world to come (Heb. 2:5) clues the reader to the reason for the emphasis of Christ's exaltation over the angels in Hebrews 1–2. He points out that the apocalyptic writings of the Second Temple period stressed the functions of angelic hosts in the national deliverance of Israel.

"The denial," therefore, "that God 'did not subject to angels the world to come' (Heb 2:5) was a direct challenge to the

---

2. John Brown, *Hebrews* (Edinburgh: Banner of Truth, 1983), 41.

prominence of angels in the national hopes of Israel. No angelic army would come to deliver the Jewish patriots from their Roman oppressors."[3] Therefore, the author exhorts his readers to seek help from Christ rather than from the angelic beings as was done in the overinflated valuation of angels in Jewish life. Gleason's view may very well add a layer to our understanding of this passage, if not providing the entire reason for the writer's stress on Christ's superiority over the angels.

Whatever the reason for the contrast between Christ and angelic beings, the need for the contrast was peculiar to the context in which Hebrews was written long ago. Of what value is this contrast to us then? The contrast is valuable to us because it heightens our awareness of who Christ is and the wonder of the revelation that has come to fulfillment through him. Hearing this contrast, we all should desire to take our place before the throne, worshiping, acknowledging the Son's Lordship. There is no such thing as an "almost God," and the angels, despite their splendor, are infinitely less than infinite. When we see in this section that the Son's place is on the throne while the angels' place is before it, we exalt the Son in our hearts and are put in our place as well—our place before his footstool.

The seven Old Testament quotations are words of the Father to or about his Son. You and I are permitted to listen in and hear the Father speak of the transcendent dignity of Jesus Christ. Also, you and I are called to put our faith in this Son of transcendent worth. We here learn something of the Son's *name*, his character, value, worth, privileges. Brown says: The angels' "name is created spirits; His name is the only-begotten Son of God."[4]

---

3. Randall C. Gleason, "Angels and the Eschatology of Heb 1–2," *New Testament Studies*, 49 (2003), 104.

4. Brown, *Hebrews*, 41.

Christ: Essentially Supreme

First, the writer references Psalm 2:7: "For to which of the angels did God ever say, 'You are my Son, today I have begotten you'?" In Psalm 2:7 God proclaims the Messiah to be his Son. To which of the angels did God ever say words like these? The answer is, to none of them. The uniqueness of Christ as the Son of God is underscored profoundly here. What do these words mean? It is typical nowadays to deny that Psalm 2:7 refers to the "eternal generation of the Son," a mysterious and true doctrine by which we are not to understand the generation of Christ's deity but of his person, as person begets person, though the mode of this eternal generation is beyond our comprehension.[5]

Rather, since Peter applies this passage to the resurrection of Jesus from the dead (Acts 13:33) and Hebrews applies Psalm 2:7 to the exaltation of Christ in his priestly office (Heb. 5:5), exegetes often argue that we are led to understand that these verses apply to the public declaration of Christ's Sonship (Rom. 1:4) in Christ's resurrection from the dead and the exaltation to the Father's right hand after having completed once for all his sacrifice for our sins. The Son is exalted to the heights of glory. The "day" envisioned by the writer is the "day" of resurrection, ascension and glorification. His exaltation makes possible the believer's exaltation; his inheritance makes sure the believer's inheritance.

---

5. I want to be perfectly understood that I regard the eternal generation of the Son to be essential to a biblically grounded doctrine of the Trinity. I agree with John Gill, cited in the introductory essay in his *Exposition of the Old and New Testaments*, lxv that: "It is easy to observe, that the distinction of Persons in the Deity depends on the generation of the Son. Take away that which would destroy the relation between the first and second Persons, and the distinction drops. And that this distinction is natural, or by necessity of nature, is evident, because had it been only arbitrary, or of choice and will, it might not have been at all, or have been otherwise than it is—and then he that is called Father might have been called the Son, and he that is called the Son might have been called the Father. This has so pressed those who are of a contrary mind as to oblige them to own it might have so happened, had it been agreeable to the will of God."

While it is true that Psalm 2:7 is applied to the resurrection/exaltation of Christ, which the older exegesis never questioned, the older approach may well be correct in seeing Psalm 2:7 first as a reference to the eternal generation of the Son, an affirmation of Christ's eternal Sonship and deity. The application of Psalm 2:7 to the resurrection and ascension of Christ is due to the fact that the Sonship of Christ provides the efficacy of Christ's exalted life. Sonship, after all, is ontological and Gill is right when he wrote: "his office is not the foundation of his sonship, but his sonship is the foundation of his office." He continues: "the date of it, *to-day*, designs eternity, as in Isa.xliii.13 which is one continued day, an everlasting now. And this may be applied to any time and case in which Christ is declared to be the Son of God" because Christ's divine sonship "more manifestly appeared" in his resurrection and ascension.[6]

Second Samuel 7:14 is next referenced by the writer: "I will be to him a father, and he shall be to me a son." Once again, these words were never said by God to angels, but the Father did speak these words pertaining to his Son. In this passage Nathan the prophet informs David that the Lord did not intend for him to build the temple but the Lord did promise to David a dynasty. The text has for its first reference Solomon but the language bursts its banks and spills forward into the future. David's dynasty through Solomon is typological of David's Greater Son, the Lord Jesus Christ. From David's line would come the eternal kingdom of the Messiah and the promise, "I will be to him a father, and he shall be to me a son." To none of the angels did God ever promise such relationship and blessing. One greater than Solomon has come.

In these verses, Psalm 2:7 and 2 Samuel 7:14, the writer affirms the *essential* supremacy of Christ over the angels. Angels are dignified and powerful creatures; but, they are simply crea-

---

6. John Gill, *Exposition of the Old and New Testaments, Psalms*, 3.531.

tures. Angels are subordinate to the Son. The unique Sonship of
Christ is seen both in his resurrection and exaltation and in the
eternal kingdom promised from of old.

Christ: The Object of Angelic Worship

Not only is the uniqueness and superiority of Christ seen
in his exaltation and the promise of his messianic kingdom,
but also in the truth that the angels themselves worship the
Son. In verse 6 the writer cites Psalm 97:7 (or possibly Deut.
32:43, LXX): "And again, when he brings the firstborn into
the world, he says, 'Let all God's angels worship him.'" We
are faced daily with the tragic reality that not all worship the
Son, but this is not true in heaven. The angels worship Christ.
The triumphs of the Messiah in the book of Revelation are
marked by angelic worship, a carefully choreographed liturgy of praise (e.g. Rev. 5:6–13). In Psalm 97 the angels themselves are called gods (*Elohim*) as a class in a lesser sense
(compare Psalm 29:1). But, these "gods" are called, one and
all, to worship the true Son who is himself the Lord God.
Christ alone is to be revered and adored.

The interpreter is faced with interesting questions as he approaches this verse. Does *again* simply announce that another
verse is being introduced or does *again* refer to a future event,
the coming of Christ? If *again* modifies the verbal phrase *brings
in*, it may well refer to the future coming of Christ as in Hebrews 9:28. The writer would be referencing the time when God
would again lead his firstborn into the world. This seems a bit
forced to me. It is best to see the *again* of 1:6 and the *again* of
1:5 as fixed forms (the *de palin* of 1:6 *and again* follows after
hotan because *de* is typically postpositive). If *again* simply introduces another quotation as in verse 5 the reference is to the
incarnation of our Lord when the angels worshiped the child
Christ (Luke 2:13–14). Whether or not the writer of Hebrews

had Luke as a source, the angel's announcement of the birth of Christ to the shepherds would have undoubtedly been known through the apostles' preaching. So, the *again* of verse 6 functions like the *again* of verse 5, as a rhetorical marker introducing another Old Testament reference.

Is the verse, then, to be translated "when he brings again," a reference to the return of Christ at the end of the age, or does "he says again" simply introduce another verse from the Old Testament and, therefore, is a reference to the incarnation of our Lord? A third view sets aside both of these possibilities by considering the meaning of the term *world* (*oikoumenē*), "when he brings the firstborn into the world." In Hebrews 2:5, it may be argued, we are explicitly told "now it was not to angels that God subjected the world to come (*oikoumenē tēn mellousan*), of which we are now speaking" thus linking the two passages together.

The reference to Psalm 97:7 with Deut. 32:43 in the backdrop, then, is neither a reference to the incarnation nor to the return of Christ but to his exaltation to the right hand of God. After atoning for sin the risen Christ ascended on high and was greeted by the worship of angels. However, it is not clear that *oikoumenē* in 2:5 means anything other than the inhabited world. Certainly, a look at standard lexicography (BDAG[7]) offers no suggestion of anything other than the inhabited world.

The writer is saying that the dominion over the creatures that Adam lost in the fall is restored in the new heavens and earth and that Jesus' exaltation demands the restoration of that original dominion since he has now been crowned with glory and honor. It seems, then, that Hebrews 1:6 is a reference to the incarnation of our Lord when the angels worshiped the Son in the announcement of his birth before the shepherds. What a

---

7. *A Greek-English Lexicon of the New Testament and Other Early Christian Literature*, 3rd Edition, eds. Walter Bauer and Frederick William Danker (Chicago: University of Chicago Press, 2001). This was formerly abbreviated as the BADG before the 3rd edition.

wonderful thought to occupy the minds of believers under the strain of Christian living in a fallen world. The Lord has come and the angels worshiped him!

When the text references the Son as *firstborn* (*ton prōtotokon*) it does not mean that Christ had a beginning, that is, the term is not a reference to a temporal birth. *Firstborn* refers to Christ's position and Mediatorial prerogatives and appointment as heir of all things (1:2). Just as the oldest son in Hebrew culture was in a position of favor receiving a double portion of inheritance and other positional prerogatives, so Christ possesses primacy, superiority and dignity. When God speaks of Israel in Exodus 4:22 as "firstborn" he indicates Israel's favored position. So here, in an infinitely greater way, favored position is ascribed to the Son.

Lane suggests a possible parallel with Psalm 89:27 where the Lord says to David, "and I will make him the firstborn, the highest of the kings of the earth." "In this context 'firstborn' is a title of honor expressing priority in rank. The reference to covenantal appointment (Ps 89:27–28) and to the establishment of a throne that will endure as long as the heavens (v 29) served to bring Ps 89 into close association with Ps 2 and 2 Sam 7, already cited in v 5."[8]

Paul refers to Christ as "the Firstborn from the dead" in Colossians 1:18 presenting before our eyes the vision of the risen Lord who is also described as "first fruits" in 1 Corinthians 15:20. Similarly, Christ is designated "the firstborn over all creation" (Col. 1:15), "so that the parallelism between Christ's relations to the Universe and to the Church is thus emphasized."[9] The people of God are "the assembly of the first born who are enrolled in heaven" (Hebrews 12:23) in union with him who is "the firstborn among many brothers" (Rom. 8:29) to whom God's

---

8. Lane, *Hebrews*, 26.

9. J. B. Lightfoot, *Saint Paul's Epistles to the Colossians and to Philemon*, 158.

people are being conformed. Christ the firstborn possesses, in an absolute sense, privilege and superiority, to whom the angels bow in worship. In both his essence and office, Christ is superior. If Christ is the object of angelic worship, should he not be the object of *your* worship?

Christ: Infinitely Above the Angels

"Of the angels he says, 'He makes his angels winds, and his ministers a flame of fire.'" This quotation from Psalm 104:4 (LXX) tells us that angels are great beings indeed, created beings who resemble the wind and lightning who serve God. Just as wind and fire, perhaps the lightning that accompanies a storm, carry out the sovereign will of God the Creator, so angels minister to accomplish the Sovereign's will. But, whatever the angels do, however great may be their power, they are creatures, ministers and mere servants of the Lord, subordinate in every way to God's desire and design to determine and order their rank.

However grand angels may be, they are infinitely below Christ; they are his creatures who do his bidding. The angels are *his angels.* All that has been said of the Son clearly teaches that Christ is infinitely above all creatures, including the angels. He who is "the radiance of the glory of God and the exact imprint of his nature" who "upholds the universe by the word of his power" (1:3) must be infinitely above even the greatest of angelic beings. The character and worth of Jesus are truly overwhelming.

Christ: Enthroned Above the Angels

The fifth Old Testament citation is Psalm 45:6–7 and is found in Hebrews 1:8–9: "But of the Son he says, 'Your throne, O God, is forever and ever, the scepter of uprightness is the scepter of your kingdom. You have loved righteousness and hated wickedness; therefore God, your God, has anointed you with the oil of gladness beyond your companions.'"

What is so very remarkable about this quotation from Psalm 45 is that, in this passage, God speaks to God. This is one of the many passages to be considered when gathering the biblical data concerning God's triune nature. Here the Father speaks of the Godhead of the Son. Kidner well observes that the form of address in this Psalm "is consistent with the incarnation, but mystifying in any other context. It is an example of Old Testament language bursting its banks, to demand more than human fulfillment (as did Ps. 110:1, according to our Lord)."[10]

The throne inhabited by the Son is "the throne of God and of the Lamb" (Rev. 22:1) and is established *forever and ever*. The Psalm underscores that God's kingdom is invariably just, "the scepter of uprightness is the scepter of your kingdom. You have loved righteousness and hated wickedness." Christ wields the symbol of royal justice with absolute uprightness. Isaiah describes Christ's reign: "Of the increase of his government and of peace there will be no end, on the throne of David and over his kingdom, to establish it and to uphold it with justice and with righteousness from this time and forevermore" (Isa. 9:7).

Indeed, this reality, "you have loved righteousness and hated wickedness," is what makes the cross of Christ necessary. If sinners are to be saved, since God is just in all that he is and in all his ways, a means must be devised by God himself that meets the demands of justice so that God can, consistently with his nature, justify sinners. The means—the *only* means—for the justification of sinners is the obedience and sacrifice of Jesus, God's own Son. In him the demands of the law of God are met and justice is thoroughly satisfied, so that

10. Derek Kidner, *Psalms, An Introduction and Commentary,* 1.172.

God "might be just and the justifier of the one who has faith in Jesus" (Rom. 3:26).

Since full deity is ascribed to the Son who reigns on the throne, establishing justice forever, the Son must be worshiped. The Son holds kingly power and governance over all, yes, even over the angels. His throne is forever, he will reign forever, and the scepter of righteousness is in his hand. The once crucified, now glorified Lord holds out that scepter in mercy and grace to his people declaring their pardon on the basis of his costly sacrifice. The one who "loved righteousness and hated iniquity" may now save lost sinners consistently with his righteousness.

The Son who is true God, has "loved righteousness and hated wickedness; therefore God, your God, has anointed you with the oil of gladness beyond your companions." The Son was anointed as Mediator, not with literal oil but with him to which the oil points, the Holy Spirit (Acts 10:38). Kings in ancient Israel were anointed to establish their reigns (1 Sam. 10:1; 16:13; 2 Sam. 19:21) as we read in Psalm 89:20: "I have found David, my servant; with my holy oil I have anointed him." Messiah, we must remember, means "anointed one." Designated Mediator from eternity, the Son was specially anointed in his baptism; but, probably the reference here is to an "anointing" with *the oil of gladness* as a result of his finished work in his ascension as the Son took upon himself the role of Mediatorial intercession on the throne of God.

This anointing, pointing to his entry into heaven, when he received his office as glorified Mediator, enabled him as risen, ascended Lord to pour out the Holy Spirit upon his church. As Peter preached on Pentecost: "This Jesus God raised up, and of that we are all witnesses. Being therefore exalted at the right hand of God, and having received from the Father the promise of the Holy Spirit, he has poured out this that you yourselves are seeing and hearing" (Acts 2:32–33 compare John 15:26). Through the powerful work of the Holy Spirit in his people—calling, saving, keeping, maturing—the sweet aroma of Christ's anointing is diffused.

Brown summarizes this section splendidly: God "has given Thee a kingdom which, for extent and duration, and multitude and magnitude of blessings, as far exceeds any kingdom ever bestowed on man or angel as the heaven is above the earth."[11] No wonder the anointing is that of *gladness* (Isa. 61:3), as the Psalmist and writer of Hebrews contemplate this "priest on his throne" (Zech. 6:13). The Son is *on* a throne; the angels worship *before* the throne!

Christ: Eternal and Immutable

Hebrews 1:10–12 brings a sixth Old Testament reference to bear upon Christ's superiority to the angels:

> And, "You, Lord, laid the foundation of the earth in the beginning, and the heavens are the work of your hands; they will perish, but you remain; they will all wear out like a garment, like a robe you will roll them up, like a garment they will be changed. But you are the same, and your years will have no end."

Psalm 102: 25–27, from which this quotation is taken, refers to Jehovah, the Creator of the heavens and the earth. Here in Hebrews 1:10–12 the writer applies these verses to the Son, of whom the author has already said is "the appointed heir of all things, through whom also he created the world" (Heb. 1:2). These words from Psalm 102, referencing Jehovah, are applied to Christ because Christ *is* Jehovah. How far above the angels is Christ? Christ is infinitely above them; Christ is Jehovah, the Creator of the earth and heavens. "You, Lord, laid the foundation of the earth in the beginning, and the heavens are the work of your hands." The Psalm wonderfully contrasts the finitude of

---

11. Brown, *Hebrews*, 59.

God's creation with the Creator's infinite nature: "They will perish, but you remain; they will all wear out like a garment, like a robe you will roll them up, like a garment they will be changed. But you are the same, and your years will have no end." The Son is the Creator of the heavens and the earth and when Christ returns to consummate his kingdom, and the present creation is rolled up like a garment, the Son will remain the same and will never perish.

This speaks of the yet future time in which the form of this world will pass away, the vestiges of the curse will be removed, and the Lord will establish the new heavens and the new earth. What radical alteration there shall be; but, in the Son there shall be no alteration whatsoever. He is unchangeable both in his nature and in his eternal priesthood. When the earth passes away as we now know it and the heavens are rolled up like a garment, Jesus the Son of God will remain immutable.

Guthrie reminds us that "there was a widespread belief in the Graeco-Roman world that the world and indeed the universe was indestructible."[12] The Scriptures teach otherwise. The present created order as we now see it will be folded and put away, grown old and in need of renewal, but what is said of Jehovah is said of Jesus: "You are the same, and your years will have no end." Brown says: "In His nature there is no change; in His duration, no circle to run—no space to be measured—no time to be reckoned—all is eternity infinite and onward."[13] And, believer, when the cosmic order is shaken prior to the consummation, you will remain because he remains, you will endure because his character makes his oath secure (6:16–20). Christ's person will remain the same and the value of his sacrifice will remain efficacious forever and ever.

---

12. Donald Guthrie, *Hebrews*, in *The Tyndale New Testament Commentaries* (Grand Rapids: Eerdmans, 1983), 78.

13. Brown, *Hebrews*, 63–64.

Superior to Angels

Christ: The Ruler of the Universe

The seventh Old Testament reference in Hebrews (1:13–14) is Psalm 110:1.

> And to which of the angels has he ever said, "Sit at
> my right hand until I make your enemies a footstool
> for your feet"? Are they not all ministering spirits
> sent out to serve for the sake of those who are to
> inherit salvation?

In Psalm 110 David as prophet is enabled to see prophetically into heaven itself and to hear also the voice of Jehovah invite the Messiah to sit down with him on his throne. This is Jehovah in heaven; the Son reigning with his Father. Psalm 110:1 must be understood within the Trinitarian frame of reference, "the LORD says to my Lord." Our Lord Jesus taught us to interpret the Psalm that way in Matthew 22:41–46 and in synoptic parallels. Psalm 110 teaches the unique Sonship of Jesus, the full deity of Christ.

The Son sits at the right hand of the Father, in the position of sovereign, universal authority which is elsewhere confirmed in Scripture. First Peter 3:21–22 speaks of "the resurrection of Jesus Christ, who has gone into heaven and is at the right hand of God, with angels, authorities, and powers having been subjected to him." Ephesians 1:20–21 brings the same truth to the fore. This text speaks of the Father's "great might that he worked in Christ when he raised him from the dead and seated him at his right hand in the heavenly places, far above all rule and authority and power and dominion, and above every name that is named, not only in this age but also in the one to come. And he put all things under his feet and gave him as head over all things to the church, which is his body, the fullness of him who fills all in all."

Similar implications may be drawn from Colossians 1:16 and 18 in which we are told that by Christ "all things were created , in heaven and earth, visible and invisible, whether thrones

33

or dominions or rulers or authorities—all things were created through him and for him" and that further, "he is the head of the body, the church. He is the beginning, the firstborn from the dead, that in everything he might be preeminent."

Christ is superior to the angels. "To which of the angels has he ever said, 'Sit at my right hand until I make your enemies a footstool for your feet'?" If the enemies of the Lord are made a footstool under his feet as he rules and defends his church in sovereign power, then what power do his enemies have? What can disturb him? Who or what can curtail his omnipotent reign? "Christ executeth the office of a king in ruling and defending us, and in restraining and conquering all his and our enemies" says the Westminster Assembly's *Shorter Catechism.* This is the prerogative of Christ, God who became man who is our Mediator; this can be said of no angel no matter how great or grand.

Therefore the writer concludes: "Are they not all ministering spirits sent out to serve for the sake of those who are to inherit salvation?" Reflecting Psalm 104:4, already referenced by the writer in verse 7, we are encouraged to remember that the angels have a subordinate role to play as *ministering spirits.* The angels serve before the throne and, therefore, serve God's people at Christ's bidding. How magnificent is the Son to whom angels bow!

Let us not miss that angelic beings serve the Lord "for the sake of those who are to inherit salvation." The Lord has designed that the angels serve the people of God during their earthly pilgrimage. "The angel of the LORD encamps around those who fear him, and delivers them" (Ps. 34:7). The angels of the Lord are sent to minister protection and deliverance to the elect of God in their earthly struggles (2 Kings 6:15–17; Dan. 6:22; Acts 5:17–19; 12:6–9) and all the way home to our heavenly inheritance. In Luke 16 we read that "the poor man died and was carried by the angels to Abraham's bosom" (Luke 16:22). Bunyan has Christian and Hopeful "upon the bank of the

River on the other side" met by "two shining men" who salute them saying: "We are ministering Spirits sent forth to minister to those that shall be Heirs of Salvation;" and, entering in the believers were "swallowed up with the sight of Angels, and with hearing their melodious notes."[14]

Yes. The Lord will take his people all the way home to their inheritance just as he has promised. Who knows along the way how he chooses to use his angels in our lives? Surely, it is a marvel to contemplate.

Final Applications

Inferences abound as we consider this majestic passage. I limit myself for the sake of clarity to two important remarks. First, Christian, do you see how glorious is your Lord, how exalted is Christ our Priest who is also King upon his throne? Beware, then, of the death of awe. Impress his greatness on your heart. And, as you do this hear the exhortation that comes repeatedly in Hebrews: don't drift. If these Hebrew Christians had kept their minds fixed here on the truths of this chapter and throughout Hebrews they would not have been tempted to drift; on the contrary, they would have kept to their place before Christ's throne. And you, believer, are you tempted to drift? If you kept your mind stored with the truths of this chapter and if your affections were drawn toward your majestic Lord, do you think you would drift? No indeed; therefore, fix your gaze on your exalted Great High Priest.

Second, do you rest on Christ's omnipotence? Jesus Christ our Lord rules and reigns, carrying creation to its appointed end. Both as to his *essence* and his *office*, Christ is transcendently great. The angels worship him. God has established the Mediator upon his throne; he reigns by the Father's ordination. Christ

---

14. John Bunyan, *The Pilgrim's* Progress (Edinburgh: Banner of Truth, 2009), 183, 186.

will defend his church and "the one who falls on this stone will be broken to pieces" (Matt. 21:44). In Psalm 2 God says "I have set my king"—God has decreed his Meditorial glory. The Lord says, "My counsel shall stand, and I will accomplish all my purpose" (Isa. 46:10).

Diocletian and others like him arise in the course of history saying the name of Christians is being extinguished.[15] This is not so. God the Father raised his Son from the dead; he elevated him to the highest place. Christ is not in a tomb but on the throne. God has promised ultimate victory to his people and ultimate success for his kingdom. Christ has been given dominion over the nations (Psalm 2:8; Matthew 28:16–20). The world belongs to Christ our Mediator. Christ did not enter the world to be defeated. He came to crush Satan's head (Gen. 3:15), to purchase his people from sin, and to restore this fallen world. The passages cited to show that Christ is superior to the angels give the ultimate encouragement that the Father does everything for Christ the King—Priest of his people.

Do these truths encourage you? Do you take the preached Word home and to the work place? You will be encouraged to the extent that you are preoccupied with the glory of God and the grandeur of Christ. Verse 4 reminds us that the Son has inherited a name more excellent than that of the angels. The Son inherits as Mediator a name above all names (Philpplans 2:9). The Son is essentially supreme, the object of angelic worship, infinitely above the angels, enthroned above the angels, eternal and immutable, and the Ruler of the universe. He rules, as Mediator, in regal splendor and brings the universe to its appointed end. The hymn writer reminds us:

---

15. "Monuments were raised to commemorate the [Roman emperor Diocletian's] zeal as a persecutor [of Christians] . . . On one of them is an inscription, 'For having extinguished the name of Christians who brought the Republic to ruin.'" James E. Talmage, *The Great Apostasy: Considered in the Light of Scriptural and Secular History* (Salt Lake City: The Deseret News, 1909), 74–75.

Superior to Angels

This is my Father's world
O Let me n'er forget
That though the wrong seems oft so strong,
God is the Ruler yet.

This is my Father's world
the battle is not done
Jesus who died shall be satisfied
and earth and heav'n be one.

None can overthrow omnipotence. The angels worship Christ; they bow before his impenetrable light. They adore his name and sing his worth in the heaven of holiness. Since this Lord Jesus Christ rules, since he is exalted, can you exalt him in your heart too much? Will you exalt him in your affections all you can? Will you find ways of doing so today?

3

Drifting

HEBREWS 2:1–4

Therefore we must pay much closer attention to what we have heard, lest we drift away from it. For since the message declared by angels proved to be reliable, and every transgression or disobedience received a just retribution, how shall we escape if we neglect such a great salvation? It was declared at first by the Lord, and it was attested to us by those who heard, while God also bore witness by signs and wonders and various miracles and by gifts of the Holy Spirit distributed according to his will.

My friend and former teacher, Sinclair Ferguson, held his first pastorate on the Isle of Unst, the northernmost inhabited island in Britain. I have heard him tell of bird watchers that would sometimes come from the mainland to observe the unusual bird and wild life on that rocky island. Dr. Ferguson said something like this: "Suppose one of those bird watchers came and looking up paid no heed to the sheer drop that was before his feet. Would you not feel compelled to cry out, 'Beware, beware!'" So it is with the gospel minister. All around us are sinners who are oblivious of the sheer drop into an eternal hell that awaits them for their unbelief. Are we not obligated to cry out "Beware!" Do we not owe it to them?

The writer of Hebrews 2:1–4 similarly warns his readers. The writer, as we shall see, is thoroughly committed to the final perseverance of the saints; a true believer cannot be lost. Indeed, Hebrews is pervaded with and encourages full assurance of faith. However, the writer also knows that the Lord uses warnings to preserve his people and that, in the church visible, there are false professors who must be warned: "How shall we escape if we neglect such great salvation?" Therefore, in this passage we are lovingly and sternly warned.

The truth of the gospel calls us to faithful steadfastness in the gospel. Do you wish to be established in the gospel, established in faith and growing in your commitment to the truth? This passage will help you to understand the trajectory of Hebrews and the writer's goal of seeing his hearers grounded in the good news of Jesus. The writer begins with our responsibility to hear the Word.

The Christian's Obligation to Hear

We are obligated to hear God's Word and gospel *because Christian doctrine is essential and practical.* The text begins with the word *therefore*, pointing us back to all that we have seen thus far in the first chapter of Hebrews. What have been the emphases thus far? Christ is more glorious than the prophets, he is glorious as the Son (the appointed heir, the Creator, the radiance of God's glory, the exact imprint of God's nature, the Cosmic Sustainer), more glorious than the angels, having inherited a more glorious name than theirs.

In light of these truths it is important to remember the practical and pastoral matter with which the writer is concerned. The author of Hebrews is preoccupied with Hebrew Christians who are nearing exhaustion and are tempted to turn back from their profession of faith in Christ. How then does the writer address this grave matter? Though it may surprise many in the church today, the writer addresses the practical matter of exhaustion in the Christian life by bringing theology to bear on the situation.

There is an attitude that prevails in the church today that sees theology as impractical, that declares creeds, confessions, catechisms, and the idea of a system of theology to be passé and even detrimental to Christian living. But, commitment to doctrine does not detract from vital Christian living. On the contrary, decrying the value of theology has dimmed the brightness of the gospel in our churches and has harmed forthright, confident Christian living. The writer's answer to the cry "give me something that I can use" is to point to theology, a theology that should govern thinking, feeling, and living. Theology and life are inseparable.

What does the author do to encourage faithful Christian living? He begins by arguing from the glory and excellence of Christ. As Owen remarked, the writer argues that "seeing the gospel hath such a blessed Author, we ought to take care that we forfeit not our interest in it."[1] Indeed, the author "minds them and us in general, that in handling of the doctrines of the gospel concerning the person and offices of Jesus Christ, we should not satisfy ourselves in a bare *notional speculation* of them, but endeavour to get our hearts excited by them unto faith, love, obedience, and steadfastness in our profession."[2]

Further, Owen reminds us that "constant high thoughts, then, of the necessity, worth, glory, and excellency of the gospel, as on other accounts, so especially of the author of it, and the grace dispensed in it, is the first step in that diligent heeding of it which is required of us." And, without such searching of the Scriptures, Owen solemnly adds, "no man will hold fast his profession."[3]

---

1. John Owen, *Hebrews* (Edinburgh: Banner of Truth, 1991), 3.259.

2. Owen, *Hebrews*, 3.257.

3. Owen, *Hebrews*, 3.265.

We are not only obligated to hear the gospel message because of the way it addresses the immediate need of perseverance in the battle of Christian living, we also are obligated to hear *because it has eternal consequence.* The author of Hebrews argues that, indeed, believers must not turn from what they have heard in the preaching of the gospel matters, because it has eternal consequences. Are we in danger of forgetting the uniqueness of the gospel? Let us not be too sure that we are not. Remember the example of the Galatians to whom Paul wrote. To his utter amazement, they had forgotten the uniqueness and exclusivity of the gospel very soon after Paul had founded their churches (Gal. 1:7–9). The gospel is not something to be forgotten, but clung to. The gospel is crucial—vital. It is not something we can take or leave. We are under moral obligation to hear the gospel.

Hebrews 2:1 calls upon us to "pay much closer attention to what we have heard," to attend to, and to give heed to the gospel. This means that we must earnestly apply ourselves to knowing, understanding, and putting to use the truth of the gospel in our lives. Christ is our prophet, and we must hear his word; he is our priest, let us receive his work by faith; he is our king, therefore let us bow before him.

Paying heed to the gospel is not just a notional knowledge of the gospel, but faith in the gospel, love for its truth, and steadfastness in following it. Lane points out that in this verse, the word *prosechein* (pay attention to, heed), when connected to the peril of drifting off course may have a nautical overtone "to hold a ship toward port, or to fasten the anchors to the sea bed." The image of a drifting ship "warns his readers that they are in danger of losing sight of the reality of Christian salvation."[4]

---

4. William L. Lane *Hebrews* in *Word Biblical Commentary* (Dallas, Word Publishers, 1991), 1.37.

Drifting

The Dangerous Consequences of Not Hearing

Having reminded his hearers of the obligation to hear the gospel message, the writer then underscores the dangerous consequences that follow upon refusing to hear the gospel. Indeed, *we* (he includes himself in the warning) may "drift away from it." *Drift* is from the verb *pararreō* meaning "to flow by" or "slip away." Imagine reclining on a raft in the ocean. All seems well. The sun is shining, and then you become drowsy in the warmth of the sun, falling asleep. When you finally sit up, you are arrested suddenly by the awareness that you have drifted far from the shore! There you are, surrounded by a deep and dangerous sea with no landmark and no bearings. Such a circumstance well illustrates the warning of this text.

Hebrews is overflowing with warning and exhortation to continue faithfully in the gospel of grace (3:12; 4:11, 14; 5:11–12; 6:1; 10:35–36; 12:1; 12:12; 13:9). Hughes summarizes: "From sheer apathy they are in grave peril of drifting away from the essentials of the gospel."[5] It is in this emotionally charged context, under the serious weight of the reality of the eternal issues that are at stake, that the text reminds us of the authority of the message.

The Authority of the Message

Verses two and three tell us that "since the message declared by angels proved to be reliable, and every transgression or disobedience received a just retribution, how shall we escape if we neglect such a great salvation?" The writer is underscoring the gravity of the message of Sinai. Angels mediated to Moses what God said on the Mount. Although the Scriptures do not altogether tell us what that means, Deuteronomy 33:2 says that "the LORD came from Sinai and dawned from Seir upon us; he shone

---

5. Philip E. Hughes, *Hebrews* (Grand Rapids: Eerdmans, 1977), 74.

forth from Mount Paran; he came from the ten thousands of holy ones, with flaming fire at his right hand." Psalm 68:17 may indicate something similar: "The chariots of God are twice ten thousand, thousands upon thousands; the Lord is among them; Sinai is now in the sanctuary." Paul reminds us that "the law was put in place through angels by an intermediary" (Gal. 3:19). And, in Acts 7, Stephen said of his opponents that they were those "who received the law as delivered by angels and did not keep it" (Acts 7:53). The writer underlines again the place of angels in God's service.

What was said at Sinai was God's Word, hence "reliable" (*bebaios*, dependable, certain) and "every transgression or disobedience received a just retribution," as shown time and again in the Old Testament. How then will those who deny and despise the gospel escape the judgment of God? Now a Mediator of far greater importance than Moses has been manifested, who came with greater attestation than the Law. The Son of God is the Mediator of the New Covenant (8:6; 9:15; 12:24). So, the writer's argument is profound and arresting: if under Moses, the law with its penalties brought consequences of eternal weight, what will the consequences be if we neglect the Word that came by Christ? After all, as Hebrews tells us, there is no more sacrifice for sin; refuse Christ and there is no salvation anywhere else. If we refuse what Christ proclaimed in the gospel we are lost.

There is no additional revelation, no other atonement, no other sacrifice for sin. Hence the gospel is called "such a great salvation." Given the description of Christ and his work in the opening verses of Hebrews (1:1–3), the grandeur, greatness, and exclusivity of the gospel has been established by the writer from the start. "The salvation is so great, because everything is to be put under his feet. The world subjected to angels is the *old* world; the new is under the man Christ, and with Him is under all mankind."[6] For those Hebrew Christians tempted to turn back, where can they go? What will the result be for those who despise this once for all, finished atonement of Christ and his gospel of grace?

"How shall we escape if we neglect such great salvation?" The verb *ameleō* is applied to a person's attitude that doesn't care or is not concerned with the gospel. It means to disregard, reject or neglect. The answer to the question, "How shall we escape if we neglect such great salvation?" is: "We shall not escape." *If we neglect* is a circumstantial participle that is conditional. It is used in Matthew 22:5 of those who neglect the invitation to the wedding feast. So here, to be careless of the gospel or to turn a deaf ear to its messengers is to despise it, to neglect the only message of salvation. No one can escape divine vengeance who neglects the truth of the gospel. There is no other atonement.

The coming of Christ does not lessen but heightens the serious call to hear God's Word. The coming of Christ is what makes the salvation *such great salvation*. As Calvin put it, "God wishes his gifts to be valued by us at their proper worth. The more precious they are, the baser our ingratitude if they do not have their proper value for us. In accordance with the greatness of Christ, so will be the severity of God's vengeance on all despisers of the gospel."[7]

Neglecting *such great salvation* is terribly serious for at least three reasons: *First,* there is life in no one but Christ. It had its beginning, *was declared at first by the Lord.* Prior prophecies and announcements of the gospel find their final fulfillment and exegesis in Christ and his atoning work. *If* we neglect the salvation God has revealed in his Son, there is no one else who can save us from our sins.

6. Geerhardus Vos, *The Teaching of the Epistle to the Hebrews* (Grand Rapids: Eerdmans, 1956), 41.

7. John Calvin, *Hebrews and I and II Peter,* in *Calvin's New Testament Commentaries: A New Translation* (Grand Rapids: Eerdmans, 1979), 19.

Second, undoubtedly, the writer is indicating that neglecting salvation in Christ results in eternal punishment. It is not popular today to bring such warning to those who neglect the gospel message, but the gospel is not just another philosophy that one can take or leave without consequence. To quarrel with God's punishment of sin is to quarrel with God for being holy and just. That which God's nature requires is good, even the eternal punishment of the wicked.

Third, to true believers, every threatening of the gospel proclaims saving grace to believers. While encouraging the believer, those rejecting the gospel must give an account for rejecting the gospel that they have seen operative in the lives of God's people, thus exacerbating their own judgment.

The Place of Warning in the Church and the Christian Life

As we see here, the place of warning in the church and in the Christian life rises to the fore very early in *Hebrews.* The theme will come up many times as we proceed. For now it will help to make a few observations about these warnings. The Scriptures clearly teach that when a professing Christian walks away from his profession that he was never a true believer to begin with. As we read in 1 John 2:19: "They went out from us, but they were not of us; for it they had been of us, they would have continued with us. But they went out, that it might become plain that they all are not of us." Until such time as an apostate actually shows his true colors, he will be addressed as a believer by virtue of his profession and membership in the visible church. Warning, then, comes to the visible church, which is made up of true and false professors.

Furthermore, the Lord uses warning in the lives of true believers to spur them on continually to see their need of Christ. Is not salvation certain for true believers? Yes. Those who are truly saved from sin must—by virtue of the Father's electing decree, the blood of Christ who bought them, and the Holy Spirit's effectual application of Christ's atonement—infallibly persevere to the end. But the way to heaven is not easy, and the Lord uses instruction, encouragement, discipline, and even warning to bring us home.

The use of warning as a part of God's purpose may be illustrated in this way. Suppose you are about to make a trip from New York to London on a jet liner. Suppose also that you knew infallibly that God had decreed that you land safely in London. Now, we cannot know such a thing, but suppose it for the sake of the illustration. Would that certain knowledge make buying a ticket and being at the airport on time unnecessary? Would certain knowledge that you will arrive in London make it unnecessary that you actually get on the plane? And, would certain knowledge of your arrival in London make the pilot, crew, safety precautions, and warning signals unnecessary? Would it make turbulence less violent?

All illustrations of divine things are inadequate, but may we not see that the Lord who has ordained the end has ordained also the *means* to take us to the appointed end? In this illustration, that means you heed the warning not to be late, arrive in time to catch the plane, and that the mechanics also heed the warning to repair stress fractures in the wing. God has ordained not only the end but the means, and warning is one of his means for accomplishing his purposes. Warning is as much a means for accomplishing the end as encouragement and rebuke and instruction. The Lord does not deal with us as stocks and blocks but as human beings who need discipline and warning, as well as encouragement and instruction, to arrive at the end the Lord has decreed.

My airline illustration might remind us that in Acts we are told that in Paul's voyage to Rome he had a direct revelation from God that he would reach Rome and that his fellow passengers would survive the impending shipwreck (Acts 23:11; 27:23–24). However, this did not hinder the emphasis on the means of accomplishing the decree which included that the sailors must remain on the ship until it ran aground (27:30–32) telling them that otherwise "you cannot be saved." In addition, God's decree was served when the centurion's order was carried out to spare the prisoners despite the soldiers' plan to kill them (27:42–44). The God who decrees also determines the means of accomplishing the decree. This may be applied to the solemn matter of warning which is one of many means the Lord uses to fulfill his decree to bring his elect home.

Any reader of Bunyan's *The Pilgrim's Progress* has another illustration of these matters ready at hand. The Lord delivers Christian from his awful burden of sin. It is certain that Christian and Hopeful will reach the Celestial City; perhaps you have read the end before the beginning. But, the certainty that Christian and his companion will reach the Celestial City did not make the instructions, rebukes, encouragements, and warnings less needful. The certainty of Christian's arrival did not make the Slough of Despond less real, or Doubting Castle less troublesome, or Vanity Fair less tempting, or the battle with Apolyon less fierce, or Valley of the Shadow less menacing.

The Lord will use instruction, encouragement and discipline to bring us home, but also in the midst of "many dangers, toils and snares" the Lord will use warnings. Again, we are not stocks and blocks but human beings in need of such means. Faith in Christ will show forth and be strengthened as we heed the warnings of Scripture. It is an awesome consideration that many a false professor will show himself to be lost and undone when he does not heed the warnings of Scripture. Those who appear to lose faith never had saving faith at all.

Drifting

Remember, there are three tenses to salvation: true believers *have been* saved, *are being* saved and *will be* saved. Indeed, one chief role given to ministers of the gospel is to be used of the Lord through the preaching of the Word every week to bring Christ's flock all the way to glory. It is certain that true believers will be saved and endure to the end; it is just as certain that the Lord uses the means of Word, sacrament, prayer, and the fellowship of God's people to bring his own home. And, the faithful preaching of the Word includes warning.

The Assembly's *Confession of Faith* (17.1) puts it this way: "They, whom God hath accepted in His Beloved, effectually called, and sanctified by His Spirit, can neither totally nor finally fall away from the state of grace, but shall certainly persevere therein to the end and be eternally saved." Yes; but, as the *Confession* also clearly acknowledges, the Lord uses means to accomplish this end.

Manifestations of the Authentic Gospel

The salvation in Christ that must not be neglected "was declared at first by the Lord, and it was attested to us by those who heard." This means that the gospel was proclaimed by the Lord Jesus Christ and was attested by his apostles or, at least, in the apostolic church. Through them "God also bore witness by signs and wonders and various miracles and by gifts of the Holy Spirit distributed according to his will." The recipients of Hebrews had seen God's work among them miraculously. These signs confirmed the apostolic gospel. The author of Hebrews calls upon his readers to remember the signs that confirmed the gospel proclamation, calling them to faithfulness in the midst of various temptations to turn aside. "Since the purpose of this evidence is the validation that God has spoken definitively in Christ, unbelief and carelessness can only be regarded as the expression of an utterly incomprehensible hardness of heart (cf. 3:7–8, 12, 15; 4:7)."[8]

---

8. Lane, *Hebrews*, 40.

I have told my congregation that we too have been witnesses to a remarkable work of God. Yes, Jesus gave the message, and his own person and work were authenticated by signs and wonders—preeminently by his resurrection from the dead. From his ascension bounty came apostles who performed miracles, and then a stream of evangelical witnesses down to the present time. Even though we have not witnessed the dead raised or withered hands restored since the cessation of apostolic sign gifts, we have seen lives changed, love demonstrated in ways that makes us marvel, acts of faith in Christ that are notable and even remarkable. Most wonderfully, the Word is preached among us and Christ is believed. We too have seen the authentic gospel in our midst. "Therefore we must pay much closer attention to what we have heard, lest we drift away from it." We also need the words burned into our consciousness: "How shall we escape if we neglect such a great salvation?"

Give Heed to the Gospel

What does it mean to give heed to the gospel? That is the question that should preoccupy the reader of this passage. John Owen, whose magisterial commentary on Hebrews still serves the church as a classic exposition, answers that question in five ways. How do we give heed to the gospel? Here is a summary of Owen's answer:

First, we give heed to the gospel by constantly maintaining high thoughts of the excellence of the gospel. Indeed, "if we consider it not as that wherein our chief concernment lies, we consider it not at all as we ought . . . . If the gospel be not more unto us than all the world besides, we shall never continue in a useful profession of it."[9] The ministration of the gospel is full of

---

9. For the references in this section to John Owen's thoughts see Owen, *Hebrews*, 3.264–268.

glory; let us keep the glory and wonder of the gospel ever before our eyes.

Second, Owen instructs us to make a diligent study of the gospel "searching into the mind of God in it, that so we may grow wise in the mysteries" of the gospel. To hold the gospel is to dig it up like treasure. We must set aside the many distractions of our modern world and take time alone with God and his inerrant Word eagerly studying the Scriptures so that we may deepen our understanding of the gospel of free grace. Owen says clearly that "studying of the word is the security of our faith."

Third, to truly heed the gospel we must "mix the word with faith." Citing Romans 10:10–11, Owen declares: "as good not hear as not believe. Believing is the end of hearing." We must not be like the person who sees food but does not eat or like a dry stick that cannot absorb water.

Fourth, heeding the gospel means conforming our hearts and lives to the gospel. "When the heart of the hearer is quickened, enlivened, spirited with gospel truths, and by them is moulded and fashioned into their likeness, and expresseth that likeness in its fruits, or a conversation becoming the gospel, then is the word attended to in a right manner. This will secure the word a station in our hearts, and give it a permanent abode in us." In this way, the Word becomes abundant and plentiful to our souls.

Fifth, giving heed to the gospel means becoming watchful against all that opposes the truthfulness of the gospel. The thoughts, attitudes, false doctrines, and living that oppose the gospel are many; therefore, we must learn to become watchful against all that would unseat truth in our lives and seek to preserve the truth in our hearts.

To these methods for taking heed of the gospel, Owen adds additional observations. He underscores three settings in which some lose what they have heard. Again, Owen, the renowned Calvinist who wrote forthrightly on the final perseverance of the saints, also knows from God's Word that the Lord uses warning in the maintenance of his grace within our hearts.

First, Owen warns us, some people lose what they have heard in times of peace and prosperity. Prosperity sometimes ruins a soul. As a pastor I have seen with sadness some professing Christians who have seemed to walk well in times of adversity, but then fell away when prosperity returned. This is the point of Owen's warning. "The warmth of prosperity breeds swarms of apostates, as the heat of the sun doth insects in the spring."

Second, some people lose what they have heard in times of persecution. "'When persecution ariseth,' saith our Saviour, 'they fall away.' Many go on apace in profession until they come to see the cross; this sight puts them to a stand, and then turns them quite out of the way." Perhaps even Christians in the West will have opportunity to practice faithfulness in persecuting times as overt antipathy to the gospel continues to grow. Persecuting times can be marvelous times in which to bear faithful witness before the world; they can also be times of danger calling for watchfulness.

Third, some lose what they have heard in times of temptation. If we slumber (Matt. 25:5) and become negligent in temptation, professors may "awake and look about them, the whole power of the word is lost and departed from them." Owen concludes with this warning: "let us not deceive ourselves; a slothful, negligent hearing of the word will bring no man to life. The commands we have 'to watch, pray, strive, labor, and fight,' are not in vain. The warnings given us of the opposition that is made to our faith, by indwelling sin, Satan, and the world, are not left on record for nothing; no more are the sad examples which we have of man, who beginning a good profession have utterly turned aside to sin and folly."

Drifting

Taking Heed Lest We Drift

Let the warnings of Hebrews and John Owens's comments upon them enter believing and sincere hearts. Open your heart to the full force of the warning so that the Spirit of God may press his truth more deeply upon your soul. Let us "pay much closer attention to what we have heard, lest we drift away from it." In what contexts may drifting take place?

Drifting can happen *ecclesiastically*. Paul wrote Galatians to Christians who had only recently professed faith in Christ. Paul was astonished to find that they were "quickly deserting" the gospel of free grace (Gal. 1:6). The church at Geneva had experienced Reformation under Calvin, blessing under Beza, and great theological teaching from Francis Turretin. But Geneva had declined so precipitously by the nineteenth century, that a visiting Robert Haldane discovered the theological faculty, students, and churches were all Socinian, having deeply departed from God's Word, the confession of the Trinity, and the Biblical doctrine of salvation.

Today, once again evangelical churches are drifting into Arminianism and the "openness of God" heresy. "Emergent churches" are denying substitutionary atonement, and the so-called New Perspective on Paul and the Federal Vision deny the imputed righteousness of Christ. We could go on and on citing contemporary aberrations and departures from the faith—all because the church is not heeding the Word.

Second, drifting can happen *personally*. Personal declension in knowing and loving the truth and living for Christ is the saddest and most tragic thing for a pastor to observe in his flock. It usually happens in small steps; absences from worship, undervaluing the church, personal time with God slips, attitudes become critical of God's people and this is often accompanied by moral failing and collapse. Heed the warning: "How shall we escape if we neglect such a great salvation?"

Perhaps it is wise that I end by addressing teaching and ruling elders and deacons. The men filling these offices should be men of doctrinal and moral integrity, filled with the Holy Spirit and who are committed to paying heed to the message of the gospel for all of life. Officers, don't drift! Ruling Elders, I urge you especially to be engaged in the positive, proactive ministry of discipleship. Engage in the preventative measures that help our flocks pay attention to the Word.

In the process of helping others, let the officers also take heed to themselves, their own doctrine, hearts and lives. John Murray has given us a solemn warning: "It is possible to lose our own souls in preoccupation with the needs of others. Piety must first burn in the individuality of our own hearts and lives. We shall not be the faithful keepers of the vineyards of others if we have not kept up our own."[10]

---

10. John Murray, *Collected Writings* (Edinburgh: Banner of Truth, 1976), 1.267.

4

Everything Subject to Christ

HEBREWS 2:5–9

Now in putting everything in subjection to him, he left nothing outside his control. At present, we do not yet see everything in subjection to him. But we see him who for a little while was made lower than the angels, namely Jesus, crowned with glory and honor because of the suffering of death, so that by the grace of God he might taste death for everyone.

Oh, what a glorious thing it is to be a Christian! When you became a Christian you became a part of something incomparably big—God's kingdom. Paul tells us that, at the end of time, Christ the Mediator will hand over that kingdom to his Father and that God will be all in all (1 Cor. 15:24–28). Surely, we have received a "great salvation" (2:3).

We easily lose perspective on the wonder of being a Christian and a member of God's kingdom. We also lose perspective on Christian living when we fail to see that we are a part of something bigger than meets the eye. This depressed experience was true of those to whom Hebrews was written and is often true of Christians today. Hebrews 2:5–9 helps us to regain true perspective on the grandness of knowing Christ and living for him.

Keep in mind that Hebrews was written to Jews who confessed faith in Christ but who, under the stress of persecution were exhausted, weary, and forgetful of the uniqueness of the Christian faith. Aware of their temptation to return to old, Judaistic religion, the author of Hebrews reminds them that Jesus is better—infinitely superior. Hebrews points these stressed and strained Christians to the glory of Jesus, the unique Son of the Father who is more glorious than the prophets and glorious in his Deity and Sonship.

That the Son is more glorious than and superior in every way to angels was demonstrated by a chorus of Old Testament texts the last of which cited Psalm 110:1. *And to which of the angels has he ever said, "Sit at my right hand until I make your enemies a footstool for your feet?"* Hebrews reminds us that the Christian walk is sustained by the constant preaching of the Word in our lives (remember, Hebrews is a sermon-epistle) through which we are constantly taught to look up as we move to the celestial city and to keep our gaze on Christ.

Appeal to Psalm 8

It is in this context that the writer now appeals to Psalm 8. He begins by saying: "Now it was not to angels that God subjected the world to come, of which we are speaking." The writer, pointing back immediately both to Psalm 110—which was not spoken to angels, but by the Father to the Son—and to the other Old Testament references—demonstrating the Son's transcendent dignity, reminds us that the angels serve the Lord in the governance of *this* world, but that the world *to come* has not been subjected to angels. There is in this consideration a reminder to the readers that their heritage is not found in this fallen world through which they travel as pilgrims but is found in the world to come secured by Jesus' atonement and enthronement.

The *world to come* refers to the new heavens and new earth, where the dominion lost by Adam will be restored to humanity in Christ. It is future in its consummation, but impinges upon God's people in the present. In Christ's triumphant death, resurrection, and ascension, the *world to come* is present and determinative of the believer's life and focus. "Remember!" the author is saying, "Your inheritance is not here but in the world to come, secured by your exalted Savior. The new heavens and the new earth are promised and coming. Let this spur you on." This "world to come, of which we are speaking" is the heart of the writer's concern throughout his epistle.

The writer appeals to additional Old Testament references in order to point to the Son's transcendent dignity. In this passage, he appeals solemnly ("it has been testified somewhere") to Psalm 8. Lane correctly notes that

> the vagueness of the formula of quotation is consistent with the strong emphasis throughout Hebrews on the oracular character of Scripture. Precisely because it is God who speaks in the OT, the identity of the person through whom he uttered his word is relatively unimportant. A vague allusion is sufficient. It is the substantial authority of what is said, not its source, which is of primary importance.[1]

The writer, then, turns to Psalm 8, where David dwells with astonishment on God's attentiveness to man:

> What is man, that you are mindful of him,
> or the son of man, that you care for him?
> You made him for a little while
> lower than the angels;

---

1. William L. Lane, *Hebrews*, in *Word Biblical Commentary* (Dallas: Word Publisher, 1991), 46.

> you have crowned him with glory and honor,
> putting everything in subjection under his feet.

This psalm is based on Gen 1:26 that points to man as the image bearer of God: *Let us make man in our image, after our likeness. And let them have dominion . . . over all the earth.* The Psalmist is overwhelmed when he considers what man was created to be, in contrast to what he has become. As he contemplates the majesty of God revealed in nature, David wonders that God deals with humans at all: "When I look at your heavens, the work of your fingers, the moon and the stars, which you have set in place, what is man that you are mindful of him, and the son of man that you care for him?" (Ps. 8:3–4).

The Psalmist knows, however, that man has a special place in the created order. Man is a creature of great dignity. Though created, for a time, a little lower than the angels, God has given the stewardship of creation to man. God put everything in the terrestrial order under human dominion. As Delitzsch put it: "Man, all but a divine being, like the angels, and royally crowned, is no landless king: the world is given him to rule over; the creature far and near is his dominion."[2] The Psalm points us back to Genesis and to Adamic kingship.

But how deeply has man fallen from that kingship. "For although they knew God, they did not honor him as God or give thanks to him, but they became futile in their thinking, and their foolish hearts were darkened. Claiming to be wise, they became fools, and exchanged the glory of the immortal God for images resembling mortal man and birds and animals and reptiles" (Rom. 1:21–23). Man fell from the kingship assigned to him in the garden. He fell hard, down into death and woe, and this leaves the question: Will man ever fulfill the calling and task that God gave him?

---

2. Franz Delitzsch, *Commentary on the Epistle to the Hebrews* (Grand Rapids: Eerdmans, 1952), 2.106.

Use of Psalm 8

Will man ever fulfill the goal of kingship? The writer appeals to Psalm 8 in order to demonstrate the Lordship of man over creation. Psalm 8 finds its fulfillment in Christ. "What the Psalm attributes to man in the totality of his race we see not (he argues) realized; *but* (so he proceeds in the following ver. 9) we do see man already even as the psalmist here depicts him, and by way of anticipation, in Jesus, that One Man who has for all our sakes already passed through death, and entered into glory and world-wide dominion."[3]

Christ is the last Adam under whose feet all things have been placed. Notice the connection the writer draws between 1:13 and 2:8. In 1:13 we read: "And to which of the angels has he ever said, 'Sit at my right hand until I make your enemies a footstool for your feet'?" Now, in 2:8 the author declares: "Now in putting everything in subjection to him, he left nothing outside his control." These thoughts in turn remind us of the affirmations of 1:3: "He upholds the universe by the word of his power. After making purification for sins, he sat down at the right hand of the Majesty on high." All things are now subjected to the chosen and only Mediator, including even the angels. As Paul also argues in 1 Corinthians 15:27, nothing in the created order is excepted.

The text affirms the marvelous truth that Christ, the Representative of the new humanity, is the One under whose feet all things have been submitted. Lane correctly points out that, in the New Testament, Psalm 8 is most often cited in association with Psalm 110:1 (1 Cor. 15:25–27; Eph. 1:20–22; cf. Phil. 3:21; 1 Pet. 3:22).[4] That all things are under the feet of our Lord fulfills the call of man to subdue the earth and restores man to his original dignity and calling. As Philip Hughes notes, "In Christ

3. Delitzsch, *Hebrews*, 2.109.

4. Lane, *Hebrews*, 1.46.

the dominion for which man was originally created is everlastingly established."[5] How did that come about? By what road did it happen? The author of Hebrews is keen that we know. The first step to Christ's sovereign exaltation was, strangely, his humiliation.

The Humiliation of the Son of God: Incarnation

In 2:7a we are told about man from Psalm 8: "You made him for a little while lower than the angels; you have crowned him with glory and honor." God's purpose to raise man above the angels is achieved by Christ. But first, before exaltation, the Son of God had to come low and be deeply humiliated. Here the writer affirms the incarnation of our Lord.

The words "for a little while" may also be translated "to a small degree." The latter fits the context of Psalm 8, but "for a little while" better fits the context of this portion of Hebrews, which is transitioning to the incarnation and humiliation of the Son and stressing that this humiliation was real but temporary. The term translated "angels" ("You made him for a little while lower than the angels") is *Elohim*, usually a name of God, but sometimes signifying angelic beings. See, for example, Psalm 97:7; 138:1; and Psalm 82:1, 6 where the LXX appropriately renders *Elohim* "angels."[6]

Pause and consider how deep was the humiliation of the Son of God. Consider first of all that the one who became man was God. In Psalm 113:4–6, we read of God: "The Lord is high above all nations, and his glory above the heavens. Who is like the Lord our God, who is seated on high, who looks down on the heavens and the earth?" Infinite perfection is his and infinite distance is between him and his creation. Isaiah 40:15, 17 says of him: "Behold the nations are like a drop from the bucket,

---

5. Philip E. Hughes, *Hebrews* (Grand Rapids: Eerdmans, 1990), 86.

6. See Hughes, *Hebrews*, 85.

and are accounted as the dust on the scales; behold, he takes up the coastlands like fine dust." Isaiah 57:17 speaks of the Lord as "the High and lofty One who inhabits eternity." The Lord is totally self-contained needing no one and nothing outside of Himself. But, now think on this; not only did the Son of God become man, but he came to redeem *fallen* humanity. The Son of God, took upon himself human nature to save sinful creatures. If there can be such a thing as more than infinite condescension then this is it! The Creator, the upholder of the universe became frail, suffering, mortal man to redeem us.

The Humiliation of the Son of God: Atonement

The infinite Son of God, the second person of the Trinity, took upon himself human nature, so that he might make atonement for his people. The Son endured "the suffering of death so that by the grace of God he might taste death for everyone." When the text tells us that the Son came that "he might taste death," "taste" does not mean simply to "sip" death. Various writers point out that this expression is a Semitism alluding to the violence of death. Notice that the writer always includes the term "suffer" or "suffering" with the death of Christ in Hebrews. That "he might taste death" (from *geuomai*—taste, experience) means that the Son became man that he might experience death to the full, experiencing the wages of sin by bearing the infinite displeasure and wrath of God. We read in John 8:52 *if anyone keeps my word, he will never taste death;* but Christ tasted death and experienced all that death involves.

The Son of God did not become man primarily to become an *example* for us, but that he might be a *substitute* atoning for the sins of sinners. The Son redeemed us from the curse of death by taking our lot. As the Westminster *Larger Catechism* (49) so provocatively puts it, Christ "having also conflicted with the terrors of death and the powers of darkness, felt and borne the weight of God's wrath, he laid down his life an offering for sin, enduring the painful, shameful, and cursed death of the cross." And we are told in that same catechism (38) that it was requisite that the Mediator be God "that he might sustain and keep the human nature from sinking under the infinite wrath of God, and the power of death; give worth and efficacy to his sufferings, obedience and intercession; and to satisfy God's justice . . ."

When the text says that Christ suffered "so that he might taste death *for everyone*," this does not mean universal atonement, that is, that Christ died for every single human. First, this would contradict the plain teaching of Scripture. Christ in his death was a real substitute for those for whom he died. He actually accomplished the salvation of his elect by his atoning death. Second, the term *everyone* proves nothing. That term is often used in a limited sense. Note for example Colossians 1:28 in which Paul says, "Him we proclaim, warning everyone." No one reading this verse would view it in an absolutely universal sense. Third, the context describes clearly the meaning of the *everyone* for whom he tasted death when, in 2:10, they are described as the *many sons* whom Christ brings to glory. The *everyone* of 2:9 is defined as *many sons* in 2:10. These are in turn the "sanctified" and "brothers" of 2:11, the "children that God has given [Christ]" in 2:13, and those delivered from the bondage of death in 2:15. There is nothing in the context to suggest a universal atonement and everything in the context to express its particular and definite nature.

The humiliation and suffering of the Son of God for our sake was accomplished "by the grace of God." What Jesus the Son achieved in his active and passive obedience was preceded by and engulfed in the freeness of God's sovereign grace. The vicarious atonement by which we are redeemed and reconciled to God excludes all claims to human merit and causes the believer to rest completely in Christ who has done for us what we never could have done for ourselves. Grace has accomplished a free and finished salvation. Christ's sufferings were a real punishment for the real sins of particular chosen sinners that achieved a real salvation for them. This is the truth upon which the believer may live and die. It is all of grace from first to last. Bless the Lord that salvation is by grace! Had it depended on our merit, we all should have been lost forever. If the Lord had waited until there was something good within us or about us to save, we would have never been saved. Salvation is by free, unconditional grace. As some old hymn line written long ago put it: "Thy rich gospel scorns conditions/Breathes salvation free as air."[7] Thank God for the grace of the cross!

We are answering the question: by what road have all things been placed under Christ's feet? The first part of the answer is through the incarnation and atonement of the Son of God, by means of his utter humiliation and infinite condescension by which he paid the price of our sins. The second part of the answer to the question, by what road have all things been placed under Christ's feet, is his exaltation to God's right hand.

The Exaltation of Christ the Mediator

In verse 9, we are told that "we see him crowned with glory and honor because of the suffering of death," and in verse 8: "Now in putting everything in subjection to him, he left nothing outside his control." *Glory and honor* may serve as a possible allusion to priestly splendor (Exod. 28:2, 40), thus moving his readers along to the major theme of the heavenly ministry of Christ as high priest. "So far from the humiliation and suffering endured by Christ tarnishing His glory, they were the meritorious cause

---

7. Richard Burnham, "O! Thou great eternal Jesus," from *Hymns of Praise: A New Selection of Gospel Hymns, Combining All the Excellencies of Our Spiritual Poets with Many Originals, for the Use of All Spiritual Worshippers*, compiled by E. Mote (London: Nichols and Son, 1853), 412–413.

of His exaltation."[8] All things then are now "in subjection under his feet" (v. 8) as he rules and reigns in his mediatorial exaltation at the right hand of his Father. F. F. Bruce rightly says: "The sovereignty which man has proved unable to exercise thus far is already wielded on man's behalf by the true Son of Man; His suffering and triumph constitute the pledge of His eternal kingdom."[9] This glorified Lord and Savior *we see*, that is, we *apprehend*, by faith.

Here we find the answer to what must have been a dilemma for those addressed in the book. How do we relate Psalm 110:1 and Psalm 8:4–6? How do we relate the promise of a *future* subjection of all things to Christ with the *present* reality of all things subject to Christ? Delitzsch put it elegantly:

> The old world, indeed, lost all its *right* to existence and continuance when Christ first came but continues nevertheless to exist still as the outward shell of that hidden world of the future which is not fully formed within it, but will one day burst from its encasement as a new heaven and a new earth at Christ's second coming . . . According to its hidden principle and spirit, this world is already present; according to its glorified manifestation and body, it is yet future.[10]

So, the kingdom is here, yet we pray *thy kingdom come!*

All things have been placed "in subjection under his [Christ's] feet"; but, "we do not yet see everything in subjection to him." The way this state of affairs has come about, humiliation and exaltation, brings with it profound implications for Christian living.

---

8. A. W. Pink, *Hebrews* (Grand Rapids: Baker, 2004), 95.

9. F. F. Bruce, *Hebrews* (Grand Rapids: Eerdmans, 1979), 37.

10. Delitzsch, *Hebrews*, 2.102.

Implications for Christian Living

First, the humiliation and exaltation of Christ provides the pattern for Christian living. Humiliation precedes exaltation; the cross goes before the crown. This was true of our Lord and is true of those united to him. As the author was writing, the cross was particularly heavy. His message points to the pattern of Christ which spoke loudly, "Do not go back!" They needed to see, and we do as well, that pain, suffering, rejection and persecution is not abnormal Christian living but is our calling as believers. "Through many tribulations we must enter the kingdom of God" (Acts 14:22). "If we died with him, we will also reign with him; if we endure, we will also reign with him" (2 Tim 2:11–12). In Berkhof's *Systematic Theology*, there is a profound little paragraph on the nature of our union with Christ which speaks right to our point:

> By this union believers are changed into the image of Christ *according to his human nature*. What Christ effects in His people is in a sense a replica or reproduction of what took place with Him. Not only objectively, but also in a subjective sense they suffer, bear the cross, are crucified, die, and are raised in newness of life, with Christ. They share in a measure the experiences of their Lord, Matt. 16:24; Rom. 6:5; Gal. 2:20; Col. 1:24; 2:12; 3:1; I Pet. 4:13.[11]

A second implication for Christian living is the encouragement that comes from the passage that the rule of Christ is indefectible. No one and nothing can pull the once humiliated and now exalted Christ from his throne! The whole theme argues, "How can you go back? Jesus reigns! And, as his redeemed ones you share in his reign." Does not Paul remind the tried people of God that if we are children we are also heirs, "heirs

---

11. Louis Berkhof, *Systematic Theology* (Grand Rapids: Eerdmans, 1972), 451.

of God and fellow heirs with Christ, provided we suffer with him" (Rom. 8:17)? Indeed, the Christ who conquered our sin and who, as the last Adam, brings all things to their appointed end, promises that "the night will be no more. [God's people] will need no light of lamp or sun, for the Lord God will be their light, and they will reign forever and ever" (Rev. 22:5).

A third implication for Christian living from this text is that the believer must not allow his troubles to obscure the throne. That is what the believers who first read this book were doing. Do not allow troubles to keep your gaze from Jesus; rather adorn the doctrine you profess by faithfulness. Christ is not less Lord, he is no less King, when you are denounced for holding the faith, or when you are losing a battle with illness, or when you are without a job. I do not minimize the struggles of the Christian life. However, these things must be seen as part of a larger battle. The struggles and hardships of Christian living have a part to play in Christ's reign. We are—even in these struggles—a part of something bigger than we are, indeed something of cosmic scope. The ways in which we respond show how we view the Kingship of Christ. Our problems may indeed be large, "but we see Jesus, crowned with glory and honor." I may not see how my trials fit his rule, but by the grace of God I do see Jesus and that is what matters. Do not lose your bearings! Stay the course!

A marvelous, moving example of such exhortation comes from the Reformation, as John Calvin encouraged the five young theological students of Lyon, who were prepared at Geneva and Lausanne to preach the gospel, to stand fast in their confession of Christ as they were in sight of martyrdom. To these stalwart young men, Calvin wrote:

> Our heavenly Father has so expressly proved by ac-
> tion how much His strength is mighty in you that we
> doubt not that He will perfect His work. You know
> that in leaving this world we do not go away on an

uncertain venture; in addition to the confidence of eternal life, you have the assurance as children of His gratuitous adoption to enter your inheritance. That God should have appointed you His Son's martyrs should be an added sign of this . . . Beloved brethren, act according to the word of David, 'My soul is continually in my hand: yet do I not forget Thy law,' and be ready to give your life at any time. Seeing that the Lord employs your life in so worthy a cause as is the witness of the Gospel, doubt not that it is precious to Him. The hour draws nigh when the earth shall disclose the book which has been hid, and we, after having been disencumbered of these fading bodies, shall rise. Meanwhile be the Son of God glorified by our shame. Let us be consoled with the sure testimony that we are persecuted and mocked for no other reason than that we believe in the living God. This is sufficient cause to despise the whole world with its pride, till we be gathered into that everlasting Kingdom where we shall fully enjoy those blessings which we now only possess in hope.[12]

Led to the stake, these young men sang the ninth Psalm, recited Scripture and the Apostles' Creed, and died bravely as Christians. "But we see Jesus, crowned with glory and honor."

One final application follows. Is Christ "crowned with glory and honor"? Every knee will bow before him. The theme of this passage parallels Philippians 2:5–10. The one who humbled himself to death upon the cross has been highly exalted. Before him, every knee will bow to the glory of God the Father. Is there some person, lost and undone, reading this page? You need a Savior; you need the King, Jesus. May the Lord dethrone your idols and enable you by faith to bow before him now, depending upon him alone for salvation.

---

12. Cited by Emanuel Stickelberger, *Calvin* (London: James Clarke, 1959), 116–117.

Hebrews

At the Name of Jesus
Every knee shall bow,
Every tongue confess Him
King of glory now;
'Tis the Father's pleasure
We should call Him LORD,
Who from the beginning
Was the Mighty Word.

At His voice creation
Sprang at once to sight,
All the Angel's faces,
All the hosts of light,
Thrones and Dominations,
Stars upon their way,
All the heavenly Orders,
In their great array.

Humbled for a season,
To receive a Name
From the lips of sinners
Unto whom He came,
Faithfully He bore it
Spotless to the last,
Brought it back victorious,
When from death He pass'd:

Bore it up triumphant
With its human light,
Through all ranks of creatures,
To the central height;
To the Throne of Godhead,
To the Father's breast,
Fill'd it with glory
Of that perfect rest.

Name Him, brothers, name Him
With love as strong as death,
But with awe and wonder

Everything Subject to Christ

And with bated breath;
He is God the Saviour
He is Christ the Lord,
Ever to be worshipp'd,
Trusted and adored.

In your hearts enthrone Him;
There let Him subdue
All that is not holy,
All that is not true;
Crown Him as your Captain
In temptation's hour;
Let His Will enfold you
In its light and power.

Brothers, this Lord Jesus
Shall return again,
With His Father's glory,
With His Angel train;
For all wreaths of empire
Meet upon His Brow,
And our hearts confess Him
King of glory now. Amen.[13]

---

13. *The Book of Common Prayer*, Hymns A and M, 306

5

Why Did Christ Suffer?

HEBREWS 2:10–18

Since therefore the children share in flesh and blood, he himself likewise partook of the same things, that through death he might destroy the one who has the power of death, that is, the devil, and deliver all those who through fear of death were subject to lifelong slavery. For surely it is not angels that he helps, but he helps the offspring of Abraham. Therefore he had to be made like his brothers in every respect, so that he might become a merciful and faithful high priest in the service of God, to make propitiation for the sins of the people. For because he himself has suffered when tempted, he is able to help those who are being tempted.

Nothing could be more important to the man, woman, or child in the pew than this passage. In 2:5–9, the writer of Hebrews set forth the humiliation and exaltation of Christ for his people. He concluded by saying that Jesus "was crowned with glory and honor because of the suffering of death, so that by the grace of God he might taste death for everyone." Now, in 2:10–18, the author answers the question: Why did Christ suffer? He does not, of course, give a comprehensive answer to that question. For that we must turn to all of the Word of God. But here the writer gives his readers the answers that most comport with the purpose of his sermon-epistle, especially as they relate to the heavenly high priestly work of the Son of God.

Christ's Suffering Was Planned by God

The death of Christ was no accident. It was planned in the eternal counsels of the Godhead. When we read in verse 10 that "it was fitting that he, for whom and by whom all things exist, in bringing many sons to glory," we have before us a strong affirmation of the sovereignty of God. The writer's point is that the death of Christ, his theme in this passage, is intimately and inseparably related to the overarching purpose and plan of God. Since it is true that for him and by him all things exist, the death of Christ participates in this comprehensive purpose and plan. The passage reminds us of that paean of praise coming at the end of Paul's contemplation of divine sovereignty, in Romans 11:33 and 36: "Oh, the depth of the riches and wisdom and knowledge of God! How unsearchable are his judgments and how inscrutable his ways! . . . For from him and through him and to him are all things. To him be glory forever. Amen."

So here in Hebrews, as the writer approaches the theme of Christ's suffering, he reminds his readers that the death of Jesus achieves the design of God's sovereignty, and that the restoration of all things in Christ will be achieved as the result of his sacrifice. In his high sovereignty, God formed a purpose of mercy to bring "many sons to glory," and that purpose must be fulfilled. Here also the believer finds his ground of confidence, a necessary plank of assurance. God's sovereignty undergirds the death of Christ and therefore undergirds our salvation. How long has God loved you? God has loved you, believer, as long as he has had a plan to save you, that is, from eternity past. Will his saving purpose fail? It is the saving purpose of the sovereign

God; it cannot fail. Atonement is planned and accomplished "for whom and by whom all things exist." Your salvation cannot fail; the glory and honor of God are at stake.

Does the sovereignty of God in salvation mean that God could have saved sinners by divine fiat? No, indeed; there was no other way to save us from our sins but the cross of Christ.

No Other Way but Incarnation and Atonement

The Son identified himself with us; the sovereign Son took upon himself human nature. This is part of the meaning of the term *fitting* in verse 10. *Fitting* implies that his method of redeeming sinners was true to his own nature and purpose. It was *fitting* that the Son save us by incarnation and atonement because there was no other way to save us that was consistent with his nature. No other way was available for the salvation of sinners but the route taken by Christ in his active and passive obedience.

The great presupposition of this portion of Hebrews is the holiness and justice of God. God cannot overlook sin. If a less costly method of saving sinners had been possible, if another way would have served the purpose of redemption, that route would have been taken. But no other way was available that was consistent with God's own nature. If God would be the justifier of the ungodly, Christ must propitiate the wrath of God through the shedding of his own blood. There was no other way. If you, reader, are seeking some other way, cease your vain effort and put your trust in Christ alone—the redeemer of sinners. Since God could save only in a way consistent with his character, then we cannot be saved apart from total reliance on Christ, who accomplished the unique way to salvation.

The Westminster Assembly's *Larger Catechism* well summarizes this point in Q&A 152:

> Q: What doth every sin deserve at the hand of God?

> A: Every sin, even the least, being against the sover-
> eignty, goodness, and holiness of God, and against
> his righteous law, deserveth his wrath and curse,
> both in this life, and that which is to come; and can-
> not be expiated but by the blood of Christ.

That we sinners might be saved it was necessary for God the Son to take human nature and sacrifice himself on the cross of Calvary.

Identification with Us

The goal of incarnation and atonement was "bringing many sons to glory." Here is the inner logic and necessity of the church's doctrine that Jesus possesses two natures in one person. Leo's dictum is correct: "We should not be able to make use of the Conqueror's victory, if it had been won outside our nature."[1] This theme bears constant repetition and emphasis. We find this theme in our text in two ways.

First, we find the two natures doctrine necessitated by the reality of the real, human sufferings of the Son. Of the Son we know that he is "the radiance of the glory of God and the exact imprint of his nature, and he upholds the universe by the word of his power" (1:3). But, we have already read in 2:9 that this same Divine Son "was crowned with glory and honor because of the suffering of death, so that by the grace of God he might taste death for everyone." And, now, in 2:10 we find the writer saying that "the founder of their salvation" was made "perfect through suffering."

The Divine Son has become "the founder of their salvation." That is, Christ is the pioneer or pathfinder who leads his peo-ple on to heaven (6:20). *Ton archēgon*, translated *the Founder* in the ESV, means "originator, founder" hence the "pioneer" of

---

1. *Letters of Leo the Great,* in *A Select Library of Nicene and Post-Nicene Fathers of the Christian Church,* eds. Philip Schaff and Henry Wace (Peabody, MA: Hendrickson, 1994), 12.45.

his people's salvation. Without him we could have no access to heaven, no relationship with God. He wears our nature on the throne on high. Christ's human nature is as real as his deity. Christ came as man; Christ ascended to heaven as man. The dust of earth sits regnant upon the heavenly throne. This is the result of his real, human *suffering*. Christ's human suffering in the place of sinners realized the goal of the incarnation, namely, the glorification of the Father through the salvation of God's people. As Spurgeon so beautifully put it:

> A God bowing his head, and suffering, and dying in the person of manhood, puts such a singular efficacy into every groan and every pang, that it needs not that his pangs should be eternal, or that he should die a second death. The dignity of the person adds a special force to the substitution, and thus one bleeding Saviour can make atonement for millions of sinful men, and the Captain of our salvation can bring multitudes into glory.[2]

But what does Hebrews mean when it says that the Son incarnate, the founder of his people's salvation, was made "perfect through suffering"? The writer here speaks of the goal for which he became incarnate. The Lord's complete victory over all temptations fitted him for his present work of High Priestly intercession. Obedience, total, complete, unreserved could be offered only through Christ. He met these qualifications perfectly "through suffering." Real, human suffering brought Christ to the goal for which he became incarnate.

Lane points out that made "perfect through suffering" draws upon certain texts in the LXX which speak of the consecration of the priest to his office (Exod. 29:9, 29, 33, 35; Lev. 4:5; 8:33; 16:32; 21:10; Num. 3:3). He rightly sees a relationship with

---

2. Charles H. Spurgeon, "Expiation," in *Metropolitan Tabernacle Pulpit* (Pasadena, TX: Pilgrim), 10.176.

vv. 10–11 in which "he who sanctifies" means "a consecrating priest" (NEB). He adds that "the pattern of suffering and exaltation found in v 9 finds its equivalent in the reference to suffering and perfection in v 10." The emphasis, then, is on the reality that Jesus was being fully equipped to serve in his High Priestly office. William Lane remarks: "God qualified Jesus to come before him in priestly action. He perfected him as a priest of his people through his sufferings, which permitted him to accomplish his redemptive mission."[3]

Second, we see the two natures doctrine necessitated and taught by a proper understanding of 2:11: "For he who sanctifies and those who are sanctified all have one origin." *He who sanctifies* is a reference to the atonement. *He who sanctifies* parallels *those who are sanctified*. Hebrews 10:10, 14, 29 and 13:12 make it plain that *he who sanctifies* refers to Christ in his atoning work while *those who are sanctified* is a reference to those set apart for worship, service, and glory as a result of Christ's atonement. Furthermore, Lane points out that "he who consecrates" is Old Testament language that refers to God and the formula "I am the Lord who consecrates you" (Exod. 31:13; Lev. 20:8; 21:15; 22:9, 16, 32; Ez. 20:12; 37:28).[4] The reference here is explicitly to Christ who consecrates his own by his own shed blood. Our cleansing from the defilement of sin is through Jesus' blood.

But what does the writer mean when he says that "he who sanctifies and those who are sanctified all have one origin" (*ex henos*, literally "of one")? By this expression the writer stresses the common and shared humanity of Christ and those he came to save. The writer is glorying in the Son's identification of himself with us. The Son is God *and* man. "It is no more permissible to

---

3. William Lane, *Hebrews* (Dallas: Word, 1991), 1.57–58. Lane relies in part on insights of M. Silva, *WTJ* 39 [1976], 62–68.

4. Lane, *Hebrews*, 1.58.

comingle the two natures in Christ than to pull them apart."[5] Hebrews affirms Christ's true deity and true humanity; the Son took human nature to save us. This reality is at the core of our faith and is worthy of constant meditation. "Here is something marvelous: the Son of God descended from heaven in such a way that, without leaving heaven, he willed to be borne in the virgin's womb, to go about the earth, and to hang upon the cross; yet he continuously filled the world even as he had done from the beginning!"[6]

Once again our author turns to the Old Testament to unpack the meaning of this new covenant revelation. That the Son shares "one common humanity" (as Phillips translates) with those for whom he came is first demonstrated by referencing Psalm 22:22: "I will tell of your name to my brothers; in the midst of the congregation I will sing your praise." He also turns to Isaiah 8:17–18 (LXX): "And again, 'I will put my trust in him.' And again, 'Behold, I and the children God has given me.'" Psalm 22 reveals the triumphant communication of salvation for those for whom Christ died. Isaiah 8 stresses the Savior's dependence upon the Father and God's sovereignty in making us his children. All emphasize that Christ indentified himself with us.

In this sense, he calls those he redeems his *brothers* (see 11:16) thus emphasizing that the Son assumed human nature though free from the contamination of sin. Lane points out that *he is not ashamed to call them brothers*, "may contain an allusion to Jesus' warning that the disciple who seeks to evade the cost of discipleship by denying his relationship to Jesus will find that the exalted Son of Man is ashamed of him"[7] (Mark 8:38; Luke 9:26).

Note that verses 10 and 13 bring the pinnacle of our salvation to the forefront, namely, our adoption by the Father and entrance into his redeemed family. This is not the place for a

---

5. John Calvin, *Institutes* (Philadelphia: Westminster, 1960), 2.14.4.

6. Calvin, *Institutes*, 2.13.4.

7. Lane, *Hebrews*, 1.59.

thorough Biblical survey of this theme, but it bears remembering that the utter humiliation of the Son was for you, believer. He took on flesh that he might make us sons (2:10) and children (2:13). We also must take heart in the first person personal pronouns from the Septuagint quotations in verses 12 and 13. *I will tell . . . I will sing . . . I will put my trust . . . Behold, I and the children*; all of which remind those tempted to go back that the ultimate issue is God's faithfulness to his covenant. Here we are reminded of his promise in the midst of real human history and temptation to accomplish his sovereign purpose of salvation and to bring many sons to glory.

The author envisions the day in which the singing Savior and High Priest of his people will lead the paean of praise, as his own are gathered for eternity in the adoration of the true and living God. Was not the Savior's trust in God's covenant faithfulness absolutely vindicated and demonstrated ("I will put my trust in him")? Therefore, the readers should know that the same Lord will see them through their troubles in union with the Son.

Christ Came to Destroy the Devil's Work

The writer of Hebrews has been stressing the true humanity of the Son in his incarnation and suffering for our sins. Now he stresses that the destruction of the devil's work required that the Son assume genuine humanity. In 2:14, he writes: "Since therefore the children share in flesh and blood, he himself likewise partook of the same things, that through death he might destroy the one who has the power of death, that is, the devil." Humans sinned; therefore, if human sinners were to be saved it required that God the Son assume human nature. That is the clear meaning of the first portion of this verse. "We observe a certain reflective attention to the significance of the pre-existent Son's having as a matter of considered choice, accepted the conditions of human existence."[8]

In the remainder of the verse we are told that the purpose of the death of the Son who was also true man was that "through death he might destroy the one who has the power of death, that is, the devil." The death of Christ defeated the devil. How?

First, the Son defeated the devil by removing the grounds for the devil's accusations against us. The justified sinner can now cry out against all accusers of his conscience "if God is for us, who can be against us? He who did not spare his own Son but gave him up for us all, how will he not also with him graciously give us all things? Who shall bring any charge against God's elect? It is God who justifies. Who is to condemn? Christ Jesus is the one who died—more than that, who was raised— who is at the right hand of God, who indeed is interceding for us" (Rom. 8:31–34). So, the efficacious death of the Son who assumed human nature removed the grounds of the devil's accusations against our consciences. The stress of the text is that the death of Christ destroyed the chief accuser, the devil, and his primary accusing work, the fear of death.

The Son came to destroy "the one who has the power of death, that is the devil, and deliver those who through fear of death were subject to lifelong slavery." The consciences of sinners testify within them of a day of judgment and fill the heart of the unbeliever with a gruesome fear of death. The unbeliever is in bondage to death (*douleia*). True, a suicide bomber may so suppress what he knows to be true that he goes to his death in false ecstasy. Even then, however, the bomber has gone through

---

8. C. J. A. Hickling, "John and Hebrews: The Background of Hebrews 2:10–18," *New Testament Studies* 29 (1983), 112–116. This author notes many fascinating connections between the thought of this passage and the prologue to John's gospel and also comments on "the depth and imaginative quality of its reflection, as evidenced by the features learned from it by two of the most theologically creative minds in the New Testament."

a process of deep, long-term denial of the truth and must drug himself to delirium with falsehood to carry out his deadly deed. Still, the fear of death fills the heart and soul of the unbeliever, but for the believer, Christ's death and resurrection have removed the sting of death (1 Cor. 15).

The reality of death confronts us all, unbeliever and believer alike. The believer in Christ, however, has no reason to fear death. Death is the result of the fall; it is not natural. Death is fearful to contemplate. However, the believer knows that Christ has come to remove the sting of death and with it the fear of death that otherwise would occupy our minds and fill our hearts. In Christ the Christian is victorious over death. There is natural apprehension in the Christian's heart as he contemplates the experience of death; after all, it will be something we all face if Jesus tarries. But there is no reason to fear the consequences of death and every reason to rejoice that we will be in the presence of God. We may also rejoice in the knowledge of the resurrection at the last day since Jesus "abolished death and brought life and immortality to light through the gospel" (2 Tim. 1:10).

Hughes tells us that Chrysostom deplored the ostentatious lamentations at Christian funerals in his day. Must they not be ashamed to act this way before unbelievers? This church father thought that such behavior encouraged unbelievers to remain unbelievers. Are not the unbelievers who die without Christ really the ones to be lamented? "May God grant that you all depart this life unwailed."[9] Chrysostom did not say *unmourned* but *unwailed*. Grief is appropriate, indeed right. But, the grieving of the Christian over believers who have gone to be with the Lord must be gospel grieving.

What is gospel grieving? It is grieving that never forgets in the midst of genuine sorrow the victory of the cross and resurrection of Jesus. At the core of the Christian's heart, in the midst of tears,

---

9. Cited by Philip E. Hughes, *Hebrews* (Grand Rapids: Eerdmans, 1977), 115.

memories, and longings, is the glory of God and Christ's defeat of death. The world needs the testimony of biblical grieving. Do not allow yourself to fall into worldly sentimentality, or into a pop culture psychotherapeutic mentality. What you and I need for Christian growth does not somehow change when death enters our homes. As we live as believers, drawing our sustenance from the means that God has appointed for our growth and maturity—namely the Word, sacraments, prayer, and the communion of the saints—we are prepared to grieve when death comes, but not as those who have no hope (1 Thess. 4:13–18).

With what triumph the Christian dies who is steeped in these realities! Pastor and hymn-writer Augustus Toplady spent his ministerial life defending the doctrines of grace. On his death bed, being told that his pulse was growing weaker, he said, "Why, that is a good sign that my death is fast approaching, and blessed be God I can add that my heart beats every day stronger and stronger for glory." Then came the question, did he doubt the doctrines of grace that he had so long preached and defended. He responded:

> Doubt! Doubt, sir! Pray use not that word when speaking of me; I cannot endure the term, at least while God continues to shine upon my soul in the gracious manner he does now; not but that I am sensible that while in the body, if left of him, I am capable, through the power of temptation, of calling in question every truth of the gospel, but that is so far from being the case that the comforts and manifestations of his love are so abundant as to render my state and condition the most desirable in the world, and with respect to my principles, those blessed principles which I have been enabled in my poor measure to maintain, appear to me more than

> ever most gloriously indubitable. My own existence
> is not, to my own apprehension, a greater certainty.[10]

Thus die those whose hearts are filled with the truth and reality of sovereign grace.

The writer would have us remember that "surely it is not angels he helps, but he helps the offspring of Abraham." The Lord Jesus took on human nature, became incarnate, and died for sinful humans thereby helping us and not angels. "Help" is a rather weak translation. The word *epilambanetai* means "to take hold of in order to help." The Son incarnate, our great high priest, takes us upon himself as his responsibility. Angels do not die nor fear death (though fallen angels will endure eternal punishment), but the *offspring of Abraham* suffer death and are in desperate need of a Redeemer. It is for them that the Son came to help, to take hold of, for whom he has taken responsibility.

The writer has in mind *effectual* help. Christ became man to save sinful men who needed saving, and he destroyed the devil's work, removing the curse of death, by effectual means. Therefore, we should not fear the grave since our Savior has preceded us and was raised from the dead. The words of F. F. Bruce should be contemplated in full:

> It calls for an exceptional effort of mind on our part
> to appreciate how paradoxical was the attitude of
> those early Christians to the death of Christ. If ever
> death had appeared to be triumphant, it was when
> Jesus of Nazareth, disowned of His nation, abandoned by His disciples, executed by the might of
> imperial Rome, breathed His last on the cross. Why,
> some had actually recognized in His cry of pain and
> desolation the complaint that even God had forsaken Him. His faithful followers had confidently expected that He was the destined liberator of Israel;

---

10. Cited in J. H. Oliphant, *The Doctrine of the Final Perseverance of the Saints* (Streamwood, IL: Primitive Baptist Library, 1979), 104–105.

but He had died—not, like Judas of Galilee or Judas Maccabaeus, in the forefront of the struggle against the Gentile oppressors of Israel, but in evident weakness and disgrace—and their hopes died with Him. If ever a cause was lost, it was His; if ever the powers of evil were victorious, it was then. And yet—within a generation His followers were exultingly proclaiming the crucified Jesus to be the conqueror of death and asserting, like our author here, that by dying He had reduced the erstwhile lord of death to impotence. The keys of death and Hades were henceforth held firmly in Jesus' powerful hand, for He, in the language of His own parable, had invaded the strong man's fortress, disarmed him, bound him fast and robbed him of his spoil. This is the unanimous witness of the New Testament writers; this was the assurance which nerved martyrs to face death boldly in His name. This sudden change from disillusionment to triumph can only be explained by the account which the apostles gave—that their Master rose from the dead and imparted to them the power of His risen life.[11]

Why did Christ suffer? First, his suffering was identification with us; second, Christ delivered us from the devil and the fear of death by paying sin's penalty. Now the writer adds another layer of understanding to the meaning of Christ's suffering for sinners. He speaks of the priestly work of Christ, the grand theme of the epistle.

Christ Suffered to Qualify for Priesthood

Having told us that "it is not angels he helps, but he helps the offspring of Abraham," the writer unpacks that connection in this deep and meaningful way:

---

11. F. F. Bruce, *Hebrews* (Grand Rapids: Eerdmans, 1964), 49.

> Therefore he had to be made like his brothers in every respect, so that he might become a merciful and faithful high priest in the service of God, to make propitiation for the sins of the people. For because he himself has suffered when tempted, he is able to help those who are being tempted.

For the Son to save us from our sins, real manhood was required; "he had to be made like his brothers in every respect." No pretence of humanity would do only genuine, real involvement in human life. Picking up the theme of verses 12 and 13, the author reminds us that for his *brothers*, for his *children*, Jesus took upon himself human nature, yet without sin (4:15; 7:26). Sin is contrary to God's holiness and is a denial of our humanity, a rebellion against what it means to be created in God's image. He took on human nature "so that he might become a merciful and faithful high priest in the service of God."

This is the first use of the language *high priest* in the book of Hebrews. It harks back to Old Testament revelation, to Aaron and the Day of Atonement, which prefigured Christ and his atoning work. Hebrews will make plain that "it is impossible for the blood of bulls and goats to take away sins" (10:4), but Christ is "a sacrifice of nobler name and richer blood than they" as Watts so beautifully phrased it in his great hymn *Not All the Blood of Beasts.* There is only one who was qualified to redeem sinners, and that is the Son who became man without ceasing to be God the Son. He alone could show us the saving mercy we needed, and he alone could be completely dependable. How could we sinners approach the blazing glory of God but on the basis of the all sufficient sacrifice of Christ? Hence we are told that it is Christ who made "propitiation for the sins of the people."

Few doctrines have had such opprobrium and aspersions heaped upon them as the truth and reality of Christ's propitiatory sacrifice. For those who deny the wrath of God, the reality of propitiation is explained away, and the texts of Scripture that teach wrath and propitiation are softened or diluted. Then there are some who have failed to stress the Father's love in the offering up of his Son to satisfy wrath, though the number of those is greatly exaggerated in the minds of those who question this biblical teaching. Biblical orthodoxy has been accused of teaching that the cross causes the Father to love sinners. But, orthodox preachers have never taught such falsehood. Propitiation is not the turning of wrath into love; propitiation is the provision of the Father's love for his elect. First John 4:10 tells us that "in this is love, not that we have loved God but that he loved us and sent his Son to be the propitiation for our sins." Romans 3:25 teaches us that Christ the Redeemer is the one "whom God put forward as a propitiation by his blood, to be received by faith." The Father's love is manifested most wonderfully, most stupendously, in the sacrifice of his own dear Son in the place of sinners as he took the penalty for our sins.

All the fury of heaven was poured out on the Son in the place of his people, and thereby he satisfied the wrath of God for his elect. Owen observes that

> in the use of this word (propitiation), then, there is always understood—(1st) An *offence,* crime, guilt, or debt, to be taken away; (2ndly) A person *offended,* to be pacified, atoned, reconciled; (3dly) A *person offending,* to be pardoned, accepted; (4thly) A *sacrifice* or other means of making the atonement. Sometimes one is expressed, sometimes another, but the use of the word hath respect unto them all.

Leon Morris, after quoting these lines, adds that "it is a valuable point that the verb often implies more than is explicitly expressed."[12]

---

12. Leon Morris, *The Apostolic Preaching of the Cross* (Grand Rapids: Eerdmans, 1982), 204.

In bearing the wrath of God for the crimes of his people against the infinite majesty of God and perfection of his law, the Son of God did the almost inexpressible. Who can rightly comprehend the wrath of the holy and awe-inspiring God? Who can comprehend the love of the Father in sending his own Son to bear his wrath in our place, the love of the Son in coming, and the wondrous work of the Holy Spirit who applies the Son's finished work to our lives? The Son, our high priest, did this "for the sins of the people," an expression used in the LXX referring to Israel (Lane cites especially Deut. 7:6–8; 14:2; 21:8), but now used of the new covenant people of God, for whom Christ gave his life by suffering, bleeding, and dying as their substitute.

As the God-man who sacrificed himself on the cross and satisfied the wrath of God as propitiatory sacrifice, Christ can now provide help for the tempted, "for because he himself has suffered when tempted, he is able to help those who are being tempted." Christ was victorious over every single temptation (4:14–16). His fellowship in human suffering enables him to identify with our moral struggles, so that he brings a twofold help—the forgiveness of sins *and* the power to overcome temptation. Remember, the writer is addressing tempted people who are facing the greatest temptation of the Christian life: the temptation to turn back. Jesus alone can provide forgiveness for sinners, and he alone can provide for deliverance from temptation, as one who also knew the power of Satan's subtle approaches, the siren call to turn from the Father's Word.

Christ was victorious over every single temptation. He alone passed the test, overcame temptation over unbelief, presumption and idolatry (Heb. 4:14–16; 5:7–9). As Hughes so aptly put it:

Why Did Christ Suffer?

> Fellowship in human suffering and testing begets fellow feeling; that true compassion which is the hallmark of his priestly identification with our moral nature . . . It is precisely because we have been defeated that we need the assistance of him who is the victor.[13]

Therefore, Christ brings the two-fold help of both forgiveness and the power to overcome temptation. Jesus does not bring this help just as a man to men, as human to humans, but as the God-man—as the Redeemer and high priest of his people.

For these reasons, the Son incarnate, who propitiated God's just wrath, who overcame our sin and bore our sorrow is our "merciful and faithful high priest." He wears our nature as High Priest upon the throne; his true humanity is as real as his Deity. He came as man, ascended to heaven as man, and intercedes for his people in the flesh. The writer virtually cries out by these facts, "You may entrust yourself to him. He is God; he is man. He came to care for his relations. This is why he suffered. This is the ground of your confidence. He knows how to send the right grace at the right time. For his people the Son is compassionate and faithful in his High Priestly work."

Did not the Lord promise this? "And I will raise up for myself a faithful priest, who shall do according to what is in my heart and in my mind. And I will build him a sure house, and he shall go in and out before my anointed forever" (1 Sam. 2:35). Whatever types and shadows may be indicated here, surely the ultimate fulfillment is found in the merciful and faithful high priest of his people, the Lord Jesus:

> It has its full accomplishment in the priesthood of Christ, that merciful and faithful high priest whom God raised up when the Levitical priesthood was thrown off, who in all things did his father's mind, and for whom God will build a sure house, build it

---

13. Philip E. Hughes, *Hebrews*, 123.

on a rock, so that the gates of hell cannot prevail against it.[14]

Is one who is lost reading these pages? Dear, fellow sinner, you need a High Priest. Put your trust in the only Savior of sinners, the only one whose sacrifice can save the most vile, the darkest heart, the gravest deeds of enmity that stem from a depraved heart. And, when you come to him you will find that he has in grace been seeking you all along.

All who know Christ and contemplate the reality of the incarnation, propitiatory sacrifice, and high priestly work of Christ know the sheer wonder of it and that our all depends upon him. The writer of Hebrews wanted his first readers to understand this, and the the divine author wants his people to understand it now. Just think, as Rutherford said, here is "a wonder! that the God-head should be knit in personal union with the Man of Sorrows!" Here we see

> his *personal subsistence* to stand connected with wounds, blood, curse, and shame! For the God-head to breathe, live in, and dwell as one with the person shamed, cursed, hanging on the cross, dead and buried, is truly wonderful! Here God is made a curse, God is made a shame; and the personality of the God-head still abiding with the shame and the curse, howbeit neither cursed nor shamed. . . . He cannot be set too high; nay, if there were ten thousand times ten thousand heavens, and each to be above another, and Christ to be set in the highest of them all; yet were He too low.[15]

Amen and amen. Watts reminds us of the greatness of our Savior's sacrificial blood in this wonderful hymn:

---

14. Matthew Henry, *A Commentary on the Whole Bible* (Old Tappan, NJ: Revell, 1983), 2.294.

15. Samuel Rutherford, *Communion Sermons* (Blue Banner: 1986), 27–28, 18.

Why Did Christ Suffer?

Jesus, my great High Priest,
offered his blood and died;
my guilty conscience seeks
no sacrifice beside.
His pow'rful blood did once atone,
and now it pleads before the throne.

To this dear Surety's hand will
I commit my cause;
he answers and fulfills
his Father's broken laws.
Behold my soul at freedom set;
my Surety paid the dreadful debt.

My Advocate appears
for my defense on high;
the Father bows his ears
and lays his thunder by.
Not all that hell or sin can say
shall turn his heart, his love, away.

Should all the hosts of death
and pow'rs of hell unknown
put their most dreadful forms
of rage and mischief on,
I shall be safe, for Christ displays
his conqu'ring pow'r and guardian grace.[16]

---

16. Isaac Watts, "Jesus My Great High Priest," from *Trinity Hymnal*, rev. ed.,
(Suwanee, GA: Great Commission Publications, 1990), selection 306.

6

Christ Superior
to Moses

HEBREWS 3:1–6

Therefore, holy brothers, you who share in a heavenly calling, consider Jesus, the apostle and high priest of our confession, who was faithful to him who appointed him, just as Moses also was faithful in all God's house. For Jesus has been counted worthy of more glory than Moses— as much more glory as the builder of a house has more honor than the house itself. (For every house is built by someone, but the builder of all things is God.) Now Moses was faithful in all God's house as a servant, to testify to the things that were to be spoken later, but Christ is faithful over God's house as a son. And we are his house if indeed we hold fast our confidence and our boasting in our hope.

The writer of Hebrews relentlessly conveys the theme that Christ is better, better than the old, the fulfiller of the prophetic writings, the goal of God's saving purpose, superior to all that had preceded in God's redemptive plan. For the Hebrew Christians addressed in this sermon-epistle to return to Judaism would mean to return to Moses for salvation and to abandon Christ the great High Priest of his people. Moses cannot save; only the Son can save. The Hebrew Christians addressed in this letter, in short, are in danger of trusting Moses to save them. There is immediate application to our lives as we perceive the warning directed to these Hebrew Christians. In whom do we put our trust? Must we not beware of any and everything that would tempt us away from Christ alone? Hebrews, let us remember, is not only God's Word then and there, but is God's Word to us here and now.

Importance of the Writer's Address

The author's mode of address is instructive. Having included himself in prior addresses, he now speaks directly to his audience. He confronts them as a preacher who is preaching for a verdict. He writes to "holy brothers, you who share in a heavenly calling." The word *holy* summarizes the defining characteristic of God's people. To call the people of God *holy* points back to the thought of 2:11—"for he who sanctifies and those who are sanctified all have one origin." "Those who are sanctified" are so because the "one who sanctifies" shed his blood to purchase them from their sins. Those who are *holy* are bought at the awful and infinitely high cost of the propitiatory sacrifice of the incarnate Son.

In addition to being *holy*, the readers of Hebrews are also addressed as *brothers*. To call them *brothers* means that they are part of the holy fellowship of those purchased by Jesus' blood, those who are unified together because they are one in Christ. Here the truths of Hebrews 2:11 inform his address. "For he who sanctifies and those who are sanctified all have one origin:" they are one in union with the great High Priest who purchased them, the incarnate Lord who bought them.

These *holy brothers* also "share in a heavenly calling," that is, a calling that is both heavenly in origin and heavenly in goal (Heb. 11:16, 22). The tempted, tried Hebrew Christians are therefore encouraged to remember that their security is in heaven from whence the Son came to save them, and that the heavenly goal is secured and assured by his infinitely valuable blood. It is ever the encouragement of God's people that our salvation is all of grace from first to last, anchored in the heavenly plan of the Triune God from eternity to eternity.

The way in which the author addresses these Hebrew Christians who are tempted to turn back is instructive to us. He speaks plainly in this sermon-epistle, but he does not berate. The writer reflects the fatherly character of God throughout, speaks in love and concern, urges them on, and points them to their sacred privileges. In the midst of their temptation, he reminds them of the security that belongs to all who truly know Christ. The author speaks with pathos and with firm conviction, calling them to faithfulness, but always in the context of the gospel of free grace.

Consider Jesus

Most importantly, the author constantly points the Hebrew Christians to Jesus, as he now does in 3:1. "Consider Jesus, the apostle and high priest of our confession." *Jesus*, of course, is the Son's earthly name. In Matthew we are told that the angel of the Lord appeared to Joseph in a dream saying, "Do not fear to take Mary as your wife, for that which is conceived in her is from the Holy Spirit. She will bear a son, and you shall call his name Jesus, for he will save his people from their sins." The name "Jesus" has already been used in 2:9 and, in addition to the reference in 3:1, will be found in Hebrews 4:14; 5:7; and 6:19–20.

The earthly name of Jesus would recall his sinless life, obedience, sufferings and death on the cross, his resurrection from the dead and intercession as one of us, the Son who became incarnate, the Savior who is "the only Redeemer of God's elect" who "being the eternal Son of God, became man, and so was, and continueth to be, God and man in two distinct natures, and one person, for ever" (*Shorter Catechism*, answer 21). The call is to consider this same Jesus when we are tempted to desert him, to consider him who considered us from eternity, who considered us in his life of perfect obedience, who considered us while paying the debt of our sin on the cross, who considered us in his resurrection from the dead, and who even now in his heavenly high priestly work still considers us.

The Jesus that the readers are called to consider is "the apostle and high priest of our confession." Hebrews reserves the word *apostle* for Christ alone, emphasizing that the Son is sent by the Father and is the messenger of peace who brings to culmination the progressive redemptive revelation of God (Heb. 1:1–2). The truth that Christ is sent by the Father appears often in the New Testament, especially in the gospel of John (e.g., John 3:17, 34; 5:36; 10:36; 11:42; 17:3). Such texts point back to the eternal covenant of grace established in the Trinitarian counsel. The Son as *apostle* is divinely authorized to achieve his work as High Priest. As *apostle* Christ is sent, as the text will indicate, to establish God's house. Jesus is *apostle and high priest*, not only the Revealer of the Father but also the embodiment of man's obedience to God, the one who obeyed where Adam and his race failed, the one who paid the debt of their sins and, as Hebrews consistently emphasizes, the one who intercedes effectually for them on the basis of his own complete and full merit. *Apostle* may anticipate the comparison with Moses who, in Exodus 3:10 (LXX), is sent (*aposteilō*) to Pharaoh.

Jesus is "the apostle and high priest *of our confession*." Here the author reminds his readers that they have together made a common commitment to Christ. They have acknowledged the Sonship of Jesus and have renounced the world in order to follow him.

Having called upon his readers to "consider Jesus, the apostle and high priest of our confession" the author of Hebrews contrasts Jesus with Moses and points out three truths that should capture the believer's consideration.

Jesus is the Faithful Architect of God's House

The first two truths revealed in this passage are these: that Jesus is faithful and the architect of God's house. Jesus "the apostle and high priest of our confession" was "faithful to him who appointed him, just as Moses also was faithful in all God's house. (For every house is built by someone, but the builder of all things is God.)" In Numbers 12, the Lord reveals to us that Moses was unique in regard to the directness with which God spoke to him in contrast to the prophets that would come after. "Hear my words: If there is a prophet among you, I the LORD make myself known to him in a vision; I speak with him in a dream. Not so with my servant Moses. He is faithful in all my house. With him I speak mouth to mouth, clearly, and not in riddles, and he beholds the form of the LORD" (Num. 12:6–7). Lane thinks that the greater reference is to 1 Chronicles 17:14 ("I will confirm him in my house and in my kingdom forever, and his throne shall be established forever") in which the oracle delivered by Nathan to David becomes "a testimony for a royal messianic figure" and finally a testimony to Jesus as faithful High Priest, providing the contrast between the Son and Moses.[1]

The contrast in Hebrews 3:3–4 is between Christ who is the builder of the house and Moses who is a part of the house that Christ builds." The architect is superior to the house just as Sir Christopher Wren is superior to St. Paul's Cathedral."[2] Let us remember that the Jewish Christians to whom the author of

---

1. William Lane, *Hebrews* (Dallas: Word, 1991), 1.76.

2. A. T. Robertson, *Word Pictures in the New Testament* (Grand Rapids: Baker, 1932), 5.354.

Hebrews writes are tempted to go back to their pre-Christian, Jewish commitment. In Jewish thought, Moses was incredibly influential. Lane reminds us of a passage from *The Exodus* by Ezekiel the Tragedian, cited by Eusebius, in which Moses is shown in a dream that he will be placed on a heavenly throne invested with crown and scepter; so highly did Jewish Hellenists regard Moses.[3] However, despite Moses' faithfulness, the honor goes to the architect and builder of the house. Jesus is better; the exalted Son is superior to Moses who was a type of Christ.

The house is God's people as we read in verse 6, "we are his house if indeed we hold fast our confidence and our boasting in hope." In 2 Samuel 7:13, God promised David that he would raise up for him a son who would build up a house for God: "He shall build a house for my name, and I will establish the throne of his kingdom forever." Jesus, David's greater Son, is the builder of that house, the sovereign king reigning on the throne of the promised kingdom. Jesus is worthy of more glory than Moses as the faithful architect of God's house, the builder of the new creation. The point, of course, is that our faithful high priest is the culmination of revelation; no one holds a higher place in redemptive revelation than Jesus the faithful Savior (Hebrews 1:1–3)—who was anticipated in all prior revelation.

The flesh does not want to see this, but the Spirit of God enables us to see and bow before the throne of this faithful redeemer who removes the ugly, hideous idolatry that keeps us from him. After all, the text makes plain that the builder of God's house who is Jesus is God himself. Comparing verses three and four demonstrates a ringing affirmation of the Deity of Christ. Jesus is the builder; God is the builder; therefore, Jesus is God. Jesus, then, is the faithful architect of God's house; he cannot and will not fail in his purpose. This builder has promised to

---

3. Lane, *Hebrews*, 1.74.

build His church (Matt. 16:18). But, there is a third truth about Jesus revealed here. Jesus is the Son over God's house.

Jesus is the Son Over God's House

> Now Moses was faithful in all God's house as a servant, to testify to the things that were to be spoken later, but Christ is faithful over God's house as a son. And we are his house if indeed we hold fast our confidence and our boasting in our hope. (3:5–6)

Moses was a faithful *servant* in God's house; Christ is faithful over God's house as a *Son* and is, therefore, absolutely sovereign. Indeed, Moses spoke of Christ; it was his role to point to Christ, "to testify to the things that were to be spoken later." Moses spoke of Christ's greatness when he said, "The LORD your God will raise up for you a prophet like me from among you, from your brothers—it is to him you shall listen" (Deut. 18:15). Christ is superior to any servant; he is Son over God's house. Christ delivered God's people from "a more terrible tyrant than Pharaoh (Heb. 2:14) and" has brought them "to an inheritance better than that of Palestine (Heb. 11:13–16; 13:14)."[4]

The immediate implication is, of course, that Jesus is Lord over the house that he builds. Temple and Tabernacle language is here applied to the people of God as is found elsewhere in the New Testament (Eph. 2:21; 1 Pet. 2:5). Hughes rightly observes that "there is genuine continuity between the Old Israel and the New Israel, or rather, there is one true Israel of the people of God throughout all the ages of human history."[5] Among the people of God, Jesus is faithful High Priest superior to Moses and all who preceded him. Therefore, when the writer describes his readers as *his house* there is an implied call to faithfulness, perseverance, and submission to his Lordship.

---

4. Philip E. Hughes, *Hebrews* (Grand Rapids: Eerdmans, 1977), 136.

5. Philip E. Hughes, *Hebrews*, 132.

In addition, there is a call to perseverance within the context of the communion of the saints ("we are his house"). We are called to help one another to walk in faithfulness, to recognize ourselves as believers to be a part of the Son's great house, to "exhort one another" (3:13), to act as members of the "people of God" (4:9), to serve the saints (6:10), and to consider how we may "stir up one another to love and good works" as we meet together and encourage one another (10:24–25). The text simply will not permit a low view of God's church. We are called to be committed members of a local body and to faithfully attend to the means of grace in public worship. God's people are to see themselves as part of the Son's house and are to recognize, as the *Confession of Faith* put it, that "being united to one another in love, they have communion in each other's gifts and graces" (21.1). Having reminded his readers of their relationship to God's house, the Lord of the house and the people of the house, he once again brings warning and encouragement to these tried and tested professors of faith in Christ.

Warning and Encouragement

We find warning and encouragement in verse 6, "And we are his house if indeed we hold fast our confidence and our boasting in our hope." F. F. Bruce observes that the writer "in deep concern urges upon them that they have everything to gain by standing fast, and everything to lose by slipping back."[6] The author of Hebrews addresses his hearers as believers, as responsible human beings, but he also recognizes that some may not be what they profess themselves to be. As John wrote in his first epistle, "They went out from us, but they were not of us; for if they had been of us, they would have continued with us. But they went out, that it might become plain that they are all not of us."

---

6. F. F. Bruce, *Hebrews* (Grand Rapids: Erdmans, 1979), 60.

Christ Superior to Moses

So here, those holding fast to the confidence that comes from true assurance of faith and the certain hope set before God's people will ever rally to the call of Hebrews to live in the fullness of the context of gospel truth and will overcome their temptations to return to the old and to forsake Christ. How we should hate all that would pull us from Christ and his people! How we should hate the sin that nailed our Savior to the tree! As an old hymn so movingly put the matter:

> Yes, my Redeemer, they shall die,
> My heart has so decreed;
> Nor shall I spare the guilty things
> That made my Savior bleed.
>
> Whilst with a melting, broken heart,
> My murdered Lord I view,
> I'll raise revenge against my sins,
> And slay the murderers too.

A weakening of confidence leads to a weakening of Christian hope. The writer must address his readers so pointedly because "they showed signs of ceasing to belong to the number of those who look for the dawning of his appearing."[7] Here as in other places in the New Testament we are called to remember the purifying effects of keeping our gaze on the Christ who is coming again (2 Pet. 3:11; 1 John 3:2–3). Since Jesus is the Son, faithful in all things, he is worthy of your complete confidence (10:19–23). Surely the history of Israel under Moses calls the professing people of God now to be utterly sincere in that profession and to not play games with the gospel. We are again reminded of the solemn warning "how shall we escape if we neglect such great salvation?" (Heb. 2:3).

---

7. Philip E. Hughes, *Hebrews*, 139.

In Conclusion: Consider Jesus

The writer, then, takes his readers full circle. *Consider Jesus*, he wrote in verse 1. To him give "serious attention," "careful study," literally, "apply the mind." The alternatives seem so attractive. "What does it profit a man if he gains the whole world and forfeits his life?" (Matt. 16:26). Do not go back; do not return to the old. Moses was a faithful servant, but Moses did not die for you, rise and ascend for you, or take the merit of his blood into the sanctuary for you. The Son has come as "the apostle and high priest of our confession"; consider him. Consider the one who came and finished his task of saving us. Moses could not finish his task. Jesus once for all died and accomplished the marvel of salvation as the architect of God's household.

The words of John Brown are deeply pertinent:

> It is because we think so little, and to so little purpose, on Christ, that we know so little about Him, that we love Him so little, trust in Him so little, so often neglect our duty, are so much influenced by "things seen and temporal," and so little by "things unseen and eternal." . . . It is because men do not know Christ that they do not love Him; it is because they know Him so imperfectly that they love Him so imperfectly.[8]

Do you agree with that? If you do, as every believer must in submission to God's Word, then seek Christ with all of your heart. Live on the Word preached and read. Eagerly gather with God's people for worship. Read good materials that help fix your gaze on Christ. Take time to praise and pray, turn your trial upward, learn to suffer like Christ, walk with care and faithfulness, keep out of your life what tempts you to drift, put in your life what helps you to be faithful. In all of these ways we learn to *consider Jesus*.

---

8. John Brown, *Hebrews* (Edinburgh: Banner of Truth, 1983), 157.

7

A Rest for God's People

HEBREWS 3:7–4:13

---

*. . . But exhort one another every day, as long as it is
called "today," that none of you may be hardened by
the deceitfulness of sin. For we have come to share in
Christ, if indeed we hold our original confidence firm
to the end. As it is said, "Today, if you hear his voice,
do not harden your hearts as in the rebellion." Let us
therefore strive to enter that rest, so that no one may
fall by the same sort of disobedience. For the word of
God is living and active, sharper than any two-edged
sword, piercing to the division of soul and of spirit,
of joints and of marrow, and discerning the thoughts
and intentions of the heart.*

That the Holy Spirit calls upon us to regard "Today" as the
day for hearing the voice of God for salvation is a solemn
matter indeed. Millions regret that they did not hear that voice
and cry out to God; but it is too late now. For those Christ rejec-
tors and false professors who have gone from this world, there
is no more "today" to which to respond, only endless years of
despair and countless moments of torment. The text virtually
cries in our ears to hear, "Oh eternity, oh eternity, press upon

my heart the reality of God's judgment. Do not permit me to put off until tomorrow response to the gospel of grace for tomorrow may never come." The solemnity of "today" is driven home by repetition in verses 7, 13, 15 and twice in 4:7. The apostle Paul pressed the call of the gospel day upon his hearers similarly in 2 Corinthians 6:2: "Behold, now is the favorable time; behold, now is the day of salvation."

Let us recollect the context. Christ is glorious; superior to Moses. That was the author's stress in the previous passage. Now, with the contrast between Moses and Christ in mind the writer brings a warning from the time of Moses. We have been prepared for this emphasis by our investigation of 3:1–6, in which the author has demonstrated Christ's superiority to Moses, but also by the call for members of his house to "hold fast our confidence and our boasting in our hope" (3:6). *Therefore*, that is, in view of these previous things, take heed to the warning that comes to us from the very time of Moses, who points beyond to Christ.

It is wise for us to keep in mind the place of warning in the preaching of God's Word to the church. Let us remember that the Word comes as an instrument of judgment on those who "neglect such great salvation" (2:3). The preaching of warning calls unbelievers to faith in Christ. That is not all. We also have seen that warning is one of the various means that the Lord uses to fix the Christian's gaze on Christ. Addressing us as responsible human beings, warning, exhortation, encouragement, and other elements of proclamation are used in the Holy Spirit's hand to fix the believer's gaze on Jesus. In ways that do not in the least contradict the gospel and the certainty of faith, warning spurs on the hearts of true believers to greater faith and deeper commitment to the truth of God's Word, and to a resolute determination to continue toward the heavenly city.

The importance of Hebrews 3:7–4:13 in a context of a people tempted to turn back is apparent. Every Christian should desire that these texts come to us with the same intensity with which the writer preaches them, that the eschatological urgency of these Scriptures rivet our attention on Christ and that our souls become more resolute in following him.

Rebellion in the Wilderness

The passage begins with a long quotation from Psalm 95 prefaced by the words, "Therefore, as the Holy Spirit says." The writer knows nothing of modern denials of the inspiration and authority of the Bible; rather, he is confident that the words of the Holy Scriptures are those of the Holy Spirit. The background to this passage is primarily Numbers 13 and 14 in which Israel received fearfully the report of the spies and refused in unbelief to attempt the conquest. It was in this context of unbelief that the Lord swore that that generation would not "see the land that I swore to give to their fathers" (Num. 14:23). *Therefore*, the writer of Hebrews quotes the Lord as saying, "I was provoked with that generation, and said, 'They always go astray in their heart; they have not known my ways.' As I swore in my wrath, 'They shall not enter my rest.'" (Num. 14:20–23; 28–35).

God solemnly swore "they shall not enter my rest" and the writer of Hebrews presents that ancient warning before those tempted to go back. "Remember the wilderness generation," the writer in essence is saying; "apply these truths to your own hearts." To this was prefaced in 3:7 the reminder that this was not only God's Word back then but is God's Word to us here and now: "Therefore, as the Holy Spirit *says*"! He holds the warning up to true faith to embrace it with repentance; he holds the warning up to those to whom it might apply in their unbelief. The words of God back then apply to us now as we also are tempted to go back.

Do you read the Scriptures this way? Do you read them in faith applying the precious words of the text to your own heart and circumstances? Having determined the historical setting, and understood what the Lord said to his ancient professing people, does your heart leap out toward the Lord crying, "Lord I believe, help my unbelief?" Perhaps it is you who needs to consider this point and to adjust your approach to reading the Bible so that you receive it for what it is, the authoritative Word of the Lord to you.

Warning Against Unbelief

The writer of Hebrews certainly wants his readers to hear the ancient message ringing with present application in their ears. He warns in verse 12, "Take care, brothers, lest there be in any of you an evil, unbelieving heart, leading you to fall away from the living God." To *fall away* is translated from *apostēnai* which implies active rebellion. To have "an unbelieving heart" (*apistias*) is to have an apostatizing heart, one that rebels against the Lord. Unbelief and apostasy are coordinate. What leads a professor of Christ to show that he may not be a possessor of what he professes? The answer of the text is "an evil, unbelieving heart." It is that which is "leading you to fall away from the living God." This harks back to Psalm 95 as quoted in verses 7 and 8: "Today, if you hear his voice, do not harden your hearts as in the rebellion."

"A hardening of the heart by the people of the new covenant will have as devastating an effect on God's people today as it did for the original wilderness generation."[1] Oh, contemplate the danger of a hard heart toward God. Sin deceives; then sin hardens; then, it can leave the hardened sinner in utter darkness (compare 10:26–31). The wilderness generation that fell in the desert fell because of unbelief that was manifested in idolatry, selfishness, and complaining. Unbelief can take many forms. One of those forms prevalent among professors today is clinging to "our own

---

1. O. Palmer Robertson, *God's People in the Wilderness: The Church in Hebrews* (Ross-shire, Scotland: Christian Focus, 2009), 144.

righteousness" as if we had righteousness apart from Christ. This is the greatest deceit of all that leads to the most profound hardness of heart. Our greatest problems are not those things that are outside of us, our circumstances, the way we are or have been treated, but our own smug self-righteousness that comes from within. Self righteousness produces hardness of heart so that life is like a frozen pond—cold and stagnant. Self righteousness is rank unbelief and it fights to dominate the sinner's heart. But, self-righteousness must die if we are to live upon another's righteousness, that which is received by faith and comes from the obedience and death of Christ for sinners.

> The believer who answers the Today of the Holy Spirit with the Tomorrow of some more convenient season, knows not how he is hardening his heart; the delay, instead of making the surrender and obedience and faith easy, makes it more difficult. It closes the heart for today against the Comforter, and cuts off all hope and power of growth.[2]

Indeed, one who closes his heart in such a fashion may find that he is not a believer at all.

The leading questions put forth in 3:16–18 are calculated to smoke the readers out of their refuge in self-righteousness and to drive them to Christ alone. Having cited again from Psalm 95 ("Today, if you hear his voice, do not harden your hearts as in the rebellion"), he asks:

> For who were those who heard and yet rebelled? Was it not all those who left Egypt led my Moses? And with whom was he provoked for forty years? Was it not with those who sinned, whose bodies fell in the wilderness? And to whom did he swear that they would not enter his rest, but to those who were disobedient?

2. Andrew Murray, cited by O. Palmer Robertson, *God's People in the Wilderness*, 124.

Then the writer concludes, "so we see that they were unable to enter because of unbelief."

What needed changing for those who rebelled in the wilderness? Was it their wilderness setting? This is what they argued: "Our circumstances need changing." But, God's answer to the question, "What needs changing?" was, "Your hearts." Here then, by means of these profound and probing questions is a call to demolish those things to which we falsely cling for salvation and comfort in the place of God. The gospel appropriated by faith changes for whom and for what we live. Paul stresses this very truth in 2 Corinthians 5:14–15: "For the love of Christ controls us, because we have concluded this: that one has died for all, therefore all have died; and he died for all, that those who live might no longer live for themselves but for him who for their sake died and was raised."

The Call to Encourage

It is within this context of profound warning that the call to mutual encouragement comes. Having warned his readers to take heed against "an evil, unbelieving heart, leading you to fall away from the living God," he next calls upon the readers to live as a communion of saints and to "exhort one another every day, as long as it is called 'today,' that none of you may be hardened by the deceitfulness of sin." Daily encouragement of one another within the household of faith is ordained by God as a means for bringing his people home. A faithful walk does not happen alone. It is God's design that believers understand the importance of the communion of the saints. "Exhort one another every day."

The encouragement that comes through the preached Word is to take such hold of the hearts of God's people that they learn to repeat the encouragement of God's promises to one another in the common course of life. Each believer should ask himself, "Am I exhorting my brothers to walk faithfully, or am I more like those who incite rebellion and unbelief?" Exhortation and the encouragement to walk faithfully that stems from it comes in many forms. Often such exhortation is overt. At other times it comes as a willingness to forgive, to show compassion, or to confront in grace without self-righteousness. Sometimes exhortation comes as a heart that cheers others on, and it shapes cruciform relationships.

This text can be taken seriously by Christians who look for ways to encourage others by letters, emails, phone calls, praying for others, and cheering the fainthearted with kind words and deeds. The term *parakalein* is very comprehensive, including entreaty, admonition, exhortation, encouragement, and comfort. We are to speak to our brothers according to their needs.

That such exhortation is essential to Christian living is underscored by the preacher's call to "exhort one another *every day,*" with frequency and regularity as long as the temptation of unbelief persists. Believers should exhort in this ongoing manner "as long as it is called 'today.'"

What does this imply? *Today* in verse 7 above cited from Psalm 95 was the *today* of the wilderness wandering; but, the *today* for the believer is that of daily gospel provision and promise, as the writer says in 4:1, it is the time "while the promise of entering his rest still stands." The call to "exhort one another every day, as long as it is called 'today'" implies that the Christian must understand his place in redemptive history, the *today* of God's promise and provision between the ascension and return of Christ. It is this redemptive historical reality that provides a context in which the exhortations of fellow believers are powered by more than their own words, but by the Holy Spirit who indwells them and the omnipotent assistance of the great high priest who rules on the throne on high.

Today must take in all that has thus far been said about the Son who saves and all that will be said in chapters to come about the glories of Christ. The exhortations of believers are not vain, frivolous efforts but have for their context the supremacy of Christ. In such a setting the writer wants them to remember that they may believe the promise that will not fail and to encourage others to do so as well. The writer will later say, "let us hold fast the confession of our hope without wavering for he who promised is faithful. And let us consider how to stir up one another to love and good works, not neglecting to meet together, as is the habit of some, but encouraging one another, and all the more as you see the Day drawing near" (10:23–25). Exhort, while it is today in view of the Day that is approaching when Christ returns.

This exhortation has as its goal "that none of you be hardened by the deceitfulness of sin. For we have come to share in Christ, if indeed we hold our original confidence firm to the end." The writer then calls to mind the results of sin's deceitfulness in 3:17–19:

> And with whom was he provoked for forty years?
> Was it not with those who sinned, whose bodies fell
> in the wilderness? And to whom did he swear that
> they would not enter his rest, but to those who were
> disobedient? So we see that they were unable to en-
> ter because of unbelief.

The deceitfulness of sin! Unbelief! What warning is here for us? The writer is concerned, as we should be concerned in the church, "that none [in the church] be hardened by the deceitfulness of sin." The passive *be hardened* shows the progressive nature of unbelief and its inevitable consequence of apostasy where it is not checked by truth and grace. The Lord has ordained mutual exhortation as one of the means to keep us in the way. Let us take heed to the call to warn and exhort one another.

As a minister of the Word and pastor of a flock I have seen the wondrous effects of exhortation. I have also seen situations where exhortation was needed and not given until it was too late to recover a professor to his profession. Do not mistake me; a saved person cannot be lost. God has, however, ordained means for his people's perseverance, for holding "our original confidence firm to the end." One of those means that we must grasp and apply *today* is mutual encouragement, confrontation, and exhortation of one another. That every true believer will cross the finish line is guaranteed; that the Lord has ordained that the runner's compatriots cheer him on to the finish line is also ordained of the Lord as one means to bring the runner to victory. Cheer your fellow believer on.

Do Not Miss God's Rest

Believe in Christ alone and be fearful of all substitutes. "Therefore, while the promise of entering his rest still stands, let us fear lest any of you should seem to have failed to reach it" (4:1). *Let us fear* is a hortatory subjunctive and is first in the sentence in the Greek text. There is a kind of fear that checks self-confidence, that is completely compatible with full assurance of faith (10:22), because it is a vigilance in Christ-confidence. This promise is held out to faith "today" and the *fear* is one that is compatible with the call to faith. It is not a fear that sets aside "the promise of entering his rest" but that believes the promise. M'Cheyne called this "a sweet, holy jealousy which the most solid Christians will always exercise over themselves." "True," he reminds us, "the fear of wrath is taken away when the soul comes into the perfect love of God. But the fear of self-jealousy remains. The spouse that loves her husband truly will be jealous over herself lest in anything she is unfaithful."[3] This is the kind of *fear* that will continue to characterize the true people of God.

Unbelief was the source of the wilderness generation's condemnation:

---

3. Robert Murray M'Cheyne, *Sermons on Hebrews* (Edinburgh: Banner of Truth, 2004), 14–15.

> For good news came to us just as to them, but the
> message they heard did not benefit them, because
> they were not united by faith with those who lis-
> tened. For we who have believed enter that rest, as
> he has said, "As I swore in my wrath, 'They shall not
> enter my rest,'" although his works were finished
> from the foundation of the world. (4:2–3)

How important it is that we see the continuity of God's
way of salvation throughout redemptive history, that we grasp
the unity in the diversity. The text plainly says that the gospel
that comes to us and that which came to the wilderness generation is the same gospel; "good news came to us just as to
them." No sinner has ever been saved but by faith in Christ. In
the Old Testament, saints were saved by Christ anticipated;
we are saved by Christ who has come, and only on his finished
work. Believers belong to that great stream of saints who have
been saved by the blood of the Lamb. The gospel proclaimed
was then to be received by faith and is now to be received by
faith. The gospel proclaimed through types and shadows and
held out in the promise of rest did not deliver ancient Israel in
the wilderness, because that gospel was rejected. The gospel
must be believed to do us good, not only heard with the hearing of the ear but in the heart by faith. The gospel proclamation "did not benefit them, because they were not united by
faith with those who listened."

This gospel then and now proclaims rest (katapau*sis*). What
is the rest to which the writer refers? It is the rest that was
founded on God's rest, that is, upon his satisfaction at the conclusion of creation. "For he has somewhere spoken of the seventh day in this way: 'And God rested on the seventh day from
all his works'" (4:4). By faith believers will enter God's rest. "For
we who have believed enter that rest" (4:3). The present tense in
verse three is not intended to detract from the future promise

of rest but "is used in a generalizing sense: entry into [that] rest is for us who have believed."[4]

The reference to Genesis 2:2 must be placed within the eschatological focus of redemptive history that presses on toward the consummation of all things. Believers have entered into the eschatological rest by faith, and that same faith presses us forward to the joyful Sabbath that awaits us. So the writer is keen to point out that the *rest* was not fulfilled in the conquest under Joshua "(For if Joshua had given them rest, God would not have spoken of another day later on)," but that *rest* points believers to the consummation of all things. "So then, there remains a Sabbath rest for the people of God, for whoever has entered God's rest has also rested from his works as God did from his" (4:8–10).

This forward looking call is found elsewhere in Hebrews. The patriarchs desired "a better country, that is, a heavenly one. Therefore God is not ashamed to be called their God, for he has prepared for them a city" (Heb. 11:16; see also 12:22ff). The "Sabbath rest" that "remains for the people of God" (4:9), therefore, is the eschatological heritage for which the Christian longs at the return of Christ. It is the "inheritance that is imperishable, undefiled, and unfading, kept in heaven for you, who by God's power are being guarded through faith for a salvation ready to be revealed in the last time" (1 Pet. 1:4–5). It is not a rest from toils, trials, temptations and tribulations in this life, but the rest that awaits God's people after the toils of life are ended and in the eternal state after Christ's return.

In this life there is toil, indeed the writer calls upon us to "*strive* to enter that rest, so that no one may fall by the same sort of disobedience." This *toil* is not works righteousness. It corresponds to a life of faith. How do we earn this rest? We do not earn it at all; Jesus has earned it and we receive that rest by faith.

---

4. F. F. Bruce, *Hebrews* (Grand Rapids: Erdmans, 1979), 73 footnote 17.

This has been the decisive point all along. Why did the wilderness generation fail to enter the rest of Canaan? "They were unable to enter because of unbelief" (3:19). The true Christian life, then, is characterized by ongoing, lively faith in Christ. It is by faith we enter into the rest that awaits us. Those who turn back have abandoned that hope because they have not trusted Christ by faith.

One passing remark that is of some importance relates to the concept of the perpetuity of the fourth commandment. Since the Sabbath (now the Lord's Day) is a sign of the rest that awaits us, the sign remains until we actually enter that rest. The rest awaits us, so the sign remains. Therefore, the Sabbath commandment to rest from our labors (now on the first day of the week, the day of resurrection) remains as a vital foretaste pointing us forward. It is a blessing for the church until the end of the age. The Westminster Confession says with clarity:

> As it is the law of nature, that, in general, a due proportion of time be set apart for the worship of God; so, in His Word, by a postitive, moral, and perpetual commandment binding all men in all ages, He hath particularly appointed one day in seven, for a Sabbath, to be kept holy unto him: which, from the beginning of the world to the resurrection of Christ, was the last day of the week; and, from the resurrection of Christ, was changed into the first day of the week, which, in Scripture, is called the Lord's Day, and is to be continued to the end of the world, as the Christian Sabbath (XXI.VII).

How much time do you spend thinking upon the ultimate glory and rest that awaits the people of God? It should be so determinative that the world looking on should see a resemblance of the end in believers now. There is no place for despair in the Christian life, only a walk by faith that looks forward to the promised Sabbath rest. Life has meaning and an ultimate goal of delight in the glory of God. Every view of the world espouses "eschatology," a view of the end, but only the Christian faith, grounded in the revelation of God in history in the person and work of Christ, can give us an eschatology of life, hope, and victory. Only those who have faith in Christ can look to the future and not only avoid Voltaire's wish that he had never been born but, on the contrary, be filled with longing for the end, a consummation which, for the believer, is a new beginning. "Therefore let the sabbath bells ring out! Let them ring till they are silenced by the very fulfillment of their message. Let them ring for the sun which will not be needed in the city forensically called to wondrous light." Let them ring for the day when "we shall sing, unceasingly—*Te Deum Laudamus!*"[5] Living by faith in God's promise causes the bells of Sabbath rest to peal out now in anticipation of that joyful day.

The Penetrating Word

Believing the Lord and receiving his promises means hearing the testimony of his covenant faithfulness in his Word. That Word fell on deaf ears in the wilderness generation, but we will hear it if we are the true people of God. That Word now confronts the congregation in its preaching every Lord's Day.

> For the word of God is living and active, sharper than any two-edged sword, piercing to the division of soul and marrow, and discerning the thoughts and intentions of the heart.

The penetrating Word lays bare the heart bringing us face to face with the eternity and the judgment to come.

There have been innumerable attempts to find here a reference to Christ, as the Word incarnate, rather than to the writ-

5. Klass Schilder, *Heaven What Is It?* (Grand Rapids: Eerdmans, 1950), 117–118.

ten and proclaimed Word of God. In addition to the fact that it is inappropriate to sever Christ the Word from the written Word, the context makes clear that the writer has the written Word in mind. It was God's Word of promise that ancient Israel failed to believe and his Word of judgment came upon them. The writer desires the church to hear that now this Word of the Lord comes with the same call to believe it and with the same warning if we do not.

Geerhardus Vos wrote that "reception of truth on the authority of God is an eminently religious act. Belief in the inspiration of Scripture can be appraised as an act of worship under given circumstances."[6] The point that must not be missed is that belief and unbelief, reception and rejection of God's Word are not primarily matters of the intellect. They are essentially moral issues. The Word is "living and active" in its application by the Holy Spirit (3:7). The Lord will accomplish his purpose and will do what he has said he will do either in faithfulness to true believers or judgment upon those who fail to be what they profess themselves to be. The Word is "sharper than any two-edged sword." Just as the unbelieving generation was cut down by the sword (Num. 14:43–45), God's Word is an awful sword of judgment to unbelievers.

Finally, the Word of God "pierces to the division of soul and of spirit, of joints and of marrow, and discerning the thoughts and intentions of the heart." There is no crevice of the heart unreachable by the Word of God; all thoughts and intentions are open to the Lord and his Word. There is nothing that can be hidden from the Lord's omniscient eye. "And no creature is hidden from his sight, but all are naked and exposed to the eyes of him to whom we must give account" (4:13). The heart is naked and exposed to the Lord who judges apostasy. When one hears the Word and does not believe it, let him hear as well that to be

---

6. Geerhardus Vos, *Biblical Theology* (Grand Rapids: Erdmans, 1948), 18.

exposed by God's Word is to be exposed by God and none can help him.

The text speaks with such glowing language of the power of God's Word we should be reminded that the Lord will accomplish through His Word the purpose for which he sends it (Isa. 55:11). I have read a number of times of a member of the "Hell-fire Club" in the time of the Evangelical Awakening in England. The purpose of this club was to gather members who would mock the Awakening and the ministers who led it. On one occasion, a member preached a sermon of George Whitefield's intending to mock this man of God, but in the process of mocking the man, was converted by the gospel he had despised. The club was dissolved and the man became a preacher greatly used of the Lord in the conversion of sinners.

The same Word can be heard or read by an unbeliever and a believer to totally different ends. We are reminded of the awesome reality that the gospel is "to one a fragrance from death to death, to the other a fragrance from life to life" (2 Cor. 2:16). The solemn message to all is that "no creature is hidden from his sight, but all are naked and exposed to the eyes of him to whom we must give account." In solemnity the writer brings to a close the second admonition of his sermon-epistle. May we hear it by faith.

8

Since We Have a Great High Priest

HEBREWS 4:14–16

Since then we have a great high priest who has passed through the heavens, Jesus, the Son of God, let us hold fast our confession. For we do not have a high priest who is unable to sympathize with our weaknesses, but one who in every respect has been tempted as we are, yet without sin. Let us then with confidence draw near to the throne of grace, that we may receive mercy and find grace to help in time of need.

A. T. Robertson, the great scholar of New Testament Greek, once lectured on the sympathy of Jesus for us his people in our daily needs. Having spoken on the present helpfulness and tenderness of Jesus for us, he returned to his study from class. After this, his biographer tells us, a beloved student followed him into his seminary study. There the student found his teacher surrounded by his books, sitting in his chair, "his eyes swimming in tears which overflowed to his cheeks." Dr. Robertson broke out in words of adoration for Jesus saying to his student: "And to think, Brother . . . , he's the same Jesus now, the same Jesus now."[1] That is the point the writer of Hebrews would impress upon our hearts in this unforgettable passage. Our great High Priest is the same Jesus now.

We must remember as we read Hebrews that this epistle is also a sermon. The writer preaches to the Hebrew Christians who are tempted to defect. Every preacher knows that all sinners that sit before him have the same basic needs but also that their circumstances and "cases" will vary. One may need encouragement and another rebuke and another more instruction. The sermon-epistle of Hebrews shows that the writer is a pastor without peer. Having concluded a section that ended with solemn warning he immediately adds some of the most encouraging words found in the entire book of Hebrews. Of course, behind this we see the supreme care of the great Shepherd of the sheep (Heb. 13:20) and the inspiration of the Holy Spirit throughout. The word we read is God's Word.

The theme revealed in this passage should thrill the Christian's soul. We have a great high priest. This priest stood in the place of his people in the judgment of the cross and Hebrews emphasizes that he now stands as an advocate of sinners in the throne room of God. Here Christ's righteousness, his perfect merit, effectually pleads for his people. Only a people who do not understand this or who have forgotten this life changing reality could miss the old ways, the old priesthood, wanting to go back. Do you understand that you have a great high priest through whom you are acceptable to God? No Old Testament priest was ever designated *great* high priest. The Son is no ordinary priest; he is incomparable.

Bear in mind also the eschatological setting of Hebrews. We need more of the early church's mentality that we are living in the last days. Without remembering this emphasis, we will not

---

1. Everett Gill, *A. T. Robertson, A Biography* (New York: Macmillan, 1943), 221–222.

understand Hebrews. This reality for them also presented a problem. How can the exaltation of Jesus co-exist with crises and testing for the church? The crises of persecution and the stresses constraining their livelihoods—all due to their commitment to Christ—strengthened the temptation to return to, and long for, the old pattern of things. By divine inspiration, the writer brings perspective to the relationship between Christ's exalted priestly work and the crises that, in the time between the ascension and return of Christ, inevitably attend Christian living.

Christ Passed Through the Heavens

The Language of Priesthood

"Since then we have a great high priest who has passed through the heavens" brings to mind Aaron's approach to God as the representative of God's people on the Day of Atonement (Lev. 16). Vos points out that in Hebrews "where a comparison with Aaron is expressed or implied, Christ is called *High Priest* (2:17; 4:14; 5:1; 7:26, 28; 8:13; 9:11–12). When the comparison is between Christ and the Levitical order, He is called *priest.*"[2] The comparison between Christ and Aaron is primarily before us here. The very language reminds us from the start that bulls and goats could not remove sin (10:14). It required a great high priest who has accomplished a finished redemption on the cross and is now our representative in heaven.

Of course, the great presupposition is that God must judge sin and that Christ has paid the penalty for the sins of his people and now presents the fruit of atonement in heaven's court as our Advocate (2:17). How could we approach the blazing glory of God apart from our high priest? All the fury of heaven was borne by him in our place; there he now sits on the throne on high in the splendor of his finished accomplishment. If a less

2. Geerhardus Vos, *The Teaching of the Epistle to the Hebrews* (Grand Rapids: Eerdmans, 1956), 84.

costly sacrifice would have served the purpose of our redemption then that route surely would have been taken. God is just; no other could redeem than the Son and no other can represent us in heaven's court but the one who paid the price.

The Language of Transcendence

The comparison between Aaron and Jesus, our great high priest, also finds expression in the transcendent language of the text, "since then we have a great high priest who has passed through the heavens, Jesus, the Son of God." Even *passed through the heavens* speaks to the contrast between Jesus and Aaron. This is probably not a reference to the multi-layered heavens in Jewish thought but "is intended to contrast with the limited entrance of the Aaronic high priest within the veil. Our high priest penetrates to the very presence of God."[3] Aaron passed from the altar through the outer court through the holy place to the holy of holies beyond the veil passing from view. Jesus in his ascension has passed from view. He has ascended through the heavenly regions to the actual throne room of which the inner sanctuary of the earthly Tabernacle was but a copy (8:5; 9:24). Does the absence of Jesus from the sight of the believer present any disadvantage to the believer in Christ? The answer unequivocally is "no." Christ accomplished redemption, finishing his atoning work on the cross and now represents us in the heavenly court to which Aaron could only point.

Who did this for us? The "great high priest who has passed through the heavens" is "Jesus, the Son of God." The name Jesus is the name that the Father gave to him at his birth, thus pointing to his true humanity (Matt. 1:2; Luke 1:31; 2:21). The same incarnate Lord Jesus born in Bethlehem endured the cross, rose from the dead, ascended on high and serves his people as *great high priest*. Jesus is *the Son of God* (see 2:9; 3:1). The writer in-

3. Donald Guthrie, *Hebrews* in the *Tyndale New Testament Commentaries* (Grand Rapids: Eerdmans, 1983), 120.

tends to stress the deity of Christ (Heb. 1:1–4), and therefore his ultimate qualification for the office of high priest. He can accomplish as man what man needs in the strength of his deity because he perfectly unites in one person the two natures forever, as Chalcedon says, "inconfusedly, unchangeably, indivisibly, inseparably." Hebrews stresses that the humanity of Christ is a necessary qualification for his high priestly work, but Hebrews also stresses that Christ's deity is a necessary qualification as well (1:3; 3:6; 4:14; 5:5; 7:28).

The Language of Exhortation

The union of Deity and humanity in one person who serves his people as high priest to bring them to God provides the context for the exhortation of verse 14, "let us hold fast our confession." The term *confession* here is the same as in 3:1, "Therefore, holy brothers, you who share in a heavenly calling, consider Jesus, the apostle and high priest of our confession." *Our confession* is the truth as it is in Jesus embraced by faith and acknowledged clearly before the world. It is in essence the same concept expressed by Paul in Romans 10:9, that "if you confess with your mouth that Jesus is Lord and believe in your heart that God raised him from the dead, you will be saved."

Have you confessed faith in Christ who propitiated the wrath of God on the cross, who rose from the dead and intercedes for his people? Have you begun to wander? Stand firm; stay the course. What could be more senseless than going back? Indeed, it is impossible for a true believer to go back; but, the Lord uses the call to know and contemplate these things to keep his people in the way. Thank God, Christ pleads for his people in heaven.

Does this speak to our time and need? Without question it does. Our Lord has passed through the heavens. He is exultant and regnant. This is no disadvantage to us, rather we are provided with the greatest possible advantage and blessing. Our

Mediator who holds heaven and earth in his hands brings us to God and serves us as our "great high priest." What incentive, then, to "hold fast our confession"; what a guarantee that all who are truly his will do so.

Omnipotent Sympathy

The Importance of Christ's Humanity

We are next reminded that the exalted Son sympathizes with his people—not with pathetic, ineffective sympathy, but the omnipotent sympathy that only the Son of God who took our flesh can provide: "For we do not have a high priest who is unable to sympathize with our weaknesses, but one who in every respect has been tempted as we are, yet without sin." Forbid the thought that our high priest in heaven is a poor substitute for one upon the earth. Quite the contrary. Christ's presence in heaven, the exercise of the Son of God's high priestly office for us, presents no disadvantage, but a wealth of advantages.

Perhaps the connection of verse 15 to 14 by "for" (*gar*) is that the greatness and grandeur of the "Son of God" who indeed "has passed through the heavens" should not hinder us from thinking that he is far removed from our needs. Here the importance of the humanity of Christ is stressed. "We do not have a high priest who is unable to sympathize with our weaknesses" (the writer uses a double negative stressing the impossibility of the proposition). Rather, "Jesus, the Son of God" who is "our great high priest" understands us from a human point of view. Here the writer reflects once again upon thoughts similar to those expressed in Hebrews 2:17–18:

> Therefore he had to be made like his brothers in every respect, so that he might become a merciful and faithful high priest in the service of God, to make propitiation for the sins of the people. For because

he himself has suffered when tempted, he is able to
help those who are being tempted.

Our great high priest is fully able to sympathize with us in our
weaknesses as the incarnate Son. Lane points out that the special nuance of the word *sympathize* is not only sharing of feelings but "the element of active help." "In this context the stress
falls on the capacity of the exalted high priest to help those who
are helpless."[4]

Christ's Victory Over Temptation Sufferings

Christ's fellowship in human sufferings and testing begets his
true human compassion. The proof of the Son's sympathy is derived from his own experience of overcoming temptation. Immediately we are confronted with great mystery when we think
of the Son of God incarnate overcoming temptation. Yet, that
he did endure temptation is the direct teaching of Scripture. He
who was sinless (John 8:46: Luke 1:35; 2 Cor. 5:21; 1 Pet. 2:22;
3:18; 1 John 3:5; Heb. 4:15; 9:14) nonetheless was tempted. Dabney puts the axe to the root of the tree of those who teach that,
even theoretically, Christ might have sinned, by reminding us
that "the human nature of Christ never had its separate personality. It never existed, and never will exist for an instant, save in
personal union with the Word. Hence, . . . since only a Person
can sin, the question is irrelevant."[5]

However, because of who he is, his temptations were more
intense than those that we endure. Who of us has experienced
the direct confrontation of Satan in the wilderness, or the struggles of Gethsemane, or the call "if you are the Son of God, come
down from the cross"—the temptation to abandon his mission
at the point of culmination? These examples were unique to the
Son of God but were, nonetheless, temptations that came to

---

4. William Lane, *Hebrews* (Dallas: Word, 1991), 1.114.

5. R. L. Dabney, *Systematic Theology* (Edinburgh: Banner of Truth, 1985), 471.

him in his incarnation, in his true humanity. His entire life was one of temptation.

Many Christians are tempted to think that given his impeccability, the Son's sufferings were mere phantasms; that is, since he could not yield, the temptations were of little consequence. Nothing could be further from the truth. The Son was indeed sinless, at the cross he "offered himself unblemished to God"; however, in his life he "was tempted in every respect" just "as we are, yet without sin." The Son's impeccability did not make the temptations irrelevant. Christ battled as he lived under the promise of God's Word and walked by faith, and as the horror of sin was presented to his holy mind. The holiness of the Son made the temptations more black and offensive.

It was actually *because of* the Lord's complete and perfect holiness that when his sinless, truly human soul was confronted with temptations, they were greater than we experience. There is a real mystery for us here, but the Word is plain, and to it we bend. Hoeksema captures the mystery and reality of this matter when he says that "the trial or test of anything does not become less real because it is certain from the outset that it will not and cannot break. The strain put upon the obedience of Christ in his sufferings and death is nonetheless real and heavy because it was *a priori* established that He could never be crushed under the strain. Also in this respect Christ was separate from sinners. He could never fall. In Him the realization of God's everlasting covenant is assured from the beginning, because He is the Word become flesh."[6]

The point of Hebrews, however, is not simply that the Lord can sympathize with us from the standpoint of humanity. The point is that the Son was truly tempted and can really sympathize with us because he was tempted *yet without sin*. This is

---

6. Herman Hoeksema, *Reformed Dogmatics* (Grand Rapids: Reformed Free, 1985), 358.

essential to the accomplishment of our redemption. The incarnate Son was completely victorious over every single temptation. Had he given in, he would have needed a redeemer! The incarnate Son did not give in, could not have given in, and so was the impeccable sacrifice for our sins and the sympathetic high priest of his people. Aaron the high priest sacrificed for his own sins and then for the sins of the people, but the great high priest of God's people did not offer sacrifice for his own sins, for he was without sin. Had he been stained, he could not have been the Lamb of God that takes away sin. The Son was the active conqueror of temptation doing battle for our fallen souls in obedience to his Father.

So our *great high priest* has "an unequaled capacity for sympathizing with them in all the dangers and sorrows and trials which come their way in life, because He Himself, by virtue of His likeness to them, was exposed to all these experiences."[7] Not only was the Lord Jesus exposed to these temptations, he was triumphant. Never once did his faith weaken; never once did he disobey his Father. As difficult as all of this is for us to understand, to paraphrase Westcott, sympathy with the sinner does not depend upon the experience of sin, but on the strength of the temptation overcome. Let us put stress on this point in our understanding.

Grace Enthroned

The Throne of Grace

"Let us with confidence draw near to the throne of grace." What is this "throne of grace"? It is that throne upon which Jesus sits in the splendor of his finished work. "After making purification for sins, he sat down at the right hand of the Majesty on high" (1:3). As the antitype of the mercy seat in the Tabernacle, this

---

7. F. F. Bruce, *Hebrews* (Grand Rapids: Eerdmans, 1979), 85.

throne upon which Jesus sits is the seat of grace because grace is enthroned there. Our great high priest is grace personified. It is at "the throne of grace" that we find our Savior applying to our souls the value of his once for all sacrifice. Brown says beautifully, "In the expression, 'the throne of grace,' there is undoubtedly an allusion to the mercy-seat in the Holy of Holies, over which the Shekinah, the emblem of the divine presence, hovered: and which might therefore with sufficient propriety be represented as the throne of Jehovah, who 'dwelt between the cherubim.'" That "throne of grace" Brown goes on to say "is a figurative expression for God as seated on a throne of grace,— 'the God of peace,' the propitiated Divinity."[8] Yes; and it is upon this very throne that the Lord Jesus "sat down at the right hand of the Majesty on high" (1:3).

In a truly pious and affecting manner John Duncan applied these themes to himself and his hearers and so should every believer. John Macleod cited a communion table address taken down by shorthand by one who heard this godly man; his words are deeply moving:

> Methought then I stood on *Calvary* and heard these words "It is finished." God said, "Look into the heart of Christ and behold Him in His vicarious death. Behold Him, and know the grace of the Lord Jesus Christ, that, though He was rich, yet for your sakes, He became poor, that ye through His poverty might be rich." The greatest depth of this poverty being not in His incarnation—though that was a wondrous depth—look at it in His death.
>
> Then methought also that God said, "Come by the blood to the Mercy-Seat." And I heard a voice speak from the Mercy-Seat from between the Cherubims. And what voice was that? "This is My beloved Son (not merely with Whom, but) in Whom I am well

---

8. John Brown, *Hebrews* (Edinburgh: Banner of Truth, 1983), 233–234.

pleased, hear Him," said He from the Mercy-Seat, between the Cherubims. "The Lord is well pleased for his righteousness' sake," said He from the Mercy-Seat, from between the Cherubims. "I, even I, am He that blotteth out thy transgressions, and will not remember thy sins," said He from the Mercy-Seat, from between the Cherubims. Sweet invitation to me, a departer, "Return unto Me," God assigning to the sinner the saving clause, "For I have redeemed thee."[9]

Confidence

The moving words of John Duncan lead us well into the theme of confidence. Christians are exhorted here to "with confidence draw near to the throne of grace" since we have a great high priest, a Savior who did not fail, and who presents the merit of his sacrifice for his people. Christ *did not fail* in his priestly sacrifice and *will not fail* in his high priestly work. He has gone within the veil with the full value of his infinitely worthy sacrifice for his own. Our case will never come up for condemnatory judgment before the throne; that throne is "the throne of grace" for his people. To *draw near* is priestly language taken from the Old Testament ritual (Lev. 16) where God prescribed how Aaron was to draw near to him on the Day of Atonement in contrast to the way in which his sons Nadab and Ahibu "drew near before the Lord and died" (Lev. 16:1). Amazingly, in Christ our high priest we have access to God and confidently "draw near to the throne of grace."

It is true that Hebrews includes many warnings; it is also true that those warnings are never intended to distract true believers from full assurance of faith but, on the contrary, to draw us to such assurance. The *confidence* to which believers are called is cultivated in the context of who Jesus is and what he has done and is doing for his elect. James Haldane tells of

---

9. John Macleod, *Scottish Theology In Relation to Church History* (Edinburgh: Banner of Truth, 1974), 285.

how he once desired to rest on "frames and feelings, instead of building on the sure foundation." This brought him no comfort.

> Gradually becoming more dissatisfied with myself, being convicted especially of the sin of unbelief, I wearied myself with looking for some wonderful change to take place,—some inward feeling, by which I might know I was born again. The method of resting simply on the promises of God, which are yea and amen in Jesus Christ, was too plain and easy, like Naaman, the Syrian, instead of bathing in Jordan and being clean, I would have some great work in my mind to substitute in place of Jesus Christ.

The Lord wrought comfort in his soul on the basis of the promises of Christ. Haldane adds that "when I have the most comfort, then does sin appear most hateful."[10] This is the comfort of the gospel to which the Lord calls his people and, if the Lord's people followed the exhortation "let us then with confidence draw near to the throne of grace" the church would abound in assured, strong, and growing Christians who hate sin and love God's law.

Even though the text instructs believers to come boldly to the throne of grace, it is possible for troubled hearts to demure. What will help us to come boldly, with confidence, to the Lord on the throne? The answer is to remember the ground of our confidence. Robert Traill reminds us of the ground of our confidence in this beautiful passage:

> It is a mistake in Christians to think, that they cannot come to the throne of grace with boldness, because of the many infirmities in their hearts, and in their addresses. Your complaint may be just and true; but the inference is not good. Do you never, in your counting your infirmities, put in this great

---

10. Alexander Haldane, *The Lives of Robert and James Haldane*, 76–78.

one amongst them in your confessions, the want of boldness of faith? For this boldness stands not in any thing in us, and done by us. We must not come boldly, because we can pray well, and plead hard; we must not think to be heard in heaven, neither because of our much speaking, nor well speaking, Matth. vi. 7. as the Pharisees did. The boldness of faith hath a higher, and more noble and firm foundation, even Jesus Christ.[11]

That is the truth to be grasped, the truth that will give us confidence to come to Christ upon his gracious throne. That boldness is not grounded in us but in Christ who achieved our redemption and intercedes for us. As Traill adds: "There is more of grace in the promise, than there can be sin and misery in the man that pleads it."[12]

Access to God

The exhortation to *draw near* may be translated "let us keep on coming." The heavenly high priestly work of Christ should engender confidence and the desire for access into his presence. We have a friend in the court of heaven, and advocate. Let this animate you to *draw near*. Come! The Father will not deny the Son. Thomas Watson reminds us that "prayer, as it comes from the saints is but weak and languid; but when the arrow of a saint's prayer is put into the bow of Christ's intercession it pierces the throne of grace."[13] As Palmer Robertson says:

Rather than having to conquer a land such as Canaan, or to be transposed into heaven itself by death or by rapture, you as a Christian believer may now

---

11. Robert Traill, *The Works of Robert Traill* (Edinburgh: Banner of Truth, 1975), 1.65.

12. Traill, *Works*, 1.74.

13. Thomas Watson, *A Body of Divinity* (London: Banner of Truth, 1970), 183.

> constantly enter the very presence of God by focusing on Jesus. His most holy dwelling place does not only exist in heaven. Instead, it can be found among believers today since they are constituted as the "house" of God.[14]

The access that we have through our great high priest brings to us needed assistance in our pilgrimage to heaven. We "draw near" with "confidence that we may receive mercy and find grace to help in time of need." The Greek text indicates "timely (*eukairon*) or opportune help." The present ministry of Christ as our great high priest is to bring such "timely help" to the tempted and tried people of God on our way to heaven. Knowing this, the believer throws himself by faith into the arms of Christ and there finds that, with dependence on his sacrifice and reliance on his merit, all is well.

Similarly Richard Sibbes encourages confidence through our great high priest saying, "We may with a heart sprinkled with the blood of Christ now ascend into heaven, answer all objections, and triumph against all enemies. We may go boldly to God, and demand the performance of his promises."[15] Sibbes does not mean by "demand" an irreverent approach to the living God, but a Christ-centered faith that boldly trusts the Word of promise. Among the best examples of such confident prayer on the basis of the promise of God through our great high priest is that of Martin Luther. Luther's associate Dietrich wrote to Melanchthon during the Diet of Augsburg:

> I cannot admire enough [Luther's] steadfastness, his joy, his faith and hope in these desolate days. He strengthens himself each day in his convictions by a constant application to the Word of God. Not a day

---

14. O. Palmer Robertson, *God's People in the Wilderness: The Church in Hebrews* (Ross-shire, Scotland: Christian Focus, 2009), 123.

15. Richard Sibbes, *Works* (Edinburgh: Banner of Truth, 1982), 7.483.

passes but he reserves *three hours at least* for prayer out of the portion of the day which is most suitable for work. One day I had the privilege of overhearing him pray. Great God! what a spirit, what a faith in his words! He prays with all the devotion of a man before God, but with all the confidence of a child speaking to his father. "I know" said he, "that Thou art our good God and our Father; that is why I am persuaded that Thou wilt exterminate those who persecute Thy children. If Thou dost not do it, the danger is to Thee as much as to us. This cause is Thine; what we have done, we could not have done otherwise. It is for Thee, merciful Father, to protect us." When I heard him from a distance praying these words with a clear voice, my heart burned with joy within me, because I was hearing him speak to God with altogether as much fervor as liberty; above all he supported himself so firmly upon the promises in the Psalms, that he seemed fully assured that nothing he asked could fail to be accomplished.[16]

Our great high priest helps us in our time of *need*. Already that need has been spoken of by the writer when, in verse 15, we were instructed that Christ sympathizes with our *weaknesses*. It is through the natural weaknesses of our humanity that we come into times of *need*. It is through his own temptation and sufferings that he is able as great high priest to sympathize with us weak and needy but blood-bought people. This points, as John Murray observed, to "the continuity and inter-dependence of our Lord's earthly and heavenly ministries." That is:

His obedience, sufferings, and temptations covered the whole course of his humiliation. And it is the experience derived from these sufferings and temptations that equips him with fellow-feeling or sym-

16. Cited by Adolphe Monod, *Adolphe Monod's Farewell* (London: Banner of Truth, 1962), 79.

pathy so that he is able to support and succor his own people in their sufferings and temptations. His earthly undertaking, therefore, was not only that he should offer himself once for all as a sacrifice, not only that he should learn obedience through sufferings so as to be able in obedience to fulfill the climactic demand of his commission, but also that he might be fully equipped with the fellow-feeling requisite to the discharge of his priestly ministry of succour.

To which professor Murray added:

To view the heavenly sympathy of our Lord from the aspect of our existential need, how indispensable to comfort and to perseverance in faith, to know that in all the temptations of this life we have a sympathizer, and helper, and comforter in the person of him from whom we must conceal nothing, who feels with us in every weakness and temptation, and knows exactly what our situation—physical, psychological, moral, and spiritual—is! And this he knows because he himself was tempted, like as we are, without sin. That he who has this feeling with us in temptation appears in the presence of God for us and is our advocate with the Father invests his sympathy and help with an efficacy that is nothing less than *omnipotent compassion*.[17]

Allow this to fill your meditations, child of God. "The Father invests his sympathy and help with an efficacy that is nothing less than *omnipotent compassion*." As A. T. Robertson said to his student, "And to think, Brother . . . , he's the same Jesus now, the same Jesus now."

---

17. John Murray, *The Heavenly, Priestly Activity of Christ, Works* (Edinburgh: Banner of Truth, 1976), 1.49–50.

9

Greater than Aaron

HEBREWS 5:1–10

In the days of his flesh, Jesus offered up prayers and supplications, with loud cries and tears, to him who was able to save him from death, and he was heard because of his reverence. Although he was a son, he learned obedience through what he suffered. And being made perfect, he became the source of eternal salvation to all who obey him, being designated by God a high priest after the order of Melchizedek.

C hrist in his great, once for all sacrifice accomplished salvation for his people, and in his high priestly work does for his people what only he is qualified to do to meet the needs of our souls. Only he can cleanse the conscience and give peace. It is only through Jesus that we may have free access into the Father's presence and so become obedient to the exhortation "let us then with confidence draw near to the throne of grace, that we may receive mercy and find grace to help in time of need" (Heb. 4:16). The text before us begins to unpack a dominant theme in Hebrews—Christ's heavenly high priesthood—by drawing parallels and contrasts with Aaron's priestly work in the Old Testament. Pursuing this provides matter for contemplation, praise, and encouragement to persevere. As we grasp the theme of Christ's priestly work, we come to understand what a mercy it is that we have such a high priest. We deepen our confidence and longing to come to the mercy seat "that we may receive mercy and find grace to help in time of need" (Heb. 4:16).

Aaron's Priesthood

The writer begins by underscoring the principle that "every high priest chosen from among men is appointed to act on behalf of men in relation to God, to offer gifts and sacrifices for sins." This truth is connected to the immediately preceding text by the word *for* (*gar*), by which it is evident that the writer is demonstrating the connection between the sympathy of the incarnate Lord (4:14–16) and the qualifications for high priestly office. Aaron's priesthood was based on two qualifications. First, he was *appointed* to act as priest. Aaron did not take this calling upon himself but was appointed by the Lord for the sacred task of offering "gifts and sacrifices for sins." In like manner, Christ did not usurp the role of High Priest but received it from the Father's hand and for his glory.

The second qualification for priesthood was that the high priest had to be "chosen from among men," so that "he can deal gently with the ignorant and wayward, since he himself is beset with weakness." Hebrews 5:1 underscores the human nature of the High Priest. Vos comments, "The direction is toward God. Note the use of the present participle, not the aorist: *being taken from among men.* This is significant, as indicating a present requirement. Otherwise He could not function as a priest."[1] Aaron was a part of the nation of Israel. He knew their needs and wants, their problems and sins, their heart rebellion and longings. In a far greater way, Christ the Son entered into

---

1. Geerhardus Vos, *The Teaching of the Epistle to the Hebrews* (Grand Rapids: Eerdmans, 1956), 85.

the world, shared the human experience, and brings us home to God through his service as incarnate Lord.

The Old Testament high priest, then, was chosen, selected, ordained by God to offer sacrifices for sins. Why is this significant? It is significant for a number of reasons. First, the High Priest offered sacrifices "in relation to God." The High Priest brings men near to God. Therefore, only God can appoint the high priest of men's souls. The sinner may not select his own high priest. God knows what is required and he supplies the need. God appointed Aaron and his descendents; man did not and could not appoint the high priest. Exceptions were by God's own command (1 Sam. 16:1–3) and violators were severely punished (e.g. Korah, Num. 16; Uzziah, 2 Chron. 26:16ff). All of this points to the truth that only God can ordain the priest for sinners.

Second, the Old Testament high priest was selected from among men that he might be sympathetic. "He can deal gently with the ignorant and wayward, since he himself is beset with weakness. Because of this he is obligated to offer sacrifice for his own sins just as he does for those of the people." The sinfully "ignorant and wayward" need a Savior and intercessor and a high priest with inner feelings for the needy sinner for whom he offered atonement and intercession. When the Israelite came to the presence of God he found someone who understood him and his need. He did not come to an angel, to a cold and inert statue, or to a calloused, careless, unholy man. He came to God's appointed high priest who was also a fellow man, tempted, tried, experiencing infirmities and weakness; one who shared his suffering. In Aaron's case, of course, he must "offer sacrifice for his own sins just as he does for those of the people." Aaron could be a better priest because, as a sinner, he could sympathize. Christ, the high priest of his people, had no sin of his own needing atonement, but he still suffered as a human in all the ways a human could suffer.

To be qualified as high priest, the one appointed by God must have profound sympathy for those for whom he offers gifts and sacrifices. He must know their fundamental problem and need and minister to their utter weakness and inability. These then were the qualifications of the high priest in ancient Israel. He must be moved with inner feelings to serve sinners and be called of God. Christ loves his people, is moved with emotion for us, longs to help us, and his feelings for us are effectual.

However, there is an immense distinction made between the inner feelings of Aaron as high priest and those of the Lord Jesus Christ as the high priest of his people. Aaron could fulfill his task as high priest with inner feelings expressed by the term *metriopathein*. The Revised Version translates "who has no excess of indignation," and BDAG has "moderate one's feelings." Vos points out that this term could not be used of Jesus. He is correct. To "moderate one's feelings" indicates a sinner who must change, transform, grow, or address possible feelings of hostility—especially at the inconsistencies and frequent failures of those he serves. For Jesus the word used is *sumpathein*, sympathy, since he is without sin.[2]

Hebrews 5:2 references the sin of ignorance. Sin offerings were prescribed in the law for those who sinned after the common manner of fallen man. No provision was given for defiance (Num. 15:30), but the law prescribes that "if anyone sins unintentionally in any of the LORD's commandments about things not to be done, and does any one of them" that the sin offering was to be offered (Lev. 4:2). Andrew Bonar well comments:

> So deceitful is sin, we may be committing that abominable thing which cast angels into an immediate and an eternal hell, and yet at the moment

---

2. Geerhardus Vos, *The Teaching of the Epistle to the Hebrews,* 100.

be totally unaware! Want of knowledge of the truth, and too little tenderness of conscience, hide it from us. Hardness of heart and a corrupt nature cause us to sin unperceived. But here again the form of the Son of man appears! *Jehovah,* God of Israel, institutes sacrifice for *sins of ignorance,* and thereby discovers the same compassionate and considerate heart that appears in our High Priest *"who can have compassion on THE IGNORANT!"* (Heb. v. 2). Amidst the types of this Tabernacle we recognize the presence of Jesus—it is His voice that shakes the curtains and speaks in the ear of Moses—*"If a soul sin through ignorance!"* The same yesterday, today, and for ever![3]

Christ's Priesthood

Having shown that Aaron's qualifications for high priestly office were twofold—God's call to the office and deep sympathy—the writer now turns to Christ who fulfills these qualifications consummately. For Christ, as for Aaron, the first qualification for high priestly office is the call of God.

> And no one takes this honor for himself, but only when called by God, just as Aaron was (5:1).

> So also Christ did not exalt himself to be made a high priest, but was appointed by him who said to him,
>> "You are my Son,
>> today I have begotten you";
>> as he says also in another place,
>> "You are a priest forever,
>> after the order of Melchizedek." (5:4–6).

The writer quotes Psalm 2:7 wherein the one installed is the Messianic king, acknowledged as God's Son. No Old Testament

---

3. Andrew Bonar, *Leviticus* (London: Banner of Truth, 1972), 65–66.

priest was so designated. This high priest will unquestionably be received of the Father and is capable of fulfilling his calling. The high priest is the Son. The writer also cites Psalm 110:4, a reference to the king of Salem in Genesis 14, also designated priest of the Most High. We will speak more of this when we come to Hebrews 7. For now it is important to note that God the Father addressed the Messianic King as Priest forever. The facts thus far bring with them tremendous implications. Think upon the following points:

- One cannot appoint his own high priest; he is the one appointed by God.

- Christ completely understood what it meant to receive this calling. Self-abasement, rejection, humiliation, agony, death, bearing our sins, and the wrath of God all preceded his exaltation to the right hand of the Father. He loved us and gave himself for us (Gal. 2:20).

- In Christ's heavenly high priesthood we find the antitype pointed to by the Aaronic priesthood, but infinitely superior.

- Our high priest is a royal priest. He is the high priest who carries with his office the authority of kingly rule. The perfect representative of his people is compassionate and has authority to apply that compassion because he reigns. So, experientially, when God's people do not feel that they have a priest touched with the feeling of their infirmities, or feel abandoned by his loving care, the reality is that he rules, reigns, and applies his compassion with sovereign right and authority. We must learn to live in accordance with what is true, not how we may feel, and to bring our feelings in line with reality.

The second qualification of our heavenly high priest is *sympathy* (compare 2:17f; 4:15f):

> In the days of his flesh, Jesus offered up prayers and supplications, with loud cries and tears, to him who was able to save him from death, and he was heard because of his reverence. Although he was a son, he learned obedience through what he suffered. (5:7–8)

If Aaron was qualified by inner feelings for the people how much more so is Christ? The argument is from the lesser to the greater. The writer points us to Christ's earthly ministry when "in the days of his flesh, Jesus offered up prayers and supplications, with loud cries and tears, to him who was able to save him from death, and he was heard because of his reverence." This is a reference to Gethsemane when Jesus prayed on the eve of his crucifixion. Mark tells us that "he began to be greatly distressed and troubled," and the Lord Jesus said, "My soul is very sorrowful even unto death." He also prayed, "Abba, Father, all things are possible for you. Remove this cup from me. Yet not what I will, but what you will" (Mark 14:32–36). How sympathetic is Jesus our high priest? He was willing to face the overwhelming horror of the cross, to anguish passionately before the Father, travail in prayer, and to undergo the divine judgment as a substitute for our sins—draining the cup of God's wrath down to the bitter dregs. His is sympathy far greater than that of Aaron; his is a sympathy that saves.

How should the believer read the experiences of the Christian life knowing that this high priest rules and pleads his merit for us with omnipotent compassion—a compassion even to the cross? The believer should remember that Christ's sympathy is not sentimentalism but an almighty sympathy that saves. This sympathy does not look on our plight helplessly but is capable of working our good with holiness as the goal. Moreover, the believer should draw encouragement from the surprising character of grace. Too often believers are prone to think, "Where is grace?" when things do not fall out in a way that appears favorable to us. Rather, we should remember that our high priest sits upon the throne. Again, let us not confuse sympathy with helpless sentimentalism.

Our high priest dispenses his grace in surprising ways; in sickness and trouble, as well as in happier ways. Our high priest is bringing us to our appointed goal and breaking us loose from this world, continuing to knock out from under us the props of self-righteousness and supposed self-sovereignty. In leading us with such sympathy, we are led to let go of the imaginary reins. We then learn to be calm and to stop trying to manipulate life in the way we might want things to be. It is a true saying that "grace runs downstream," and the Lord humbles us that he may lift us up in due season. Our high priest understands our weaknesses. He was tempted from the manger to the cross. He wears our nature upon his throne. He fellowshipped in human suffering more intensely than any human suffering that we will know. He did not sin in the process of suffering and knows how to apply his merit for our intercession; he knows our need precisely, and he knows how to meet it. Our high priest is no dormant, torpid, motionless stained glass window, but the God-man, our truly human priest. You cannot see what he is doing; but, you are not disadvantaged to have a priest in heaven and you can trust his intercession. In Gethsemane, Christ was "heard because of his reverence," and the Savior's merit effectually cries out for us now.

Christ's Priesthood is Sufficient

The writer now takes up the efficacy of Christ's priesthood emphasizing this in two ways. First, the writer speaks of the effectual answer to the Savior's prayers in Gethsemane.

> In the days of his flesh, Jesus offered up prayers and supplications, with loud cries and tears, to him who was able to save him from death, and he was heard because of his reverence.

The efficacy of the Savior's prayer in Gethsemane was answered by his resurrection from the dead. The writer says that Jesus prayed "to him who was able to save him from death." The writer expresses the answer to Jesus' prayer as *ek thanatou,* out of death, rather than *apo thanatou,* from death. Even though prepositions can be pressed too far, it is likely that the use of *ek* rather than *apo* is significant in this context. Jesus' prayer was answered when he was saved *out of* death by his resurrection on the third day. His prayer in Gethsemane was heard and answered in that way which would best serve God's glory and our good.

F. F. Bruce suggests that the writer reflects upon Psalm 22, "loud cries and tears," referencing the supplication and complaint of the Psalm's first portion, while "he was heard because of his reverence" references Psalm 22:24: "He was heard when he cried to him."[4] Though it is true that the author is emphasizing the sympathy of the Savior, it seems to me that he wants us also to have in mind the efficacy of his cry to the Lord heard in resurrection. The Savior's intercession for his people was heard in Gethsemane, for in praying regarding himself he did so in his capacity as our head and representative.

This has not changed; the intercession of Christ is still heard and effectually answered for his people. Moreover, to stress what

4. F. F. Bruce, *Hebrews* (Grand Rapids: Eerdmans, 1964), 100–101.

the text stresses, since he drank the cup, he is not less but *more* qualified to sympathize with his people for whom he died and for whom he intercedes. He endured the cross but also endured the strain of unanswered prayer (in the short term) and his holy soul knew what we can never know. We cannot truly imagine what it meant for the holy, sinless soul of the Son of God to be burdened with all of the sins of all of his elect throughout all of the ages. In *reverence* the Savior tread the path to the pain, agony, and holy wonder of the cross.

That Christ's priesthood is sufficient is also demonstrated by his cumulative obedience. That the Son "learned obedience through what he suffered" and his "being made perfect" do not point to moral inadequacies that he needed to overcome as he grew; he possessed moral perfection from the point of conception by the work on the Holy Spirit in the virgin's womb. Rather, this refers to obtaining qualifications to be our high priest by the experience of life and death, thus overcoming the natural inclination to avoid suffering (5:7). Had he failed at any point he would have been disqualified; but he could not and did not fail. "His *learning* is not equivalent to acquiring something new, as if He would only have the obedience after learning it. For in this case He would have been imperfect before the learning took place" (see 10:7). "Therefore in 5:8 *learning obedience* signifies *bringing out into the present conscious experience of action* that which was already present in principle."[5] Note as well that it is as a Son that Christ learned obedience. "The contrast is not between *Son* and *obedience,* as though it were strange for a son to be obedient, but rather between *Sonship* and having to learn obedience *through suffering,* which was unnatural for one who was a Son."[6]

---

5. Geerhardus Vos, *The Teaching of the Epistle to the Hebrews,* 94.

6. Geerhardus Vos, *The Teaching of the Epistle to the Hebrews,* 94.

Greater than Aaron

This provides a huge contrast with Aaron's priesthood. On the Day of Atonement, the high priest made atonement first for his own sins and then for the sins of the people. Before killing the goat of the sin offering for the people and sprinkling the blood within the veil of the Holy of Holies, he first entered the veil with the blood of the bullock which he offered for himself and his family. Then he offered a goat for the sin offering for the people. Jesus needed to offer no sacrifice for himself. The writer makes this explicit in 7:27 saying "he has no need, like those high priests, to offer sacrifices daily, first for his own sins and then for those of the people, since he did this once for all when he offered up himself." Hughes rightly said that "for him to have been our fellow in defeat would have been of no worth to us"[7]; he was not one who shares our defeat, but who gives us victory over our sins because he was not a sinner but a Savior from sin. Blessed contrast!

Possibly, as F. F. Bruce suggests, the Suffering Servant passage of Isaiah 50:4ff was in the writer's mind. "The Lord has opened my ear, and I was not rebellious; I turned not backward" (Isa. 50:5). Then, following the statement of the Servant's heartfelt and complete obedience, comes this amazing statement of his willing suffering for his people: "I gave my back to those who strike, and my cheeks to those who pull out my beard; I hid not my face from disgrace and spitting" (Isa. 50:6). The obedience of our Lord for his people's salvation necessitated his willing suffering for God's glory and our good. So, the Savior's example of obedience and perseverance and especially the knowledge of his present intercession provided immense encouragement for those who were tempted to go back; it should also encourage us. The one who set his face like flint (Isa. 50:7) to move toward the cross is able to keep his people in the way of life.

---

7. Philip E. Hughes, *Hebrews* (Grand Rapids: Eerdmans, 1977), 177.

Therefore, this high priest is in a class by himself. This uniqueness is pointed to in two ways in the text. First, in verse 9 the writer makes plain that Jesus is in a class by himself as high priest by insisting that he is able by himself alone in his perfection to be "the source of eternal salvation to all who obey him." *Being made perfect* refers to the fitting for his office. "The experience of learning was a moral experience to be sure; but the perfection attained was not moral perfection, but a perfect fitness for His office."[8] The "source" (*aitios*) means that he alone is the author and there is no other for our eternal salvation (compare 2:10). Jewish atonement could not remove moral guilt, could provide no permanent salvation. The gift of God is eternal life through Jesus Christ our Lord.

The uniqueness of Jesus' high priesthood also is pointed to when he is "designated by God a high priest after the order of Melchizedek." The opening of Psalm 110 was referenced in Hebrews 1:3. Now the writer appeals to the fourth verse of that Psalm in Hebrews 5:6–9. The writer will unpack the significance of this statement in chapter 7, but for now let it suffice to point out that the Son's high priestly office is distinguished from the Aaronic high priesthood by this designation and points to him as the perpetual priest of the order, not of Aaron, but of Melchizedek.

Note that the salvation procured by the Savior is *eternal*: "He became the source of eternal salvation." What encouragement to tempted believers who wished to go back to the old and to forsake the new. Jesus is the "source of eternal salvation," aitios, meaning the "cause" of our eternal salvation. By all the means of God's appointment, the true believer, though tempted, will not return to the old. Christ is the "cause" of our salvation and the salvation procured is *eternal*. "But Israel is saved by the Lord with everlasting salvation; you shall not be put to shame or confounded to all eternity" (Isa. 45:17).

---

8. Geerhardus Vos, *The Teaching of the Epistle to the Hebrews*, 94.

Greater than Aaron

Believer, behold your great high priest in the throne room of God, your divinely appointed, sympathetic high priest. Grace is there enthroned and we are compelled by the weight of his glorious office to come with boldness in free access to the God of our salvation. Make use of your privileges in Christ. J. C. Ryle challenges us:

> If Christ is really the Priest of our souls, let us use Him regularly, and keep back nothing from Him. It is a sorrowful fact that many believers enjoy the Gospel far less than they ought to, for lack of boldness in using the priestly office of Jesus Christ. They go mourning and weeping along the way to heaven, perplexing themselves by poring over their infirmities and sins, and carrying ten times as much weight on their backs as Christ ever meant them to bear. Ignorance, sad ignorance, is too often the simple account of the condition of these people. They think only of the death of Christ, and not of the life of Christ. They think of His finished work on the cross, but forget His priestly intercession. If this be our case, let us turn over a new leaf, and change our plan this very day. Let us think of Jesus Christ as a loving Friend, to whom we may go morning, noon, and night, and get relief from Him every day. "Cast thy burden on the Lord, and He will sustain thee." (Psalm lv.22) Let us live the life of faith in the Son of God, and hold communion with Him continually. Let us use Him every morning as a Fountain of grace and help, and drink freely from that Fountain. Let us use Him every evening as a Fountain of absolution and refreshment, and draw out of Him living water. He that tries this plan will find it for the health of his soul.[9]

---

9. J. C. Ryle, "The Priest," in *Knots Untied* (London: William Hunt and Co., 1879), 310.

Perhaps you are an unbeliever reading this exposition of Scripture. My friend, you cannot know God without Christ. You cannot *be* your own priest, and you cannot even *appoint* your own priest. Apart from Christ, we are condemned by our own guilt in his court. Without Christ, your case is coming up, and your doom is sure. With Christ, you can confidently live in view of the coming judgment because, for those who believe in Jesus, our condemnation took place over 2,000 years ago when Jesus died on the cross, and because the efficacy of that once for all sacrifice avails through our great high priest in heaven.

10

A Solemn Warning and A Sure Promise

HEBREWS 5:11–6:20

Therefore let us leave the elementary doctrine of Christ and go on to maturity

---

By the grace of God, he <u>gives us warning</u>. That statement may surprise some who think that warning and grace are contradictory. If God saves and keeps his people by grace, why is warning necessary? However, as we have already made plain, the same God who promises to keep his people addresses his people as responsible persons who make choices and whose decisions relate to their eternal welfare. The promise of God that none of his elect shall be lost does not make warning unnecessary. The Lord keeps his people by the application of his Word of sovereign grace and addresses his people in that Word with proclamations of encouragement, descriptions of privileges, chastisements, exhortations, promises, rebukes, and warnings.

The assured perseverance of the saints is the fruit of the Holy Spirit's saving operations in his people's hearts through the written Word of God. The regenerating work of the Holy Spirit produces carefulness in the hearts of God's true people so that they may hearken to all of God's Word. Christ did not die so that some for whom he died may perish. The final perseverance of his elect is infallibly secured. Nonetheless, as Jonathan Edwards noted:

> There is just the same reason for those commands of earnest care and laborious endeavours for perseverance, and threatening of defection, notwithstanding its being certain that all that have true grace shall persevere, as there is for earnest endeavours after godliness, and to make our calling and election sure, notwithstanding all that are elected shall undoubtedly be saved. For as the case with respect to this is the same, decree or no decree, every one that believes shall be saved, and he that believes shall not be damned. They that will not live godly lives, find out for themselves that they are not elected; they that will live godly lives, have found out for themselves that they are elected. So it is here: he that to his utmost endeavours to persevere in ways of obedience, finds out that his obedience and righteousness are true; and he that does not, discovers that his is false.[1]

Pastoral Concern for Spiritual Maturity

The writer begins, in 5:11–14, by expressing his pastoral concern for the spiritual maturity of those to whom he writes. "About this we have much to say, and it is hard to explain, since you have become dull of hearing" (5:1). That is, there is much regarding Christ's High Priestly office after Melchizedek's order that the writer wants to say but his readers are lazy, sluggish, or dull (*nōthros*) of hearing. This dullness did not happen at once but was the result of a process of defection; "you have become [*gegonate*] dull of hearing." The writer will unpack this matter of Christ's High Priesthood after the order of Melchizedek (7:1–

1. Jonathan Edwards, *Concerning the Perseverance of Saints*, in *The Works of Jonathan Edwards* (Edinburgh: Banner of Truth, 1974), 2.596.

28), but he must first register his hesitance and stir them up to the matter by his argument from 5:11 to 6:20.

Note how often the author reminds his readers to listen (2:1; 3:7–8, 15; 4:1–2; 7). By this time, given their exposure to the gospel, opportunities for growth and suffering for his name, these Hebrew Christians "ought to be teachers" but due to their digression they are still in need of being taught the ABCs of God's Word, "the basic principles of the oracles of God. You need milk, not solid food." These Hebrew Christians have become distracted, interested in things other than and contrary to God's Word. They have become infantile, confined to baby food. They are incapable of taking in any nourishment but the simplest spiritual truths. They are tempted to forsake "the word of righteousness," that is, the most basic foundational truths.

The readers of Hebrews do not see how the doctrinal content, learned and digested, leads to discernment. "But solid food is for the mature, for those who have their powers of discernment trained by constant practice to distinguish good from evil" (5:14). They need to mature, to grow up, and to learn doctrine. They need solid food to become spiritually discerning. These Hebrew Christians need to be "trained by constant practice" just as an athlete shows his zeal to become healthy and strong by habitual exercise. Christians learn "to distinguish good from evil" by saturating their minds with the gospel of grace, the deep truths of the faith, and by constant application to the Word of God.

Is that true of you? It is simply true that if we do not saturate our minds in the Word of God, we will be deceived. Just think how quickly the Galatians deserted the gospel only recently preached by Paul (Gal. 1:6–9), how soon after the apostolic era the church was thrown into confusion by Gnostic errors. In our day, we are inundated with messages through media that may seem plausible on the surface but are truly insidious and soul destroying. Were it not for God's Word constantly poured into the soul who could survive the deceiving words and messages that stream into our senses?

In 6:1–3 this pastor calls upon the Hebrew Christians to grow up. He does not pander to them: "Let us leave the elementary doctrine of Christ and go on to maturity." Literally, the writer would have them be "borne on" to maturity. Submit to God's ordained influences; rely on your great high priest and the hidden but powerful energy of the Holy Spirit. Stop dallying with everything that hinders your growth. Deepen your knowledge and application of the truth. Grow up into adulthood. To "leave the elementary doctrine of Christ" does not mean to fail to rely upon fundamentals as ever significant but rather, to learn to deepen your understanding of these truths and to apply them more effectively. This is what the early church did when "they devoted themselves to the apostles' teaching and fellowship, to the breaking of bread and the prayers" (Acts 2:42).

The author mentions six foundational truths. The first two relate to conversion: "not laying again a foundation of repentance from dead works and of faith toward God." Repentance, turning from our sins to the Lord, forsaking the evil of our hearts and in turn embracing by faith Jesus freely offered in the gospel is meant here. "Dead works" are those from which those who trust in Christ have been cleansed by his blood (9:14). They are works that stem from hearts far from God, from hearts dead in trespasses and sins. "Faith toward God" had been proclaimed in God's own Word to them and by the apostolic witnesses.

The next expression relates to "instruction about washings," probably referring to Old Testament washings, truths that relate closely to the regenerating work of the Holy Spirit and to the sacrifice of Christ for our sins (Ezek. 36:25; Heb. 9:13 with Num. 19). Debates relating to ritual baptisms were a significant part of first century Judaism, many going far beyond anything prescribed by God's Word on the matter. "The laying on of hands" in the Old Testament related to installation to office and to animal sacrifice (for example, Num. 27:18, 23; Lev. 1:4). "The resurrection of the dead" is next referenced. Nothing is more fundamental than the resurrection of Jesus from the dead. The resurrection of believers clearly was taught in the Old Testament (Isa. 26:29; Dan. 12:2). "Eternal judgment" was again a large part of Judaism and was taught in no uncertain terms in the Old Testament revelation (Isa. 33:22; Dan. 7:9).

Clearly, no Christian can overestimate the importance of truths relating to these weighty matters. The writer's point is that the Hebrews must have a right understanding and estimate of these truths and all that relates to them; they must learn how to apply them, live them out and practice them in Christian experience. Perhaps he means also that they must not reinterpret them or practically forsake them by attempting to fit them into a distorted context that would in essence eradicate them. This would be the result if they returned to the old order of things. This would be, in effect, "laying again a foundation" rather than building upon the foundation of apostolic truth already given. With God's blessing, as the Hebrews dwell on God's truth in gospel context and deepen their knowledge and application of the truth, they will grow. "And this we will do if God permits."

If this rebuke and encouragement applies to you open wide your heart to receive it. Bestir yourself in dependence upon God's grace and grow. Read the Scriptures, attend upon the means of grace, seek God in the preached Word, learn the Scriptures, and do away with "boxes" by which we attempt to be Christians yet hold onto autonomy in some areas of life. Take Hebrews seriously; grow, change, and feed on the truth.

Warning Against Apostasy

In 6:4–6 the writer warns against apostasy ("for" [*gar*] connects this with the prior discussion about prolonged immaturity).

His concern is grave. In light of the spiritual immaturity and the general program of defection, the writer is not concerned simply with stunted growth but with the possibility of apostasy. ✓ This passage has been variously interpreted and almost endlessly debated. The main viewpoints on this matter are as follows:

According to the first view, the text teaches that truly regenerated persons *can become lost*. This Arminianism is contrary to the whole tenor of Biblical teaching that the truly regenerate person cannot be lost (Heb. 8:12; John 10:28–30; Rom. 8:28–39; Phil. 1:6; and many other places). Behind the salvation of the sinner is God's eternal election and character, the plan of the Triune God—the choice of God's people by the Father, the purchase of that people by the Son, and the effectual application of the gospel by the Holy Spirit. The true minister of the gospel can hardly pour adequate opprobrium upon such a view that detracts from God's glory and leaves the people of God in despair. Comparing Scripture with Scripture makes this view impossible as does the end of this very chapter. There the sure promises of God in securing his people are underscored (Heb. 6:13–20).

A second view is that the text references truly regenerate people who backslide. The "falling away" is, according to this view, a falling into serious sin exposing true believers to chastisement. There is little to commend this view, and it should not take our time.

A third view is that the text is merely referencing a hypothetical; that is, that the threat of going back to Judaism, were such a thing possible for a true believer, would lead to lostness. This could not in reality happen, but were such a thing possible, the apostasy would be irrecoverable. This view seems to undremine the serious intent of the author, as he sees some on the verge of a perilous return to Judaism.

A fourth view commending itself to this writer is that the warnings of Hebrews 6 address professing believers who may not in reality possess ~~what they profess~~. The writer is not concerned with spiritual immaturity alone, but with apostasy as a real alternative. Of course those who apostatize are not real, genuine Christians. However, the temptation to turn back brings the writer to apply deep and pointed warning to his readers. It is as if he were saying, "Are you who you say you are? Do you realize what going back really means?"

The warning against apostasy (6:4–6) therefore is solemn and grave. He mentions six characteristics of those who turn back.[2]

First, they professed repentance. "For it is impossible to restore again to repentance" indicates that they had once professed repentance and evidenced, at least publicly, a turning to Christ away from sin. With F. F. Bruce we insist that "continuance is the test of reality. In these verses he is not questioning the perseverance of the saints; we might say that rather he is insisting that those who persevere are the true saints."[3]

Second, those who turn back are among "those who have once been enlightened." They have evidenced for a time minds and hearts that were temporarily awakened to need and that seemed to walk in the light of the gospel. Some see this as a reference to baptism called "enlightenment" in the second century but there is no textual support for that.

Third, the apostates "have tasted the heavenly gift." They have had a taste of the Lord's goodness in the gospel of God's Son. There is no need to see this as a reference to the Lord's Supper, though this is possible.

---

2. Dave Mathewson, in his article *Reading HEB 6:4–6 In Light of The Old Testament, WTJ* 61.2 (1999), 209–225, makes a strong case for seeing OT allusion undergirding this section repeating and working out the warning against apostasy in the wilderness. I am still considering his thesis. His reading could underscore the severity of apostasy at the time of the writing of Hebrews.

3. F. F. Bruce, *Hebrews* (Grand Rapids: Eerdmans, 1979), 118.

Fourth, those who turn back "have shared in the Holy Spirit" that is, in his common operations, his presence in the Christian congregation, and his conviction of sin. Remember that Jesus taught that many who exercised spiritual gifts would hear from the Lord on Judgment Day, "I never knew you; depart from me, you workers of lawlessness" (Matt. 7:23).

Fifth, they have "tasted the goodness of the word of God." They seemed to have responded to God's Word, to delight in its preaching and teaching, and to have submitted to its authority for a while. Jesus spoke of the one "who hears the word and immediately receives it with joy, yet he has no root in himself, but endures for a while, and when tribulation or persecution arises on account of the word, immediately he falls away" (Matt. 13:20–21). The situation addressed by the writer seems to echo these words of Jesus.

Sixth, the apostates have in a measure tasted "the powers of the age to come." In becoming a member of the church visible, they have known something of the eschatological powers, the coming of the kingdom, the anticipation of the end, and the glories that belong to God's redeemed people who long for Christ's coming and live in its reality. Those miracle-working Christ-professors in Matthew 7 are examples of those who tasted "the powers of the age to come," but were lost. Such tasting is no evidence in itself of a genuine conversion. The writer speaks of those who have been in the sphere of the church, but who have never been regenerated, converted, or justified.

Many members of the church visible are characterized by carnal confidence and presumption. In these days when the "charismatic movement" has made inroads into almost every denomination, there are undoutedly multitudes who rely on what they consider to be displays of miraculous powers, rather than on Jesus Christ. How many in the churches of our day know anything about the heart's corruption, the necessity of regeneration, or of our danger outside of Christ? Yet, they base their eternal welfare upon experiences that move them.

Of those who have so tasted, the writer says solemnly, "if they then fall away, since they are crucifying once again the Son of God, to their own harm, and holding him up to contempt . . . it is impossible to restore . . . [them] again to repentance" (Heb. 6:6, 4). Holding Christ in contempt! Guthrie notes, "In no more vivid way could the position of the apostatizers be identified with those whose hatred of Christ led them to exhibit him as an object of contempt on a hated Roman gibbet."[4] Miserable apostates! As the great Puritan commentator Matthew Henry notes:

> They declare that they approve of what the Jews did in crucifying Christ, and that they would be glad to do the same thing again if it were in their power. They pour the greatest contempt upon the Son of God, and therefore upon God himself, who expects all should reverence his Son, and honour him as they honour the Father. They do what in them lies to represent Christ and Christianity as a shameful thing, and would have him to be a public shame and reproach. This is the nature of apostasy.[5]

The writer's concern here is not a single act of sin but obviously a state of mind, a commitment, an attitude. Of this attitude, John wrote in 1 John 5:16: "If anyone sees his brother committing a sin not leading to death, he shall ask, and God will give him life—to those who commit sins that do not lead to death. There is sin that leads to death; I do not say that one should pray for that. All wrongdoing is sin, but there is sin that does not lead to death." It seems reasonable as well to identify the apostasy of this passage with the blasphemy against the Holy Spirit

---

4. Donald Guthrie, *Hebrews*, in *The Tyndale New Testament Commentaries* (Grand Rapids: Eerdmans, 1983), 144.

5. Mathew Henry, *A Commentary on the Whole Bible* (Old Tappan, NJ: Revell, 1983), 6.913.

of which Jesus spoke in Mark 3:29: "But whoever blasphemes against the Holy Spirit never has forgiveness, but is guilty of an eternal sin" (see also Matt. 12:22ff).

It is difficult to say precisely where the line is crossed into the land of no return. That is one of the frightening realities of this discussion. There seems to be an attitude that says: "I now sin deliberately against the gospel I once professed; I sin deliberately against the knowledge of the truth" (Heb. 10:26). Perhaps this attitude is reflected in those of whom John wrote in 1 John 2:19: "They went out from us, but they were not of us; for it they had been of us, they would have continued with us. But they went out, that it might become plain that they all are not of us."

Not all who profess the truth possess the truth; not all who have acknowledged the truth are permanently and savingly changed and given abiding affections. Just as it was true that "not all who are descended from Israel belong to Israel" (Rom. 9:6), so it is true that not all who have had connections to the church really belong to this new Israel of God. Jesus spoke of the various soils upon which the Word of God falls. Of the third class of hearers we are told: "The cares of the world, and the delight in riches, and the desire for other things, enter in and choke the word, and it proves unfruitful" (Mark 4:19). Demas, Simon Magus, Judas Iscariot all stand out in Scripture to warn professing believers to truly possess what we profess. The parable of the sower stands as a scriptural monument to this very reality.

It is possible for one to have been in some measure enlightened, to have tasted the heavenly gift, and have shared in the common operations of the Holy Spirit, to have tasted the goodness of the word of God, and the powers of the age to come and not be regenerated. From the remains of the Puritan Philip Henry, we are reminded of this awesome possibility:

How far may a man go towards heaven, and yet fall short? In general; a great way, Mark xii. 34. *Almost* a Christian, Acts, xxvi. 28.

In particular; a man may have a great deal of knowledge, 1 Corinthians, xiii. 1, 2; even so much, as to teach others, Matthew, vii. 22. He may be free from many, nay, from any gross sins, Luke, xviii. 11; he may perform, not only some, but all manner of external duties of religion;—pray, fast, give alms, Matthew vi. 1, 2, etc. He may be a lover of good men, as Herod, Pharaoh, Darius. He may repent after a sort, as Ahab; and believe, after a sort, as Simon Magus. He may suffer much for religion, as, no doubt, Judas did, while a retainer of Christ. If a man go thus far, and yet fall short, then what will become of those who go not near so far? Then, what need have we to look about us, and to make sure of regeneration, and sincerity, which are things that certainly accompany salvation![6]

A true believer cannot and will not apostatize. True believers are elect by God's sovereign will, purchased by Christ's blood, regenerated by the Holy Spirit, and are granted persevering grace. When Hymaneus and Philetus defected from the faith, Paul encouraged Timothy with the truth of God's foundation that is firm and secure (2 Tim. 2:19) bearing this seal: "The Lord knows those who are his." He knows that some who have professed faith and have, on at least one level, enjoyed Christian fellowship and the blessings of God's kingdom, may not be what they profess to be.

It is in the context of warning against apostasy that the writer of Hebrews brings a small parable to bear:

For land that has drunk the rain that often falls on it, and produces a crop useful to those for whose sake

---

6. J. B. Williams, *The Lives of Philip and Matthew Henry* (Edinburgh: Banner of Truth, 1974), I.359.

it is cultivated, receives a blessing from God. But if
it bears thorns and thistles, it is worthless and near
to being cursed, and its end is to be burned (6:7–8).

Having been much cultivated, such hearts that deny the
Lord bring forth only "thorns and thistles." This expression,
bringing Genesis 3:17–18 to mind, reminds us of the curse resulting from the rebellion of Adam. According to Henry,

> [The bad ground] is not only barren of good fruit,
> but fruitful in that which is bad, briers and thorns,
> fruitful in sin and wickedness, which are trouble-
> some and hurtful to all about them, and will be
> most so to sinners themselves at last; and then such
> ground is rejected. God will concern himself no
> more about such wicked apostates; he will let them
> alone, and cast them out of his care; he will com-
> mand the clouds that rain no more upon them. Di-
> vine influences shall be restrained; and that is not all,
> but such ground *is nigh unto cursing;* so far is it from
> receiving the blessing, that a dreadful curse hangs
> over it, though as yet, through the patience of God,
> the curse is not fully executed.[7]

"Its end is to be burned" points to the tragic end of the apostate, "for our God is a consuming fire" (12:29). The text calls
upon all who read to be sure that their faith is in Christ alone
for redemption.

> You are a member of the church; you have been bap-
> tized; you take the Lord's supper; perhaps you are a
> deacon, or an elder; you pass the sacramental cup
> round, you are just all that a Christian can be, ex-
> cept that you are without a Christian heart. You are
> whitewashed sepulchers, still full of rottenness with-
> in, though garnished fairly on the outside. Well, take
> heed, take heed! It is an astonishing thing, how near

---

7. Matthew Henry, *A Commentary on the Whole Bible,* 5.914.

> the painter can go to the expression of life, and yet
> the canvas is dead and motionless; and it is equally
> astonishing how near a man may be to a Christian,
> and yet, though not being born again, the absolute
> rule shuts him out of heaven; and with all his profes-
> sion, with all the trappings of his professed godliness,
> and with all the gorgeous plumes of experience, yet
> must he be borne away from heaven's gates.[8]

The writer is not attempting to keep people in suspense about their faith; rather, he is encouraging full assurance upon the proper foundation. He insists upon this in verse 11: "And we desire each one of you to show the same earnestness to have the full assurance of hope until the end." He encourages assurance by turning the eyes of his readers to the promise of God in Christ. It does no harm for a Christian to ask about his foundation and can only encourage genuine faith, where it exists, to be reminded again of the foundation of our faith in the promises of God.

The Sure Promises of God

Obviously the writer does not see most of his readers as apos-tate. "Though we speak in this way, yet in your case, beloved, we feel sure of better things—things that belong to salvation" (6:9). "We feel sure" (*pepeismetha*) comes first in the Greek text for emphasis. He calls them *beloved*. He sees them as brothers and is assured of their foundation in Christ. Their love shows God's work in their lives, and their diligence in serving others will also show in their diligent focus on the gospel:

> For God is not so unjust as to overlook your work
> and the love that you showed for his sake in serving
> the saints, as you still do. And we desire each one of
> you to show the same earnestness to have the full
> assurance of hope until the end, so that you may not

---

8. Charles Haddon Spurgeon, "Regeneration," in *New Park Street Pulpit* (Pasadena, TX: Pilgrim, 1975), 3.186–187.

> be sluggish, but imitators of those who through faith
> and patience inherit the promises. (6:10–12)

Apostates are not focused on the gospel, and the promises of God in Christ are far from their thoughts. The writer longs for his hearers to be firm in the truth and points them to *full assurance*; it is not his purpose to tear down but to build up a sure hope in Christ. He knows that if their convictions become unsettled, their gaze will be distracted from the certainty of hope in Christ. How does assurance grow and prosper? It grows by attention to God's truth until the end, shaking off sluggishness and imitating "those who through faith and patience inherit the promises." The writer knows that spiritual sloth is ruinous. In view of the apostasy outlined above the call is to go on in Christian commitment and growth.

Having mentioned "those who through faith and patience inherit the promises," the writer now turns the attention of his readers to God's promise given to Abraham:

> For when God made a promise to Abraham, since he had no one greater by whom to swear, he swore by himself, saying, "Surely I will bless you and multiply you." And thus Abraham, having patiently waited, obtained the promise. For people swear by something greater than themselves, and in all their disputes an oath is final for confirmation.

God's Word is totally trustworthy. Behind that Word is God's own character and integrity. "He had no one greater by whom to swear." This passage reminds the readers of God's promise to Abraham after the offering of Isaac when God said: "By myself I have sworn, declares the LORD, because you have done this and have not withheld your son, your only son, I will surely bless you, and I will surely multiply your offspring as the stars of heaven and as the sand that is on the seashore." This is a repetition of the promise of Genesis 12:2ff in Genesis 22:16. Abraham believed God's promise regarding the child of promise and the blessing flowing from him so that by faith he obtained the promise of God. Behind this promise, and behind all of God's promises to his people, are the two realities of God's oath and the impossibility that God can lie. "God is not man that he should lie, or a son of man that he should change his mind" (Numbers 23:19). This is the believer's comfort.

"By two unchangeable things," God has as it were lifted his sovereign hand in oath to save his people; that is, by both the unchangeable Word of promise and the oath based upon his character, he keeps his own (compare v. 17). Behind our salvation is the reality that God has sworn on the authority of his own character (Isa. 45:23). The writer uses the term *boulomenos* speaking of God's sovereign resolve—his firm desire and will. Therefore, with the whole weight of his character thrown behind his oath, his promise is irrevocable. God's purpose is *unchangeable.*

> His oath, his covenant, his blood,
> support me in the whelming flood;
> when all around my soul gives way,
> he then is all my hope and stay.[9]

Christ Our Refuge

In view of these things, the pastoral writer of Hebrews utilizes three figures to stress the certainty of God's promise in Christ. The first figure, found in verse 18, is the city of refuge:

> So when God desired to show more convincingly to
> the heirs of the promise the unchangeable character
> of his purpose, he guaranteed it with an oath, so that
> by two unchangeable things, in which it is impossi-
> ble for God to lie, we who have fled for refuge might

---

9. Edward Mote, "My Hope is Built on Nothing Less," from *Trinity Hymnal*, rev. ed., (Suwanee, GA: Great Commission Publications, 1990), selection 521.

have strong encouragement to hold fast to the hope
set before us.

Certain Levitical cities served as asylums for accidental
manslayers (Num. 35:6; Josh. 21:13, 21, 27, 32, 38). When the
manslayer fled to the city, he was safe from his pursuer. As long
as one was in the city of refuge, he was safe. We who have fled
from the coming wrath have found refuge in Christ and this
has removed the dread of eternity. The *hope* described here and
opened up in verse 20 is the expectation that awaits us based on
the gospel promise that is dependent on God's sure character
and oath. Those who believe the gospel promise can be sure of
what awaits them in the future. Ultimately, the "hope set before
us" is Christ himself as Paul reminds us in 1 Timothy 1:1: "Paul,
an apostle of Christ Jesus by command of God our Savior and
of Christ Jesus our hope." It is through Christ that "a better hope
is introduced, through which we draw near to God" (Hebrews
7:19). Relying upon no false hope, we have sound and solid hope
in Christ. This provides "strong encouragement to hold fast." Indeed, this hope is presented for us as "behind the curtain"—so
sure is it there in the person of our great high priest. This moves
us to the second figure.

Christ Our Anchor

The second figure that stresses the certainty of God's promise in
Christ is that of an anchor: "We have this as a sure and steadfast
anchor of the soul, a hope that enters into the inner place behind the curtain." The anchor is "sure and steadfast." The place-
ment of the anchor is all important, "the inner place behind the
curtain" (Lev. 16:2, 12, 15). Hidden but secure, this anchors our
hope, that is, the certainty of our future that determines our
present. Our salvation is anchored in the priestly work of Christ.
F. F. Bruce has beautifully commented:

> We are refugees from the sinking ship of this present world order, so soon to disappear; our hope is fixed in the eternal order, where the promises of God are made good to His people in perpetuity. Our hope, based upon His promises, is our spiritual anchor. The figure of the anchor is not pressed; all that is meant is that "we are moored on an immovable object" and that immovable object is the throne of God Himself.[10]

Christ Our Forerunner

The third figure by which the author grounds our hope in God's promise is that of Christ as forerunner:

> We have this as a sure and steadfast anchor of the soul, a hope that enters into the inner place behind the curtain, where Jesus has gone as a forerunner on our behalf, having become a high priest forever after the order of Melchizedek.

"Forerunner," (*Prodromos*) anticipates our being with him eventually, where he is. In its classical use the term has military overtones which may still linger about the term. *Prodromos* was used with the meaning of "*running before, going in advance*" frequently used of "horsemen *in advance of* an army."[11] One whose faith is in Christ, who relies upon his promise, can never apostatize, and will never fall away. *Forerunner* anticipates what E. K. Simpson calls the "care-quelling utterance"[12] of Jesus in John 14:1ff: "Let not your hearts be troubled. Believe in God; believe also in me. In my Father's house are many rooms. If it were not so, would I have told you that I go to prepare a place for you? I

---

10. F. F. Bruce, *Hebrews*, 131.

11. Entry for *prodromeuo* in H. G. Liddell and R. Scott, *Greek-English Lexicon With a Revised Supplement* (Oxford: Clarendon Press, 1996), 1475.

12. Cited in F. F. Bruce, *Hebrews*, 132.

will come again and will take you to myself, that where I am you may be also." Our hope is "a sure and steadfast anchor of the soul." The anchor was taken ahead of us by our Forerunner who will bring us to our appointed end.

By his very name, God has sworn and it will come to pass. Do not doubt his word of promise but believe.

11

Our Priest Forever

HEBREWS 7:1–28

For it was indeed fitting that we should have such a high priest, holy, innocent, unstained, separated from sinners, and exalted above the heavens. He has no need, like those high priests, to offer sacrifices daily, first for his own sins and then for those of the people, since he did this once for all when he offered up himself. For the law appoints men in their weakness as high priests, but the word of the oath, which came later than the law, appoints a Son who has been made perfect forever.

On the road to Emmaus after his resurrection from the dead, our Lord taught the disciples that the Scriptures comprehensively point to Him (Luke 24:27). Throughout the various genres of Old Testament literature, Jesus the expected Messiah, is the theme. One expression of this truth is found in typology in which a symbol is historically and vitally held together by the ultimate fulfillment in Christ and his kingdom. Melchizedek is one of those types, to whom the writer has already pointed, the significance of whom the readers have failed fully to appreciate (5:1–11). Now the writer will help his readers see the significance of this Old Testament type, and through him to value even more the symbolic fulfillment in Christ our king-priest.

"See how great this man was to whom Abraham the patriarch gave a tenth of the spoils" (7:4). A great man indeed was Melchizedek King of Salem; great because he pointed beyond himself so remarkably to the Lord Jesus Christ. The Hebrew Christians were tempted to return to the old Jewish ways, to trust in Aaron rather than Christ. Now, in a thrust of the sword of God's Word right to the heart of the matter, the author points these tempted and tried Christians to Melchizedek, King of Salem. This may seem strange to us, as it may have to the original hearers, until we follow the Biblical logic of the writer.

Remember that Hebrews has already mentioned Melchizedek in 5:6, 10 and 6:20. There was essential teaching for the Hebrew Christians through this Old Testament type and there is essential teaching for us as well—teaching that encourages forthright, persevering Christian living. The writer is showing that Jesus' priesthood is superior to the Levitical priesthood, and he does so by pointing to Christ through Melchizedek the priest-king of Salem. He has already spoken of Jesus the forerunner "having become a priest forever after the order of Melchizedek" (6:20), and now the preacher will unpack the significance of this *forever* priesthood for God's people.

Melchizedek: A Type of Christ

The writer points back to Genesis 14:17–24 when, after the battle of the kings, Abraham gave tithes and offerings to Melchizedek, king of Salem (compare Psalm 76:2, an early name for Jerusalem), and was blessed by him. How wonderful that in the midst of the paganism of Canaan, the Lord had appointed a unique and wonderful type of Christ. Knowing little about him serves to make Melchizedek a superior type of Christ, as we shall see. The type is unusual, but for believers in the verbal inspiration of the Bible, we find God's explanation of the facts to be both intriguing and edifying. Melchizedek is a divinely inspired type. Why should the writer have dwelled upon him?

"Why should he have done so? Because Melchizedek already in a measure possessed what Abraham still only hoped for—he reigned where Abraham's seed were destined to reign, and exercised a priesthood which in future generations was to be committed to them. The union of the two in Melchizedek was in itself a great thing—greater than the separate offices of king and priest in the houses respectively of David and Aaron; but it was an expiring greatness: it was like the last blossom of the old rod of Noah, which thenceforth became as a dry tree. In Abraham, on the other hand, was the germ of a new and higher order of things—the promise, though still only the budding promise, of a better inheritance of blessing; and when the seed should come in whom the promise was more especially to stand, then the more general and comprehensive aspect of the Melchizedek order was to reappear, and find its embodiment in one who could at once place it on firmer ground, and carry it to unspeakably higher results. Here, then, was a sacred enigma for the heart of faith to ponder, and for the spirit of truth gradually to unfold: Abraham, in one respect, relatively great, and in another relatively little; personally inferior to Melchizedek, and yet the root of a seed that was to do for the world incomparably more than Melchizedek had done; himself the type of a higher than Melchizedek, and yet Melchizedek a more peculiar type than he! It was a mystery that could be disclosed only in partial glimpses beforehand, but which now has become comparably plain by the person and work of Immanuel. What but the wonder-working finger of God could have so admi-

rably fitted the past to be such a singular image of
the future![1]

Again, if this seems strange to us, let us remember that by
divine inspiration these words of the writer of Hebrews draw
upon what John Murray called in another connection "the perspective of organic relationship and dependence." We must
view the Old and New Testaments in terms of the unity of both
remembering that "the Old Testament has no meaning except
as it is related to the realities that give character to and create
the New Testament era as the fullness of time, the consummation of the ages."[2] We may only be on the threshold of understanding the depth of the Bible's unity, as it has been obscured
by unbiblical, rationalist critical assumptions.

Melchizedek was king of Salem (Gen. 14:18).[3] Evidently, in
ancient Canaanite law, the king was at the same time the priest,
but this king-priest (Gen. 14:18) was also a believer in Jehovah (Gen. 14:18–20). Despite the efforts throughout history to
identify Melchizedek more precisely, we know nothing about
his identity beyond what the text tells us. After the battle and
Abraham's offerings, Melchizedek blessed Abraham—a priestly
act (Deut. 21:5: Num. 6:24, 26). In blessing Abraham, the father
of the faithful, Melchizedek blessed Abraham's posterity.

By divine inspiration, the writer sees in this king-priest a
type even in his very title: "He is first, by translation of his name,
king of righteousness, and then also king of Salem, that is, king
of peace." This king of righteousness who was also a king of
peace is a fitting type of Christ, who is the preeminent king of
righteousness and peace for his people. There is no peace apart

1. Patrick Fairbairn, *The Typology of Scripture* (Grand Rapids: Guardian
Press, 1975), I.303.

2. John Murray, *The Unity of the Old and New Testaments* in *Collected Writings of John Murray* (Edinburgh: Banner of Truth, 1976), 1.26.

3. Ursalim is mentioned in the Tel el Amarna letters (c. 1300 BC). "Ir," or
"Ur," means "city" while "Salem" corresponds to "Shalom," peace.

from righteousness. Never has the Lord set aside righteousness to grant peace, but ever is peace accomplished on the basis of righteousness. His very title points to the work of the Mediator. He is our peace and through his propitiatory sacrifice we have peace with God (Rom. 5:1).

If you are reading this and have a guilty soul and a troubled conscience and tremble within knowing that you need to be at peace with God, then realize that this peace comes at the cost of Jesus' shed blood. He met the requirements of God's righteous throne that all who believe might be reconciled to God. He is our peace (Eph. 2:14). Come in faith to this King of Salem. In Christ you can be forgiven righteously.

In another way, Melchizedek is also a remarkable type of Christ. "He is without father or mother or genealogy, having neither beginning of days nor end of life, but resembling the Son of God he continues a priest forever" (Heb. 7:3). As king- priest of Salem, Melchizedek is a fitting type of Christ, the king-priest of righteousness and peace, but he also points to the eternal Godhead—the dignity of his person and the perpetual priesthood of the Son—since there is no record of the beginning or ending of his days (Ps. 110:4). The writer also points out that Melchizedek as type of Christ is superior to the Old Testament priesthood of Aaron and of the Levitical system. Silence regarding Melchizedek's origins and succession foreshadows Christ's eternal priesthood.

Melchizedek: Superior to the Old Testament Priesthood

The superiority of Melchizedek's priesthood, as it points beyond to the Lord Jesus the priest of his people, is clearly stated in verses 4–10. First, the superiority of Melchizedek's priesthood is shown by the tithes Abraham brought to this king-priest of Salem. "See how great this man was to whom Abraham the patriarch gave a tenth of the spoils!" (7:4). Levites received tithes from fellow Israelites (Num. 187:21–24; Luke 1:9); Melchizedek was not a Levite, but he received tithes of the booty taken from the defeated kings. These tithes were taken by Melchizedek right from father Abraham himself. Therefore, Melchizedek is much more distinguished than the Levites. "And those descendants of Levi who receive the priestly office have a commandment in the law to take tithes from the people, that is, from their brothers, though these also are descended from Abraham" (7:5). It was Abraham *the patriarch* that gave a tenth of his spoils and received Melchizedek's blessing. *Patriarch* is emphasized because Abraham is the representative of his descendants.

Next we note that Melchizedek blessed Abraham implying his superior priesthood to that of the Levitical law. "But this man who does not have his descent from them received tithes from Abraham and blessed him who had the promises" (7:6). Melchizedek's genealogy is not traceable to the Levites. Melchizedek granted and bestowed blessing on the father of the faithful. Since Abraham is the father of all who believe (Rom. 4), how great is the dignity of the one who blesses *him* and, in him, all believers who come after Abraham.

Then, the writer adds that the priesthood of Melchizedek, unlike that of Aaron, knows no succession. "It is beyond dispute that the inferior is blessed by the superior. In the one case tithes are received by mortal men, but in the other case, by one of whom it is testified that he lives" (7:7–8). Levites died and there must be a succession of priests. Contrasting with their mortality, there is no record of the death of Melchizedek, pointing to a living priesthood.

Finally, the superiority of Melchizedek's priesthood over that of Aaron and the Levitical law is seen in the fact that Levi, not yet born, tithed to Melchizedek since Levi was present in Abraham. Here the writer insists on the unity of the human family. "One might even say that Levi himself, who receives tithes, paid tithes through Abraham, for he was still in the loins of his ancestor when Melchizedek met him" (7:9–10). "Although Levi was as yet unborn when Melchizedek met Abraham, the tithe Abraham gave to Melchizedek was a gesture that anticipated the subordination of Levi and the Levitical priesthood to the priesthood like Melchizedek's that would be inaugurated at God's appointed time."[4]

By the Scripture's silence on Melchizedek's ancestry (3a, "without geneology"), he is a type of Christ. The writer of Hebrews is speaking typologically of an eternal priest who points to the Lord Jesus, our eternal priest in fulfillment. Our priest has no beginning and no ending; his person and priesthood last as long as you have need—forever!

If Melchizedek as type is superior to the priesthood of the Levitcal law, itself typological, then how much better is Christ himself, the fulfillment of both.

The Superiority of Christ's Priesthood after the Order of Melchizedek

Christ's superiority after the order of Melchizedek to that of Leviticus is seen in at least five ways:

First, *our Lord's priesthood is superior because he is a priest without limits.* This is made plain in verses 7:11–14. Levitical priesthood had its limits as indicated in verse 11:

> Now if perfection had been attainable through the Levitical priesthood (for under it the people received the law), what further need would there have been for another priest to arise after the order of Melchizedek rather than one named after the order of Aaron?

---

4. William Lane, *Hebrews* (Dallas: Word, 1991), 1.171.

The limits of the Levitical priesthood are seen in the succession of priests and of sacrifices. If all was provided for with permanence in the Levitical system, then why did Christ come? Rather than another priest arising "after the order of Aaron" what was needed was a final priest "after the order of Melchizedek." Christ's coming and priesthood show that the old has passed, that a change in economy has arrived, and that the Levitical system is now obsolete since it was unable to bring about a perfect relation to the Lord. A "change in the law" has taken place, that is, the Mosaic economy has been set aside. "God's choice of another kind of priesthood for his Son, left the Levitical line off to one side, forever discounted, passed by 'the order of Aaron.'"[5]

There is no reference here to the moral law but to service at the altar and Levitical descent (vv. 13–14). Indeed, "another priest" (literally: "a different priest") was necessary for God's people. Those to whom the writer of Hebrews preaches strongly desired to go back. They wanted to return to Aaron, but Christ's coming set aside the Levitical law (v. 12), so that any objection that Christ, after all, is not a priest of Aaron's line fails. Jesus was not a Levite but was of the tribe of Judah (v. 14), showing that the law has been done away. Therefore the limits of the Levitical priesthood as type and shadow are done away. Perfection was not obtainable through the Levitical system but only through Christ (2:9; 5:9). "For by a single offering he has perfected for all time those who are being sanctified" (10:14). Through Christ our Priest are the spirits of just men made perfect (12:23).

Second, the superiority of Christ's priesthood after the order of Melchizedek is shown *because the Lord Jesus, our priest, is alive.* This is made plain in verses 15–19:

---

5. A. T. Robertson, *Word Pictures in the New Testament* (Grand Rapids: Baker, 1932), 5.383.

Our Priest Forever

This becomes even more evident when another priest arises in the likeness of Melchizedek, who has become a priest, not on the basis of a legal requirement concerning bodily descent, but by the power of an indestructible life. For it is witnessed of him,

> "You are a priest forever,
> after the order of Melchizedek."

For on the one hand, a former commandment is set aside because of its weakness and uselessness (for the law made nothing perfect); but on the other hand, a better hope is introduced, through which we draw near to God.

The priesthood of Melchizedek typifies the coming of Christ the superior priest in that there was no record of Melchizedek's beginning or ending. Unlike in the Levitical law, there was no "legal requirement concerning bodily descent." Rather, the efficacy of Christ's priesthood depends on "the power of an indestructible life" (v. 16; indissoluble, 2 Cor. 4:1) as is testified by divine inspiration in Psalm 110, wherein Christ is foreshadowed: "The Lord has sworn and will not change his mind, 'You are a priest forever.'" On the cross, the Father poured out his just wrath on the Son as the sinner's substitute, but that sacrifice could not destroy the life of our priest who in love sacrificed himself for us. The indestructible life and eternal priesthood of Christ, typified by Melchizedek fulfilled in Christ' intercessory work, introduces "a better hope" through which God's people now in Christ "draw near to God" (v. 19). This solid hope replaces the imperfection of the law. "The law made nothing perfect." Owen observes:

> It made "nothing," that is, none of the things which we treat about, "perfect." It did not make the church-state perfect, it did not make the worship of God perfect, it did not perfect the promises given unto

Abraham, in the accomplishment, it did not make a perfect covenant between God and man; it had a shadow, an obscure representation of all these things, but it "made nothing perfect."[6]

Through the means of the Levitical priesthood and sacrificial system the Lord moved his people along in redemptive history to the one who alone can save, to a better hope that can bring us near to God (4:16; 6:18–20;). Through that system he taught the need for the Redeemer. The knowledge of sin was constantly addressed, and the condemnation of the law, as well as the temporary ordinances, all led God's people to the coming of Christ in the fullness of time (Gal 4:4ff). A solid hope was needed and came in the person and work of Christ.

This solid hope (a "better" hope, 7:22; 8:6; 9:23) is completely effective and pours tremendous energy into the prayers of the saints and their communion with God as we realize that we come into God's presence, as Luther put it, "in his skin and on his back" (compare 4:15ff; 10:19ff).[7] The "better hope" is Christ himself and it is by him that "we draw near to God" (Lev. 10:3; 2:21). In proportion as we are drawn to Christ and approach the Father through Christ we are drawn away from sin. This implies real peace of conscience as we come into the presence of the Holy God through the work of our Intercessor. Calvin observes:

There is an implicit contrast between us and the fathers. We excel them in privilege in the fact that God has made Himself known to us face to face, whereas He appeared to them only at a distance and in shadows. Allusion is made here to the form of the tabernacle or the temple. The people stood far off in the courtyard, and no one was allowed any closer approach to the sanctuary except the priests. Only

---

6. John Owen, *Hebrews* (Edinburgh: Banner of Truth, 1991), 5.471.

7. Martin Luther, *Luther's Works: Devotions I*, edited by Jaroslav Pelikan, vol. 42 (St. Louis, MO: Concordia, 1958), 23.

the high priest went into the inner sanctuary. But now that the tabernacle has been abolished God admits us into His intimate presence, from which the fathers were prohibited. Anyone who still holds to, or wants to restore, the shadows of the Law not only obscures the glory of Christ, but also deprives us of a great blessing in that he puts a barrier of space between us and God, to approach whom freedom is given us by the Gospel. Whoever sticks to the Law, knowingly and voluntarily deprives himself of the nearness of God.[8]

Third, the superiority of Christ's priesthood is evident because *it is based on an oath*. This is revealed in verses 20–22:

And it was not without an oath. For those who formerly became priests were made such without an oath, but this one was made a priest with an oath by the one who said to him:

"The Lord has sworn
 and will not change his mind,
 'You are a priest forever.'"

This makes Jesus the guarantor of a better covenant.

No oath guaranteed the perpetuity of the Levitical priesthood. Christ's priesthood after the order of Melchizedek, however, is unique and permanent, an oath guaranteed forever. Already the writer has pointed to the oath-guaranteed nature of Christ's priesthood in Hebrews 6:17–18. Now the writer connects that oath (from Ps. 110:4), as typified in Melchizedek's "eternal" priesthood, with the realization that Christ stands as the Surety of his people. "This makes Jesus the guarantor of a better covenant," since it is God the Father who swears to his own Son. "The oath marks not only the importance, but the stability,

---

8. John Calvin, *Hebrews*, in *Calvin's New Testament Commentaries* (Grand Rapids: Eerdmans, 1979), 100.

of the economy in reference to which it is made. God is never represented in Scripture as swearing to anything but what was fixed and immutable."[9]

Christ is "guarantor," that is, the Surety of this better covenant of grace set up by God's own authority. The promise is totally reliable. The term "guarantor" (*enguos*) in the papyri was common in legal documents of the first century. For example, in one document we read that "the father assents to the marriage, and is surety (enguatai) for the payment of the aforesaid dowry."[10] That is to say, the father in this case bears the legal obligation of payment; he is "good for it." Christ our priest has borne the legal obligations of his people, he is good for them, and so can stand as the "guarantor of a better covenant." The hymn writer spoke the thrilling language of Hebrews when he wrote, "before the throne my Surety stands, my name is written on his hands."[11] Verse 22 contains the first of seventeen references to "covenant" in Hebrews, that "bond in blood sovereignly administered."[12] The security of believers is not found in their effort but in the value of the blood of Christ, in the achievement of their Surety. "The covenant of grace is not built upon the faithfulness of a poor fallible, changeable creature, but upon the never-failing faithfulness of an unchangeable God."[13]

As Surety, Christ paid the debt of his people and can intercede for them on the value of that payment. Spurgeon rightly preached:

---

9. John Brown, *Hebrews* (Edinburgh: Banner of Truth, 1983), 350.

10. J. H. Moulton and G. Milligan, *Vocabulary of the Greek Testament* (Peabody, MA: Hendrickson, 1997 reprint from 1930 original), entry 1450.

11. Charles Wesley, "Arise, my soul, arise," from *Trinity Hymnal*, rev. ed., (Suwanee, GA: Great Commission Publications, 1990), selection 305.

12. O. Palmer Robertson, *The Christ of the Covenants* (Phillipsburg, NJ: Presbyterian and Reformed, 1980), 4.

13. Letter of George Whitefield in Arnold Dallimore, *George Whitefield* (Westchester, IL: Cornerstone, 1980), 2.342.

Now, the sinner is not saved in a way which casts a slight on justice, for Jesus has honoured the law, and borne its penalty on the behalf of the men whom the Father gave him. It was a wonderful act of grace on Christ's part thus to become our surety before the throne of justice, but he did it, and smarted for it, and fulfilled all that it involved. Beloved, I would not like to have gone to heaven over a broken law: no right minded man could be eternally happy and yet know that the law of God had to be dishonoured before he could be rescued from hell. What would the universe say but that God was unrighteous, for he had saved the ungodly, and tarnished the honour of his justice by allowing sin to go unpunished: thus proving that the law was needless, and the punishment superfluous. But now they cannot thus speak concerning any one of us who are saved in Christ Jesus. The saved one's sins have been punished: every believer has borne the punishment of his guilt in the person of his great Substitute. The law is satisfied; we owe it nothing, for we have obeyed it actively and passively in the person of our surety. Even the infinite holiness of God can demand nothing of any believer but what the Lord beholds and accepts on the believer's behalf in Christ Jesus our representative.[14]

Fourth, the superiority of Christ's priesthood is seen in that *his priesthood is not interrupted by death.*

The former priests were many in number, because they were prevented by death from continuing in office, but he holds his priesthood permanently, because he continues forever. (7:23–24)

The Aaronic priesthood was interrupted by death. Josephus calculated eighty-three High Priests from Aaron to the end of

---

14. Charles Haddon Spurgeon, "The Priest Ordained By The Oath of God," in *Metropolitan Tabernacle Pulpit* (Pasadena, TX: Pilgrim, 1984), 27.267.

the second temple in AD 70.[15] Christ your High Priest will need no replacement. His priesthood is permanent; he remains our High Priest *aparabaton* without fail. No death will ever prevent Christ from carrying on his priestly work. "Consequently, he is able to save to the uttermost those who draw near to God through him, since he always lives to make intercession for them" (7:25). His finished, once for all sacrifice has continual efficacy, is not partial nor ineffectual; his "saving power is available without end . . . He is the unique Mediator between God and man because He combines Godhead and manhood perfectly in His own person; in Him God draws near to men and in Him men may draw near to God, with assured access." These lines from F. F. Bruce conclude with this observation:

> [Christ our intercessor] is not to be thought of "as an orante, *standing* ever before the Father with outstretched arms, like the figures in the mosaics of the catacombs, and with strong crying and tears pleading our cause in the presence of a reluctant God; but as a *throned* Priest-King, asking what He will from a Father who always hears and grants His request. Our Lord's life in heaven is His prayer." His once-completed self-offering is utterly acceptable and efficacious; His contact with the Father is immediate and unbroken; His priestly ministry on His people's behalf is never-ending, and therefore the salvation which He secures to them is absolute.[16]

Christ's intercession is efficacious through the crimson blood of the everlasting covenant of grace shed once for all for God's people. Through him we may now "draw near to God." Spiritual paupers are now infinitely rich in Christ. "He is able

---

15. The reference to *Ant.* xx. 227, cited by F. F. Bruce, *Hebrews* (Grand Rapids: Eerdmans, 1979), 152

16. F. F. Bruce, *Hebrews*, 153–155. Bruce quotes H. B. Swete, *The Ascended Christ*, 95.

to save to the uttermost." Do we have guilt? He has removed it. Do we need access? Through Christ we have it. Are we distressed? Here is our comfort. All this and more is ours because the source is in the shed blood of Christ. The mercy he extends to his people has no limit.

Fifth, the superiority of Christ's priesthood is found in *his unique qualifications*. Here the text discloses Christ's *absolute moral purity*. This has already has been stressed in 4:15–16. "For it was indeed fitting that we should have such a high priest, holy, innocent, unstained, separated from sinners, and exalted above the heavens" (7:26). The now exalted Christ (compare 1:1–3) was morally perfect, sinless, and stainless in heart and soul for the accomplishment of his work. Our Lord's heart and life are described by a succession of wondrous adjectives: "holy" (*hosios*) in the absolute sense; he is God in the flesh; "innocent" (*akakos*), that is guileless (Rom 16:18); "unstained" (*amiantos*), without moral corruption, totally untainted.

"Separated from sinners" (perfect passive participle) may be a further description of his moral holiness or it may more likely refer to Christ's exaltation (9:28). These truths are inseparable of course. Only our Christ in his moral perfection could purchase our redemption and serve as Priest before God for desperate, wicked, rebellious sinners. This High Priest is now "exalted above the heavens" (9:28). The Father conferred upon him his mediatorial reign as the reward of his suffering and there he serves his own in the perfection of his office.

It is because of our Priest's eternal nature and absolute moral purity that the writer can next speak of Christ's vicarious, unrepeatable sacrifice. "He has no need, like those high priests, to offer sacrifices daily, first for his own sins and then for those of the people, since he did this once for all when he offered up himself" (7:27, compare 10:12). Christ offered himself up (*anapherō*, "old verb for sacrifice, to place on the altar"[17]). Christ's sacrifice was "once for all" (*ephapax* 9:12; 10:10).

This and other texts like it are very important for our understanding of the completed work of Christ and were of immense consequence for the Reformers' conflict with Rome. Teaching the Word and defending the church against error required the Reformers to attack the Roman Mass as sacrilege. Conflict with Rome was necessary for the truth to triumph. "What sacrilege under heaven is more execrable than the Mass?"[18] asked Calvin. As early as 1534 Hebrews 7:27 held prominence when in the famous placards incident notices were posted all over France (including the antechamber to the king's bedroom!) assailing the Mass with its reenactment of Christ's sacrifice. The *Placards* insisted that Christ was the sole and only Mediator and that this truth was compromised by the Roman Mass.

Bernard Cottret reminds us that "even more than Romans, Hebrews was the cornerstone of the French Reformation"[19] with its insistence on the "once for all" sacrifice of Christ. This issue in church history helps to highlight the importance of the finished work of Christ, the finality and sufficiency of his once for all, never to be repeated sacrifice for sin. The Reformer's conflict with Rome were not over inconsequential matters.

On these points in Hebrews, Calvin beautifully wrote on the defects of the old Levitical system:

> One was the defect in the old priesthood that the high priest offered sacrifices for his own sins. How could he have appeased God for others when God was rightly wroth with him himself? They were quite unequal to the task of atoning for sins. The second defect is that they offered various sacrifices every

---

17. A. T. Robertson, *Word Pictures*, 5.387.

18. Cited by Bernard Cottret, *Calvin A Biography* (Grand Rapids: Erdmans, 2000), 103.

19. Cottret, *Calvin*, 83.

day, and it therefore follows that there was no true atonement because when the cleansing is repeated the sins remain. The case of Christ is quite different. He needed no sacrifice inasmuch as He was not tainted by any stain of sin. His sacrifice was such that its once-for-all oblation sufficed to the end of the world. He offered Himself.[20]

In view of these truths Christ's sacrifice is immeasurably superior to Aaron's priesthood: "For the law appoints men in their weakness as high priests, but the word of the oath, which came later than the law, appoints a Son who has been made perfect forever" (7:28). He, as our Priest, is fit for the Father's presence, absolutely qualified by his absolute moral purity and once for all sacrifice for sin. In heaven the value of the cross appears for believers now. He needs no cleansing for himself and "the word of the oath, which came later than the law," was God's own appointment of his Son ("a son" in contrast to mere men, God's Son in the unique, ontological sense) "who was made perfect forever." The Father was behind the Lord Jesus fitting the Savior for High Priestly office (as in 5:8)—his work of atonement is done, perfect, and complete, needing no supplement.

These Hebrew Christians had allowed the world into their hearts in the guise of religion. They allowed their troubles to obscure the throne. The author of Hebrews in essence pleads: "Why return to that worn out system? Why are you tempted to leave, or forget, or minimize the gospel of grace? We have nothing to pay. God demanded that the complete debt be paid by his own Son. The connection between his death and life for us as our living High Priest is inseparable." And the writer could not plead more powerfully than by appealing to the finished work of the Redeemer. Romans 5:10: "For if while were enemies we were reconciled to God by the death of his Son, much more, now that

---

20. Calvin, *Hebrews*, 103.

we are reconciled, shall we be saved by his life." The answer to our struggles and temptations to turn back can not be found in a Christless gospel, which is no gospel, and certainly not in a return to types and shadows, but only in refocusing our gaze on the sinless substitute for sinners who rose from the dead and ever lives to make intercession for his people.

12

In the Sanctuary

HEBREWS 8:1–6

Now the point in what we are saying is this: we have such a high priest, one who is seated at the right hand of the throne of the Majesty in heaven, a minister in the holy places, in the true tent that the Lord set up, not man. For every high priest is appointed to offer gifts and sacrifices; thus it is necessary for this priest also to have something to offer. Now if he were on earth, he would not be a priest at all, since there are priests who offer gifts according to the law. They serve a copy and shadow of the heavenly things. For when Moses was about to erect the tent, he was instructed by God, saying, "See that you make everything according to the pattern that was shown you on the mountain." But, as it is, Christ has obtained a ministry that is as much more excellent than the old as the covenant he mediates is better since it is enacted on better promises.

In life as we face hardship in the service of Christ, and our hearts are burdened with everything from personal sin struggles to the needs of a fallen world, there is no greater encouragement to us than the knowledge that Jesus Christ is interceding for us in heaven. The true but tried believers to whom the writer preaches in Hebrews also needed the encouragement of this reality for their perseverance in the faith and energy in Christ's service. They were severely tried and tempted to return to the old covenant and forsake the blessing of the new covenant in Christ. Indeed, the writer begins this section by asserting that the heavenly high priestly ministry of Christ is the main point of his entire epistle.

The Main Point

The exhilarating main theme of the entire book of Hebrews is found in the first two verses of chapter 8. He begins by saying: "Now the point in what we are saying is this," and follows on with a description of Christ's priestly work. This high priestly work is not only the summary of the main point of what has thus far been written in Hebrews but is the main point of the entire book. 8:1 should be taken together with 13:22 where we read: "I appeal to you, brothers, bear with my word of exhortation, for I have written to you briefly." That is, the entire book is to be read as a word of exhortation.

It's clear that the "word of exhortation" refers to the entire book on the face of things, as he writes this summary at the end of the book, but it is also clear considering that the "word of exhortation" follows a grand summary of the themes of Hebrews in 13:20–21, which connects the priestly work of Christ with God's equipping believers "with everything good that you may do his will." The book of Hebrews is an exhortation through and through.

In 8:1, we are told the *point* in what the writer is saying. The "point" (*kephalaion*) means the "sum" or "main point" of what the writer is saying. Note that he writes "now the point in what we *are saying* is this". What Christ is now, *at present*, doing in heaven—the import of "are saying"—is an integral and inseparable part of his high priestly work, not an addendum to it.

In the Sanctuary

Therefore, the main "point" of Hebrews is the heavenly, high priestly work of Christ. When Hebrews 8:1, which reveals the high priestly theme of the whole book, is taken together with Hebrews 13:22, which characterizes the book as an "exhortation," we conclude that *the book of Hebrews is an exhortation in which the heavenly high priestly work of Christ is the main point.*[1]

This brings to the fore a much needed lesson for the church of Jesus Christ today. An exhortation is ethical in nature; that is, Hebrews is concerned with our heart's response toward God and to our moral foundations and behavior. Yet, the exhortation is based on the doctrine of Christ's heavenly, high priestly work. Therefore, the conclusion is that the life of the believer is based on doctrine. J. Gresham Machen put the matter in his crucial, splendid, and in many ways timeless book, *Christianity and Liberalism*, something like this: Christianity is not a way of life; Christianity is a way of life based on a message. If we take away the message, then there is no Christianity.[2]

When reading Hebrews, the reader may be tempted to think that all of this detailed writing on Christ's heavenly priesthood is high flown and esoteric. What does all of this have to do with living on Monday? Even though this attitude is unhappily very prevalent among Christians today, it misses the essential point of Hebrews, a point which applies to all Christian theology—doctrine is an essential means of grace, and without it there can be no genuine Christian living.

Redouble your efforts to learn Christian doctrine according to the method of the writer of Hebrews, never severed from exhortation, and you will find yourself growing in understanding and capable of applying the truth to everyday needs and

---

1. This connection was drawn and made plain to me by Dr. Richard Gaffin, under whose lectures on the theology of Hebrews I sat as a student at Westminster Theological Seminary.

2. J. Gresham Machen, *Christianity and Liberalism* (New York: Macmillan, 1930), 19ff.

circumstances. Doctrine, imbibed, digested, understood, meditated upon, and applied to life will make us strong when otherwise we would be weak, will make us valiant for truth when the world is filled with lies, will make us joyful when we would be dejected. As Machen said: "Indifferentism about doctrine makes no heroes of the faith."[3] The writer of Hebrews wants his readers to see the inseparable connection between doctrine and life so that we may be heroes of the faith.

Who Is Jesus?

"Now the point in what we are saying is this: we have such a high priest, one who is seated at the right hand of the throne of the Majesty in heaven." These words were intended to prick the memory of the original hearers of Hebrews and subsequent readers. Our minds are turned back to the opening verses of the sermon-epistle where we were told that Jesus is the Son, the appointed heir of all things, the creator, the radiance of the glory of God, the exact imprint of God's nature who sustains the universe by the word of his power. This Son, "after making purification for sins, . . . sat down at the right hand of the Majesty on high" (1:1–3).

The writer of Hebrews begins this section, in which he deepens his readers' understanding of the high priestly ministry of Christ, by reminding the Hebrews of who Jesus is and by underscoring his enthronement as the Mediator and Savior of sinners. Having seen that he is a priest that is far superior to Aaron, that truth becomes all the more glorious when we are told that in his high priestly office he "is seated at the right hand of the throne of the Majesty in heaven." The writer turns our eyes upward to remind us that, no matter what the trouble may be below, the eternal Son who became man to save us and who purified sins, now reigns over all in Mediatorial power and splendor. This high

---

3. Machen, *Christianity and Liberalism*, 51.

priest does not serve on earth but in heaven; but his heavenly high priestly ministry has everything to do with us on earth. He rules and reigns for his people here and now from the throne on high.

The work of Christ the Redeemer is done, accomplished. Since his one, never to be repeated offering of himself for sinners is completed he "is seated." Where does he sit? He sits "at the right hand of the throne of the Majesty in heaven." Again, the readers' thoughts are drawn to the opening verses of Hebrews, and we are once again reminded that our high priest, to whom as Mediator "all authority in heaven and on earth" has been given (Matt. 28:20), reigns with God as the Son who redeemed us. The writer wants us to think:

- His mission is accomplished, never to be repeated.

- He was once humbled, but now is exalted above all.

- His high priesthood is superior, since no Jewish high priest sat down in the Holy of Holies.

- Our high priest sat down in the Divine Presence and on the Divine throne, from where he holds sway over the universe.

All of these thoughts are gloriously gathered up into one powerful incentive for perseverance as the writer says "*we have* such a high priest." *We have*, the blessed present tense (*exomen*) indicating the privileges and provision granted to the believer in Jesus *right now*. Is it not deeply, richly meaningful for us to dwell upon this *doctrine*? Will not this encourage any believer in Christ no matter his circumstances? We are reminded how that blessed present tense is applied to the priestly work of Christ by John in his first epistle in words that Luther said should be written with golden letters and painted in the heart: "My little children, I am writing these things to you so that you may not sin. But if anyone does sin, we have an (*exomen*) advocate with the Father, Jesus Christ the righteous. He is the propitiation for our sins, and not for ours only but also for the sins of the whole world" (1 John 2:1–2). The words of F. F. Bruce on 7:23–25 also summarize the powerful theme of these verses with succinct potency:

> His once-completed self-offering is utterly acceptable and efficacious; His contact with the Father is immediate and unbroken; His priestly ministry on His people's behalf is never ending, and therefore the salvation which He secures is absolute.[4]

Where Is Jesus?

Our enthroned priest—king sits on the throne above, but where does he minister? The writer makes a great point of emphasizing the place of the present ministry of Jesus our high priest. The Lord Jesus ministers in the sanctuary, he is "a minister in the holy places, in the true tabernacle[5] that the Lord set up, not man." Our Lord ministers in the Father's presence in heaven. *True* here means "original," that is, it is not a copy, not an imitation. The Holy of Holies, the writer will later say, is heaven itself: "For Christ has entered, not into holy places made with hands, which are copies of the true things, but in heaven itself, now to appear in the presence of God on our behalf" (9:24). Our ascended Lord has entered into that "better country" mentioned in 11:16; he has blazed the trail for us to go in union with him into the presence of God, and to our heavenly home. John 14:1ff, once again, is applicable here. The Lord Jesus has gone to prepare a place for us. Before that day comes in which he comes to take us unto himself we are already there in union with Christ and have free access to the Father through his efficacious shed

---

4. F. F. Bruce, *Hebrews* (Grand Rapids: Eerdmans, 1979), 155.

5. "Tabernacle" is the marginal reading in the ESV and is preferred to "tent" selected by the translators. "Tabernacle" brings to mind the worship of the people of God in the wilderness.

blood. Since our Lord serves now in heaven "the true taber-nacle," we are led to ask, "What is he doing there?"

What Is Jesus Doing?

Jesus our great high priest "is seated at the right hand of the throne of the Majesty in heaven" serving there as "a minister in the holy places, in the true tabernacle that the Lord set up, not man." The Lord Jesus is ministering in heaven as our high priest. Catch the argument of verses 4 and 5:

> Now if he were on earth, he would not be a priest at all, since there are priests who offer gifts accord-ing to the law. They serve a copy and shadow of the heavenly things. For when Moses was about to erect the tent, he was instructed by God, saying, "See that you make everything according to the pattern that was shown you on the mountain."

The writer impresses on us that if Christ remained on earth, he would not be serving as priest. The Levitical system is obso-lete, there is no earthbound priestly caste; but, there is Jesus ministering in the "true tabernacle" in heaven. His ministry, then, is superior to the earthly. The death of Jesus rent the veil and closed the Old Testament economy. The earthly sanctuary was no more than a copy; the real and original is heaven itself. Therefore, our Savior's priestly service in heaven is far superior to the service of the old. The writer's purpose in reminding the readers of Exodus 25:40 where God instructs Moses about the Tabernacle is, observes Guthrie, "not to reduce the glory of the shadow, but to enhance the glory of its substance." Indeed, he adds: "All the meticulous detail in the Exodus account would have little purpose if some better antitype was not being fore-shadowed by them."[6]

---

6. Donald Guthrie, *Hebrews*, in *The Tyndale New Testament Commentaries* (Grand Rapids: Eerdmans, 1983), 172–173.

Christ's ministry in heaven is conducted on the basis of his once for all finished sacrifice: "He has no need, like those high priests, to offer sacrifices daily, first for his own sins and then for those of the people, since he did this once for all when he offered up himself" (7:27). What constitutes the ministry he offers on the basis of his finished work on Calvary's mountain? It is his work of intercession for his people:"Consequently, he is able to save to the uttermost those who draw near to God through him, since he always lives to make intercession for them" (7:25).

Do not allow the intercessory work of Christ to remain indistinct and ethereal for you believer. Through his shed blood, Christ accomplished his redemptive purpose, and his blood effectually pleads for his people. This is not ethereal; indeed, it has everything to do with practical Christian living. This truth of the intercession of Christ is essential to your piety and walk and is applicable to your life every day. Again we see that doctrine is necessary to Christian living. Here are a few reasons that this is the case. Ponder them and thank God for them:

1. Christ your priest appears in heaven in the presence of God in your stead. You are seen in your great high priest, in union with him.

2. Christ your priest exhibits an accepted offering for our sins.

3. Christ is interceding for the elect of God who have yet to believe so that they must come to faith in him.

4. Christ is interceding for his people and that intercession cannot fail so that all of those for whom Christ intercedes must persevere to the end.

5. Christ's intercession enables parental pardon and the efficacy of Christ's blood prevails for us when we sin (1 John 1:9; 2:1–2).

6. Christ's intercession protects us from Satan's accusations.

7. Christ's intercession delivers us from temptation and leads us homeward when we fail.

8. Christ's intercession enables us to progressively grow in grace, again, guaranteeing our perseverance.

9. Christ's intercession maintains the bond of peace and communion between us and God.

10. Christ's intercession makes our service acceptable.

11. Christ's intercession presents our prayers in perfection to the Father. He ever lives to make intercession for us (7:25)!

Why Is Jesus' Ministry Superior?

The writer has labored to emphasize that Jesus our high priest's ministry is superior to the old system to which the readers are tempted to return. He now gives two additional, potent reasons for this superiority. First, Christ is the true and final mediator between God and man. Second, the promises of the new covenant are better than the old. "But as it is, Christ has obtained a ministry that is as much more excellent than the old as the covenant he mediates is better since it is enacted on better promises" (v. 6).

The superiority of Christ as true and final Mediator summarizes the pith of Hebrew's message. Christ is the mediator of the new covenant, the fulfiller of that to which the old pointed, and the terminal goal of the redemptive purpose of God. "Long ago, at many times and in many ways, God spoke to our fathers by the prophets, but in these last days..." (1:1,2). Christ is *mediator* and in this mediation he excels (*diaphorōteras*) over the old. As "mediator" (*mesitēs*) our Lord has drawn the embattled parties together in agreement through his own shed blood reconciling God and the sinner. In the papyri the term *mediator* was typically used in legal settings of an "arbiter." Sometimes the *mesitēs* was the "surety" for a debt[7] which fits well the context and both the idea of arbiter and surety may be implied here (7:22). It is through the work of Christ who bore our legal obligations that we his people may now count on the "better promises" of the new covenant.

Similarly Paul writes in 1 Timothy 2:5: "For there is one God, and there is one mediator between God and men, the man Christ Jesus." In our mediator the believer finds complete reconciliation with God from whom we were otherwise separated by our sin. The glory of it all moves us to worship and the sinner sees this only by the work of the Holy Spirit. Owen well wrote:

> To come unto God by Christ for forgiveness, and therein to behold the law issuing all its threats and curses in his blood, and losing its sting, putting an end to its obligation unto punishment, in the cross; to see all sins gathered up in the hands of God's justice, and made to meet on the Mediator, and eternal love springing forth triumphantly from his blood, flourishing into pardon, grace, mercy, forgiveness,— this the heart of a sinner can be enlarged unto only by the Spirit of God.[8]

The second reason the writer gives for the superiority of Christ's high priestly ministry is that the promises of the new covenant are better than the old. The "better promises" of the new covenant are summed up in verses 10–13 to which we turn in the next chapter. For now, keep in mind the "better promises"

---

7. Moulton and Milligan, *Vocabulary of the Greek Testament* (Peabody, MA: Hendrickson, 1997 reprint from 1930 original), entry 3316.

8. John Owen, *Works of John Owen* (Edinburgh: Banner of Truth, 1987), 6.407.

are inseparable from the new thing God has done in Christ and the new covenant instituted by him. Indeed:

> The old covenant had hardly any promises. The old covenant says, "If you will be obedient, and do what I command, you shall have life." But the new covenant says, "If you are sinners, believe and you shall be saved." The new covenant says, "I will be merciful to their unrighteousness, and their sins and their iniquities will I remember no more." And again, it says, "I will give unto him that is athirst of the fountain of the water of life freely."[9]

Oh! How we should take to heart the grandeur of the gospel as displayed in the mediation of our great high priest and Lord, Jesus Christ.

Meditating on Christ's Intercession

By divine inspiration the writer of Hebrews has preached that our Savior "always lives to make intercession for" his people (7:25), and that he is "seated at the right hand of the throne of the Majesty in heaven, a minister in the holy places, in the true tent that the Lord set up, not man" (8:1–2). William Symington in his book, *The Atonement and Intercession of Jesus Christ*, beautifully summarizes the properties of Christ's intercession. We encapsulate and paraphrase his remarks here, providing matter for praise and meditation for the believer. He argues that "from the character of the advocate, we may judge what will be the qualities of his advocacy."[10]

1. Christ's intercession is skillful. Your needs, sins, and infirmities are better known to Christ than to your-

---

9. Robert Murray McCheyne, *Sermons on Hebrews* (Edinburgh: Banner of Truth, 2004), 112–113.

10. For what follows see, William Symington, *On the Atonement and Intercession of Jesus Christ* (New York: Robert Carter, 1839), 264–274.

self. We are often ignorant of ourselves and our true needs. Moreover, we are often incapable of expressing what we feel. Not only is it true that Christ our high priest know us, but since "no one knows the Father but the Son" our high priest's intercession is skillful on two fronts.

2.   Christ's intercession is morally pure. We, in ourselves, are impure. Christ's intercession is as pure and sinless as is his person and sacrifice.

3.   Christ is a compassionate intercessor. His exaltation has not changed his nature and affections. Human blood flows in his veins and human sympathies in his heart. The dust of earth sits upon the throne on high.

4.   Christ's intercession is prompt. "He is never absent from his place; they (God's people) know always where he is to be found: he is ever at the right hand of God, waiting to undertake what they may commit to his charge."

5.   Christ' intercession is earnest. Your prayers for yourself are not anything like the fervency of his intercession for you.

6.   Christ's intercession is authoritative. He has a special commission; his intercession is utterly exclusive and there is not another like it. In the Old Testament not even the King himself could intrude into the priestly office; only the high priest could carry incense into the holy of holies. He did not take this honor unto himself. Christ is the king-priest who has as his peculiar honor, the regal intercession at the right hand of God.

In the Sanctuary

7. Christ's intercession prevails. The most urgent entreaty among men can go unheard among men; but Christ the Father always hears. As Symington declares, Christ "asks for nothing for which he has not paid the full price of his precious blood." We, then, have no excuse to neglect coming to him who is our great high priest and intercessor.

8. Christ's intercession is constant. His understanding is infinite; he can care for ten thousand needs as easily as for one. You never have to take a number. Moreover, his intercession will never come to an end; never shall his people cease to be the objects of his care.

This Christ does for his people in the sanctuary. Symington writes a beautiful and powerful conclusion worthy of much meditation:

> [Christ] entered into heaven, not without blood, to appear in the presence of God for us. He goes to the portals of the upper sanctuary, holding in his hand the memorials of his sacrifice; at his approach the celestial gates fly open; he enters in the name and on the behalf of his people; he opens and no one can shut, till all his redeemed and chosen have followed him thither; and, then, he shuts and no one can open, either to invade their peace or to pluck one of the countless multitude from their happy abode.
>
> The permanent continuance of the redeemed in the state of glory stands connected, in the same manner, with the intercession of Jesus. 'He is a priest *for ever.*' Not only is everlasting glory the *effect* of his intercession; but it is the *subject of* everlasting intercession. 'He *ever liveth* to make intercession.' The perpetuity of heavenly blessings, and the acceptance of celestial services, must all be traced to this source.

Not a ray of light, not a smile of favour, not a thrill of gladness, not a note of joy, for which the inhabitants of heaven are not indebted to the Angel standing with the golden censer of incense, before the throne. Remove this illustrious personage from his situation; divest him of his official character; put out of view his sacerdotal function; and all security for the continuance of celestial benefits is gone,—the crowns fall from the heads of the redeemed, and the palms of victory drop from their hands, the harps of gold are unstrung, and the shouts of hallelujahs cease for ever; nay, heaven must discharge itself of its human inhabitants, and the whole be sent away into irremediable perdition! But no such appalling catastrophe need ever be feared: CHRIST EVER LIVETH TO MAKE INTERCESSION![11]

---

11. Symington, *On The Atonement and Intercession of Jesus Christ*, 263–264.

13

The New Covenant

HEBREWS 8:7–13

In speaking of a new covenant, he makes the first one obsolete. And what is becoming obsolete and growing old is ready to vanish away.

When the Lord saves a sinner he changes his heart. What once was hateful to him, now he loves. One great theme of this passage is the way in which the Lord writes his law on the heart in fulfilment of his covenant promise. Spurgeon told a most interesting story about this theme. A friend of Spurgeon's gave him an expensive walking stick. Made of ebony with a gold head and California quartz worked into it, the gift must have been costly. One night a thief broke into Mr. Spurgeon's home and stole the precious gift which meant much to Spurgeon because it was a gift from his dear friend. The thief took a portion of the stolen item to the pawn broker; he had broken the head off and battered it, but all of his hammering could not hide the word *Spurgeon*. The thief got away, but the shop owner returned the gold to Pastor Spurgeon who said: "though the man hammered it, there was my name, and the gold was bound to come back to me, and so it did." Spurgeon then pressed the point of the illustration:

> Now, when the Lord once writes his name in your
> heart, he writes his law within you; and through the
> devil may batter you, God will claim you as his own.
> Temptation and sin may assail you, but if the law of
> the Lord is in your heart, you shall not give way to
> sin, you shall resist it, you shall be preserved, you
> shall be kept, for you are the Lord's.[1]

This is a summary of the theme of our text, to which we now turn.

Jesus is the true and final Mediator. "The covenant he mediates is better, since it is enacted on better promises" (8:6). As we have seen "mediator" was a common word in legal transactions of the first century sometimes associated with the idea of a "surety." Our Mediator and high priest, the Lord Jesus Christ, has brought God and the elect sinner together by bearing the legal obligations of God's chosen people. "For there is one God, and there is one mediator between God and men, the man Christ Jesus" (1 Tim. 2:5).

In view of the political correctness and "tolerance" of our culture, surely one of the greatest issues faced by the church today is stating forthrightly the uniqueness of Christ as Mediator and the indispensability of his blood atonement. I cannot help but think of the "Insider Movement" endorsed by many "missiologists." The gospel going into a Muslim country, for example, is so trimmed in many cases that the exclusive claims of Christ are not recognizable—all in the name of cultural anthropology. In other cases, substitutionary atonement is denied because it is distasteful to proponents of feminism. The uniqueness of Christ and of his gospel, however, may never be compromised by those who would be faithful. There is none like him. No work but his saves from sin, and there is no effectual intercession but what flows from the only Mediator between God and men, our Lord Jesus Christ.

---

1. C. H. Spurgeon, *Metropolitan Tabernacle Pulpit*, 43.107.

This unique Mediator is the Mediator of a better covenant "enacted on better promises" (8:6). The truth that the new that has come with Christ is "better" or more excellent is a constant claim of the writer of Hebrews. The writer never wearies of relentlessly presenting the supremacy of Christ. "Intensely zealous that God's honour should contract no stain, this ideal Mediator, having secured that supreme end, will with equal zeal seek the offender's rescue and reclamation. Such an unique Intermediary evangelical faith recognizes in her beloved Lord."[2]

The question will arise to every thoughtful reader: What is this "new covenant"? What does the writer propose by it and why is it important for us? In what ways does the new contrast with the old? Moreover, what makes the new covenant new and better? Verses 7–13 begin to answer that question and the answer extends into the glorious chapters that follow.

Imperfection of the Old

Keep in mind that the writer of Hebrews is concerned to call professing Jewish Christians to faithfulness. Under the threat of persecution, they were tempted to go back to what appeared to be the safer life of Judaism. To them, the writer bluntly says: "For if that first covenant had been faultless, there would have been no occasion to look for a second." The preacher's argument here is similar to that of 7:11: "Now if perfection had been attainable through the Levitical priesthood (for under it the people received the law), what further need would there have been for another priest to arise after the order of Melchizedek, rather than one named after the order of Aaron?" In essence, the argument is that the old covenant could not

---

2. E. K. Simpson, cited in F. F. Bruce, *Hebrews* (Grand Rapids: Eerdmans, 1979), 168.

bring salvation, so God instituted a new covenant according to his plan.

It would be wrong to see this in a way characteristic of the older dispensationalist view of the kingdom. That well known view insisted that God offered the kingdom through Christ (Plan A), and when the Jews rejected it, he instituted salvation through Christ's atonement (Plan B). One cannot read Hebrews without noting the author's deep appreciation for the unity of God's plan of salvation. However, the writer also wishes to draw the contrasts between the old and the new. The old was provisional and typological while the new fulfills the old and brings to fruition the plan of salvation determined from the beginning. The old was inadequate, and God institutes the new. The Levitical system was inadequate, and the type pointed ahead, by its very inadequacy, to a replacement by a new kind of priest.

Here in the passage before us is made plain that the old covenant could not bring salvation, but God institutes the new. If the old were not inadequate, there would be no need for the new. The new makes the old obsolete. This brings us face to face with the fundamental unity of the Old and the New Testaments in bringing us a complete picture of our sin and of the Savior Jesus Christ. But we are also brought face to face with the radical newness of the accomplishment of Jesus to save us from our sins. As the Old Testament scholar Franz Delitzsch put it:

> The Old Testament may be compared to the starry night, and the New Testament to the sunny day, or, as we may also say, the New Testament period, in its beginning, is related to the Old Testament as the coming of spring to winter. The spring in the kingdom of God suffered itself to be long waited for; and when at length spring days seemed to announce the end of the darkness and coldness of winter, the winter soon made its presence felt again. Then, however,

> when the Lord appeared, it became spring. He was
> indeed predicted as the embodiment of spring.[3]

Verse 8 therefore points to the perfection of the new, the coming and embodiment of the new.

> For he finds fault with them when he says: "Behold
> the days are coming, declares the Lord, when I will
> establish a new covenant with the house of Israel
> and with the house of Judah, . . ."

Note once again how the writer revels in the authority of Scripture. *He* says. The author is not mentioned because the authority of the ultimate author is the essence of the matter. Any true doctrine of Scripture's inspiration and authority must start with the ultimate author, and only then take into account the human authors of God's Word.

The writer cites Jeremiah 31:31–34, demonstrating the Lord's promise that the new will supersede the clearly provisional old. This, Hebrews insists, has taken place in the coming of Christ. Why return to the old when the new has come? Why return to the old when the Lord himself has promised, in the midst of the old, that the better would arrive in Christ?

Israel had entered into the old covenant given at Sinai in the most fearful manner with fire and earthquake accompanied with blessings and the promise of terrible cursing for disobedience. In Exodus 24 Israel was sprinkled with the blood of the covenant. However, within seven days of that sacred moment, they danced idolatrously before the golden calf. This becomes a paradigm of disobedient covenant breaking as we find in the prophet Jeremiah (7:24–26).

The law was defective in two ways. First, the law could provide no atonement adequate for the sins of sinners. The blood

---

3. Franz Delitzsch, *The Messianic Prophecies of Christ* (Minneapolis, MN: Klock and Klock, 1983 reprint of 1891 edition), 4.

of bulls and goats could not satisfy divine justice. Second, there was no spiritual efficacy in the law. The law's very nature was to point ahead to the Redeemer and the work of the Holy Spirit due to the law's inability to redeem and to transform the heart. Indeed, in verse 8 as Guthrie notes, the writer stresses the "fault finding function of the law"[4]: "For he finds fault with them when he says." Similarly, Paul tells us in Galatians 3:23–24: "Now before faith came, we were held captive under the law, imprisoned until the coming faith would be revealed. So then, the law was our guardian until Christ came, in order that we might be justified by faith." The law can provide no righteousness for sinners; it cannot justify but does demonstrate our transgressions and our need of a Savior.

God promised the new covenant. When Jeremiah announced the new covenant by divine inspiration, the Northern Kingdom had long been taken captive by Assyria, and Judah, the Southern Kingdom, was nearing its destruction by the Babylonians. Though Jeremiah saw a revival under King Josiah, he also saw the beginning of the captivity of Judah. In this sad and dark hour, God himself promised a new covenant that would bring to pass the salvation that the first covenant could not. Jeremiah was enabled to see great promise in the midst of spiritual disaster.

What brilliance is shown in these wondrous promises to lighten the darkness of Jeremiah's day. The new covenant would be "enacted on better promises" (8:6) and the "fault" of the covenant at Sinai was superceded by the glory of the promise of the new:

> For he finds fault with them when he says: "Behold,
> the days are coming, declares the Lord, when I will
> establish a new covenant with the house of Israel

---

4. Donald Guthrie, *Hebrews*, in *The Tyndale New Testament Commentaries* (Grand Rapids: Eerdmans, 1983), 174.

and with the house of Judah, not like the covenant
that I made with their fathers on the day when I took
them by the hand to bring them out of the land of
Egypt. For they did not continue in my covenant,
and so I showed no concern for them, declares the
Lord." (8:8–9)

Of course, it would be a great mistake to think that this new
covenant would be established only with the natural seed of
Abraham. The Scriptures make plain that the new covenant in
Christ's blood is made with all of God's people, the new Israel of
God (Luke 22:20; 1 Cor. 11:25; 2 Cor. 3:6). The reason that Hebrews does not stress this is solely due to the Jewish-Christian
audience to whom the epistle is addressed.

The writer of Hebrews develops the idea of contrast in the
progress and unity of redemptive history. We find this elsewhere, for example in the writings of Paul, where the contrasting features of the old and new covenants are clearly drawn. For
example, in 2 Corinthians 3, the apostle contrasts:

- The tablets of stone with tablets of human hearts (vv. 3, 7)

- The letter of the law with the Spirit (v. 6)

- The killing of the old with the life giving power of the new (vv. 6–7)

- The lesser glory of the old with the greater glory of the new (vv. 8–10)

- The condemnation of the law with the justifying righteousness of the new (v. 9)

- The passing nature of the old with the abiding na-ture of the new (v. 11)

- The veiling of the old with the unveiling of the new (vv. 12–18)

So also the writer of Hebrews draws stark contrasts between the old and the new in order to wake up these Hebrew Christians tempted to return to the old. In essence, the author of Hebrews is asking, "Why would you return to the old when it has been superseded by the redemption that comes in Christ with all of its 'better promises'?" The tried Christian today must be confronted with this same reality when tempted to turn aside. Can you not see the glory of the gospel of free grace? How totally impoverished will be that person who goes to any other than the Lord Jesus our high priest?

Perfection of the New

With the pastoral concern for recovering the erring, the writer now turns to three wondrous perfections of the new covenant. The writer will focus on the promises of the new covenant in 10:15–17, but here he focuses on what makes the new covenant new. Of course, this focus is inseparable from the promises and intersects with the promise theme at every point.

The first perfection of the new covenant is that the Lord internalizes his law in the members of the new covenant.

> For this is the covenant that I will make with the house of Israel after those days, declares the Lord: I will put my laws into their minds, and write them on their hearts and I will be there God, and they shall be my people. (8:10)

The text stresses divine monergism: *I* will. By the regeneration of the Holy Spirit the Lord implants into minds and hearts the very law of God (Ezek. 11:19–20; 36:26–27). This does not mean that no one before the institution of the new covenant had a renewed heart. The covenant in the Mosaic law, however, made no provision for it. The history of Israel demonstrated that, at many points in her history, only a remnant knew the

The New Covenant

Lord. Those who trusted in Christ by believing the promises of the new covenant in advance, did so with immensely fewer advantages than believers have had since the coming of Christ.

With all of her advantages over the nations, Israel could not keep God's law and was not faithful to the Lord. What was needed was a new nature. The old, unregenerate heart of the nation was too black upon which to write, and too stony to take the imprint of God's law. But now, the law is written on the heart and the greater work of the Holy Spirit impresses the soul with a love for God's Word and way. Bunyan speaks of Little Faith who was met in Dead Man's Lane by three villains. They robbed him of his money but could not steal his jewels because he carried them in his heart. So, the new covenant writes God's law on the hearts of God's people.

The staging principle of revelation means that since the coming of Christ, his ascension, and the pouring out of the Holy Spirit at Pentecost, the greater role of the Holy Spirit in the lives of God's people is to draw their hearts out toward God in communion, uplift the Savior, and magnify the place of God's law in their lives. Put another way, the antinomian view that the new covenant believer can now disregard God's law is in direct contradiction to the teaching of Hebrews. Rather than ignorance of or apathy toward God's law, there is now given a great internal commitment to the law and an earnest desire for obedience. With those upon whose hearts the Lord writes his law, the covenant formula comes to fruition:" and I will be their God, and they shall be my people" (v. 10; see Rev. 21:3).

The second perfection of the new covenant is knowledge of God: "and they shall not teach, each one his neighbor and each one his brother, saying, 'Know the Lord,' for they shall all know me, from the least to the greatest" (v. 11). John Brown observed:

> The words in the 11th verse are not to be understood absolutely, but comparatively. They intimate, that

> under that covenant there shall be a striking con-
> trast to the ignorance which characterized the great
> body of those who were under the Old Covenant;
> that the revelation of the divine will shall be far more
> extensive and clear under the new than under the
> old economy; and that there shall be a correspond-
> ingly enlarged communication of the enlightening
> influences of the Holy Spirit.[5]

This knowledge of God is not mere intellectual assent, even though the intellectual component must not be minimized. The knowledge is one of saving interest, of true communion, and an experiential reality that will be found in the lives of all of God's true children among whom there is no Gnostic style class system ("for they all shall know me from the least of them to the greatest"). The new covenant brings true knowledge of God. One who knows God has a sense of sin, recognition of need, an understanding of his hell deservedness, and a trust in Christ as all-sufficient.

In his justly famous sermon *A Divine and Supernatural Light*,[6] Jonathan Edwards unpacks the essence of this knowledge of God by expounding on Matthew 16:17. This "divine and supernatural light" is not simply the conviction of conscience known by the unregenerate, it is not impressions made upon the imagination, it is not the impartation of new revelation apart from Scripture, nor is it to be confused with those moments in which unregenerate men are moved by religious notions. Rather, this knowledge of God, this "divine and supernatural light" is "a true sense of the divine excellency of the things revealed in the Word of God, and a conviction of the truth and reality of them thence arising."

---

5. John Brown, *Hebrews* (Edinburgh: Banner of Truth, 1983), 373.

6. For what follows, see Jonathan Edwards, *The Works of Jonathan Edwards* (Edinburgh: Banner of Truth, 1974), 2.12–17.

The New Covenant

A true knowledge of God is given by the Holy Spirit so that a person will not merely have a rational notion that God is glorious but will have a true sense of the gloriousness of God within his heart. It is one thing to know that God is holy; it is another to have a sense of the loveliness of God's holiness in your heart:

> There is a difference between having a rational judgment that honey is sweet, and having a sense of its sweetness. A man may have the former that knows not how honey tastes; but a man cannot have the latter unless he has an idea of the taste of honey in his mind. So there is a difference between believing that a person is beautiful, and having a sense of his beauty. The former may be obtained by hearsay, but the latter only by seeing the countenance.

When God reveals himself to a sinner, it "destroys the enmity, removes those prejudices, sanctifies the reason, and causes it to lie open to the force of arguments for their truth." This knowledge, that is, "the subject matter of this light, are conveyed to the mind by the Word of God; but that due sense of the heart, wherein this light formally consists, is immediately by the Spirit of God."

Edwards has captured the essence of the issue revealed by divine inspiration in this portion of Hebrews. A chemist may be able to analyze honey and speak very precisely of its properties, but if he has never tasted honey, his knowledge is not experiential. So it is that the believer's knowledge of God in the new covenant is real, genuine, and experiential by the supernatural light of the Holy Spirit.

It is also wonderful to consider that the Spirit of God often accelerates this knowledge and applies it widely as the Lord has gathered his elect in various seasons of church history. Early eighteenth-century England, for example, was a dark time indeed in which there was very little knowledge of God in this land once favored with the light of the Reformation and the truly wonderful gift of a Puritan ministry. The religious and moral condition of England at that time was deplorable. Hogarth's sketches show the moral condition quite accurately, and Blackstone, the noted lawyer, went throughout London to hear preachers early in the reign of George III, and said that "he did not hear a single discourse which had more Christianity in it than the writings of Cicero, and that it would have been impossible for him to discover, from what he heard, whether the preacher were a follower of Confucius, of Mahomet, or of Christ!"[7]

It was in the midst of this sad and miserable condition that the Lord intervened in grace, raising up a host of ministers to preach the unsearchable riches of Christ. Their preaching, accompanied by the power of the Holy Spirit, was used to turn England around, and thousands were supernaturally regenerated and granted a true knowledge of Christ and responded to the gospel in faith.

The third perfection of the new covenant in this portion of Hebrews is the promise of sin not remembered: "For I will be merciful toward their iniquities, and I will remember their sins no more" (v. 12). Knowledge of God comes through the forgiveness of sin. This forgiveness comes through sovereign mercy. One of the great truths distinguishing the Christian faith from the religions of the world is found right here. In every world religion, man is thought to make his way to God, indeed in some instances to actually *become* God. The Biblical view is that fallen man could never make his way to God. God must come to man if sinners are to be saved. "I will be merciful; I will remember their sins no more."

The covenant at Sinai showed the need for the forgiveness of sins, but it could not provide the forgiveness of sins. The law is a

---

7. J. C. Ryle, *Five Christian Leaders of The Eighteenth Century* (London: Banner of Truth, 1963), 12.

mirror; mirrors show stains but cannot remove them. The Lord has promised that in the new covenant he would look merciful-ly upon criminals against his law and that he would "remember their sins no more." Oh! The immutability of the divine pardon through Jesus Christ our Lord; how wondrous, comprehensive and liberating! Consider these Old Testament promises fulfilled in the new covenant:

> He does not deal with us according to our sins, nor repay us according to our iniquities. For as high as the heavens are above the earth, so great is his stead-fast love toward those who fear him; as far as the east is from the west, so far does he remove our trans-gressions from us. (Psalm 103:10–12)

> I, I am he who blots out your transgressions for my own sake, and I will not remember your sins. (Isaiah 43:25)

> I have blotted out your transgressions like a cloud and your sins like mist; return to me, for I have re-deemed you. (Isaiah 44:22)

> Who is a God like you, pardoning iniquity and pass-ing over the remnant of his inheritance? He does not retain his anger forever, because he delights in steadfast love, He will again have compassion on us; he will tread our iniquities under foot. You will cast all our sins into the depths of the sea. (Micah 7:18–19)

F. F. Bruce notes:

> Now the assurance of the forgiveness of sin is writ-ten into the very terms of the covenant in the most unqualified fashion: "I will forgive their iniquity, and their sin will I remember no more." For the Hebrew, "remembering" was more than a mental effort; it car-ried with it the thought of doing something to the

> advantage, or disadvantage of the person remembered . . . If men's sins are remembered by God, His holiness must take action against them; if they are not remembered, it is because His grace has determined to forgive them—not in spite of His holiness, but in harmony with it.[8]

"Christ has obtained a ministry that is as much more excellent than the old as the covenant he mediates is better, since it is enacted on better promises" (8:6). The better promises are founded upon the perfections of the new covenant as we find them in verses 8–12:

1. In the new covenant, God puts his law into our hearts.

2. In the new covenant, God gives a true knowledge of himself.

3. In the new covenant, God has no remembrance of his people's sins.

Therefore he concludes in verse 13: "In speaking of a new covenant, he makes the first one obsolete. And what is becoming obsolete and growing old is ready to vanish away." The old is now obsolete (stressed by the perfect tense in the Greek text). The sacrificial system is done away by the one who "bore our sins and carried our sorrows" (Isa. 53). Now a new way is open through Jesus' perfect, unrepeatable sacrifice. We have received a gift, not a wage, and are enabled to believe the word of promise. The words "growing old" and "is ready to vanish away" may be an opaque reference to the continuance of temple ceremony as the writer preaches his message of the newness of the new covenant. The destruction of the Temple was right around the historical corner.

---

8. F. F. Bruce, *Hebrews* (Grand Rapids: Eerdmans, 1979), 175.

The New Covenant

In Hebrews 10:15, the writer will once again cite the new covenant spoken of by Jeremiah, as he does here in chapter 8. The writer is keen that we understand that what Jeremiah wrote about the new covenant and the "better promises" (8:6) is the Holy Spirit bearing witness to us. These things are for *us*; for Christians here and now and until the coming of Christ. To read about this new covenant and the better promises and to apply them to the Jews only or to limit them to some future recovery of Israel would entirely miss the point. We who trust in Christ enjoy this covenant relationship now. We sup on the covenant meal (Luke 22:20; 1 Cor. 11:25).

The covenant of grace made with Abraham, Moses, and David finds fulfillment in the new covenant instituted by Christ and will continue into the consummation of all things. While the original prophecy of Jeremiah referenced the house of Judah and the house of Israel, these references are now applicable "to us" who are in Christ forming the new Israel. Any dispensational approach limiting the words of Jeremiah to the return of the Jews to their land violates the unity of the redemptive purpose of God. As Calvin said:

> Whenever the Prophets prophesied of the return of the people, they extended what they taught to the whole kingdom of Christ. For liberation from exile was no more than the beginning of God's favour: God began the work of true and real redemption when he restored his people to their own country; but he gave them but a slight taste of his mercy. The prophecy, then, with those which are like it, ought to be extended to the kingdom of Christ.[9]

---

9. John Calvin, *Calvin's Commentaries, Commentaries on the Book of the Prophet Jeremiah and The Lamentations, Volume Third* (Grand Rapids: Baker, 1979), 207–208.

Some Differences Between Law and Gospel

The new covenant in Christ's blood has now come and we who believe are in that covenant. The old covenant at Sinai demanded works; the new covenant in Christ's blood is all of grace. The old and the new; this entire section implies a contrast. What is that contrast? Where do the contrasts lie?

Before looking at a few essential points of contrast, let us remember that the contrasts do not in the least rupture the unity of God's redemptive purpose for his people. The covenant of grace, though administered differently in various ages, is essentially one through history. There is contrast, but not disunity, and the contrast furthers the consistent pressing forward in unity to the coming of Christ and the establishment of the new covenant. The new covenant is not new in the sense that it had no antecedents, but it is new because Christ has come fulfilling the purpose of redemption in history.

The law in the Mosaic economy was intended to lead to Christ, to move the people on to grace by a sense of their own inability (Gal. 3:24). Indeed, the apostle Paul must oppose the Judaizers for the very reason that they failed to understand this essential point and believed that they had the resources for justification in God's court by their own obedience rather than by the work of Christ alone. It is only as we understand that we are incapable of keeping the law for justification and so find our salvation in Christ alone that the law has its rightful place in the Christian walk as a rule of life. With that in mind the following contrasts will be helpful to us.

1. The law requires perfect obedience; the gospel sees us as helpless, and condemned. We are righteous only by the imputed righteousness of Christ.

2. The law shows what we ought to be; the gospel actually changes us.

3. The law says, *Do and live.* The gospel says, *It is done.* "The law is God in command, but the gospel is God in Christ."[10]

4. The law promises life upon obedience; the gospel promises life to the ungodly upon the obedience of Christ for us.

5. The law condemns and cannot justify; the gospel justifies. It cannot condemn the sinner who believes in Jesus; rather, it declares "not guilty" and positively righteous.

6. The law aggravates sin; it rouses it. The gospel renews the heart.

The gospel is pure promise having nothing to do with tables of stone. It all points to 8:6: "Christ has obtained a ministry that is as much more excellent than the old as the covenant he mediates is better since it is enacted on better promises." Jesus obeyed the law and its demands; Jesus suffered to pay its penalty. Look to the crimson blood of Christ and there see this pronouncement: *Done! Finished!* The law can crush no believer. There is no "if" in the new covenant! God's covenant of grace cannot fail, it will not fail:

> Firm as the lasting hills,
> This covenant shall endure,
> Whose potent *shalls* and *wills*
> Make every blessing sure:
> When ruin shakes all nature's frame,
> Its jots and tittles stand the same.
>
> Here, when thy feet shall fall,
> Believer, thou shalt see
> Grace to restore thy soul,

10. John Colquhoun, *A Treatise on The Law and The Gospel* (Morgan, PA: Soli Deo Gloria, 1999), 149.

And pardon full and free;
Thee with delight shall God behold
A sheep restored to Zion's fold.

And when through Jordan's flood
Thy God shall bid thee go,
His arm shall thee defend,
And vanquish every foe;
And in this covenant thou shalt view
Sufficient strength to bear thee through.[11]

---

11. John Kent, "With David's Lord and Ours," in *Our Own Hymn-Book: A Collection of Psalms and Hymns for Public, Social, and Private Worship*, compiled by C. H. Spurgeon (London: Passmore and Alabaster, 1883), selection 227.

14

The Blood of Christ

HEBREWS 9:1–14

But when Christ appeared as a high priest of the good things that have come, then through the greater and more perfect tent (not made with hands, that is, not of this creation) he entered once for all into the holy places, not by means of the blood of goats and calves but by means of his own blood, thus securing an eternal redemption. For if the blood of goats and bulls, and the sprinkling of defiled persons with the ashes of a heifer, sanctify for the purification of the flesh, how much more will the blood of Christ, who through the eternal Spirit offered himself without blemish to God, purify our conscience from dead works to serve the living God.

The powerful words to James George Deck's hymn, "The Veil is Rent," provides a meditative introduction to the themes in this chapter. The ground of the believer's confidence is the precious shed blood of Christ; and that blood now avails for us in heaven.

> The veil is rent: our souls draw near
> Unto the throne of grace;
> The merits of the Lord appear,

They fill the holy place.

His precious blood avails us there
As we approach the throne;
And His own wounds in heaven declare
The atoning work is done.

'Tis finished: here our souls have rest,
His work can never fail;
By Him, our Sacrifice and Priest,
We pass within the veil.

Within the holiest of all,
Cleansed by His precious blood,
Before the throne we prostrate fall,
And worship Thee, O God.

Boldly the heart and voice we raise,
His blood, His name, our plea;
Assured our prayers and songs of praise
Ascend, by Christ, to Thee.[1]

Hebrews 9 dwells on the thrilling theme that should always be at the forefront of the church's thinking and the Christian's thought and life. Here the writer takes us into the inner sanctum and shows us by divine inspiration what the precious blood of Christ accomplished and how that relates to the ongoing life of Christ for his people.

The writer has been dwelling on what makes the new covenant new. The old covenant had two principle defects. First, the law could offer no adequate atonement. Second, the law had no spiritual efficacy within itself; it could not bring about what it demanded. The gospel, however, is sheer promise. The gospel can achieve its intention, and the writer demonstrates

---

1. James George Deck, "The veil is rent: our souls draw near," from *Hymns of Grace and Truth* (New York: Loizeaux Brothers, Bible Truth Depot, 1903), selection 4.

this by pointing to the perfection of the new covenant. The new covenant:

- Internalizes God's law

- Brings a true knowledge of God

- Does not remember sin against us

Now the writer proceeds in his argument and shows how the inadequacies of the old are met in Christ and his work for us. The writer begins by continuing his contrast between the old and the new and demonstrating the inadequacy of the Tabernacle.

Inadequacy of the Tabernacle

The writer continues to expound on the theme of 8:13: "In speaking of a new covenant, he makes the first one obsolete. And what is becoming obsolete and growing old is ready to vanish away." So now, the writer in 9:1–5 dwells on the inadequacy of the tabernacle. Hebrews 9:1 says literally "the place of holiness" not "*a* place of holiness." In the tabernacle, the Lord manifested his earthly presence. It was "an earthly place of holiness." The sanctuary was a tent with moveable furnishings and repeatable sacrifices pointing to its temporary and impermanent quality. The Tabernacle comprised two chambers: the Holy place (9:2) and the Most Holy Place (9:3–4). In the Holy Place were the lamp stand, the table where the twelve loaves were placed weekly, and the altar of incense.

> Behind the second curtain was a second section called the Most Holy Place, having the golden altar of incense and the ark of the covenant covered on all sides with gold, in which was a golden urn holding the manna, and Aaron's staff that budded, and the tablets of the covenant. (vv. 3–4)

Of course, "the golden altar of incense" was not found in the Most Holy Place, but as Guthrie points out, "there is clearly a close link between the altar of incense and the holy of holies," and he notes that in 1 Kings 6:22 "the incense altar is described as 'the whole altar' belonging to the inner sanctuary."[2] It is the relationship between the altar of incense and the Most Holy Place that seems to be the point. The references to manna and Aaron's budding rod point back to the Lord's divine intervention in caring for and saving his people. In the Most Holy Place, God prescribed the ark, with the gold-covered mercy seat, which was splattered with blood on the Day of Atonement pointing to the propitiation of sins. The ark contained the manna, Aaron's rod that blossomed, and the tables of the law.

In verses 2–5, the writer briefly describes the Tabernacle in order to remind the hearers of the main propitiatory themes surrounding this temporary dwelling place. The "cherubim of glory" point beyond themselves to the majesty of the holy God who shows mercy through sacrifice. The mercy seat is the place of propitiation pointing beyond itself also to the sacrifice of Christ "whom God put forward as a propitiation by his blood to be received by faith" (Rom. 3:25). The writer does not intend an exhaustive treatment: "of these things we cannot now speak in detail" (v. 5). He moves from this brief description of this impermanent tent to the inadequacy of the tabernacle ritual.

Inadequacy of the Tabernacle Ritual

In verses 6–10, the writer underscores the inadequacy of the tabernacle service in two ways. First, the tabernacle allowed at best an imperfect access into God's presence. Second, the work

---

2. Donald Guthrie, *Hebrews*, in *The Tyndale New Testament Commentaries* (Grand Rapids: Eerdmans, 1983), 181.

of the priestly service of the tabernacle could not cleanse the conscience.

First, the tabernacle ritual was inadequate, allowing only imperfect access into God's presence. The daily service of the priests was ongoing. They offered incense morning and evening, tended the candelabrum, and changed the bread of presence weekly. This was the work of Zechariah in Luke 1:9ff. He was one of the common priests who participated in these duties. The writer indicates these saying: "These preparations having thus been made, the priests go regularly into the first section, performing their ritual duties" (v. 6).

The second chamber was more restricted: "But into the second only the high priest goes, and he but once a year, and not without taking blood, which he offers for himself and for the unintentional sins of the people" (v. 7). Annually the high priest, and note—the high priest *only*—with sacrificial blood not yet finally efficacious but pointing typologically to the altogether sufficient sacrifice of Christ, entered into the Most Holy Place on God's terms and after his appointment. This showed the people the need for sacrifice for sins. Moreover, by the fact that once per year the High Priest performed this ritual, the Holy Spirit was showing that perfect access to the Father was yet to come through Christ.

The very limitations of the tabernacle service pressed the nation ahead to the greater fulfillment of these things in Christ. Access was far from free and open but was clearly prescribed. Thus the nation looked forward and awaited the finished work of Christ on the cross by which God's people have free access to the throne of grace. "By this the Holy Spirit indicates that the way into the holy places is not yet opened as long as the first section is still standing (which is symbolic of the present age)" (vv. 8–9). Thus the Holy Spirit indicates the typical and temporary character of the old pointing ahead to the new in Christ.

Since the new has come, the old has no standing. The old was a "symbol [literally, a "parable"] of the [then] present age," the age of fulfillment in Christ the ascended Lord.

The second inadequacy of the Tabernacle ritual was that it could not cleanse the conscience:

> According to this arrangement, gifts and sacrifices are offered that cannot perfect the conscience of the worshiper, but deal only with food and drink and various washings, regulations for the body imposed until the time of reformation. (vv. 9–10)

The rituals of the tabernacle, with its sacrifices, were adequate as types only. They could point ahead and prefigure the work of Christ, but for the cleansing of the conscience, they were worthless. Conscience is our moral awareness of the judgment of God that brings about a sense of guilt, the recognition that we have done wrong, that we are answerable to God.

Every person has an unworthy past and, apart from the gospel, does not know what to do about it. Every person is guilty in Adam and adds to the guilt of Adam's first transgression by his personal sin. Religion, moral systems, labeling sin with medical or psychological terms, denial of guilt, and escape mechanisms will not remove the load of guilt to which every person as a sinner is liable. The writer of Hebrews helps us to keep the question before us: How is it possible to have a clear conscience? How may the sinner have a saving relationship with God? The church today faces many important themes and issues but must at all costs keep her focus on proclaiming the gospel of Christ through whom alone we are saved from sin. Hence, the writer makes plain that the type must give way to fulfillment, "the outward and earthly copy to the inward and heavenly reality."[3]

---

3. F. F. Bruce, *Hebrews* (Grand Rapids: Eerdmans, 1979), 197.

The Blood of Christ

The sacrifices of the temple service "cannot perfect the conscience of the worshiper." The history of Israel was characterized by looking forward to the *reformation*, that is, to the coming of Christ and a reordering of things on the basis of fulfillment, on the basis of substance as over against shadow, the new as fulfilling the old and bringing to fruition the better promises based on the better and final sacrifice of the Son.

Effects of Christ's Work

The preacher now brings to his hearers and readers the implications of the "reformation" that has taken place due to the coming of Christ. He mentions four effects ("the good things that have come") of Christ's work of fulfillment.

The first effect of Christ's work for his people is access into the inner sanctum. This is implied in verses 11 and 12 and, as we shall see, is specifically worked out for us in Hebrews 10:19ff.

> But when Christ appeared as a high priest of the good things that have come, then through the greater and more perfect tent (not made with hands, that is, not of this creation) he entered once for all into the holy places, not by means of the blood of goats and calves but by means of his own blood, thus securing an eternal redemption. (11–12)

Since our Lord is in heaven, having blazed the trail for us by his own perfection and merit, his people now have free access in the heavenly court.

> Therefore, brothers, since we have confidence to enter the holy places by the blood of Jesus, by the new and living way that he opened for us through the curtain, that is, through his flesh, and since we have a great high priest over the house of God, let us draw near with a true heart in full assurance of faith, with

> our hearts sprinkled clean from an evil conscience
> and our bodies washed with pure water. (10:19–22)

Our access to the holy places is through our great high priest who is God, and entered *once for all* into the holy places. He assumed human nature and suffered and bled in that nature, rose from the dead, ascended on high, and ever lives to make intercession for us (7:25).

The second effect of Christ's work is the eternal redemption of his people. Verse 12 states explicitly that Christ secured "eternal redemption" for us "by means of his own blood." "Redemption" (*lytrōsis,* from the root *lytron,* ransom) indicates freedom and purchase from slavery by payment of a price. In 1859, the Lord sent a powerful and true revival to the churches of Northern Ireland. One of the many stories of conversion was that of a Roman Catholic woman who found a lost communion token. In the Presbyterian churches of that place and era, those desiring to come to the Lord's Table attended a preparation service the week before. After attending the service the communicant was given a communion token usually made of lead. The token served as a ticket of entrance to the communion service.

So, a Roman Catholic woman found a token that had been lost on which was embossed the words "this do in remembrance of me" (Luke 12:19). The words of the gospel were taken to her heart by the Holy Spirit, and she was deeply convicted of sin. Sending for the Presbyterian minister, this woman heard the gospel of salvation through Jesus' blood and after a short time believed on Christ. When the minister asked for the token, since they were scarce, she replied: "Oh, no I cannot give it you. I will never part with it till I put it into your hand sitting at the communion table." The writer of the narrative declared: "What a powerful preacher is that bit of lead! and what an exciting sermon the words, 'This do in remembrance of Me!' when they are blessed by the Spirit of God."[4]

The writer of Hebrews would have us know that we are saved by Jesus' blood. On the basis of his sacrifice on the cross our Lord Jesus accomplished what Aaron could only foreshadow; "he entered once for all into the holy places, not by means of the blood of goats and calves." On the basis of his once for all shedding of his blood our great high priest entered into the presence of the living God for us his people in the prevailing value of his own merit "by means of his own blood." His redemption of us through his shed blood on the cross is eternal in its effects as indicated in the aorist middle participle, "having secured" (*heuramenos*).

How can the blood of Christ enter into the courts of heaven? The blood enters through *redemption*, that is, through the deliverance from sin accomplished by the Lord Jesus. Because that redemption is accomplished by God who assumed human nature that redemption very pointedly is "eternal redemption." The redemption accomplished by Christ is eternal in its accomplishment and in its effects. No repetition is needed. "He entered once for all into the holy places . . . by means of his own blood." On the basis of his finished work our Lord entered in triumph to live for his people forever. Priest and offering are one in Christ, and our redemption can, therefore, never fail.

> It is not that the sinner is accepted, but that Jesus is accepted. God looks only on the great Intercessor, and gives Him power to give eternal life to all whose names are on His breast-plate; and when, in answer to these Divine intercessions, the Spirit is given to Christ, that Christ may give Him to us—when, in consequence of that gift, He descends not from the Father but from Christ to us, and unites us to Jesus—

4. This narrative is recorded by Ian R. K. Paisley, *The "Fifty Nine" Revival* (Belfast: Martyrs Memorial Free Presbyterian Church, 1970), 148–149.

> then, God looks upon us in the Redeemer and justi-
> fies us in consequence of that union. Here there is
> perfect harmony in the whole plan.[5]

How then can our redemption not be eternal? It is founded on Jesus' blood and intercession. If true believers to whom Christ's righteousness has been imputed could be lost, then Christ's blood would be thrown away, the purchase of his blood would be in hell, the Father would not be hearing the intercession of Christ for believers, and Jesus would be completely disappointed in his errand from heaven. In short, the devil would be the victor. Perish such blasphemy! Christ is the infinite God become man. He fulfills the eternal plan of the Triune God to redeem sinners. He will save his elect, and bring us home to glory. His redemption is eternal. We are free from the penalty of the law and Jesus has paid our debt in full. The merit of his sufferings has entered in his person right into the holy of holies to plead effectually for us. With the hymn writer John Cennick, we exclaim:

> My full Receipt may there be shew'd,
> Graven with Iron Pens in Blood,
> On Jesu's Hands and Side;
> I'm safe, I'd cry, O Law and Sin,
> Ye cannot bring me guilty in,
> For Christ was crucify'd.[6]

Yes. Our crucified Lord entered into the most holy place as our great high priest in heaven presenting the fruit of his labor on the cross, and so we are kept forever safe in his care. "The single sacrifice had eternal value, owing to his personality."[7]

---

5. James Henley Thornwell, *The Collected Writings of James Henley Thornwell* (Edinburgh: Banner of Truth, 1974), 2.283.

6. John Cennick, "A Sinner to the Lord I come," from *The Two Covenants. Being the Substance of a Discourse Delivered in London, In the Year 1745*, 3rd ed. (London: M. Lewis, 1771), 24.

7. James Moffatt, *A Critical and Exegetical Commentary on The Epistle to the Hebrews* (Edinburgh: T&T Clark, 1963), 121.

The Blood of Christ

Let it be carefully noted that there is nothing here about sacrifice in heaven; sacrifice has been accomplished once for all. There is, however, an everlasting efficacy to that sacrifice that is presented on behalf of the people of God, which is an essential plank in our security in Christ.

When and how did our Lord Jesus enter into the holy places for us (v. 11)? It is often assumed that it was at his ascension, but there are those who differ from that view. The argument that the entry was immediately after Christ's death on the cross is as follows. It is true that the great high priest pleads the merit of his blood for us in heaven. As the writer tells us in his introduction, "after making purification for sins, he sat down at the right hand of the Majesty on high" (1:3). However, in this text there is no reference to ascension but to atonement on the cross.

The "entering" of the text is the entering into the Most Holy Place through the sacrifice of Christ on the cross. The high priestly sacrifice in the old economy is referenced by the writer in verses 6–10, and the sacrifice of Christ is the counterpart according to verses 11 and 12. Just as the high priest in the old economy entered the Most Holy Place and sprinkled the blood on the mercy seat, so also in a far greater way our Lord Jesus entered into the Most Holy Place by the sacrifice of himself for our sins. The cross, the death of Christ, is in this text the entrance of Christ into the Most Holy Place. Smeaton observes:

> All the ceremonies on the great day of atonement correspond with this view, for the atonement for the people of Israel was not consummated till the sacrificial blood was sprinkled on the ark of the covenant. The figure therefore corresponds with the Lord's entrance into heaven immediately after His death, when the soul and body were sundered, and not with

the idea of a triumphant entrance into heaven, as it took place at His ascension, with all the jubilee belonging to a coronation day. In the type, everything assumes that the whole was completed on the atonement day. And Christ's resurrection on the third day, equivalent and parallel to the return of the high priest from the holy of holies, was a proof that He had entered with His own blood, and been accepted.[8]

Hence the "once for all" (cp. 1 Pet. 3:18) entry of our Savior "into the holy places . . . by means of his own blood" refers to the finished work of Christ on the cross which continues to have efficacy in the Savior's intercessory work. It is the basis of his great work of intercession. The atonement is once for all; the intercession is continuous based on the completed work (9:25–27). "A double entry into heaven is indicated in these chapters,—first at the time of Christ's death, the second when He entered with His risen body as the Melchizedek priest."[9]

While appreciating the desire to get as far as possible from a view of a continuing sacrifice in heaven, the idea that Christ entered into heaven at the hour of his death, in his intermediate state, does not seem exegetically tenable.

The point of Hebrews is to emphasize the Lord's high priestly work: "We have such a high priest, one who is seated at the right hand of the throne of the Majesty in heaven, a minister in the holy places, in the true tent that the Lord has set up, not man" (8:1a–2). The sustained emphasis on the exalted high priestly ministry of Jesus, the ascension predicate of the sermon (1:3), makes it unlikely that the writer would shift that emphasis at this point. The argument that the fulfillment of the Old Testament shadow depicted the sacrifice and sprinkling of the blood on the ark in the Most Holy Place is not decisive. The author of Hebrews clearly

8. George Smeaton, *The Apostles' Doctrine of the Atonement* (Edinburgh: Banner of Truth, 2009), 381.

9. Smeaton, *The Apostles' Doctrine of the Atonement*, 382.

stresses the finished work of Christ on the cross as presented in heaven at the Lord's enthronement at his ascension.

Heavenly enthronement took place at Christ's ascension (Acts 2:33–35; Heb. 1:3; 8:1; 10:12–13) so it seems most fitting in the context of Hebrews to believe that the Lord presented his blood upon completion of his mission—when he ascended into heaven. Hebrews emphasizes the salvific cycle of Christ's work on earth—life, death, and resurrection—climaxing with his session at the Father's right hand. The New Testament as a whole does not place enormous emphasis on the theological significance of Christ's intermediate state. There is a prudent restraint in the language of the Westminster Shorter Catechism, which says Jesus was "continuing under the power of death for a time."[10] Owen well summarizes the intent of the writer of Hebrews:

> This *entrance* of Christ into heaven upon his ascension may be considered two ways:
>
> (1) As it was *regal*, glorious and triumphant; so it belonged properly unto his kingly office, as that wherein he triumphed over all the enemies of the church. See it described, Eph. iv. 8–10, from Ps. lxviii.1. Satan, the world, death and hell, being conquered, and all power committed unto him, he entered triumphantly into heaven. So it was regal. (2) As it was *sacerdotal*. Peace and reconciliation being made by the blood of the cross, the covenant being confirmed, eternal redemption obtained, he entered as our high priest into the holy place, the temple of God above, to make his sacrifice effectual unto the church, and to apply the benefits of it thereunto.[11]

How encouraging this would have been to those to whom the writer preached these truths. The writer knows that his readers

---

10. This idea was presented to me in this context in personal conversation with Dennis Johnson.

11. John Owen, *Hebrews* (Edinburgh: Banner of Truth, 1991), 6.278–279.

are attracted to the still standing temple with its sacrifices. Notice the present reference to that system in verses 6 and 9.[12] "Does not the tangible, visible sacrificial system call us back? Is not the system still in place better than what we have heard about Jesus," they seem to ask. No; indeed, the temple on earth has nothing to offer now. We have a great high priest in the presence of God for us, and this ministry of intercession preceded by his atoning work for us on earth means that our redemption is eternal and secure. Indeed, this is better, far better. It fulfills the old and infinitely exceeds the types and shadows of the temple system on earth. Unlike the sacrifices of the temple offered over and over, the sacrifice of Jesus is a finished work, and his entrance into heaven with his blood was "once for all" (v. 12).

> This he did "once" only, "once for all." In the foregoing description of the service of the high priest, he shows how he went into the holy place "once every year;" that is, on one day, wherein he went to offer. And the repetition of this service every year proved its imperfection, seeing it could never accomplish perfectly that whereunto it was designed, as he argues in the next chapter. In opposition hereunto, our high priest entered once only into the holy place; a full demonstration that his once sacrifice had fully expiated the sins of the church.[13]

The third effect of Christ's work for his people in heaven is a purified conscience. The writer indicates this by contrasting the sanctifying influence of the old with that of the new:

> For if the blood of goats and bulls, and the sprinkling of a heifer, sanctify for the purification of the flesh, how much more will the blood of Christ, who through

---

12. By referencing the still-standing Jerusalem Temple, the writer indicates that he is writing before the destruction of Jerusalem in AD 70.

13. John Owen, *Hebrews*, 6.279.

the eternal Spirit offered himself without blemish to
God, purify our conscience from dead works to serve
the living God. (vv. 13–14)

In Numbers 19:1–18, a red heifer was slain, and its burned
ashes were stored for use in cases of ceremonial defilement.
When an Israelite was ceremonially defiled he was cleansed
by being sprinkled with the ashes of this sin offering, this red
heifer whose ashes had been dissolved in water. Access into the
sanctuary was thus restored. The sentence over our conscience,
however, is not ceremonial but moral, to which the ceremonial
of the old was an indicator. The sentence passed over us sinners
was that of death, and for this only the application of the saving
efficacy of the blood of Christ can avail. The precious blood of
Christ is efficacious; his sacrifice can cleanse our consciences
defiled by sin.

Our consciences must be purified "from dead works," those
works of the law, vaunted self-righteousness by which we
proudly think that God will accept us, or any depravity that
stems from our fallen nature (6:1). We cannot deal with such
a perverted conscience ourselves. Deep within our hearts, we
know it. Suppressing the truth in unrighteousness, we defile our
consciences, but the blood of Christ cleanses us within—in the
court of our consciences where we stand condemned by our sin.
As Smeaton says so beautifully:

A judicial exchange of persons has been effected
between Christ and sinners, by which we truly
enter into each other's position. When the man
accepts this provision, keeping in view the two
sides of that personal exchange, he says: Sin does
not attach to me, but to my Substitute, who took
it upon Him by an act allowed at the divine tribunal. Punishment is not to strike on me, for He
tasted death for every one of His people: and the

good which the divine law required in its utmost conceivable perfection I have done; for what the Surety did, I did in Him, and His merits are transferred to me with the accompanying boon of the divine good pleasure. All this is effected in a way that for ever humbles and abases the man; but that which pacifies the human conscience, the vicegerent of God. The purging of conscience is effected when we see that the law suffers no wrong, and the divine attributes no indignity.[14]

In Greek literary history, a palimpsest was a scroll page that had the original writing scraped off so that the page could be written over again. Codex *Ephraemi Rescriptus* is one example of such a Biblical manuscript. Many such manuscripts exist. The palimpsest can serve to illustrate what the Lord has done for us through the blood of Christ. Our hearts, like manuscripts written with sin, have now been scraped and cleansed, and the law of God is now written there in the crimson characters of Christ's blood. True peace of conscience comes from realizing by faith that the sentence in my conscience has been written over by another sentence, that of free grace and sovereign mercy. The Westminster Larger Catechism is quite stirring in answer 55 concerning the intercession of Christ:

Christ maketh intercession, by his appearing in our nature continually before the Father in heaven, in the merit of his obedience and sacrifice on earth, declaring his will to have it applied to all believers; answering all accusations against them, and *procuring for them quiet of conscience*, notwithstanding daily failings, access with boldness to the throne of grace, and acceptance of their persons and services. [Italics mine.]

---

14. George Smeaton, *The Apostles' Doctrine of the Atonement*, 393.

The Blood of Christ

Many true believers fall back into an empty attempt to find peace of conscience in their own performance, constantly thinking that they must lack something. Calvin rightly says that "we are not cleansed by Christ so that we can immerse ourselves continually in fresh dirt, but in order that our purity may serve the glory of God."[15] However, the believer does not find purity of conscience in his own holiness but only in the blood that bought him. We often fail to understand the absolute perfection of the work of Christ. Never are we to ground peace of conscience in our own behavior, even through Spirit-produced holiness. Peace of conscience may be found, not in ourselves, not in performing duties, and certainly not in attempts to establish our own righteousness, but only in acknowledging Christ as our righteousness and peace.

When we see ourselves to be dead with Christ, and thus free from the condemnation of the law; when we understand that all of our debt has been paid by his shed blood; when we realize by faith that we are clothed with the perfect righteousness of Christ, that we are raised with him and that he intercedes for us—this is the source, Christ alone is the source, of a clean conscience.

The fourth effect of Christ's work is the sanctification of our service as found in verse 14: "How much more will the blood of Christ, who through the eternal Spirit offered himself without blemish to God, purify our conscience from dead works to serve the living God." Outside of Christ, our works are spiritually dead. They originate in death, they are done by the living dead, and they lead to death. Things are different now for those in union with Christ. Our feeble and faltering efforts to please the Lord and serve him are accepted in his righteousness and merit. Our consciences, now purified "from dead works" are also now free "to serve the living God."

---

15. John Calvin, *Hebrews* (Grand Rapids: Eerdmans, 1979), 122.

> Because no work is so pure or free from sin as to be pleasing to God by itself, cleansing by the blood of Christ which destroys all stains must necessarily intervene. This is the true contrast between the living God and dead works.[16]

How Could the Blood of Christ Achieve These Accomplishments?

This great high priest who without spot came to sacrifice himself and shed his blood, who came according to the eternal plan of the Triune God to save his people and who intercedes in the efficacy of his blood for us, did so in the Holy Spirit's power. He is the one "who through the eternal Spirit offered himself without blemish to God" (v. 14). In the perfect union of his divine and human natures "Christ offered himself without blemish to God." His infinite divine nature gave infinite value to his human sufferings. He could offer himself acceptably only if he were "without blemish." Because of his impeccability, the Savior's sacrifice is acceptable to God. All of this was done by the Spirit's enablement.

It is important to note that the text says that Christ "offered himself." Our Lord laid down his life willingly, of his own accord; no one took his life from him (John 10:18). As Thornwell beautifully observes, "Though there was an immense cost of suffering and of blood, it was never for a moment begrudged, never for a moment sustained with reluctance." He adds: "We have no occasion for regrets that the blessings which we enjoy have been put into our hands by cruelty, injustice, or even harshness and severity to others. They are free gifts of that sublimest of all spirits—the spirit of a priest." [17]

---

16. John Calvin, *Hebrews*, 122.

17. James Henley Thornwell, *The Collected Writings of James Henley Thornwell*, 2.276.

The Blood of Christ

The text also tells us that this sinless sacrifice offered himself "through the eternal Spirit." Does this mean "through the eternal spirit" that is his own perfect human nature, or does it indicate the role of the Holy Spirit in the Savior's self-offering? There can be no doubt that, prior to this statement, the writer has the nature of the Son in mind—his impeccability and unblemished offering. However, others point out that the work of Christ, as the Suffering Servant of Jehovah, was accomplished by the empowerment of the Holy Spirit. Which does the writer mean? Does he mean that Christ's person enabled him to accomplish his work, or does he mean that the Lord Jesus accomplished his redemptive task in the empowerment of the Holy Spirit? Both are true theologically, but which is the concern of the author?

Given the concern of the writer with Christ's person, his impeccable offering, and prior references to the Lord's person and work (e.g. 7:3; 16; 24), some have thought that on balance it seems best to see "through the eternal spirit" to mean that the Son accomplished redemption by virtue of his divine nature in perfect union with his sinless human nature. Only he who was God in the flesh could offer himself without blemish to God. Moreover, the contrast in the text between the offerings of the Levitical order and that of Christ showed his offering to be "infinite rather than relative" as Hughes observes. Hughes cites Beza: "To the blood of beast our author opposes the blood of him who was not only man, like others, but also God; for by the designation 'eternal spirit' I understand the infinite efficacy of the Deity in the humanity he assumed, which consecrated the whole of his sacrifice."[18]

Vos sees "eternal" here to be synonymous with "heavenly":

> This does not refer to the Holy Spirit, but to the Spirit which was his own, that is, to *Christ's divine nature.* Also, the word *eternal* means *heavenly.* Therefore the

---

18. Philip E. Hughes, *Hebrews* (Grand Rapids: Eerdmans, 1990), 360.

meaning is that *through the heavenly aspect of His deity* Christ makes the offering. "...the Son, after he made propitiation of sins in himself." The verb here is the middle voice, which is significant, indicating something taking place *within Christ's Person.*[19]

Ebrard says of this text that it means "the finished manifestation of the fullness of the eternal being of God in time."[20] Marcus Dods similarly says "that Christ having an eternal spirit was thereby able to perform the whole work of atonement, not merely dying on the cross but passing through death to present Himself before God."[21] To these we add one more example; Alford agrees with the foregoing perspective saying that the text points to Christ who "offered Himself, with His own consent assisting and empowering the sacrifice."[22]

Essentially, the writer is saying then, according to many excellent exegetes, that the Lord achieved the wonders of salvation because of the power of his divine nature. This is why in Christ's blood, God's people can find the answer to a defiled conscience. "There is thus a moral quality in the blood of Christ not in that of other sacrifices."[23] "Eternal spirit" in 9:14, then, is seen to be the equivalent of "the power of an indestructible life" in Hebrews 7:16.

As convincing as the arguments are that the writer is referring to the person of Christ in his self-offering by the words

19. Geerhardus Vos, *The Teaching of the Epistle to the Hebrews* (Grand Rapids: Eerdmans, 1956), 104. For additional arguments, see also Delitzsch, *Commentary on the Epistle to the Hebrews,* 2.95–97.

20. John H. A. Ebrard, *Biblical Commentary on the Epistle to the Hebrews* (Edinburgh: T&T Clark, 1868), 290. Compare Moffatt, *Hebrews,* 124.

21. Marcus Dods, *Hebrews,* in *The Expositor's Greek Testament* (Grand Rapids: Eerdmans, 1990), 4.334.

22. Henry Alford, *The Greek Testament* (Cambridge: Deighton, Bell and Company, 1875), 171.

23. A. T. Robertson, *Word Pictures in the New Testament* (Grand Rapids: Baker, 1932), 5.400.

The Blood of Christ

"eternal Spirit," and as theologically true as they certainly are, I remain unconvinced. I think that "who through the eternal Spirit offered himself" refers to the empowerment of the Holy Spirit. My reasons are threefold:

First, it seems to me that the natural reading of "eternal Spirit" is the Holy Spirit. It seems more likely that a reader would take this to mean "the Holy Spirit" rather than a reference to Christ's spirit. Had he intended the latter, the writer could have said so clearly.

Second, the Scriptures everywhere affirm the empowerment of the Holy Spirit in the life of our incarnate Lord. All that he accomplished as our Mediator was accomplished in the power and fellowship of the Holy Spirit. John 3:34–35: "For he whom God has sent utters the words of God, for he gives the Spirit without measure. The Father loves the Son and has given all things into his hand." While recognizing the work of the Holy Spirit in the life of Christ may not resolve the exegetical question here, it is certainly pertinent to the discussion and may predispose one on first reading to think that "eternal Spirit" is a reference to the Holy Spirit.

Third, the background seems to be the suffering Servant passages in Isaiah. More to the point, the background to Hebrews 9 seems to be not only the Levitical priesthood but also the self-offering of the Lord as the suffering Servant of Jehovah who conducted his ministry in the power of the Holy Spirit. F. F. Bruce, pointing ahead to 9:28 ("so Christ, after having been offered once to bear the sins of many"), correctly sees an allusion to Isaiah 53.[24] There we read that "his soul makes an offering for guilt" (53:10), and the purification of conscience of Hebrews 9:14 may refer to Isaiah 52:15: "So shall he sprinkle many nations." Christ's self-offering as one with unblemished life in Hebrews 9:14 ("who through the eternal Spirit offered

---

24. F. F. Bruce, *Hebrews*, 205–206.

himself without blemish to God") seems to be a reference to Isaiah 53:9 ("although he had done no violence, and there was no deceit in his mouth"). When the suffering Servant of Jehovah is introduced in Isaiah's prophecy (Isa. 42:1), he is specifically introduced with a reference to his Holy Spirit empowered ministry: "Behold my servant . . . I have put my Spirit upon him; he will bring forth justice to the nations." Given the fact that Isaiah's prophecy formed a background for Hebrews 9, it seems likely that "who through the eternal Spirit offered himself without blemish to God" refers to the enablement of the Holy Spirit in the life of Jesus, the suffering Servant of Jehovah.

The Savior's self-offering in the power of the Holy Spirit is the ground of the believer's confidence. It is because of this once for all achievement that our Lord's High Priestly work is eternally efficacious:

> There is no direct and immediate approach to God. We come before Him only in the name of our Priest, who attracts us by the community of nature, and who presents all our worship for us before the eternal throne. Our prayers are not heard and received as *ours,* but as the prayers of Jesus; our praises are not accepted as *ours,* but as the praises of Jesus. The imperfection which attaches to our performances, our pollution and weakness and unbelief, stop with the High Priest; His intercession and atonement cover all defects, and we are faultless and complete in Him. The prayer which reaches the ear of the Almighty is from Him, and not from us, and must be as prevalent as His worth. Here is our confidence, not only that Jesus died, but that Jesus lives—that He is our intercessor in the heavenly sanctuary, and there presents, enforces and sanctifies the religious worship of earth; here is our confidence that in the whole process of salvation God regards the Redeemer and not us, and deals out blessings according to

The Blood of Christ

His estimate of Christ; here is our confidence that
if any man sin we have an Advocate with the Father,
Jesus Christ the righteous. What an encouragement
to prayer and praise! And what thanks shall we ren-
der unto God for adapting the marvelous scheme
of His grace with such consummate wisdom to the
wants and weaknesses of men![25]

What then is the power of the blood of Christ? His blood
takes hold of sinners like us and purchases us from our sins,
reconciles us to God, justifies us with Christ's righteousness,
redeems us from our guilt, regenerates our souls, gives persevering grace, and takes us all the way to heaven. All of this the
Spirit-empowered sacrifice of Christ accomplished for God's
people, and this same unblemished sacrifice continues to bear
fruit for us in the heavenly high priestly work of Christ.

---

25. James Henley Thornwell, *The Collected Writings of James Henley Thornwell*, 2.284–285.

15

The Perfect Sacrifice

HEBREWS 9:15–28

For when every commandment of the law had been declared by Moses to all the people, he took the blood of calves and goats, with water and scarlet wool and hyssop, and sprinkled both the book itself and all the people, saying, "This is the blood of the covenant that God commanded for you." And in the same way he sprinkled with the blood both the tent and all the vessels used in worship. Indeed, under the law almost everything is purified with blood, and without the shedding of blood there is no forgiveness of sins.

The English Reformation in the sixteenth century provides examples of many wondrous conversions. The gospel of grace had been overgrown with the weeds of human merit, but the Reformation was a rediscovery of the profound and simple gospel of salvation through Christ's blood. When Thomas Bilney of Cambridge was brought to a saving knowlege of Christ, the Lord laid upon his heart to share his faith with a fanatical priest, Hugh Latimer. How to do it? Bilney finally decided that the approach would be through the confessional! He would go to Hugh Latimer the priest and ask him to hear his confession.

His confession, however, would not be that of a man confessing his sin to a priest but of confessing faith in his Savior who is our great high priest. When Bilney came to "confess," Latimer thought that his preaching against Reformation "heresy" had converted Bilney back to Roman Catholic doctrine. Latimer was eager to hear Bilney's confession. Kneeling before Latimer, Bilney "related to him with touching simplicity the anguish he had once felt in his soul, the efforts he had made to remove it; their unprofitableness so long as he determined to follow the precepts of the church and, lastly, the peace he had felt when he believed that Jesus Christ is *the Lamb of God that taketh away the sin of the world.*" Upon hearing Bilney's confession, Hugh Latimer, the arch-enemy of the gospel, was himself converted, his heart cleansed through Jesus' blood, and he became a preacher of the very gospel he once despised.[1] It is the power of the blood of Christ to save us that is the theme of the text to which we now turn.

The writer of Hebrews has been directing his readers to the blessing and superiority of the new covenant over against the old. He has described the inadequacy of the tabernacle and its ritual. The Tabernacle service typified what the sacrifice of Christ fulfilled and made effectual. Christ's propitiation alone was able to "purify our conscience from dead works to serve the living God" (9:14). Nothing could be plainer: The basis of our acceptance with God and the removal of our guilt are completely founded in the substitutionary sacrifice of Christ for sinners. Lawbreakers are redeemed by Christ's shed blood. The writer now opens more fully the wonder of the sacrifice of Christ and its meaning for believers.

---

1. J. H. Merle d'Aubigne, *The Reformation in England* (Edinburgh: Banner of Truth, 1977), 1.203.

The Perfect Sacrifice

Christ's Death: An Efficacious Sacrifice

The death of Christ on our behalf was no half measure. Christ's blood establishes and validates the new covenant. "Therefore," that is, "on the basis of" the "blood of Christ, who through the eternal Spirit offered himself without blemish to God"(9:14), "he is the mediator of a new covenant, so that those who are called may receive the promised eternal inheritance, since a death has occurred that redeems them from the transgressions committed under the first covenant" (9:15). All who are *called* of God, both prior to and after Christ's death, are saved through Christ's blood. Though sinners under the old covenant committed transgressions under the temple administration ("the first covenant"), the death of Christ redeems them from those transgressions.

By "the first covenant" the writer, of course, does not have in mind the covenant made with Adam, but contrasts the first sacrificial system with its fulfillment in the sacrifice of Christ. Nor does "the first covenant" mean that the new covenant established in Christ had no antecedents. The new administration of the covenant of grace is new because it is one of fulfillment and of final and effectual accomplishment. Old Testament sacrifices found their value not in themselves but in the once-for-all sacrifice of Christ to which they pointed. Old Testament believers were redeemed from sin by the cross in anticipation. We who now believe the gospel are saved by the work of Christ on the cross in retrospect. All who are *called* by God, whether Old Testament believers or those saved after the coming of Christ, are saved in the same way, namely, through the shed blood of Christ. Hence, the sacrifice of Christ is efficacious.

This is the foundation of our acceptance with God, the foundation of our faith, the immovable Rock upon which we must build our lives. Any setting aside of the fundamental and indispensable importance of the substitutionary atonement of

Christ is to build sandcastle lives that will be eroded by the tides of life. This was the reason that the Reformers were set against the Roman idea of the sacrifice of the mass. What could embolden a man such as Wycliffe to say to his accusers that all of the doctors of the church since the year 1,000, with the possible exception of Berengar of Tours, had been wrong on the doctrine of the sacrament of the altar; what but a heart transformed by the Christ who died once for all for sinners?

> How canst thou, O priest, who art but a man, make thy Maker? What! the thing that groweth in the fields—that ear which thou pluckest today, shall be God tomorrow! . . . As you cannot make the works which He made, how shall ye make Him who made the works? Woe to the adulterous generation that believeth the testimony of Innocent rather than of the Gospel.[2]

In the spirit of the Reformers and martyrs may we never compromise the blood atonement.

Christ, then, is "the mediator of a new covenant." What makes the new covenant new is that Christ has come and achieved our salvation through his shed blood. The anticipated Christ has come. He is the *mediator*, as the author made plain in 8:6: "Christ has obtained a ministry that is as much more excellent than the old as the covenant he mediates is better, since it is enacted on better promises." On the basis of our Savior's mediation the called of God have received "the promised eternal inheritance, since a death has occurred that redeems them from the transgressions committed under the first covenant" (v. 15). What is this "promised eternal inheritance" given in grace to those redeemed through Christ's blood from transgressions?

---

2. J. H. Merle d'Aubigne, *The Reformation in England*, 1.93.

The Perfect Sacrifice

Note that the writer is focusing on the Old Testament believer. This inheritance has been spoken of already by the author in 8:8ff. Did not the Lord promise Abraham an innumerable inheritance (Gen.17:7, 9)? This was only partially fulfilled in the land and nation of Israel:

> Yet because of the transitory nature of earthly possessions and the mortality of man which makes certain his separation sooner or later from the acquisitions of this life, it was impossible that an "everlasting covenant" promising an "everlasting possession" and an "everlasting inheritance" could find the completeness of its fulfillment in the present order of things. The physical land and the posterity that in due course inherited . . . constituted a sign, visible and passing, which pointed beyond itself to a reality, as yet invisible, which would be permanent.[3]

Now this, as Hughes points out, is the purpose of the author here and we see that the "eternal inheritance" pointed the Old Testament believer beyond to a time in which all believers, both Jew and Gentile, would share in the fruit of the redemption of Christ. The patriarchs looked for a better, heavenly country (11:13–15) and by faith obtained the promise (6:15, 18). This fruit is applicable to all of the called for whom Christ is mediator (9:15). Thus the certainty of the inheritance is guaranteed by the shed blood of Christ and by the effectual call of the Father.

Of this eternal inheritance, the fruit of the new covenant accomplishment of Jesus, we also read in 1 Peter 1:3–6:

> Blessed be the God and Father of our Lord Jesus Christ! According to his great mercy, he has caused us to be born again to a living hope through the resurrection of Jesus Christ from the dead, to an

---

3. Philip E. Hughes, *A Commentary on the Epistle to the Hebrews* (Grand Rapids: Eerdmans, 1990), 367–368.

> inheritance that is imperishable, and unfading, kept
> in heaven for you, who by God's power are being
> guarded through faith for a salvation ready to be re-
> vealed in the last time.

H. A. Ironside told of a man in Montana for whom attorneys had searched for a long while because he was heir to the estate of a British nobleman. He had been eking out a living when the news came to him. How did he react? He went to town and bought a fine suit on the credit of his inheritance and started out for Great Britain. When asked by people where he was headed, he responded, "To take possession of my estate." In a far greater way believers in Christ have an unfading inheritance by virtue of Christ's shed blood. By the grace of God, we are on our way to take possession of our estate.[4]

The Power of the Blood Illustrated

The usual interpretation of verses 15–17 is to view them as pointing to the analogy of a last will and testament. The argument is as follows: The eternal inheritance that belongs to God's people as the result of Jesus' sacrifice for our sin is illustrated by the writer by means of a will and testament.

> Therefore he is the mediator of a new covenant, so
> that those who are called may receive the promised
> eternal inheritance, since a death has occurred that
> redeems them from the transgressions committed
> under the first covenant. For where a will is involved,
> the death of the one who made it must be estab-
> lished. For a will takes effect only at death, since it is
> not in force as long as the one who made it is alive.
> (9:15–17)

---

4. H. A. Ironside, *In the Heavenlies* (Neptune, NJ: Loizeaux Brothers, Neptune, 1971), 20–21.

The Perfect Sacrifice

The point of the illustration, it is said, is clear: property is bequeathed by an owner but the inheritors have no title to the property until the owner dies. Settlement of the title upon the inheritors cannot take place and no benefits can belong to them until the one who bequeathed the property has died. So also,the new covenant, in this case compared for the sake of illustration to a will, requires the death of the testator for the saints to inherit the benefits. Here we have an illustration of the necessity of the sacrifice of Christ so that "those who are called may receive the promised eternal inheritance." This illustration, however, has a truly glorious limitation. After all, Jesus not only died to bring to his people saving benefits, but he rose from the dead, and as our great intercessor, he administers the dispensing of that inheritance to the children for whom he died.

The author uses word association to make his point. The term for "covenant" and for "testament" ("will") is the same (*diathēkē*) so that the interplay between the ideas becomes obvious for the first readers. The covenant is likened to a will; the covenant is established on the basis of the death of Christ analogously to the benefits provided to beneficiaries after the death of the testator. "For a will takes effect only at death, since it is not in force as long as the one who made it is alive" (9:17).

The above, as was indicated, turns *diathēkē* into a reference to a last will and testament. However, keeping in mind that the term for "covenant" and for "testament" is the same, there is another interpretative possibility. Elsewhere in Hebrews, the term *diathēkē* refers to "covenant," and the term certainly means this in the immediate context (vv. 15; 18–20). This second interpretation argues that the term *diathēkē* should also be translated "covenant" in verses 16 and 17. These verses then should be viewed as expressions of the method of making covenants in the ancient world.

Hebrews 9:17 literally reads "a covenant is confirmed over dead bodies" (*epi nekrois bebaia*). Immediately the interpreter thinks of Genesis 15 and the animals God cut in half when he cut his covenant with Abraham. Multiple bodies, that is, animals, are mentioned here, almost necessitating a reference to ancient covenant making. Hebrews 9:16 also reads: "For where there is a covenant, it is necessary that the one making the covenant be brought out" (or "brought forward") again referring to the ancient method of covenant making. Christ has vicariously sacrificed himself for covenant breakers. Verse 17 says that "a covenant is confirmed upon death, since the covenant is not validated while the covenant maker lives," that is, death is required to confirm the covenant.

"Therefore," says v. 18—and note the connective—"not even the first covenant was inaugurated without blood." Even though Exodus 24 is primarily in view, the method of covenant making in ancient times might still inform the writer's perspective. No covenant could be valid until there was the symbolic death of the one making the covenant. Hence, the rich theme of these verses, and we think the right interpretation, sees the entire section as referring to "covenant" rather than to "testament." O Palmer Robertson summarizes:

> The contextual connection of Hebrews 9:16 with the preceding verse lends support to the assumption that "covenantal" not "testamentary" arrangements provide the framework for understanding the writer's arguments. Christ died to redeem from the transgressions committed under the first covenant (v. 15). The death was made necessary because "the death of the covenant-maker" was "brought forward"

The Perfect Sacrifice

at the point of covenantal inauguration (v. 16). By the grace of God, Christ has substituted himself in the place of covenant-violators. He has died in their stead, taking on himself the curses of the covenant.[5]

The Shedding of the Blood: Necessary for the Establishment of the New Covenant

To those doubting or perhaps—in the press of the immediate circumstances—*forgetting* what the writer is saying, he stresses that even the Mosaic covenant required the shedding of blood:

> Therefore not even the first covenant was inaugurated without blood. For when every commandment of the law had been declared by Moses to all the people, he took the blood of calves and goats, with water and scarlet wool and hyssop, and sprinkled both the book itself and all the people, saying, "This is the blood of the covenant that God commanded you." (9:18–20)

This reference to Exodus 24:1–8 demonstrates the necessity of blood to establish the covenant. Indeed, the writer goes on to show that almost everything was sprinkled with blood:

> And in the same way he sprinkled with the blood both the tent and all the vessels used in worship. Indeed, under the law almost everything is purified with blood, and without the shedding of blood there is no forgiveness of sins. (9:21–22)

---

5. O. Palmer Robertson, *The Christ of the Covenants* (Phillipsburg, New Jersey: Presbyterian and Reformed, 1980), 142. On the other hand, K. M. Campbell, "Covenant or Testament? Hebrews 9:16, 17 Reconsidered," *Evangelical Quarterly* 44 (1972), 107–111 argues that the idea of "will" and "covenant" may not be far removed from each other. He shows that from about the sixth century BC, it was customary for the wealthy without issue to adopt a son as heir. The document drawn up was a *diatheke*. From this he argues that similarities between the "covenant" and "will" can be demonstrated. Compare David B. McWilliams, *Galatians: A Mentor Commentary* (Ross-Shire, Scotland: Christian Focus, 2009), 123–125.

The necessity of sacrifice, of shed blood, for the forgiveness of sins was clearly established even in the Old Testament covenant in the Mosaic economy. Indeed, our Lord reflects the very language of Exodus 24 when he established the Supper and referred to his blood as the blood of the covenant (Matt. 26:28). What folly to turn from him whose shed blood establishes our saving relationship with God! What folly to return to the type away from its fulfillment in Christ! In this context, the writer next expounds the perfection of Christ's sacrifice. This is necessary in order to call the wandering Hebrew Christians from the temporary and typical to the permanent and fulfilled covenant in Christ.

The Perfection of Christ's Sacrifice

First, Christ's sacrifice is the basis of his representation of us in heaven. Heaven itself, as we have already observed, is the prototype of which the tabernacle and temple were the copies. If the copies were "purified with blood" (9:22), then the writer draws the line between the copy to the prototype: "Thus it was necessary for the copies of the heavenly things to be purified with these rites, but the heavenly things themselves with better sacrifices than these" (9:23). The plural word "sacrifices" means the one sacrifice of Christ fulfills all of the *sacrifices* of the old system. Here the preacher of Hebrews dwells upon the perfection of the sacrifice of Christ for sin.

> The general principle involved in these words is, plainly, that in expiation the victim must correspond in dignity to the nature of the offenses expiated, and the value of the blessings secured. "The blood of bulls and of goats, and the ashes of an heifer," may expiate ceremonial guilt, and secure external, temporary blessings; but in order to the expiation of

moral guilt, and the attainment of spiritual and eternal blessings, a nobler victim must bleed.[6]

The Tabernacle and Temple, "copies of the heavenly things," were "purified with these rites," that is, rites that required the sprinkling of blood. This was *necessary* in order to drive home the principle of sacrifice, as we read in Leviticus 17:11: "For the life of the flesh is in the blood, and I have given it for you on the altar to make atonement for your souls, for it is the blood that makes atonement by the life." The Tabernacle ritual, however, simply pointed ahead to the greater reality of the value of Christ's shed blood so that "the heavenly things themselves" are purified "with better sacrifices than these" (v. 23). Purifying or cleansing heavenly things is simply a way of saying that the blood of Christ opens the way to God, provides for our approach, and gives us free access.

Heaven itself is set aside, sanctified, in this sense *purified* for "the saint's everlasting rest," to use Baxter's well-known expression. Christ entered heaven itself as our representative. "For Christ has entered, not into holy places made with hands, which are copies of the true things, but into heaven itself, now to appear in the presence of God on our behalf" (9:24). All of the truth of the old covenant purification ritual is fulfilled in Christ, so that now, in our great high priest, we have free and open access into the court of heaven. Only Christ could do this for us, "on our behalf"; we were hopeless to accomplish this on our own.

> The imperfection which attaches to our performances, our pollution and weakness and unbelief, stop with the High Priest. His intercession and atonement cover all defects, and we are faultless and complete in Him. The prayer which reaches the ear of the Almighty is from Him, and not from us, and must be

6. John Brown, *Hebrews* (Edinburgh: Banner of Truth, 1983), 420.

as prevalent as His worth. Here is our confidence, not only that Jesus died, but that Jesus lives—that He is our intercessor in the heavenly sanctuary, and there presents, enforces and sanctifies the religious worship on earth; here is our confidence that in the whole process of salvation God regards the Redeemer and not us, and deals out blessings according to His estimate of Christ.; here is our confidence that if any man sin we have an Advocate with the Father, Jesus Christ the righteous. What an encouragement to prayer and praise![7]

Second, the sacrifice of Christ has put away sin forever. The essential point that the sacrifice of Christ has put away sin forever is established by a glorious contrast between the old and the new.

Nor was it to offer himself repeatedly, as the high priest enters the holy places every year with blood not his own, for then he would have had to suffer repeatedly since the foundation of the world. But as it is, he has appeared once for all at the end of the ages to put away sin by the sacrifice of himself. (9:25–26)

"Once for all" contrasts with the Day of Atonement repeated annually. Christ's one offering of himself dealt with sin forever and it is that finished work that is presented in the court of heaven for his people. Our Savior "once for all at the end of the ages put away sin by the sacrifice of himself"; the center of history is the cross of Christ. The purpose of the cross was that Christ's sacrifice might "put away sin." The debt is paid; he left nothing undone for the salvation of his people. The law could not do this; it showed the need of deliverance but could not save from sin. The law condemns but could not save.

---

7. James Henley Thornwell, *The Collected Writings of James Henley Thornwell* (Edinburgh: Banner of Truth, 1974), 2.284.

The Perfect Sacrifice

Moreover, the ritual of the old economy could only point forward to the sacrifice of Christ "once for all at the end of the ages" (cp. 1:2: "in these last days"). The cross of Christ is the climactic event of redemptive history—so far as the fulfillment of the sacrificial system is concerned—and the beginning of the new covenant era. An exchange was necessary for the sinner's salvation. It is tragic, indeed deadly, that the church in many places and instances no longer stresses penal, substitutionary atonement. Our salvation depends on "the sacrifice of himself" by which "he put away sin" and that "once for all" (v. 26).

Third, Christ's sacrifice secures our favorable verdict with God.

> And just as it is appointed for man to die once, and after that comes judgment, so Christ, having been offered once to bear the sins of many, will appear a second time, not to deal with sin but to save those who are eagerly waiting for him. (9:27–28)

The preacher is drawing an analogy. Man dies once, at his appointed time and the judgment follows, not implying that the Judgment Day is immediately after death but subsequent to death. Christ died once, at the time appointed by the Father at "the end of the ages," and there follows the salvation of his people. Salvation follows because the condemnation requiring the sinner's judgment is dealt with in his penal substitution by which he came to "bear the sins of many."

Christ died only once. The writer is explicit on this: "Christ, having been offered once to bear the sins of many." Salvation from sin is secure. He says in effect to those Hebrew Christians who are beginning to long for the old economy, "You want to go back, back to the inadequacies of the old, back to the repetition and uncertainty, on and on missing the point to which all of the sacrificial system points? Do you not see the superiority of the new? Christ died once for all; it is that finished work that pleads on our behalf. Christ has settled the issue between us and God for all time!" Indeed, the issue is so serious that "to refuse the cross as the instrument of salvation is to choose it as the instrument of judgment."[8] Christ is the suffering Servant who bore the sins of many (Isa. 53:10–12).

The Christian life is like a palimpsest, a papyrus manuscript that has been erased so that a new message might be written on it. Just as the papyrus manuscript has been cleansed of the former writing, the guilt of our sin has been removed. The old has been cleaned away. When we forget the cross, however, we make the Christian life to resemble an opisthograph, a manuscript that still has the writing on both sides of the leaves. Christ died for us; the handwriting that was against us has been removed. The comprehensive word "condemned" has been washed away in Jesus' blood.

"Show me the sinner that can spread his iniquities to the dimensions . . . of this grace,"[9] demands John Owen. On one occasion, I was counseling a believer who was struggling to believe fully that his sins were forgiven. I took him out of my study, had him look up at the sky, and cited Psalm 103:11, saying with some force: "For as high as the heavens are above the earth, so great is his steadfast love toward those who fear him; as far as the east is from the west, so far does he remove our transgressions from us." "Look," I said to my needy friend, "how far is East from West, can you tell? That is what the blood of Christ has done for us sinners."

---

8. Philip E. Hughes, *Hebrews,* 388.

9. John Owen, *The Works of John Owen* (Edinburgh: Banner of Truth, 1980), 2.62.

Waiting for His Coming

The text is comprehensive on the sinner's need and on the Lord's salvation of his people. Having pressed home the efficacious sacrifice of Christ, the power of his blood to remove sin, the necessity of the shed blood of Christ for establishing the new covenant and the perfection of Christ's sacrifice as the basis of our Lord's representation of us in heaven, the writer now turns our attention to the future, certain return of Christ from heaven:

> And just as it is appointed for man to die once, and after that comes judgment, so Christ, having been offered once to bear the sins of many, will appear a second time, not to deal with sin but to save those who are eagerly waiting for him.

How glad it made the old covenant people when, after making sacrifice for atonement, the high priest would emerge from the Tabernacle having accomplished his task, his presence evincing that the sacrifice had been accepted. Christ has shed his blood "having been offered once to bear the sins of many" (Isa. 53:12) and has now taken the efficacy of his atoning work before the Father on our behalf as our great intercessor. He will emerge from the heavenly precincts and with what joy shall his people greet him on the day of his coming. Jesus died; Jesus rose, ascended, and intercedes; Jesus will return.

Jesus came the first time to bear our sins; he will return to receive his reward. Jesus came the first time bowing under the awful burden of the cross; when he returns all the world will bow to him. He came at first to inaugurate the new covenant; he will return to consummate the new covenant. He came the first time as the man of sorrows; he comes again to laugh with his people in triumph. No wonder the writer speaks of his people "eagerly waiting for him." Only those who know that their sins are forgiven through Jesus' blood could possibly be eagerly expecting the return of Christ.

The writer teaches us about three essential appearances of Jesus. Jesus "appeared once for all at the end of the ages to put away sin by the sacrifice of himself" (v. 26). On the basis of that once for all accomplishment our Lord has entered heaven itself "now to appear in the presence of God on our behalf" (v. 24). Then, at the last day our great intercessor will emerge from heaven and "will appear a second time, not to deal with sin but to save those who are eagerly waiting for him" (v.28).

These three appearances of Christ are three skeins tightly woven into one unbreakable cord. That cord is one of love drawing his people homeward. Do not yearn for the old; the new has come. The work of Christ has purchased for us, his people, an undefiled inheritance ("the promised eternal inheritance," v. 15). Do not grow weary or impatient; persevere in the faith and look for Christ's coming.

16

The Finished Work
of Christ

HEBREWS 10:1–18

---

*And every priest stands daily at his service, offering re-
peatedly the same sacrifices, which can never take away
sins. But when Christ had offered for all time a single
sacrifice for sins, he sat down at the right hand of God,
waiting from that time until his enemies should be made
a footstool for his feet. For by a single offering he has perfected for all time those who are being sanctified.*

It is an old expression; one rarely heard any more: *the finished
work of Christ.* Glorious! "The finished work of Christ" is a
most fitting expression summarizing the writer's purpose in
this section of Hebrews. Here the author sums up his theological argument thus far with inescapable conclusions concerning
Christ and his atonement applied to the recipients' temptation
to apostatize. The menacing shadow of turning back to the old is
dealt a final blow by the writer's insistence on the finished work of
Christ. The preacher's powerful atonement theology is not only
a most fitting conclusion to what the writer has thus far argued,
but the once for all sacrifice of Christ is singled out as the mortal

blow to any temptation to turn back to the old. Once a person has understood what Christ accomplished, how could that person turn back to the partial shadows of Levitical law?

Inadequacy of the Old Sacrificial System

In the first ten verses of this chapter, the author of Hebrews glories in the finished work of Christ as over against the inadequacy of the old sacrificial system. He states five reasons for the inadequacy of the old system, so that he may put forward the glory of the final atonement accomplished by Christ.

First, the old sacrificial system was inadequate because it demanded repetition.

> For since the law has but a shadow of the good things to come instead of the true form of these realities, it can never, by the same sacrifices that are continually offered every year, make perfect those who draw near. (10:1)

Indeed, the old showed forth important truths. The old demonstrated that sin between God and man must be removed and reconciliation must be accomplished by another. The Levitical system demonstrated the necessity of expiation for sin and established that forgiveness can come only through sacrifice— all of these essential truths were clearly demonstrated by the sacrificial system ordained by God in the Old Testament. Still, the Levitical system was but an outline of the truth, a shadow of the reality to which it pointed. No animal sacrifice could ultimately redeem sinners. Moreover, the annual sacrifice on the Day of Atonement demonstrated its inadequacy. These annual sacrifices could not truly redeem (make perfect) "those who draw near."

Second, the old sacrificial system was inadequate because it could not remove the guilt of sin. Hence follows the rhetorical question of verse 2: "Otherwise, would they not have ceased to be offered, since the worshipers, having once been cleansed, would no longer have any consciousness of sin?" Of course, the sacrifice would not have been repeated annually if the sin had been removed by those sacrifices. The sacrifices pointed ahead to the need of the one, final sacrifice of Christ, fully efficacious for the removal of sin. The old system could point to this but could provide no assurance of pardon; additional sin called for ongoing annual sacrifice.

Third, the old sacrificial system was inadequate because it constantly reminded the worshipers of guilt. But in these sacrifices there is a reminder of sin every year. For it is impossible for the blood of bulls and goats to take away sins (10:3–4). The remembrance of sin was intensified year by year as the sacrifices were repeated. They could not bring permanent peace of conscience or an absolute erasure of sin from the Divine record. The moral and legal impossibility of the blood of bulls and goats to accomplish redemption brought with it the constant and ongoing reminder of guilt. Indeed, the believer today, with the congregation of the Lord, gratefully remembers the sacrifice of Christ, but the remembrance is not of sin unexpiated but of the once for all sacrifice that has removed our guilt.

> Not all the blood of beasts
> on Jewish altars slain,
> could give the guilty conscience peace
> or wash away the stain
> But Christ, the heav'nly Lamb,
> takes all our sins away,
> a sacrifice of nobler name,
> and richer blood than they.[1]

---

1. Isaac Watts, "Not All the Blood of Beasts," from *Trinity Hymnal*, rev. ed., (Suwanee, GA: Great Commission Publications, 1990), selection 242.

Fourth, the inadequacy of the old sacrificial system is shown by Scripture. The writer of Hebrews has Jesus quoting Psalm 40, in which we read of the sacrifice that could indeed take away sin. Having affirmed that "it is impossible for the blood of bulls and goats to take away sins" (10:4), the writer goes on to contrast the true sacrifice of Jesus that can and does take away sin:

> Consequently, when Christ came into the world, he said,
>
> "Sacrifices and offerings you have not desired,
>   but a body have you prepared for me;
>   in burnt offerings and sin offerings
>   you have taken no pleasure.
> Then I said,
>   'Behold, I have come to do your will, O God,
>   as it is written of me
>   in the scroll of the book.'"

In order to perform God's plan to save his people from their sins, the Eternal Son of God "came into the world" and required a body so that he might assume human nature as the perfect man, free from sin, whose obedience and blood could take away sin:

> When he said above, "You have neither desired nor taken pleasure in sacrifices and offerings and burnt offerings and sin offerings" (these are offered according to the law), then he added, "Behold, I have come to do your will." He abolishes the first in order to establish the second. (10:8–9)

God wants heartfelt devotion and the total, unmixed devotion he received from his Son coming into the world to achieve our redemption. Hence, our Lord could provide a sacrifice, full, perfect and sufficient, that was acceptable to God. In his incarnation, obedient life, and sacrificial death our Savior achieved our redemption.

As Edwards points out in his marvelous sermon on Psalm 40:

> Though Christ's sufferings were but temporal, yet they were equivalent to our eternal sufferings by reason of the infinite dignity of his person. Though it was no infinite suffering, yet it was equivalent to infinite suffering, for it was infinitely expensive . . .
>
> [Christ's sacrifice] was a most glorious act of obedience because it was so expensive. Christ therein showed an infinite respect to God's commands, in that he would obey it at such infinite expense. And it was therefore meritorious because Christ was not obliged to it: he was not obliged to appear in the form of a servant in such a manner to obey God. It is an act of obedience of infinite value in God's account, and a price sufficient to purchase all those eternal blessings which are promised in the gospel to believers.[2]

Fifth, the inadequacy of the old sacrificial system was shown by Christ's replacement of the former system. Had the old been adequate, would there have been need for the new? Through Christ's active and passive obedience, as shown from Psalm 40, "he does away with the first in order to establish the second" (v. 9). The Lord came to take away the first, to abolish the old, fulfill the types, and to establish the second and final order. "He does away with the first" by the once for all character of the atonement: "And by that will we have been sanctified through the offering of the body of Jesus Christ once for all" (v. 10). The sanctification spoken of here is being set apart as the purchased possession of the redeemer by means of his active and passive

---

2. Jonathan Edwards, *The Sacrifice of Christ Acceptable* in *The Works of Jonathan Edwards* 14 (New Haven, CT: Yale, 1997), 452–453; 454–455.

obedience. "The offering of the body of Jesus Christ once for all" stresses again the unrepeatable character of Christ's sacrifice.

The writer of Hebrews has stressed the once for all character of Jesus' work explicitly in 7:27, 9:26, and 10:10–14 in order to contrast the finished work of Christ and the newness of the new covenant, over against the temporary nature of the old and its ineffectual, temporary status. Christ's sacrifice brings the perfection to which the Old Testament sacrifices could only point. The perfect sacrifice demands the cessation of the imperfect; the institution of Christ's high priestly office brings to an end the Levitical priesthood. "He has no need, like those high priests, to offer sacrifices daily, first for his own sins and then for those of the people, since he did this once for all when he offered up himself" (Heb. 7:27).

Before transitioning to the culminating themes of this section of Hebrews, we do well to underscore the fact that the writer of Hebrews understands what "modern man," with his humanistic rebellion, and self love does not, namely, that there is real guilt that must be dealt with by the atonement if we are to be saved from sin. We may suppress the truth of this guilt, dress it up, call it by other names, say that it is just a bad feeling, or attempt to massage it by "therapy" or religious observances, but judgment is written on the fallen human heart and, most importantly, is revealed in the sacred Scriptures. God has holy wrath against sin. If it is not dealt with, we will perish and remain guilty forever.

How is guilt removed? How may we have clean consciences before God? The Bible's answer, the answer of Hebrews is clear: through the finished work of Christ. Christ's obedience and sacrifice were real, penal, substitutionary punishment in the place of sinners. Were this not so, then the sins of sinners had not been properly punished and we could not be saved from sin. Sin cannot be remitted without punishment; justice must be satisfied. By the strange, marvelous grace of God the iniquity of God's people was laid on Jesus and now no guilt is upon the true believer in Jesus. Hence Christ was "offered once to bear the sins of many" (Heb. 9:28).

Christ actually bore our sins to remove them. This is the newness of the new covenant in its very heart. The sins of believers are blotted out by the shed blood of Christ. This is the *offense of the cross* to be borne by the people of God, but this offense is a badge of glory, for it is delightful to bear the reproach of the One who bore our sins. Let the world scoff and mock; those saved by sovereign free grace rejoice.

The Efficacy of Christ's Self Offering

What follows in Hebrews is not only related to the preceding, necessarily and immediately, but it also powerfully draws out the saving significance of Hebrews 1:3: "He is the radiance of the glory of God and the exact imprint of his nature, and he upholds the universe by the word of his power. After making purification for sins, he sat down at the right hand of the Majesty on high." Here the writer works out the saving performance of Christ our great high priest and speaks of the efficacy of his once for all offering for sin. He shows this in several ways.

First, the efficacy of Christ's sacrifice is demonstrated by his exaltation:

> And every priest stands daily at his service, offering repeatedly the same sacrifices, which can never take away sins. But when Christ had offered for all time a single sacrifice for sins, he sat down at the right hand of God, waiting from that time until his enemies should be made a footstool for his feet. (10:11–13)

The high priest under the Levitical law could not sanctify the people "offering repeatedly the same sacrifices which could never take away sins." What was needed was that to which the repeated sacrifices pointed in God's plan of salvation—the sacrifice of Christ that could take away sins forever. The Old Testament priest "stands daily" and offers repeatedly (*pollakis*) an ineffectual sacrifice; Jesus our high priest "offered for all time a single sacrifice for sins" after which "he sat down at the right hand of God." Standing is expressive of a never finished sacrifice. Now, Christ has come and has brought a radical change with his sacrifice.

Christ sacrificed himself once and for all time in a single finished and complete sacrifice of consummate and absolute worth. In the cross, guilt truly and finally receives its death blow. The Son sits now, which guarantees that his work was done and his sacrifice was accepted for our sins. Bunyan took heart from this: "Sinner, thou thinkest that because of thy sins . . . I cannot save Thy soul, but behold my Son is by me, and upon him I look, and not on thee, and will deal with thee according as I am pleased with him."[3]

There he sits, our great high priest; his once for all sacrifice is completely accepted of the Father, and while sitting also "waiting from that time until his enemies should be made a footstool for his feet." The writer of Hebrews, applying Psalm 110:1, lifts our eyes to the future triumph of Christ as a sure result of his victorious conquering of sin for his people.

> If therefore our faith looks for Christ sitting on the right hand of God, and rests quietly in that truth, we shall at the end enjoy the fruits of this victory along with Him who is our Head, and, when our foes are vanquished along with Satan and sin and death and the whole world and when we have put off the corruption of our flesh, we shall triumph.[4]

3. John Bunyan, *Grace Abounding to The Chief of Sinners*, in *Works of John Bunyan* (Grand Rapids: Baker, 1977), 1.39, paragraph 258, also cited by F. F. Bruce, *Hebrews* (Grand Rapids: 1979), 240.

4. John Calvin, *Hebrews* (Grand Rapids: Eerdmans, 1979), 138.

The Finished Work of Christ

Second, the efficacy of Christ's sacrifice is demonstrated in that it is sufficient for all time. "For by a single offering he has perfected for all time those who are being sanctified" (10:14). Why can Jesus sit at the Father's right hand? Jesus can sit at the Father's right hand because he was successful. Unlike the priestly work of the Levitical law requiring sacrifice upon sacrifice, Christ "by a single offering" accomplished his work. Bruce has rightly pointed out that "we have been sanctified" is in the perfect tense in verse 10, stressing the unrepeatable work of the Savior, but in verse 14, the present participle is used ("are being sanctified") "indicating in timeless terms" the character of the people of God set apart by the sacrifice of Christ. "Emphasis is now laid on the fact that by the same sacrifice Christ has eternally 'perfected' His holy people." Bruce adds:

> Three outstanding effects are thus ascribed to the sacrifice of Christ: by it His people have had their conscience cleansed from guilt; by it they have been fitted to approach God as accepted worshippers; by it they have experienced the fulfillment of what was promised in earlier days, being brought into that perfect relation to God which is involved in the new covenant.[5]

Christ's "single offering" is efficacious "for all time." There will never be another sacrifice for sin and never will the people of God be placed in double jeopardy due to their sad failings. Once, I read an account of John Rippon, the eighteenth-century Baptist Calvinist minister, who had obtained a pardon for a young man related to his congregation. Then, on the eve of what was to have been his execution, the Pastor learned that the pardon had not reached the executioners! He rode all night, obtained an audience with the King in his bed chamber, and took from his gracious hands the pardon of the King. He then rode as fast as possible, arriving just in time to keep the young

5. F. F. Bruce, *Hebrews*, 241.

man from execution. Though Rippon had the King's pardon in hand, it all depended on his swift action to save the man. His effort almost failed. His effort could have failed. The atonement of Jesus is not like that. Having received the pardon of the King, there will be no "almost salvation" for God's elect. The condemnation was real; the justification is real. Christ's atonement will not leave his people in their condemned state but has achieved a sufficient atonement for our sins "for all time."

Third, the efficacy of Christ's sacrifice is shown by the removal of our sins.

> And the Holy Spirit also bears witness to us; for after saying,
>
> > "This is the covenant that
> > I will make with them
> > after those days, declares the Lord:
> > I will put my laws on their hearts,
> > and write them on their minds,"
>
> then he adds, "I will remember their sins and their lawless deeds no more." (10:15–17)

The writer cites Jeremiah 31:33 to demonstrate that Christ's blood has the power to carry out the requirements for establishing the new covenant and to give assurance that our sins and iniquities are blotted out, removed from God's record—never, never, to be brought into God's court against us. The Day of Atonement was an annual remembrance of sins with repeated offerings. Now those sins are erased irrevocably in Jesus' blood. Not *some* of the sins of God's people, not *a little* of sin, not *a few* sins, not even *most* sins—*all* our sins are eradicated in the sacrifice of Christ (Isa. 43:25; 44:22; Ps. 103:10–12; Mic. 7:18ff). God has no thought to condemn a believer in Jesus whose "hope is built on nothing less than Jesus' blood and righteousness." Suppose you owed great debts that you could never pay. Then a loving man, knowing of your debts, goes to your creditors saying, "I will pay all his debts. I will stand surety for my friend." Then the ledger is wiped clean; your debts have been paid in full. The friend of sinners has done this for his people.

The incalculable greatness of the debt paid by God's own Son who shed his blood is underscored when we think about the infinite debt we owed. I recall long ago reading an essay by Augustus Toplady entitled *The National Debt*. England at that time knew something of the greatness of national debt, just as most countries do today. However, the national debt Toplady had in mind was not the financial debt of England but the incalculable sins of the nation. Adding up the sins that might be committed by sinners in a lifetime, Toplady showed how astronomical they might be. But we do not need to do that. One sin against the holy God is deserving of God's infinite displeasure. Only the blood of Christ can blot out our transgressions.

Finally, the efficacy of Christ's atonement is shown in the finality of his sacrifice: "Where there is forgiveness of these, there is no longer any offering for sin" (10:18). Eternal redemption, unrestricted access to the worship of the living God, and freedom from guilt have been accomplished by Jesus. No work of ours contributes to his once for all achievement. The work of redemption is done, "It is finished," the veil is rent, and his atonement never fails in its power and application to the needs of the sinners for whom it was intended.

Perhaps someone is reading this who has been struggling with that essential question: "How can I be saved from my sin?" The answer: no work of your own can save you, but you can be saved by simple trust in Christ who has accomplished redemption for sinners by the sacrifice of himself on the cross. The answer is found only in the finished work of Christ. Are you willing to receive Christ and with him all the benefits of redemption?

"My will is bound; how can I come to Christ since my heart is so sinful?" If you are learning that, you are taught by God's Spirit. Only those who are regenerated by the Spirit of God can know that they are sinners deserving of God's displeasure. Heart-knowledge of our hell-deservedness is a necessary component of the faith that receives Christ.

My friend, hear this good news. Such is the finished work of Christ that he has even purchased the faith with which his people trust him. The Lord has not said in essence "I purchased salvation for them but I leave it to each one to take salvation by faith." What faith? What faith does a sinner dead in trespasses and sins possess? No, rather the Lord has done it all. On the cross, Christ purchased our salvation and also determined to give the gift of faith with which to believe in him. So sufficient is the cross of Christ!

Let me paraphrase an illustration of an old divine.[6] A man approaches a dungeon. The imprisoned one languishes helplessly in prison. The man comes to the prisoner saying, "I have gold sufficient to save you if you will just free yourself from your chains, burst open your prison doors and come forth!" "Alas!" the prisoner responds, "You can do nothing to help me then. For I cannot free myself so that your redemption money will do me good."

The illustration is well done. The gospel does not proclaim, "Free yourself and break your chains, then the blood of Christ will redeem you." The gospel proclaims: "Poor, chained sinner. There you are helpless. The cross of Christ is the battering ram that will break down the prison walls, snap your chains, and set you free!"

Believe on Christ and you will be saved. Do you feel your inability? The good news of the gospel proclaims that even the

---

6. William Rushton, *A Defense of Particular Redemption* (NY: Joseph Spencer, 1834), 34–35.

faith with which to embrace Jesus as Savior is the fruit of the cross. The Lord Jesus was given "as a covenant for the people, a light for the nations, to open the eyes that are blind, to bring out the prisoners from the dungeon, from the prison those who sit in darkness" (Isa. 42:6–7).

There he sits. Our Lord Jesus Christ reigns at the Father's right hand. His work is done. Once he hung upon a cross in bloody agony but now he wields the royal scepter in sovereign authority as the risen, ascended king-priest of his people. From there he applies his blood in sovereign mercy to his own.

17

Through the Veil

HEBREWS 10:19–25

---

*Therefore, brothers, since we have confidence to en-
ter the holy places by the blood of Jesus, by the new
and living way that he opened for us through the curtain, that is, through his flesh, and since we have a
great priest over the house of God, let us draw near
with a true heart in full assurance of faith, with our
hearts sprinkled clean from an evil conscience and
our bodies washed with pure water. Let us hold fast
the confession of our hope without wavering, for he
who promised is faithful. And let us consider how to
stir up one another to love and good works, not neglecting to meet together, as is the habit of some, but
encouraging one another, and all the more as you
see the Day drawing near.*

This section brings together what Christ has done for us with
our responsibilty to "hold fast the confession of our hope
without wavering." One of my prayers in expositing Hebrews is
that someone who may once have been commited to the Bible's
teaching on its inspiration and authority, and Hebrew's teaching on the atonement and intercession of Christ, but is now

wavering, will be called back. I well remember my undergraduate days in a University that taught "Christianity," but the Christianity taught there was not that of Biblical orthodoxy. I appreciate completely the words of C. H. Spurgeon on this theme:

> We are told today that this is an age of progress, and therefore we must accept an improved gospel. . . . We want no new gospel, no modern salvation. . . . To talk of improving upon our perfect Saviour is to insult him. He is God's propitiation; what would you more? My blood boils with indignation at the idea of improving the gospel. There is but one Saviour, and that one Saviour is the same for ever. His doctrine is the same in every age, and is not yea and nay. . . . We stand fast by the unaltered, unalterable, eternal name of Jesus Christ our Lord.[1]

Having just concluded the powerful presentation on the full, final, and efficacious sacrifice of Christ our great high priest, the writer of Hebrews now points to a grand implication of that truth. In view of what Christ has done believers have free access to the Lord. He encourages believers to make use of that access and to apply the truth that he has preached. The New Testament stresses the connection between theology and action, truth and life, and this passage presents no exception. Truth is to inform all of life. The writer now brings three exhortations to the tempted, tried Hebrew Christians. The first exhortation is to draw near to God through Christ's sacrifice.

Let Us Draw Near

"Therefore, brothers . . . let us draw near" (10:19, 22). On the basis of the once for all, sufficient atonement of Christ believers are exhorted to "draw near" to the Lord. Given the context, "draw near" is almost certainly priestly language as when Moses

---

1. C. H. Spurgeon, *Metropolitan Tabernacle Pulpit*, 34.80–81.

said to Aaron: "Draw near to the altar and offer your sin offering and your burnt offering and make atonement for yourself and the people..." (Lev. 9:7). Now, through the one sacrifice of Christ, God's people are a "kingdom of priests" (Exod. 19:6; 1 Pet. 2:9) and are privileged to "draw near" on the basis of Jesus' blood.

Draw Near With Confidence

Believers, "since we have confidence to enter the holy places by the blood of Jesus" (v. 19), are exhorted to "draw near" (v. 22). Note that the preacher does not stress the subjective feeling of confidence; rather, he stresses the objective reality of the believer's confidence. Freedom of access into the presence of God is given with the blood of Christ and is not removed by moods (4:16). The writer specifically states that on the basis of the finished work of Christ ("therefore," v. 19) "we have confidence." Freedom of access is grounded in Jesus' priestly work.

Certainly how the believer feels should be influenced positively by this reality. However, even if the believer does not feel bold and confident, his moods do not change the reality. "We have confidence" just as John reminds us "we have an advocate with the Father, Jesus Christ the righteous" (1 John 2:1). We did not gain access to God through any supposed merits of our own but by the blood of Jesus; therefore, on the basis of his self-sacrifice we have and continue to have access to God. In striking contrast to the exclusion of God's people from the Holy of Holies except through the Representative, Christ has now entered into the Father's presence, and we confidently follow having entrance "by the blood of Jesus."

Draw Near Through the Veil

By means of Jesus' blood, we enter into the presence of the just and holy God, that is "by the new and living way that he opened for us through the curtain, that is, through his flesh" (v. 20).

"The new and living way" contrasts with the old structure, the Tabernacle and its furnishings, the sacrifices of bulls and goats. There is a "new and living way" that now corresponds to the newness of the new covenant. "In speaking of a new covenant, he makes the first one obsolete" (8:13). Indeed, a "living way" is open because Christ is our living Lord. This "new and living way" is described to us as access as over against the forbidding curtain of the Tabernacle and Temple.

The inner veil of the Tabernacle separated the Holy Place from the Most Holy Place which was off limits to all but the high priest who entered on the Day of Atonement once per year (Lev. 16). When Christ shed his blood and finished his work of atonement, the veil was rent in two from top to bottom (Matt. 27:51). The way is now open though Christ's flesh, the true veil, that is, through his sacrifice. Christ "suffered for sins once, the righteous for the unrighteous, that he might bring us to God" (1 Pet. 3:18). All barriers have been removed; the "no entrance" sign has been taken down. "This was according to the eternal purpose that he has realized in Christ Jesus our Lord, in whom we have boldness and access with confidence through faith in him" (Eph. 3:12). In a monarchial nation, one might be filled with a sense of dread at the thought of entering the King's palace, but if we were befriended by the Prince of the realm and he led us in, we could enter with reverent boldness. Such Jesus has done for his people.

Draw Near Through Christ's Priesthood

We draw near "since we have a great high priest over the house of God" (v. 21). In verse 19 the writer preached that "we have confidence to enter"; now, he makes plain that we have this confidence because "we have a great high priest." He reminds us of themes traceable to the third chapter, Christ our priest "over the house of God," the new Temple of God's building and perhaps also an allusion to the true Tabernacle above (10:19 along with 6:16; 7:25; 8:1,2; 9:24). Here we have a reminder of the central theme of Hebrews as summarized in 8:1–2: "Now the point in what we are saying is this: we have such a high priest, one who is seated at the right hand of the throne of the Majesty in heaven, a minister in the holy places, in the true tent that the Lord set up, not man."

The ground of our confidence is our compassionate, glorified high priest who died for us and ascended on high in regal splendor to reign. Given our free and full access through Jesus our great high priest, it is no wonder, as Owen somewhere noted, that there is no office of Christ that Satan labors so hard to obscure and overthrow as his priestly one.

Let Us Draw Near

On the basis of these realities, the writer urges believers "let us draw near with a true heart in full assurance of faith, with our hearts sprinkled clean from an evil conscience and our bodies washed with pure water" (v. 23). The access is not fenced but is open for us so that with fully assured faith in God's promises believers may come. To have "a true heart" is to have a believing heart (11:6). It is worthy of notice that the book of Hebrews with all its warnings about apostasy was not written to discourage but rather to encourage assurance. Indeed, what are the warnings for if not to bring the people of God to trust in the promises of God alone? Christians are exhorted to come "in full assurance of faith" meaning hearts fully assured that Christ who died for them, who intercedes for them, has made the way open for them to the presence of God.

The writer enlarges upon this full assurance by speaking of our coming "with our hearts sprinkled clean from an evil conscience and our bodies washed with pure water" which is a reference to the cleansing of the soul by the blood of Christ and the renewing grace of the Holy Spirit, evoking Old Testament ritual and promise (e.g. Lev. 16:4, 14–16; Ezek. 36:25–26). The writer has already alluded to this in 9:13–14:

> For if the sprinkling of defiled persons with the blood of goats and bulls and with the ashes of an heifer sanctifies for the purification of the flesh, how much more will the blood of Christ, who through the eternal Spirit offered himself without blemish to God, purify our conscience from dead works to serve the living God.

Since by the Spirit's work, we have come to know that God is holy and that we are defiled by sin and in need of the cleansing blood of Christ, how could we think of coming in any other way? To come "with our hearts sprinkled clean from an evil conscience" is "to draw near to God as the God of peace."[2]

How important it is for believers to apply these truths to our inner moods and feelings that might hinder our prayers. With this gospel preached to our souls how can we fail to come? Of course I am a sinner, but Christ is righteous and now, clothed in his righteousness, I come boldly to my Father in prayer. James 4:7–8: "Submit yourselves therefore to God. Resist the devil, and he will flee from you. Draw near to God, and he will draw near to you." Indeed, we may draw near because he has drawn near to us in Christ (Eph. 2:11–18). "For through [Christ] we both have access [Jew and Gentile believers] in one Spirit to the Father" (Eph. 2:18).

These wonderful truths constitute an urgent plea to live in the fullness of Christ's work and to come assuredly to the Lord for prayer and communion. Access is purchased for believers. There are two additional exhortations in this section of Hebrews. The next is the exhortation to hold fast.

---

2. John Brown, *Hebrews* (Edinburgh: Banner of Truth, 1983), 461.

Let Us Hold Fast

"Let us hold fast the confession of our hope without wavering, for he who promised is faithful" (v. 23). Building on the triad of faith (22), hope (23) and love (24) this second exhortation calls upon believers to live in hope. The calling of the Hebrew Christians who are tempted to look back and to return to the old is to look forward and to live in the present in light of God's promises for the future of his people. That is what hope is all about; living in the present on the basis of the future promises of God. Holding fast is not works righteousness but is living upon the promises of God. Calvin put it well: "Just as hope is the child of faith, so it is fed and sustained by faith to the end. Moreover, he demands confession because there is no true faith that does not show itself to man."[3] Living in hope is based on the faithfulness of God to his promises; here we base our very lives upon the sure foundation that "he who promised is faithful."

Perhaps the best commentary on this text is what the Lord revealed in 1 Peter 1:3ff. The hope to which we have been born through God's sovereign grace lives on the promise of "an inheritance that is imperishable, undefiled, and unfading, kept in heaven for you, who by God's power are being guarded through faith for a salvation ready to be revealed in the last time." Indeed, by the promise of God, our inheritance is kept for us and we are kept for our inheritance. As F. F. Bruce said: "Our hope is based on the unfailing promises of God, why should we not cherish it confidently and confess it boldly?"[4]

Sadly, we do not always live confidently and confess boldly. I have read several accounts of the way in which Luther's wife Katherine helped the great Reformer remember God's promises. On one occasion, when Luther was despondent in the midst of the battle for Reforming the church, his depression so gripped

---

3. John Calvin, *Hebrews* (Grand Rapids: Eerdmans, 1979), 142.

4. F. F. Bruce, *Hebrews* (Grand Rapids: Eerdmans, 1979), 252.

him that he was sullen and non-communicative. Katie put on the black of mourning and walked about until her depressed husband noticed. "Katie, who died?" he asked. "God died," she answered. Receiving from Martin a shocked reply, Katie responded to the effect, "Well, you are acting as if God died." This jolted Martin Luther from the doldrums and renewed his sagging faith. Now that is quite the point. The promises of God are sure and certain. We who believe have an assured faith by which we may draw near through our great high priest. "Let us hold fast the confession of our hope without wavering, for he who promised is faithful."

Oh, how the church needs to remember this exhortation! Spurgeon's words in his day are imminently applicable to our own:

> There came a day when our dissenting churches almost went round to Socinianism, and then their chapels were empty, and their day of power was gone. Earnest men rose up and preached the old gospel again, and there was a grand revival. Now they are gone off again, turning every man to his own error, save that the Lord has a faithful company that hold fast the faith, and will not let it go, and these will live to see a great revulsion of feeling yet. If they do not, that is a small matter to them; to be faithful to their God is their first and their great business.[5]

By way of application, holding fast our confession should underscore the necessity of confessionalism in the church. The Bible contains a discernible system of doctrine and—for the Presbyterian Church in America, of which I am a member, as well as other Presbyterian bodies—that system is presented clearly

---

5. Charles Haddon Spurgeon, "Holding Fast Our Profession," in *Metropolitan Tabernacle Pulpit* (Pasadena, TX: Pilgrim Publications, 1986), 32.238. Socinianism was a denial of the Trinity, the Deity of Christ, of original sin, and all gospel doctrine. Unitarianism is closely equivalent.

in the Westminster Confession. In addition to witnessing before the world through an outright and human confession, the church depends on its ministers to subscribe so as to ensure a faithful succession of ministers. When we are half-hearted in confessing our faith, reserved in our subscription, or when we allow erosion of some part of what we confess to be the system of doctrine contained within the Scriptures, then we are not honest as ministers and we begin to open the church to gradual apostasy.

Becoming indifferent, for example, to the issue of evolution can lead to a denial of Adam, which in turn will lead to a denial of the atonement of the last Adam. Commitment to the seamless garment of truth can begin to unravel as a church becomes indifferent to matters that some may consider to be of only fringe importance. If the Confessional churches actually held to their confessions, despite their differences, the cause of truth overall would be fostered as well as greater unity in the body of Christ.

Let Us Consider One Another

Consider One Another

We are called to walk faithfully and in dependence on the promises of God. However, we are not called to do so alone but in the bonds of communion found in the church of the Lord Jesus Christ. Having mentioned confessionalism as an application of the theme of this text, we here see all the more reason for it. Confessionalism enhances the bond of communion found among believers. Therefore, the following exhortation naturally follows: "And let us consider how to stir up one another to love and good works" (v. 24). The people of God will live confidently when we are living together as fellow believers with constant reminders of our calling. Faith flourishes when believers think, act and serve together and admonish one another to remember service and self sacrifice for the cause of Christ.

Meet Together

This is why the writer adds: "not neglecting to meet together, as is the habit of some, but encouraging one another." How essential it is to be faithful in the local Christian fellowship if we are to learn to live upon the promises of God. It may be that out of fear of persecution some were forsaking the assembly of believers. Whatever the reason, the writer found it necessary, as we do also today, to exhort professing believers to put heart and soul into the corporate worship of God and the communion of the saints. We need this lesson deeply applied today. The Lord has promised certainly to keep his true people; none for whom Christ died will perish. However, the Lord keeps his true people through means.

What are those means? The Holy Spirit applies Word, sacrament, prayer, and the worship of the Triune God in the fellowship of God's people. There is nothing magical about it; nothing esoteric and certainly nothing "spectacular" as the world counts excitement. No, the Lord would have his people submit to the simple means of his own appointment for their growth in grace and perseverance in the faith. Thus "encouraging one another" happens in the way of God's appointment and living upon the promise of God's faithfulness will grow when we are deeply committed to the communion of the saints. Let no reader of this comment think that he can grow without the means of God's appointment. Hear the exhortation: Do not forsake the means; get deeply involved with the true people of God and do not simply live on the fringe of the church.

Rather than forsaking the communion of the saints, "encourage one another." Look around you when you are next in worship. See that person over there? He needs your encouragement, she needs a kind word, that one needs your active help. When we are so involved with one another, the ethos of the church will be good, we will not become isolated by self indulgence and fear, and the body of Christ will thrive. Do not wait for others; you obey from the heart. Indeed, live this way "all the more as you see the Day drawing near" (v. 25).

Live in View of Christ's Coming

The New Testament is pervaded with this eschatological motivation. "We should continually expect His second revelation and think of each day as though it were the last."[6] Do not let the knowledge that you live in the end time weaken. Where this reality, the return of Christ, is the absorbing consideration, we walk differently, faithfully, carefully, lovingly, helpfully, and hopefully. Paul also tells us to be alert and aware of the time between the ascension and coming of the Lord and calls us to wake up from our slumber. Thoughts of Christ's coming serve as alarm clocks every time we slumber in the presence of sin and self centeredness. So Paul says, "Besides this you know the time, that the hour has come for you to wake from sleep. For salvation is nearer to us now than we first believed" (Rom. 13:11).

The history of redemption is like a book. The body of the book includes the cross, resurrection, and ascension of Christ; the conclusion of the book is being written between Christ's ascension and return. The supremely important events of history are already accomplished but one: the return of Christ. Upon this we are called to keep our focus. This is the meaning of 1 Peter 4:7, "the end of all things is near." In Romans 13 the apostle demonstrates how such living leads to chastity and leads us to put on our day clothes, the "armor of light." Living in the epilogue of God's masterpiece, waiting for the last page to turn, keeps the people of God living for that day in which we will cast

---

6. John Calvin, *Hebrews*, 145.

our crowns before his feet. This is being so heavenly-minded that we truly become of some earthly good.

Similarly, Peter calls us to think upon the end of the age and the return of our Lord saying, "What manner of people ought you to be in lives of holiness and godliness, waiting for and hastening the coming of the day of God, because of which the heavens will be set on fire and dissolved, and the heavenly bodies will melt as they burn!" (2 Pet. 3:11–12). If we are longing for a world in which righteousness dwells (2 Pet. 3:13), does not ungodly living contradict it? Constantly the New Testament calls upon believers to live with these realities in the forefront of our thoughts. "Beloved," writes John in his first epistle, "we are God's children now, and what will be has not yet appeared; but we know that when he appears we shall be like him, because we shall see him as he is" (1 John 3:2–3).

The writer of Hebrews has already pointed to this theme in 9:28: "So Christ, having been offered once to bear the sins of many, will appear a second time, not to deal with sin but to save those who are eagerly waiting for him." Does the reality of the promise of Christ's coming control your life so that you are "encouraging one another, and all the more as you see the Day drawing near?" This keeps our feet grounded in the reality of God's objective work in history and makes our lives of faith flourish in the reality of the certainty of God's promise. This in turn frees us to think of others as we, the pilgrim people of God, move on to our final destination. Otherwise, we are drawn away from Christ as were the professing Christians addressed in Hebrews.

Schilder's illustration of the age in which we live is impressive.[7] To paraphrase his vivid image, the arch of God's judgment spans this age like a dome. This dome is upheld and buttressed

---

7. As found in Rudolf Van Reest, *Schilder's Struggle for the Unity of the Church* (Alberta: Inheritance Publications, 1990), 123–124.

by a column, the preaching of the Word. One of these days, in God's appointment, the last sermon will be preached and the last of God's elect will be saved. Then, the column of the preaching of the Word will be removed and the dome of God's judgment over this world will collapse. This world exists until the full number of God's elect is completed by the effectual drawing of God's people in grace. Yes, this indeed is true. Until then, the church is to live by faith with that Day in view, "encouraging one another, and all the more as you see the Day drawing near." Guthrie's comment here is worth pondering:

> It is worth noting in the present context that the verb is indicative and records an accomplished reality—*you see*—and is not as the preceding verbs, in the form of an exhortation. The imminence of the day was considered to be plain. It is not to be regarded as secret. Christians were to live as if the dawning of the day was so near that its arrival was only just beyond the horizon.[8]

Every summer when I was a little boy, my father would take our family to one of the "golden isles" on the coast of Georgia. Not understanding the relation of distance and time, I would regularly punctuate the family conversation with the question, "Daddy, are we there yet?" My father was patient indeed as I repeated the question with increased delight and intensity. I anticipated seeing the ocean on the other side of every hill we approached. Finally he was able to say, "Yes, we are there." This is how we should live the Christian life. We should eagerly anticipate the return of Christ, "encouraging one another, all the more as you see the Day drawing near." One day—oh, what a Day!—one day, Christ will come and take us unto himself, and our Father will say to us, "You have arrived."

---

8. Donald Guthrie, *Hebrews* in *The Tyndale New Testament Commentaries* (Grand Rapids: Eerdmans, 1983), 216–217.

18

Call to Perseverance

HEBREWS 10:26–39

Therefore do not throw away your confidence, which has a great reward. For you have need of endurance, so that when you have done the will of God you may receive what is promised.

We come now to the fourth exhortation of Hebrews 10. Here we find perhaps the greatest warning of the entire sermon-epistle. This is a powerful warning against sin that demonstrates once again that the Lord uses warnings to keep his people in the way and to bring us home. Note also that the warning comes in the context of persecution for the faith. Times of persecution can be intense times of temptation. Thomas Brooks warns that, "Some, to deliver themselves from outward tortures, have put themselves under inward torments. He purchases his freedom from affliction at too dear a rate, who buys it with the loss of a good name or a good conscience."[1] The core of his concern, the heart of the call to persevering faith, is found in verse 35: "Therefore do not throw away your confidence, which has a great reward." There are two ways in which the author

---

1. Thomas Brooks, *The Works of Thomas Brooks* (Edinburgh: Banner of Truth, 1980), 1.323.

calls these Hebrew Christians to persevering faith. The first is by means of warning.

Warning Against Apostasy

The warning found here is *awfully* impressive. The writer of Hebrews is not dealing here with the Christian's ongoing struggle or temporary failures. The writer clearly has in mind a determined rejection of Christ and his gospel. In other words, this section is about apostasy. "A [professing] Christian who, knowing what he does know, leaves the worshipping community incurs the penalty of apostasy from Israel and worse."[2]

As a wise pastor, the writer of Hebrews precedes this passage with a section on full assurance of faith (10:19–25) and will follow the warning with teaching on God's faithfulness. The Lord promises to preserve his true children. God's people cannot maintain the walk of faith by their own resources. Daily the true believer finds himself under attack. We are "by God's power . . . guarded through faith for a salvation ready to be revealed in the last time" (1 Pet. 1:5). Through oppression and attack, the true believer learns to lean more on his Lord, to find himself more and more detached from loving this present evil age from which the Lord has delivered him (Gal. 1:4) and to seek another country (Heb. 11:16). The true believer is "sure that neither death nor life, nor angels nor rulers, nor things present nor things to come, nor powers, nor height nor depth, nor anything else in all creation, will be able to separate us from the love of God in Christ Jesus our Lord" (Rom. 8:38–39).

However, seeing that some in the church are not walking faithfully, and evidently persist in a false direction, the preacher who wrote Hebrews did what any faithful pastor must do when he sees persistent rebellion. What is the pastor to do? He is to

---

2. Paul Ellingworth, *The Epistle to the Hebrews* (Grand Rapids: Eerdmans, 1993), 530.

say in essence: "If you continue on this path, you will show yourselves not to be what you profess yourselves to be. I warn you, there is but one gospel and one Savior; turn from him and all is lost." Now this is precisely what we find here. The true believer will heed the warning and turn back to his Lord; the false professor will show himself ultimately to be an apostate. The writer brings to bear on this pastoral need three marks of apostasy:

The first mark of apostasy is rejection of the truth professed:

> For if we go on sinning deliberately after receiving the knowledge of the truth, there no longer remains a sacrifice for sins, but a fearful expectation of judgment, and a fury of fire that will consume the adversaries. Anyone who has set aside the law of Moses dies without mercy on the evidence of two or three witnesses.

Note well the essential place of "the truth" in the Christian life. Apostasy is first of all a rejection of the truth found in the sacred Scriptures. The writer is not talking about isolated sin and failing or of the Christian's daily struggle to make progress in the Christian life (Gal. 6:1; Rom. 7:21–25; 1 John 1:9). He speaks of deliberate sin (the present tense denotes persistent action: "if we go on sinning") that leads to the rejection of God's Son. We should treasure the truth, steep in it, and value it with all our hearts allowing nothing to lead us from it.

This leads to the second mark of apostasy: the rejection of God's Son. This is described in verse 29 as profaning the blood of the covenant, and here in verse 26 as forsaking the only sufficient sacrifice for sin: "there no longer remains a sacrifice for sins." The one who has "profaned the blood of the covenant" (v. 29) treats the blood of Christ as if it has no more value than that of any man. Indeed, he rejects the redemptive accomplishment of Christ outright. Perhaps these professors had come to the Lord's Table up to this point with regularity and had been reminded of "the blood of the covenant" in the church's liturgy, but now they set it aside altogether, desiring instead the old life of Judaism for safety's sake. The writer is not saying that there is no hope for an apostate, for those who fall away after the manner of Peter in his denial; rather, he is saying that a person persisting in unrepentant and true apostasy has set aside the cross of Christ which is the only hope for sinners. If we do not look to the cross, we have forsaken our "only comfort in life and in death." What is that comfort?

> That I am not my own, but belong body and soul, in life and in death—to my faithful Savior Jesus Christ. He has fully paid for my sins with his precious blood, and has set me free from the tyranny of the devil. He also watches over me in such a way that not a hair can fall from my head without the will of my Father in heaven: in fact, all things must work together for my salvation.[3]

The writer wants his readers to ponder a punishment that is worse than that resulting from setting aside God's law. This punishment inevitably results from spurning the cross of Christ: "how much worse punishment, do you think, will be deserved?"

The third mark of apostasy is rejection of "the Spirit of grace." If under the law of Moses, one was guilty on the testimony of two or three witnesses, how much greater will be the condemnation of those who sin against the full revelation of the Son of God?

> Anyone who has set aside the law of Moses dies without mercy on the evidence of two or three witnesses. How much worse punishment, do you think, will be deserved by the one who has trampled underfoot the Son of God, and has profaned the blood

---

3. *Heidelberg Catechism*, Lord's Day 1.

> of the covenant by which he was sanctified, and has
> outraged the Spirit of grace?

To profane the blood of our Lord Jesus who is the Lord of the covenant underscores that sin will destroy our souls and that there is only one Savior and only one sacrifice for sins. To reject the only Savior of sinners is to outrage God's Spirit, and our reading of this should be attended with a due sense of the weight of eternal consequence.

We have already seen how the common operations of the Holy Spirit have been spoken of in Hebrews 6, where the writer says:

> For it is impossible to restore again to repentance
> those who have once been enlightened, who have
> tasted the heavenly gift, and have shared in the Holy
> Spirit, and have tasted the goodness of the word of
> God and the powers of the age to come, if they then
> fall away, since they are crucifying once again the
> Son of God. (6:5–6)

When one rejects the common operations of the Holy Spirit, meets the movement of God's Spirit with contempt, and rejects the Spirit-inspired Scripture—along with its warnings, appeals, and calls—this one "has outraged the Spirit of grace."

What are the consequences of outraging the Spirit of grace, of deliberately sinning after receiving the knowledge of the truth, and of profaning the blood of the covenant? Verse 27 tells us plainly: "a fearful expectation of judgment, and a fury of fire that will consume the adversaries." Verses 28–29 tell us of worse punishment than would befall someone who was convicted of setting aside the law of Moses. Verse 30 adds: "For we know him who said, 'Vengeance is mine; I will repay.' And again, 'The Lord will judge his people.' It is a fearful thing to fall into the hands of the living God."

The one who has "profaned the blood of the covenant by which he was sanctified" was not ever really saved. He is or was a part of the professing people of God, a part of the church in its visibility, and set apart by the blood, in the sense that he is a member of the covenant people of God by his apparent faithfulness up to a point. Oh, how destructive is sin! How the enemy of the souls of men is a liar! What tragedy when professors show themselves not to possess what they have professed! The fire of God will "consume the adversaries," a zealous consumption of the unholy by the Holy God; literally the fire will "eat" them up.

If apostates suffered physical death in the Old Testament, how much greater will the punishment be for those who reject God's Son? How deeper now in view of the revelation of Christ is the judgment of the one who said, "Vengeance is mine; I will repay" and "the Lord will judge his people" (Deut. 32:35–36; Ps. 50:4; 135:14). How deep will be the judgment upon those who reject the fullness of the revelation of the gospel in God's Son, especially having professed his name publicly without a corresponding reality in the soul?

Despite the weak and helpless view of God presented in modern theology, culture, and Arminianism, the text presses upon us the reality of God's justice and judgment: "It is a fearful thing to fall into the hands of the living God." He is "the living God" who is thoroughly capable of carrying out his judgments. The "living God" is Jehovah (Ps. 84:2). Sinners "fall into the hands of the living God," that is, they are incapable of resisting, once he moves to judge. Revelation 6:15–16 speaks of his judgment:

> Then the kings of the earth and the great ones and
> the generals and the rich and the powerful, and ev-
> eryone, slave and free, hid themselves in the caves
> and among the rocks of the mountains, calling to
> the mountains and rocks, "Fall on us and hide us

> from the face of him who is seated on the throne,
> and from the wrath of the Lamb, for the great day of
> their wrath has come, and who can stand?

Consider, however, that the judgment of our text is *even greater*, since it is judgment on those who have sat under the gospel ministry, professed faith in Christ, and have denounced the Redeemer they once confessed publicly. When the final apostate falls under this judgment,

> there will be no end to this exquisite horrible misery.
> When you look forward, you shall see a long forever,
> a boundless duration before you, which will swallow
> up your thoughts, and amaze your soul; and you will
> absolutley despair of ever having any delieverance,
> any end, any mitigation, any rest at all.[4]

Today, universalism (such as contained in Rob Bell's popular book *Love Wins*) and other errors denounce hell, leading to revisions of the atonement and the production of damnable error; but the reality of hell is anchored in God's just and unchangeable nature. In this context, false profession is very serious indeed. We must grasp the fact that dispensing with the doctrine of hell involves dispensing with substitutionary atonement. What is the most basic and fundamental aspect of substitutionary atonement? It is that Christ is the wrath bearer, the propitiation for our sins (Rom. 3:25), or put another way, Christ bore the punishment due to the sins of his people in hell.

Therefore, there is no other sacrifice, no other way for sins to be forgiven, and no other way to God than through the blood of the covenant. Every gospel minister knows that his hearers will spend an eternity in heaven or in hell. Why will you perish? Is there not a sufficient sacrifice for sin? Such is the total de-

---

4. Jonathan Edwards, *Sinners in the Hands of an Angry God*, in *The Works of Jonathan Edwards* (Edinburgh: Banner of Truth, 1974), 11.

pravity of man that it is possible to profess faith in Christ while inwardly hating him. May we heed God's Word, engage the text and be savingly engaged by it.

I cannot cite the source, but I remember hearing an interview with Adolph Coor aired on a radio broadcast some time ago. He told the story of a foggy night in which the captain of a ship noted a large object before him. He signaled, "Change your course 10 degrees west." The reply came: "Change *your* course 10 degrees east." The captain felt insulted and signaled angrily: "I am a captain and have been on the seas for 35 years; change your course 10 degrees west." The signal back: "I am a seaman, fourth class, change 10 degrees east." This was too much for the captain who, knowing a crash was imminent, replied angrily: "I am a 50,000 ton freighter; change your course 10 degrees west now!" The signal back: "I am a lighthouse. Change 10 degrees east now." So it is with us sinners. By nature, we are in the dark of night, engulfed in the fog of sin. We think we are great; we think that God should change his course for us. Yet, we are headed to destruction. We need to change our course when confronted with the truth.

This is the purpose of the warning of Hebrews 10. The writer knows that true believers will alter their course. Those who reject the warning are doomed to collision with the Almighty and they will not win. Are true Christians capable of final apostasy? No; but we are not stocks and blocks. We are human beings, creatures of history, and our decisions have consequences. Warning is a means by which the Father, through the Holy Spirit who makes the gospel effectual in the lives of God's elect, appeals to the heart and affection of his people. When God warned Joseph in a dream, "Rise, take the child and his mother, and flee to Egypt, and remain there until I tell you, for Herod is about to search for the child, to destroy him," there was no possibility from the perspective of God's decree that the

Christ child could be destroyed. The Lord, however, works in history to save his people, and it was essential that Joseph heed the warning. So here, in Hebrews 10, the moral warning against turning from grace must be heeded in faith by all who are truly the Lord's. Is that person you?

A Reminder of God's Faithfulness

The second way that the writer calls his readers to persevering faith is to remind them of God's absolute faithfulness. How essential it is that the covenant people of God remember God's faithfulness, just as we do when we come to the Table: "Do this in remembrance of me" (1 Cor. 11:24–25). Having warned those who are tempted to depart from Christ, the preacher now reminds his readers of the Lord's faithfulness to them in the midst of those trials.

> But recall the former days when, after you were enlightened, you endured a hard struggle with sufferings, sometimes being publicly exposed to reproach and affliction, and sometimes being partners with those so treated. For you had compassion on those in prison, and you joyfully accepted the plundering of your property, since you knew that you yourselves had a better possession and an abiding one.

Essentially the writer reminds his readers that, in ultimate terms, only good things have come from their trials, despite the hardship. The trials may be deep, but they are designed by God for your growth and service to the Lord. These trials were in God's providence purposed for the believer's good and for God's glory. As the *Heidelberg Catechism* so beautifully expounds it in Lord's Day 10:

> Providence is the almighty and ever present power of God by which he upholds, as with his hand, heaven and earth and all creatures, and so rules them that

leaf and blade, rain and drought, fruitful and lean years, food and drink, health and sickness, prosperity and poverty—all things, in fact, come to us not by chance but from his fatherly hand.

Therefore the writer would have them "recall the former days, when after you were enlightened, you endured a hard struggle with sufferings." When they had first confessed Christ the trials they endured were hard, their suffering great, but they were overflowing with benefit.

Trials Deepen Fellowship

"But recall the former days when, after you were enlightened, you endured a hard struggle with sufferings, sometimes being publicly exposed to reproach and affliction, and sometimes being partners with those so treated" (vv. 32–33). There was evidenced, in the past, such a love for the gospel and one another that the Christians to whom Hebrews is addressed endured hardship and were exposed willingly "to reproach and affliction."

This willing exposure to suffering for Christ's sake also bound the church together in a deeper realization of fellowship for they were "sometimes being partners with those so treated." *Partners* is from *koinonia* and stresses the communion of the saints. The *Westminster Confession* summarizes well the Biblical perspective on this matter:

> All saints that are united to Jesus Christ their Head, by His Spirit, and by faith, have fellowship with Him in His grace, sufferings, death, resurrection, and glory: and, being united to one another in love, they have communion in each other's gifts and graces, and are obliged to the performance of such duties, public and private, as to conduce to their mutual good, both in the inward and outward man. (26.1)

Call to Perseverance

This is precisely the point here in verses 32–33. These Christians risked their secure positions in society by providing for fellow believers who had already forfeited their freedom for the sake of the gospel.

Trials Deepen Compassion

Thus, in serving one another, their compassion came to the fore and was deepened. "For you had compassion on those in prison" (v. 34a). Literally, the Christians to whom this sermon-epistle is addressed had "suffered with" those in prison. The communion of the saints is evident here, and that communion is not without a sense of care and concern to alleviate the sufferings of fellow believers in Jesus. Had not our Lord pointed to this as an evidence of his grace in the lives of true believers (Matt. 25:36)? In many parts of the world, Christians already have this privilege, and the evidence is mounting that soon we in the West may also "suffer with" those imprisoned for their faith in Christ.

Trials Deepen Joy

In the process of serving one another in these desperate times of need, their joy was also deepened. "For you had compassion on those in prison, and you joyfully accepted the plundering of your property," (v. 34) writes the preacher. In this they were indeed disciples of their Lord who had taught:

> Blessed are you when people hate you and when they exclude you and revile you and spurn your name as evil, on account of the Son of Man! Rejoice in that day, and leap for joy, for behold, your reward is great in heaven; for so their fathers did to the prophets. (Luke 6:22–24)

Joy in suffering means that Christians suffer with eschatological ends in view, and hope for that which awaits them (Rom.

5:1–5). Peter wrote to the "elect exiles of the dispersion" (1 Pet. 1:1) that joy pervades the hopeful suffering of believers in Jesus.

> Beloved, do not be surprised at the fiery trial when it comes upon you to test you, as though something strange were happening to you. But rejoice insofar as you share Christ's sufferings, that you may also rejoice and be glad when his glory is revealed. If you are insulted for the name of Christ you are blessed, because the Spirit of glory and of God rests upon you. (1 Pet. 4:12–14)

Philip Hughes references John Hooper who, when facing death, wrote: "Loss of goods is great, but loss of God's grace and favour is greater . . . there is neither felicity nor adversity of this world that can appear to be great, if it be weighted with the joys or pains in the world to come."[5]

Trials Deepen a Sense of the Important

In the process of suffering and serving, the Christians to whom the writer speaks deepened their commitment to what really matters in life. He writes: "You joyfully accepted the plundering of your property, since you knew that you yourselves had a better possession and an abiding one." So gripped were they by the reality of the world to come that they were able to keep in perspective the material goods of the Lord's provision and to give them up knowing that they had "a better possession and an abiding one." This theme will be emphasized throughout chapter 11. We have already cited the deep piety of the Heidelberg Catechism summarizing the Bible's teaching that "leaf and blade . . . prosperity and poverty" come to us, not by chance, but in God's providence.

---

5. Philip E. Hughes, *Hebrews* (Grand Rapids: Eerdmans, 1990), 431.

Call to Perseverance

The Instructor in the catechism goes on to ask in Lord's Day 10, question 28: "How does the knowledge of God's Creation and Providence Help Us?" The answer:

> We can be patient when things go against us, thankful when things go well, and for the future we can have good confidence in our faithful God and Father that nothing will separate us from his love. All creatures are so completely in his hand that without his will they can neither move nor be moved.

When we think further that the providence of God takes us all the way to glory, to that "inheritance that is imperishable, undefiled, and unfading, kept in heaven for you" (1 Pet. 1:4), then the knowledge of "a better possession and an abiding one" brings perspective to the sufferings, deprivations, and persecutions of believers in this life. Calvin well said:

> Wherever the feeling of heavenly good things is strong, there is no taste for the world and its allurements, so that no sense of poverty or of shame can overwhelm our minds with sorrow. If then we wish to bear anything for Christ with patience and equanimity let us grow accustomed to frequent meditation on that happiness in comparison with which all the goods of this world are but rubbish.[6]

Believers will develop an ability to appreciate and to keep central those things that matter most here and now when they look to the promises of God for the future. Knowledge of "a better possession and an abiding one" is an essential transformative element in Christian living. On the basis of this future promise the writer calls upon his readers: "Therefore do not throw away your confidence, which has a great reward" (v. 35). Live for the things that endure! The truth of the believer's con-

---

6. John Calvin, *Hebrews* (Grand Rapids: Eerdmans, 1979), 153.

fidence is grounded in what the writer has already written in 10:35–36. The confidence given us on the basis of Christ's accomplishment presents an urgent and potent exhortation for persevering Christian living with the end result of *great reward* in view.

As I write these lines, Pastor Youcef Nadarkhani marks his 1,001st day of incarceration in Lakan, the notorious Northern Iranian prison. In Nigeria, bloody jihad is being waged against Nigeria's Christians and the Islamic organization Boko Haram is doing its best to remove all Christians from Nigerian society. Other examples abound. When you read these lines, the above examples may have changed, but new persecutions will be on the horizon. We should pray for the church persecuted around the world and encourage intervention and aid. However, it remains true that such things will be a pattern until Christ comes again. How can the believer in Christ endure such treatment? In the knowledge of "a better possession and an abiding one," the believer will retain his confidence in the battle. John Brown wrote powerfully:

> It is easy to see how the calling of these things to remembrance was calculated to serve his purpose— to guard them from apostasy, and establish them in the faith and profession of the Gospel. It is as if he had said, "Why shrink from suffering for Christianity now? Were you not exposed to suffering from the beginning? When you first became Christians, did you not willingly undergo sufferings on account of it? And is not Christianity as worthy of being suffered for as ever? Is not Jesus the same yesterday, to-day, and for ever? Did not the faith and hope of Christianity formerly support you under your sufferings, and make you feel that they were but the light afflictions of a moment? And are they not as able to support you now as they were then? Has the

substance in heaven become less real, or less enduring? and have you not as good evidence now as you had then that to the persevering Christian such treasure is laid up? Are you willing to lose all the benefit of the sacrifices you have made, and the sufferings you have sustained? and they will all go for nothing if you endure not to the end." These are considerations all naturally suggested by the words of the Apostle, and all well calculated to induce them to "hold fast the profession of their faith without wavering."[7]

The Call to Endure

This passage, then, calls upon these believers to endure in the faith they have professed. The writer of Hebrews calls upon them to remember how they have willingly suffered for the gospel in the past. He urges them to look ahead to their certain inheritance and to live out of the fullness of the Lord's faithful commitment to them. Therefore he says to them: Do not give up!

Do Not Give Up

"For you have need of endurance, so that when you may have done the will of God you may received what is promised" (v. 36). Arminianism has never been able to understand, based as it is upon a faulty view of God and man, that these exhortations do not imply that true believers may fail to arrive at the promised destination. Calvinism understands that these exhortations are essential to Christian living. God's promise does not make exhortation unnecessary. Quite the opposite. The Lord is addressing his people who will arrive at their appointed end as God has promised, but who will do so through the means of God's appointment, which include the exhortations of his Word. As Loraine Boettner has remarked:

---

7. John Brown, *Hebrews*, 483.

[Warnings and exhortations in Scripture] are inducements which produce constant humility, watchfulness, and diligence. In the same way a parent, in order to get the willing co-operation of a child, may tell it to stay out of the way of an approaching automobile, when all the time the parent has no intention of ever letting the child get into a position where it would be injured. When God plies a soul with fears of falling it is by no means a proof that God in His secret purpose intends to permit him to fall. These fears may be the very means which God has designed to keep him from falling.[8]

All of this is calculated to produce *endurance*.

Such warnings as we read in this passage should produce a great incentive to hate sin. Remember that times of persecution in particular can be times of grievous temptation. Thomas Brooks reminds us that

There is infinitely more evil in the least sin than there is in the greatest miseries and afflictions that can possibly come upon you; yea, there is more evil in the least sin than there is all the troubles that ever come upon the world, yea, than there is in all the miseries and torments of hell. . . .

The least sin is an offence to a great God, it is a wrong to the immortal soul, it is a breach of a righteous law; it cannot be washed away but by the blood of Jesus; it can shut the soul out of heaven, and shut the soul up a close prisoner in hell for ever and ever.

Brooks, as a faithful pastor, reminds us further:

The least sin is rather to be avoided and prevented than the greatest sufferings; if this cockatrice [a venemous serpent] be not crushed in the egg, it will

8. Loraine Boettner, *The Reformed Doctrine of Predestination* (Philadelphia: Presbyterian and Reformed, 1973), 195–196.

soon become a serpent; the very thought of sin, if
but thought on will break out into action, action into
custom, custom into habit, and then both body and
soul are lost irrevocably to all eternity.[9]

Do Not Shrink Back

Therefore, the writer pleads with these Hebrew Christians not
to shrink back from their movement toward the heavenly goal.

> For,
>
> > "Yet a little while,
> > and the coming one will come
> > and will not delay;
> > but my righteous one shall live by faith,
> > and if he shrinks back,
> > my soul has no pleasure in him."
>
> But we are not of those who shrink back and are
> destroyed, but of those who have faith and preserve
> their souls (vv. 37–39).

The preacher here conflates Isaiah 26:20 and Habakkuk 2:3–
4 (LXX). "Yet a little while, and the coming one will come and
will not delay" serves to keep the church alert to the coming of
the Lord and the end of the world. As in Isaiah, the Lord comes
in judgment upon the wicked and keeps his people so it will be
at the end. The passage in Isaiah, the readers would remember,
also speaks of resurrection (Isa. 26:19). John Calvin comments
on an earlier verse:

> The church was so constituted from the beginning
> of the kingdom of Christ that the faithful ought to
> imagine the coming of the Judge as imminent . . . we
> should continually expect his second revelation and
> think of each day as if it were the last.

---

9. Thomas Brooks, *Works*, 1.323.

And on this passage, he adds, "just as a general proclaims to his soldiers that the end of the war is not far off if only they hold on for a little, so the apostle declares that the Lord will soon come to deliver us from all evil if only our spirits do not give up by becoming weak."[10]

The second portion of the conflated quotations stresses themes from Habakkuk. This seventh century BC prophet called out to God in distress and concern for his nation. What did God reply to Habakkuk? The passage speaks of judgment upon the wicked and reward for those who live by faith. The passage presents a strong contrast of the wicked and the Lord's people. God's reply to the prophet's cry was that the prophet must take the posture of trust and patience: "but my righteous one shall live by faith, and if he shrinks back, my soul shall have no pleasure in him."

This is the point of the contrast between the righteous person who lives by faith and the wicked person who shrinks back from God's will. Those who rely on Christ alone may lose much in this life, but in relying on Christ, they preserve their souls. "But we are not of those who shrink back and are destroyed, but of those who have faith and preserve their souls" (v. 39). "For God has not destined us for wrath, but to obtain salvation through our Lord Jesus Christ" (1 Thess. 5:9).

The Lord's goal is not to lead his people to darkness and gloom but to the liberty and joy that comes from knowing that the foundation under our feet is Christ alone. The Lord will always keep his promises to his people. On the basis of this promise, let us never shrink back but persevere to the saving of our souls!

---

10. John Calvin, *Hebrews*, 145, 154.

19

Looking to Jesus, Part 1

HEBREWS 11:1–12:2

Now faith is the assurance of things hoped for, the conviction of things not seen. For by it the people of old received their commendation. By faith we understand that the universe was created by the word of God, so that what is seen was not made out of things that are visible.

Having concluded a ringing call to perseverance, the writer of Hebrews now shows the principle of faith in the Old Testament. Many writers and preachers of this section tend to look at the "roll call of faith" (11:1–12:2) in this passage and say, "Look at these great examples, imitate them!" Indeed, what Christian does not want to imitate the believing walk of those listed here? However, as important as that may be, I am convinced that the author's stress lies elsewhere.

As we remember that the Hebrew Christian recipients of this sermon-epistle were tempted to go back to the old ways and to forsake the truth as it is in Jesus, the point of the "roll call" in Hebrews 11 becomes clearer. It is a challenge to remember what the original purpose of the old covenant was all about. In essence, the writer is saying: "You want to go back to the old covenant? Your fathers were looking by faith to what you now possess in the gospel. Why would you want to go back since what you now have fulfills their expectations?"

If I may take a moment to address the preacher who may be reading these words (though these comments I think will be profitable for all readers), we must not lose sight of the purpose of this text. We should stress to the people of God this element of fulfillment and of longing for consummation found here. Rather than bringing the congregation a lengthy series of biographical sketches, think of what the author is doing and translate that to the needs of God's people today, who also are tried and sometimes tempted to go back.

Help your congregation to take the theme of Hebrews 11 to heart. Say to them, "Let your heart cling to the promise and long for *the city that has foundations, whose designer and builder is God* (v. 10)." Think of Hebrews 11 as broad strokes on a large canvas, or as a film moving rapidly before the eye, racing toward a goal and leaving an overall impression. That may help you to see the purpose of the text and how the Lord's people throughout redemptive history were pressing, pressing, pressing toward Christ by faith in the promise of God. They had nothing but the promise of God on which to rely. Now, in continuity with this purpose and with God's people through the ages, we can see ourselves as we are: "We are not of those who shrink back and are destroyed, but of those who have faith and preserve their souls" (10:39).

What is Faith?

Our author begins by answering the implicit question, "What is faith?" If we are "of those who have faith" (10:39), then it will help to strengthen faith if we have some definitive categories by which to build confidence. Therefore he writes:

> Now faith is the assurance of things hoped for, the
> conviction of things not seen. For by it the people
> of old received their commendation. By faith we un-
> derstand that the universe was created by the word
> of God, so that what is seen was not made out of
> things that are visible. (vv. 1–3)

Faith, then, is held up and displayed in following categories:

Assurance

"Now faith is the assurance of things hoped for." *Assurance* (*hy-postasis*) is connected to "things hoped for" because the idea of *hypostasis* related to "substance," "property," and "effects"—that is, to property that belonged to or was inherited by an owner. On the basis of the non-literary papyri, Moulton and Milligan suggest the translation, "faith is the *title-deed* of things hoped for."[1] In another place, Moulton explains this in fascinating de-tail:

> "Now faith," says the Revised Version, "is the assur-
> ance of things hoped for." The word translated "as-
> surance" occurs in a long legal document, the "Pe-
> tition of Dionysia." She was a widow who had had
> some trouble with her property, which had been
> claimed by litigious persons. She writes out a copy
> of the judgement delivered in a previous litigation,
> and a full statement of her claim is sent with this to
> the prefect of Egypt. In the course of that document
> there occurs this Greek word *hypostasis.* Drs. Gren-
> fell and Hunt tell us it was a technical legal word,
> and meant a collection of papers bearing upon the
> possession of a piece of property. When anybody
> bought a piece of land there were always some pa-
> pers connected with it. There would be old census
> papers in which the owner and his land were regis-

---

1. J. H. Moulton, G. Milligan, *Vocabulary of the Greek Testament* (Peabody, MA: Hendrickson, 1997 reprint from 1930 original), entry 5287.

tered, bills of sale, correspondence about it—in fact, any sort of thing that might be put in as evidence if any question should arise as to the title of the land. All this was carefully collected in a docket and then put into the public archives office. Each large town had a special keeper of the archives to look after the papers and produce them when demanded in order to help the security of property. In other words, this word may be translated "the title-deeds." Can we not see what a depth of meaning that puts in to the word? "Faith is the title-deeds of things hoped for."

Now do not forget what *hope* means in the New Testament. The "hope" of the New Testament means absolute certainty about the future. Things hoped for are things not yet seen, but things which God guarantees to us as something that absolutely belongs to us. Faith is the "title-deeds of things hoped for." Suppose I go to a real estate agent and buy a piece of land in Canada. I have not time to go and see it; but if I buy that land I have certain papers put into my hands, title-deeds of that property. I take these home with me, and if ever I want to realize on that land I can go to an office and say: "I have some land to sell. Here are the title-deeds." I present the paper, and that paper is accepted as being the equivalent of the land. Even if I never saw my property, that paper represents it for me. And if you look at the eleventh chapter of Hebrews you will find that this is just what faith is there. Men and women received a promise from God counted that promise as being the title-deeds to something they could not see yet, but which they were going to see some day. They were so sure of it, because God had promised it to them, that they acted upon the belief, treated it as their estate, as something absolutely theirs.[2]

2. James Hope Moulton, *From Egyptian Rubbish-Heaps* (London: Charles H. Kelly, 1916), 27–29.

Looking to Jesus, Part 1

I suppose there is no way of knowing with certainty how much of the usage of the term *hypostasis* as found in the non-literary papyri came to mind when the writer penned the words "now faith is the assurance of things hoped for, the conviction of things not seen," but as it was a common expression in business documents, it seems more than probable that this meaning would have come to the minds of those who first heard the sermon-epistle. We can imagine how hearing faith and hope related to their struggles in such a vivid way must have raised eyebrows and slackened jaws in astonishment. "Faith is the title-deeds of things hoped for." Should this not fill our hearts with astonishment as well?

In this way, the author closely allies faith with the certainty of what is promised in Christ. The writer is pushing us forward, helping his tempted and tried readers to look ahead to the promised inheritance that is ours in Christ (1 Pet. 1:3–9). We who are tempted and tried today need to take this to heart, and here we must find our encouragement to persevere. Faith in Christ is the title-deed—secure and certain—that guarantees the bright, future prospect of the believer in Jesus. How differently men live who have this hope!

My dear friend Vince Strawbridge, Jr., now with the Lord, suffered terribly as a quadriplegic. Yet, as he suffered, he was filled with hope, served his fellow Christians as a ruling elder in Covenant Presbyterian Church,[3] and even in his worst decline leading to death, Vince gave praise to God. How many conversations did we have in which I was the one leaving encouraged by this brother who knew he had an inheritance and that his title was purchased by Jesus' blood. On the other hand, I have known men who do not know Christ in similar circumstances who become cynical, bitter, and hopeless. Yes, "faith is the assurance of things hoped for." This is the reason for endurance

---

3. Covenant Presbyterian Church, PCA, Lakeland, FL.

given in the text, the motivation of the people of God from of old, and our motivation as well.

Conviction

"Faith is the assurance of things hoped for," but the writer adds that faith is also "the conviction of things not seen." Faith in Christ, belief in God's promise, is his divinely granted gift. Therefore, true faith carries with it the seed of "conviction" with regard to the Christian's inheritance, the "things not seen." *Conviction (elengxos)* was used in the papyri as "proof," "evidence," such as in a court of law when proof was gathered against an accused and sometimes for the idea of "conviction," that is, sure persuasion. The writer may mean that faith itself carries with it conviction, or the assured persuasion, as proof in itself that the "things not seen," another way of saying "things hoped for," are indeed the Christian's possession. This is because faith does not look to itself but to the object, who is Christ.

A very moving illustration of this great matter of a certain hope comes from the life of A. T. Robertson, famed for his in depth of study of the Greek of the New Testament. When his young daughter Charlotte died, those who came to his home to comfort him and his family found the great Greek scholar in deep grief walking up and down the house with his Greek New Testament in his hand. Reading the story of the raising of Jairus' daughter he said to his friends in his grief, "He raised Jarius' daughter; why not mine?"

One might think that Dr. Robertson was experiencing a crisis of faith. It seems more accurate to think that he was attempting by faith to grasp the reality of the future hope that was beyond his sight. Yes, he walked by faith and not by sight, but that faith moved his heart on to the great hope and future promised to the Lord's people in God's Word. Let us not forget that Dr. Robertson struggled, but that he struggled as all of God's people should in this world; he struggled *with a Bible in his hand!* The promises of God are found there, and they are sure.

Faith, then, is confident assurance based on God-given conviction about unseen realities, about a yet unseen and future inheritance. These invisible things are so determinative that they keep us walking in conviction of their reality even when the present evil age tempts us to embrace materialism and leave our conviction behind. This, after all, was the temptation of these Hebrew Christians who desired to go back rather than keep an unsullied eye on the promises of God for the future. Paul similarly writes:

> So we do not lose heart. Though our outer self is wasting away, our inner self is being renewed day by day. For this light momentary affliction is preparing for us an eternal weight of glory beyond all comparison, as we look not to the things that are seen but to the things that are unseen. For the things that are seen are transient, but the things that are unseen are eternal. (2 Cor. 4:16–18)

Demonstrated by the fathers

This faith has been demonstrated throughout redemptive history. What motivated the saints of old? Was it not faith in the promise? "For by it the people of old received their commendation." The saints of the past were granted confident assurance based on the God-given conviction about unseen realities as they looked in faith to things yet future and not visible to the eye. They "died in faith, not having received the things promised, but having seen them and greeted them from afar, and having acknowledged that they were strangers and exiles on the earth" (11:13). "Their commendation" may refer to the inclusion of "people of old" (literally, "elders") in the sacred Scriptures as seen in the "roll call of faith" that is to follow.

Acknowledges God as Creator

"By faith we understand that the universe was created by the word of God, so that what is seen was not made out of things that are visible" (v. 3). Faith in Christ acknowledges that God is Creator. It is an axiom in the study of the Bible that "protology leads to eschatology," that is, that first things lead to last things. Creation is fundamental to new creation, origins become the root for the unfolding of redemptive history leading on to the full flowering of consummation when Jesus comes again (vv. 39–40). Specifically, "by faith we understand that the universe was created by the word of God."

Faith grasps that "in the beginning God created the heavens and the earth" (Gen. 1:1). The new creation that has come to light in our lives by faith must look back to the Lord as the Creator of all things; new creation looks back to creation, which in turn leads us on to consummation. God spoke and matter came into existence. The earth was framed just as God says in his written Word, and faith acknowledges this. Faith knows that "what is seen was not made out of things that are visible" just as surely as it knows that our trust in Christ originates in his creative power. "For God who said, 'Let light shine out of darkness,' has shone in our hearts to give the light of the knowledge of the glory of God in the face of Jesus Christ" (2 Cor. 4:6).

How foolish it is for Christian leaders to give in to the pressure of the world on the theme of the creative power of God and his self-revelation in the first chapters of Genesis. It is Genesis to which the writer of Hebrews refers with confidence. It is there that we find the anchor for understanding the creation of the world. For Christian leaders to deny creation by divine fiat, or the historicity of Adam, or to imagine that hominids evolved into God's image bearers, and then to think that these compromises will not harm the faith and walk of the church is almost incomprehensible.

Looking to Jesus, Part 1

When I was a boy, before the Lord shone into my darkened heart and called me to him, I had suppressed the truth by doubting God's existence and by reading sophisticated evolutionary materials that fostered my humanism. When I was about 12 years old, I wrote an essay, highly praised by my teacher, about "man" and his evolution from the dimness of antiquity. But when the Lord called me to himself, all of that dropped off like the scales from Paul's eyes (Acts 9:18). I regained my sight lost in the fall, and my faith in Christ involved trusting God's Word. God's Word says that God is the Creator, therefore, the evolutionary humanism I had been reading was unmasked for the lie it was.

Soon thereafter when evolution became the topic of discussion in my public school classroom, I was the only student who did not believe it. The teacher, a strong proponent of evolution, devised a plan wherein we would be taken to the school library and, after investigating a few resources on evolution, would return to the class to report our findings. I went eagerly with the others only to find that there was not one book or article in the school library in support of the viewpoint that God was the Creator of the heavens and the earth. When we returned I had nothing to rely on but that the Word of God teaches creation.

These days, of course, I know where to turn to find answers from noted scientists to the objections of my teachers and classmates. It is important to help our young people know how to show the inconsistencies and failures of the evolutionary myth. But the underlying issue is always faith relying on God's Word. This is the point of Hebrews 11:3; faith in Christ, faith in God's promise, a faith that moves us on to the future hope, is also a faith that looks back to the Creator and sustainer of the universe. The Lord who is Creator is in sovereign control to bring about the promise of new creation. No Christian should be ashamed or intimidated by the world on this score.

Redemptive History Highlights Features of Faith

Now begins the "roll call" itself, and here we find the "people of old" set forth as those who had a true and lively faith in Christ. Let us remember that these believers are not simply held out as examples of faith. The writer is not primarily saying "be like these people of old." The writer is telling his readers, preaching to us as well, to cling to the promise, to look to Christ, to be forward-looking to the future, for that is what the Lord has produced in his people through the outworking of his plan of redemption. This was not only God's Word then and there; it is God's Word here and now.

When tempted to go back, remember that God's people have always looked ahead by faith to what we now possess and what we will share together in the consummation of all things. They had nothing but God's promise to rely on, and you and I must rely on that promise too; but, the promise is enhanced by the fulfillment seen in Christ and in the encouragement of his high priestly work. Here then, in this "roll call," is found God's faithfulness to sustain his people, as well as characteristic features of the faith God has granted us.

Before we move on, it may be wise to remember that the church must hold fast to God's promise in a world that has rejected it. Time and again in the verses that follow we will note the opposition of the world to the Word of God. Our text has stressed creation but we see the devastating results of rejecting the Creator and his revelation in wars and devastation on the earth. Thinking back to two world wars in which the philosphical commitments of Germany were to macro-evolution rather than to the Creator, the cosmic darkness of Darwinian evolution resulted in mutilation, genocide, and the total disgregard of man, God's image bearer. Ideas have consequences. When they are God's ideas, they lead to life, but when God's truth is replaced with the lies of fallen man, they lead to disaster.

Looking to Jesus, Part 1

When I lead my congregation in reciting the Apostle's Creed, following the example of the minister of my youth, I present the Creed with these words: "We live in a day of unbelief, when people all around us do not know what to believe. In such a day, O Christian, what do you believe?" The nave then fills with the sound of many voices confessing the Triune nature of God, the Father's creative power, the Son's redemptive love, and the presence of the Holy Spirit. In some ways this captures the theme of Hebrews 11; confessing the faith in a hostile world, holding fast the Word of God, and clinging to the promise though all the world deride us. May the Lord give us strength continually to confess his name!

20

Looking to Jesus,
Part 2

HEBREWS 11:1–12:2

---

*By faith Abraham obeyed when he was called to go out
to a place that he was to receive as an inheritance. And
he went out, not knowing where he was going. By faith
he went to live in the land of promise, as in a foreign
land, living in tents with Isaac and Jacob, heirs with him
of the same promise. For he was looking forward to the
city that has foundations, whose designer and builder is
God. By faith Sarah herself received power to conceive,
even when she was past the age, since she considered him
faithful who had promised. Therefore from one man, and
him as good as dead, were born descendants as many
as the stars of heaven and as many as the innumerable
grains of sand by the seashore.*

In writing of the life of Abraham, Edmund Clowney made an
arresting comment on the nature of faith:

> Faith cannot be less than total. To trust in God
> means to look to Him alone, to find in Him all our
> hope, to hold nothing back, no reserve. Faith is com-

mitment. Yet just because faith looks to God and not to ourselves, faith's giving is really a receiving.

Then Clowney clinches the idea in this provocative way: "In commitment, the price faith pays is everything. But in total trust, the price is nothing. Faith looks to God, not man, as the giver."[1] These words well summarize the thrust of our text. Faith in the Lord required everything from these Old Testament saints; yet, the faith that gave everything was itself God's gift. It did not look to self for its origin or sustenance, but to the promise.

Continuing into this eleventh chapter, let us remember that the writer is after something more profound than imitation of great men and women of the past. The writer has described the characteristics of faith in the first three verses. He has reminded us of the certain hope gripped by faith which functions as "title-deeds" to the properties we have not yet seen. The writer is not simply saying, "do as they did" but is helping us to see that, throughout redemptive history, faith has always been forward-looking.

True faith has been and still is *persevering* faith—fixed and determined by those promises of future things not yet seen with the eyes of the flesh. Why would we go back when all of the saints of redemptive history have forged ahead and have kept their eye on the invisible, yet certain, realities of God's promise in Christ? They had nothing but the promise of God on which to rely, and in continuity with this purpose, we also can see ourselves as we are: "We are not of those who shrink back and are destroyed, but of those who have faith and preserve their souls" (10:39).

Each of the persons noted in the "roll call" lived by faith, "the assurance of things hoped for, the conviction of things not seen" (11:1). The various features of faith pointed out in this chapter help us to see our privileges and also call us to faith in

---

1. Edmund P. Clowney, *The Unfolding Mystery* (Phillipsburg, NJ: Presbyterian and Reformed, 1988), 55.

the promise of God as we sojourn to our heavenly home. Here we find a powerful call to and incentive for perseverance.

Some commentators and preachers lose the forest for the trees as they examine this chapter. This is usually done when the chapter is viewed as a series of normative examples. Again, it is important that we keep in mind the goal of the saints and their experiences, so that we do not lose track regarding the overall purpose—to move us onward in our Christian walk to those unseen certainties possessed by faith alone. In other words, the examples of the saints' faith point us beyond the saints to the Christ in whom they trusted.

Features of Faith

Faith Seeks to Please God (vv. 4–7)

Hebrews 12:1–3 talks about what faith *is*, but the following verses talk about what faith *does*. In verses 4–7, we learn (through the examples of the pre-patriarchs Abel, Enoch, and Noah) that faith seeks to please God.

About Abel we read:

> By faith Abel offered to God a more acceptable sacrifice than Cain, through which he was commended as righteous, God commending him by accepting his gifts. And through his faith, though he died, he still speaks. (v. 4)

The story here is from Genesis 4:1–15. Abel offered the Lord a lamb from his flocks, while his brother Cain brought an offering of crops. Abel's offering, because it was brought in faith, was "more acceptable" than Cain's. It was "through his faith" that this pre-patriarch "was commended as righteous." The nature of that righteousness is unpacked in the remainder of the Bible, especially by Paul. We are justified by grace alone through faith alone on the ground of the work of Christ alone. "And through

315

his faith, though he died, he still speaks." Abel's *blood* cried out for vengeance, but in Hebrews, the writer would have us see that *Abel* speaks through his faith. Of what does Abel speak? Abel speaks of the place of faith in the Christian life, of that faith that is demonstrated in a heart that trusts God's promise and desires to please God.

Enoch is the next pre-patriarch mentioned.

> By faith Enoch was taken up so that he should not see death, and he was not found, because God had taken him. Now before he was taken he was commended as having pleased God.

Though the bells of death toll from the fall of man until now, they did not toll for Enoch. Enoch's righteousness and translation were by faith; he passed from this world to the next without dying (Gen. 5:21–24). Even though faith is not mentioned in the text of Genesis, the author of Hebrews understands that faith is precisely the issue in a life like Enoch's. A walk of faith can only be true for those who acknowledge God and believe his promises. "And without faith it is impossible to please him, for whoever would draw near to God must believe that he exists and that he rewards those who seek him" (11:6).

Faith receives the revelation of the living God and believes the promises sovereignly pledged to believers. Enoch shows that faith seeks to please the Lord, believes his self-revelation, and trusts his promises and provision. Faith takes the unseen God at his Word. Faith clings to the naked promise of God. We are called to walk by faith and not by sight (2 Cor. 5:7). This we see again and again in the lives of these saints.

Similarly, Noah's life was one of faith.

> By faith Noah, being warned by God concerning events as yet unseen, in reverent fear constructed an ark for the saving of his household. By this he con-

demned the world and became an heir of the righteousness that comes by faith.

It had not rained prior to the flood (Gen. 2:5), and it is likely
that Noah had never seen ships sailing on the sea. But the Lord
determined to bring judgment on the earth and on mankind
when he saw that "every intention of the thoughts of his heart
was only evil continually" (Gen. 6:5). Having "been warned by
God concerning events as yet unseen," Noah believed what the
Lord revealed to him. This was for Noah, just as it must be for
us, living out of the definition of faith found in 11:1: "Now faith
is the assurance of things hoped for, the conviction of things
not seen."

Therefore, based on the sheer Word of the Lord, Noah "in
reverent fear constructed an ark for the saving of his household."
Faith reverences the Lord, holds Him dear as holy, and catches
the theme of God's greatness that is determinative of a life that
pleases the Lord. Even though Noah had never experienced
anything like the cataclysmic flood that swept over the earth,
Noah believed the Lord and in so doing "he condemned the
world and became an heir of the righteousness that comes by
faith." Noah was "a herald of righteousness" (2 Pet. 2:5) so that,
by his words and by his life as he built the ark, "he condemned
the world."

The Christian's life and words do the same now; as we speak
for Christ and live for the glory of God (1 Pet. 2:11–12). This
does not mean that we are vitriolic, but when we live by faith,
the contrast between ourselves and the world becomes undeni-
able (Gal. 1:4). This deliverance and life by faith are by grace; we
do not produce them through our own efforts. However, not
only did Noah's life "condemn the world," but he is also thus
identified as "an heir of the righteousness that comes by faith"
(v. 7). The faith Noah demonstrated by believing God's promise
showed him to be justified by the merits of Christ, who was

anticipated in the promise that Noah believed. Let us not be ashamed of the Word of God but, in the midst of the scoffing world, embrace it by faith. This condemns the world as the world condemns us for believing what we cannot see; but, it also shows that we have faith in Christ by whose righteousness we are acceptable to God.

Faith seeks to please God. I recall years ago hearing a taped sermon by George W. Truett in which he told the story of how some young ladies stood for Christ in the midst of an unbelieving world. An infidel stood before a crowd declaiming the faith and deriding the Lord. He dared anyone to respond. Some young Christian girls who were present responded when no one else would. "We cannot preach," they said, "but we can sing." Then they began to sing: "Stand up, stand up for Jesus, ye soldiers of the cross; lift high his royal banner, it must not suffer loss: from vict'ry unto vict'ry his army shall he lead, till ev'ry foe is vanquished, and Christ is Lord indeed." When they were done the crowd was subdued and softened by the courageous witness of these young, Christian girls. That is faith in action; standing on the promises of God in the midst of a hostile world.

The Lord continued to reveal his promise in redemptive history and, as the plan and purpose of God pushed on, we see in the patriarchs another feature of faith, namely, that faith looks to the future.

Faith Looks to the Future (vv. 8–10)

Faith is hope-filled, that is, faith looks to the future with expectancy, since it clings to promises yet to be fulfilled. The writer of Hebrews now turns to the patriarchs and to Abraham in particular. "By faith Abraham obeyed when he was called to go out to a place that he was to receive as an inheritance." Abraham did not know where the Lord was leading him when he was called out of Ur of the Chaldeans (Gen. 12:1; Heb. 11:8). Abraham was called by sovereign grace and believed the promise that "he was to receive . . . an inheritance," but he knew little more than that. His faith clung to the promise and looked to its future fulfillment. Abraham trusted the Lord with a future-looking faith that knew God would keep his promise in his own way and time, though yet unfulfilled. A promise had been given to Abraham; he would act upon that promise by faith.

"By faith he went to live in the land of promise, as in a foreign land, living in tents with Isaac and Jacob, heirs with him of the same promise." The covenant included Abraham's seed, for electing grace moves through the line of the promise (Rom. 9). The land was "a foreign land," a land in which one called of God at this stage in history would not be at home. It was unfamiliar territory. Abraham knew that the promise pointed beyond the land he could see to a greater fulfillment, a land beyond his sight he believed in by faith. "For he was looking forward to the city that has foundations, whose designer and builder is God" (11:10).

Verse 16 defines this city for us clearly as "a better country, that is, a heavenly one." To this eternal inheritance, Abraham adds nothing. He seeks it by faith, receives the promise which is by sheer grace, and he yearns for this eternal city promised him by God, but he does nothing to earn it, nothing to create it, nothing to sustain it. The city is God's doing, not any man's. The call was of God, and the seeking was a seeking by faith in the promise. This is the case for the Lord's people today, as it was for Abraham and for the Hebrew Christians. The true people of God are encouraged to move on to the heavenly inheritance and indeed shall do so by grace.

Moreover, God's promise was beyond the land underneath the patriarchs' feet. Abraham, Isaac, and Jacob died without seeing their descendants possess the land irrevocably, but never at any point in redemptive history did the land embody the fullness of God's promise. The land itself pointed to the greater land of rest for the people of God. The writer, in essence, says to those to whom he wrote: "Do you want to go back? Abraham was moving forward to the promised blessings that you now possess in Christ. He was pressing on to the tangible reality of what awaits you in the new heavens and the new earth." The patriarchs' homeland was not merely Palestine, not ultimately. Their homeland and yours is the entirety of the new heavens and earth (Rev. 21:22).

Coming together in this passage are the themes of the people of God as sojourners and the return of Christ. The call comes just as it did to Abraham, and as in his case, it is effectual. We are strangers and pilgrims here on this earth, but our inheritance is sure. When Christ comes again, the whole wide, broad, deep inheritance will be tangibly possessed to the glory of Christ our Savior. Yet, we should recognize our favored place in God's plan of redemption. We know more than Abraham. We have greater promises placed before us than the patriarchs, and we live in heightened expectation of Christ's return, since the cross, resurrection, and ascension. We have greater reason to push on, to sojourn well, and to keep our gaze fixed on the mark.

It is plain that faith relies totally and utterly on the promise of God. That is clear throughout the narrative and particularly so in the account of Sarah's response to the promise of God.

Faith Relies on God's Promise (vv. 11–12)

That faith rests on the promise of God is especially clear in the promise and fulfillment of Isaac's birth. "Sarah herself received power to conceive, even when she was past the age, since she considered him faithful who had promised" (11:11). Here the people of God should take heart! Would we not say that Sarah doubted rather than believed, that she faltered and failed? Indeed, she laughed at the promise that she would conceive. The

Lord said to Abraham, in view of the promise of Genesis 17, that a son would be born to Abraham and Sarah: "I will surely return to you about this time next year, and Sarah your wife shall have a son" (Gen. 18:10). Sarah, listening at the tent entrance "laughed to herself, saying, 'After I am worn out, and my lord is old, shall I have pleasure?' The LORD said to Abraham, 'Why did Sarah laugh and say, 'Shall I indeed bear a child, now that I am old?' Is anything too hard for the LORD?" Even then Sarah denied that she laughed, but the Lord had sworn.

This shows two things of great importance. First, the Lord's promise to us does not depend upon us. Throughout redemptive history the Lord's people were swept along in the sure promise of God by means of his sovereign grace. That is what is happening in the Genesis narrative. The Lord is bringing about the salvation of his people. Ultimately, the Messiah himself came through God's sovereign promise. That promise was sure. Secondly, faith clings to the promise, and yet true faith may be stronger or weaker at various moments in the believer's life. Faith may indeed be true faith, yes even assured, though mingled at times with the weakness of our incredulity. Sarah initially faltered, but the text tells us plainly that she "considered him faithful who had promised." Faith relies on the promise.

Is the promise on which faith relies certain? The text underscores the absolute certainty of the promise. "Therefore from one man, and him as good as dead, were born descendants as many as the stars of heaven and as many as the innumerable grains of sand by the seashore" (v. 12). God promised, and there it stood. Faith is never unfruitful because the promise believed is sure. The promise has as its content the Christ of the promise; to believe the promise is to believe in Christ. God promised Abraham: "I will make your offspring as the dust of the earth, so that if one can count the dust of the earth, your offspring also can be counted" (Gen. 13:16; cp. Gen. 15:5).

The fact that Abraham had a one hundred year old body and that Sarah was long past the age of childbearing did not hinder the promise of God. God had promised that the line of electing grace would run through Isaac (Rom. 9:6–12), and so it did not matter to the sovereign God that Abraham was "as good as dead." The Lord fulfilled his promise for the sake of the Christ to come and the people of God who would believe on Him.

Faith Looks for Another City (vv. 13–16)

"These all died in faith, not having received the things promised, but having seen them and greeted them from afar and having acknowledged that they were strangers and exiles on the earth" (11:13). The eye of faith is not focused on this world. Though we live by faith in this world, the faith of God's elect keeps its gaze on another world. Here we "acknowledge" that we are but "strangers and exiles," a theme already stressed particularly in Hebrews 4. By faith we greet the promise "from afar."

This is not pietism but the essence of true piety. On Sunday morning when I am privileged to lead my congregation in worship, the first thing I do behind the pulpit is open the Bible. This is a silent reminder that we are a pilgrim people on the way to our heavenly home, "strangers and exiles" here. The open Bible reminds us that we live under the Word of promise until we arrive at our heavenly destination.

"For people who speak thus make it clear that they are seeking a homeland" (11:14). Faith knows that what is promised may not come to fruition in this life. Abraham did not see all of the promises regarding the land fulfilled in his day. The promise of the land was a promise containing a greater promise, that of the world to come. We, similarly, have the promise of the coming of Christ and the new heavens and the new earth. We may die before seeing the fulfillment of this ultimate and blessed hope.

Yet, the promise is sure. Therefore we look for another city and live for the coming of the better world.

The patriarchs, had they not been focused on the promise by faith, may well have gone back to their place of origin. "If they had been thinking of that land from which they had gone out, they would have had opportunity to return" (11:15). Here is no subtle reminder to the readers of Hebrews that their attitude of faith should be that of the patriarchs. They too should yield to no temptations to return but they should keep their gaze on the promise held out to faith. We too are called as believers to walk in light of the promise. Though we cannot yet see the complete fruition of the promise that awaits us, we trust the Lord has gone to prepare a place for us (John 14:1ff). God, after all, is not ashamed of his relationship with us due to our union with Christ. This clinches the fulfillment of the promise.

This understatement contains a great promise in itself that the Lord will bring his people home. Therefore, as with the patriarchs of old the promise must stimulate us to consistent, faithful walking in view of the covenant of grace. Does not the text say, "therefore God is not ashamed to be called their God, for he has prepared for them a city"? Despite the weakness of our faith God acknowledges us. He "is not ashamed to be called [our] God" as we press forward to the *city* that awaits us. "That city" is not the old Jerusalem but the new Jerusalem in which righteousness dwells.

John Newton captured much of the value of this line of thought for believers in a letter to a certain Miss Medhurst:

> The time is short, the world is passing away, all its cares and all its vanities will soon be at an end. Yet a little while, and "we shall see him as He is." Every vail shall be taken away, every seeming frown be removed from his face, and every tear wiped away from ours. We shall also be like him. Even now, when

we contemplate his glory as shining in the glass of the Gospel, we feel ourselves, in some measure, transformed into the same image: what a sudden, wonderful, and abiding change shall we then experience, when He shall shine directly, immediately, and eternally upon our souls without one interposing cloud between! Because He lives, we shall live also; because He shines, we likewise shall shine forth as the sun, in our Saviour's brightness: then shall we sing with understanding those glorious songs, Isaiah xii. Lxi.10; Rev. v.9, and vii. 10, without one jarring note, or one wandering thought for ever.

"Having therefore these promises, dearly loved, let us cleanse ourselves from all filthiness of the flesh and spirit, perfecting holiness in the fear of the Lord." "Let us lay aside every weight;" "Let us not be slothful," but followers of that cloud of witnesses who in every age have set their word to the truth and power of God. They were once as poor as we are now; they had their complaints and their fears, their enemies, and temptations; they were exercised with a wicked heart, and a wicked world; and I have doubt not but many of them, in a fit of unbelief, have been ready to conclude, "I shall one day perish by the hand of Saul;" but at length the "blood of Jesus, and the word of his testimony," made them more than conquerors; and now their warfare is finished, they are "before the throne of God and the Lamb, and shall go no more out." While we are sighing, they are singing; while we are fighting they are triumphing; but their song, their triumph, their joy, will not be complete till we are called up to join them. The Lord prepare us for, and hasten, the happy hour.[2]

---

2. John Newton, *Letters of John Newton* (Edinburgh: Banner of Truth, 2007), 51.

In verses 17–22, the writer takes us through the remainder of patriarchal history down to the time of Moses and the Exodus. Here he shows us that faith believes God can raise the dead.

Faith Believes God Can Raise the Dead (vv. 17–22)

> By faith Abraham, when he was tested, offered up Isaac, and he who had received the promises was in the act of offering up his only son, of whom it was said, "Through Isaac shall your offspring be named." (11:17–18)

We read in Genesis 22:1 "After these things God tested Abraham and said to him, 'Abraham!' And he said, 'Here am I.'"[3] This voice was known to Abraham; it was the voice of Jehovah who had sovereignly called Abraham out of a pagan land and promised to make him a blessing to the nations. Abraham went out, and God sealed his covenant with Abraham in blood, speaking peace to Abraham's heart: "Fear not, Abram, I am your shield; your reward shall be very great" (Gen. 15:1).

By oath, God promised Abram an heir. Abraham knew that voice; it was the God who loved him, who had promised him good, a voice of blessing. Perhaps in awe, Abraham had thrilled to hear that voice. Perhaps he pondered what blessing God would now bring upon him. Then God said, "Take your son, your only son Isaac, whom you love, and go to the land of Moriah, and offer him there as a burnt offering on one of the mountains of which I will tell you" (Gen. 22:2). Blessing? God was condemning his promised heir to death. What conflict must have churned in Abraham's heart. Yet we read: "So Abraham rose early in the morning, saddled his donkey, and took two of his young men with him, and his son Isaac. And he cut

---

3. My understanding of Genesis 22 reflects a sermon I heard in my youth by my pastor Gordon Reed. Is not the sermon the chief theological medium?

wood for the burnt offering and arose and went to the place of which God had told him" (Gen. 22:3).

Isaac was special indeed. He was God's promise personified. The salvation of the world was lost if Isaac perished, through him the Lord would fulfill his promise to bless the world. Abraham had three long days in which to turn these matters over in his heart. There was an apparent contradiction between what God promised and what he now commanded. However the point of the text is that Abraham trusted the omnipotent God in the dark, believing that "God was able even to raise him from the dead" (11:19). Calvin rightly says that "we act unjustly toward God, when we hope for nothing from him but what our senses can perceive, so we pay him the highest honor, when, in affairs of perplexity, we nevertheless entirely acquiesce in his providence."[4] Remember when the phenomena of life seems to contradict the promise of God that, as the Puritan John Flavel said, the providences of God are like Hebrew words—they can only be read backwards.

The time for the sacrifice finally came. Abraham placed the wood for the altar fire upon the back of his son Isaac, took the knife in one hand and the clay pot of fire in the other, and together they made their way up Moriah's mount. Some of the most moving words in Scripture are found here. Isaac spoke. "My father!" Abraham answered, "Here am I, my son." Isaac asked, "Behold the fire and the wood: but where is the lamb for a burnt offering?" Abraham answered, "God will provide for himself a lamb for a burnt offering, my son" (Gen. 22:7–8). Later, just as Abraham raised his knife and was about to plunge it into his son, God intervened and provided a ram for the offering.

The text in Genesis points to two fundamental principles. The first is the necessity of sacrifice. Sacrifice is necessary to restore the broken relationship between God and man. The sec-

---

4. John Calvin, *Genesis* (Grand Rapids: Baker, 1979), 568.

ond principle is that substitution of one life for another is necessary to restore fallen sinners.

The place where this took place, Mount Moriah, is mentioned again in the Bible. On that spot, on the threshing floor of Ornan, David built an altar. And later, the Temple was built there and sacrifices were offered, pointing to the sinless substitute for sinners (2 Chron. 3:1). We now receive Christ and all of his benefits by faith. For Abraham also, believing faith was the lone instrument of receiving the gospel in its then revealed form. Indeed, Abraham believed that God was able to raise the dead, and "figuratively speaking, he *did* receive him [Isaac] back" (11:19). Such is the triumph of faith! Had not Abraham said to his servants before going to the Mount of sacrifice, "I and the boy will go over there and worship and come again to you" (Gen. 22:5)? Faith, our faith, also believes in the resurrection. Our faith is anchored in the resurrection of God's Son in power and the promise of our resurrection on the last day.

The writer of Hebrews closes out this portion of the chapter of faith that dwells upon the patriarchs by pointing to Isaac and to the Jacob narrative. "By faith Isaac invoked future blessings on Jacob and Esau" (11:20). Isaac's blessing looked to things to come (Gen. 27:28–29, 39–40; 28:3–4) because he believed the promise to Abraham his father (Gen. 28:4). Despite the deception of Isaac by his son Jacob, the blessing was offered in faith, recognizing the Lord's purpose for the elect of his father's line (Gen. 27:33).

"By faith Jacob, when dying, blessed each of the sons of Joseph, bowing in worship over the head of his staff" (11:21). Jacob believed at the end of his life in the promise given through his father Isaac and grandfather Abraham. The Lord would fulfill his sovereign promise to his posterity (Gen. 47:28–49:33). Through his posterity, not one son only but all of his sons, the promise would be fulfilled. Even though all of Jacob's sons receive blessing, the writer of Hebrews stresses blessing on "each of the sons of Joseph," Ephraim and Manasseh. Despite Joseph's protest, Jacob stressed the blessing on Ephraim the younger twin, thus emphasizing the election of grace. The sovereign God guided the blessing according to his own purpose despite the reversal of the norm. That Jacob blessed "bowing in worship over the head of his staff" stresses the Septuagint reading, the consonants for "bed" and "staff" being the same in Hebrew. Perhaps the reading adopted may intend to emphasize faith depending upon God even in the weakness of the end of life.

The writer now moves from Joseph's son to Joseph. "By faith Joseph, at the end of his life, made mention of the exodus of the Israelites and gave directions concerning his bones" (v. 22). Joseph's faith is underscored in the directions he gave regarding his bones (Gen. 50:22–26). At his death, Joseph wanted care taken that when Israel was delivered from Egypt by the Lord's hand that his bones would also be taken up to the land of promise. Jacob, his father, had arranged for his burial in the land of promise (Gen. 49:29–50:13), and now his son shows similar concern. When the exodus took place under the leadership of Moses, Joseph's bones were taken with them (Exod. 13:19) and were buried in Shechem after the conquest of Canaan by Israel (Josh. 24:32).

Thus Joseph believed the gospel in its Old Testament form and trusted that the Lord would fulfill his promise to Abraham. And so we who believe in Jesus trust our Lord that our remains will be raised on the last day to enjoy the promise of the new heavens and earth. Should we turn back when all of the saints of God have looked ahead to the fulfillment of the promise of God in Christ? Press on believer, press on!

21

Looking to Jesus, Part 3

HEBREWS 11:1–12:2

Therefore, since we are surrounded by so great a cloud of witnesses, let us also lay aside every weight, and sin which clings so closely, and let us run with endurance the race that is set before us, looking to Jesus, the founder and perfecter of our faith, who for the joy that was set before him endured the cross, despising the shame, and is seated at the right hand of the throne of God.

Campbell Morgan points out that the opening line of the well-known hymn "My Jesus, I Love Thee" has been altered. In most hymnals it reads: "My Jesus, I love thee, I know thou art mine; for thee all the *follies* of sin I resign." Originally, the line read: "My Jesus, I love thee, I know thou art mine; for thee all the *pleasures* of sin I resign."[1] That largely captures the theme before us. The saints in the past and present are called to rely on the promise of God and in so doing to look ahead to the inheritance before us, not allowing our lives to be distracted by the *pleasures* of sin. The saint's great pleasure is communion

1. G. Campbell Morgan, *The Triumphs of Faith* (Grand Rapids: Baker, 1980), 125. Emphasis mine.

with God. As we are called to "lay aside every weight, and sin which clings so closely," and to "run with endurance the race that is set before us, looking to Jesus, the founder and perfecter of our faith."

We have organized our thoughts around the "features of faith" demonstrated in the chapter and now continue to recognize these features in the text.

Features of Faith (continued)

Faith Considers Christ More Valuable Than All the World's Allurements (vv. 23–32)

Having concluded the theme of the relation of faith to patriarchal history, the preacher points us to faith in the life of Moses.

> By faith Moses, when he was born, was hidden for three months by his parents, because they saw that the child was beautiful, and they were not afraid of the king's edict. (11:23)

This is undoubtedly intended to bring to mind the entire narrative of Moses' deliverance from the hand of Pharaoh as it is revealed in the first two chapters of Exodus. Moses' parents exercised faith in the Lord by hiding their child for three months.

The reference to the child as *beautiful* is interpreted for us by divine inspiration in Stephen's speech in Acts 7:20: "At this time Moses was born; and he was beautiful in God's sight. And he was brought up for three months in his father's house." Moses was beautiful to his parents supremely because he was beautiful to the Lord and perhaps his parents discerned that there was a special role for him to play in God's economy. The efforts to save their son were "by faith" and, even though they could not have known the entire unfolding of history, their faith was honored. In exercising this faith, they too were clinging to the promise of God regarding his people.

Looking to Jesus, Part 3

It is well to observe that the faith of Moses' parents enabled them to act despite Pharaoh's edict to kill Hebrew male children (Heb. 1:16). We are expressly told that "they were not afraid of the king's edict." They feared God above Pharaoh. But, as John Murray reminds us, "It is the essence of impiety not to be afraid of God when there is *reason* to be afraid."[2] Note that, as seen in Exodus and throughout the history of God's people, it often has been necessary to stand for the Lord against the power of the state. This reality is not one merely of the distant past but is very much the case for many Christians in the world today who are persecuted for faith in Christ. There are indications that this is becoming more threatening in Western countries today as well, as Christianity is more and more marginalized. "Those who identify with God's people at once become the targets of God's enemies."[3] This fact should not grip us with fear but should stabilize our faith. It is simply the case that "all who desire to live a godly life in Christ Jesus will be persecuted" (2 Tim. 3:12).

Not only did Moses' parents exercise faith, but Moses their son exercised faith as well.

> By faith Moses, when he was grown up, refused to be called the son of Pharaoh's daughter, choosing rather to be mistreated with the people of God than to enjoy the fleeting pleasures of sin. (11:24–25)

Whether this daughter of Pharaoh was Hatshepsut the daughter of Thutmose I is uncertain; it may have been any number of Pharaoh's daughters who reared Moses. At any rate, Moses did not yield to the temptation to become Egyptian and forget the people of God, though it is possible that a position of prominence and comfort was offered to him enabling him "to enjoy the fleeting pleasures of sin." Rather than give in to these "fleeting

---

2. John Murray, *Principles of Conduct* (Grand Rapids: Eerdmans, 1981), 233.

3. Donald Guthrie, *Hebrews*, in *The Tyndale New Testament Commentaries* (Grand Rapids: Eerdmans, 1983), 239.

pleasures of sin," associated with the emoluments of a position in court or nation, Moses identified himself with the poor and persecuted people of God. That is, in New Testament language, Moses shared in Christ's sufferings (1 Pet. 4:13).

Moses was willing "to be mistreated with the people of God." Notice the important point that Moses recognized the Hebrew slaves to have been "the people of God" despite their persecuted position. The "fleeting pleasures of sin" in this case may have been perfectly normal objectives in other circumstances; that is, the things in themselves might have been perfectly permissible. However, for Moses to pursue these things would have been sin due to the Lord's purpose for him and for God's people.

Moses, then, "considered the reproach of Christ greater wealth than the treasures of Egypt, for he was looking to the reward" (11:26). The wealth available to a young man adopted by one of Pharaoh's daughters in the opulent Eighteenth Dynasty would have been massive. The author specifically says that Moses' refusal of this wealth was because he "considered the reproach of Christ greater wealth than the treasures of Egypt." Here we find an essential hermeneutical key for understanding this chapter and, indeed, all of the Old Testament in relation to the new. In trusting the Lord and relying upon the promise of God, thus refusing the grandeur of Egypt and casting his lot with the despised people of God, Moses bore "the reproach of Christ."

The entirety of redemptive history, the promise, deliverance, and covenants are all about Christ. These realities point to Christ, lead to Christ, and revolve around Christ like planets around the sun. By trusting the promise, the Old Testament saints trusted Christ. Therefore, as the writer of Hebrews encourages God's new covenant people to persevere in the faith of Christ, he rightly points to the Old Testament saints who also trusted in Christ as then revealed in the promise. In trusting

Christ, believing in God's promise to his people, Moses went outside the camp bearing Christ's reproach (Heb. 13:13).

Moreover, in his willingness to bear Christ's reproach and to believe the promise, Moses was "looking to the reward." Just as Abraham "was looking forward to the city that has foundations, whose designer and builder is God" (11:10), and the patriarchs desired "a better country, that is, a heavenly one," so Moses was enabled by faith to look beyond his present circumstances to a future reward. What an encouragement to the persecuted people of God in the writer's day and in ours to persevere, also knowing the same Christ by faith and, indeed, with much more knowledge of what the reward of faith entails!

This passage then helps God's people to properly evaluate the world and its allurements in view of the promise and its reward. Erich Sauer has illustrated this interestingly:

> Many years ago I visited a Press Exhibition in Cologne. In one of the large halls the relationship between the Press and the postal services was shown by various documents and tables. I shall never forget the decoration on one of the main walls. It represented a huge eagle. The exhibition concerned itself with the attainments of the German postal services up to 1928. The effect of this huge eagle was most imposing. But when one came nearer to it and looked at it more closely one discovered that it consisted solely of postage stamps of the inflation period—hundreds of thousands of small inflation postage stamps. I said to my companion immediately: "For estimating things earthly is not this a picture of the values of this world in general? Regarded from a distance, at first sight, they seem to be grand and imposing. But the nearer one comes to them, the more one discovers that they are all inflated values—huge numbers but little worth. Not only inflation of money but inflation of words, inflation of terms, inflation of

> ideals, inflation of spirit. Behind the mighty façade
> only very little actual substance. The more one gets
> to know them the less one values them. From the
> distance like an eagle, yet in reality only inflation![4]

When Moses left Egypt, this was also by faith. "By faith he left Egypt, not being afraid of the anger of the king, for he endured as seeing him who is invisible" (11:27). The writer continues the constant refrain "by faith" as if to say, "Do you get the point? The saints of old lived by faith in the promise; are we called to less or to something different who are now blessed with incredible knowledge of the unfolding of God's redemptive purpose in Christ?" This text may point to Moses' flight to Midian or to the exodus. It seems best to see this as a reference to Moses' first flight from Egypt to Midian since the Passover next mentioned is prior to the exodus, and also due to the fact that Moses is mentioned here alone. This may at first blush seem to contradict the statement that "he left Egypt, not being afraid of the anger of the king" but the point of the text is that his flight was "by faith." Overcoming faith determined Moses' actions rather than, ultimately speaking, the threat of Pharaoh.

The point seems to be that Moses' every step was taken by faith. When Moses returned in courage and faith to lead the people of God out of Egypt the Lord established the Passover (Exod. 12) under Moses' direction. "By faith he kept the Passover and sprinkled the blood, so that the Destroyer of the firstborn might not touch them" (11:28). The Passover instituted by God under Moses in Exodus 12 included sprinkling "the blood" in anticipation of the precious blood of Christ (1 Cor. 5:7). This was originally done "so that the Destroyer of the firstborn might not touch them," that is that the Lord himself might not destroy the

---

4. Erich Sauer, *In the Arena of Faith* (Grand Rapids: Eerdmans, 1955), 16. This fine man wrote many things of value, but I cannot commend his dispensational system.

firstborn of Israel as he did the firstborn of the Egyptians from Pharaoh's firstborn down (Exod. 12:12–29).

The exodus from Egypt was by faith. "By faith the people crossed the Red Sea as on dry land, but the Egyptians, when they attempted to do the same were drowned" (11:29). Israel's crossing "the Red Sea on dry land" was by faith, at least on the part of a portion of the people (remembering that a large part of the nation died in the wilderness because of unbelief as already stressed in Hebrews 3:12, 18–19; 4:2, 6, 11). In this exodus, Moses lifted his rod over the sea and the Lord sent an east wind that blew the entire night (Exod. 14:16ff). The waters walled up on both sides and the children of Israel "crossed the Red Sea on dry land." Their pursuers, "the Egyptians, when they attempted to do the same were drowned"—completely destroyed (Exod. 14:28). The people of God led by Moses walked across by faith; the Egyptians who were profane and faithless died under God's judgment.

The conquest as a result of the exodus from Egypt was also conducted by faith. Highlighting one special event of the conquest of Canaan the writer notes that "by faith the walls of Jericho fell down after they had been encircled for seven days" (11:30). Looking at the walls of Jericho, who could ever imagine that they could come down without the miraculous work of the Lord? The people of God may not have understood why the Lord had them march around the walls with the promise that on the seventh day they would come down, but they lived by faith. The Lord kept his word and the people of God destroyed the city in conquest.

Within that city, there was one who had protected the Lord's servants and was delivered by faith when Jericho fell. "By faith Rahab the prostitute did not perish with those who were disobedient, because she had given a friendly welcome to the spies" (11:31; see Josh. 2:1–24; 6:22–25). How wondrous to see that the Lord's sovereign purpose of salvation includes this harlot (*hē pornē*), that he granted her true faith, and commended her (James 2:25). Indeed, this Rahab, transformed by grace, became part of the people of God and was an ancestress of Jesus (Matt. 1:5).

Faith Produces Magnificent Lives (vv. 32–38)

The writer moves on in rapid succession to mention others who exercised faith in the progress of redemptive history, showing that faith in the Lord and his promise produces magnificent lives despite the frailty, faults, and sins of those who truly believe. "And what more shall I say? For time would fail me to tell of Gideon, Barak, Samson, Jephthah, of David and Samuel and the prophets" (11:32). The record of redemptive history is so replete with those who exercised faith that the writer must race through some of the most important characters in the covenant, giving nothing more than honorable mentions.

He is not even concerned at this point with precise chronology (Barak came before Gideon, Jephthah before Samson, and Samuel and David were contemporaries) but to evoke remembrance of their magnificent lives by faith. "Gideon, Barak, Samson, Jephthah" were all used of the Lord during the period of the judges. Gideon (Judg. 6–9) was instrumental by faith in delivering Israel from the Midianites with a small number of three hundred men over against thirty-five thousand coalition forces (Judg. 8:10). Barak (Judg. 4–5), along with Deborah the prophetess, was used to deliver God's people from Jabin's army led by Sisera. Samson (Judg. 13–16) delivered Israel from the Philistines. Even though his life was filled with inconsistency, he believed the Lord and at the end of his life greatly exercised faith in the Lord when he brought down in God's strength the temple of Dagon (Judg. 16:27–30). Jephthah delivered God's people from the Ammonites (Judg. 11–12).

He moves on to tell "of David and Samuel and the prophets." David the King's faith in the Lord could fill reams, and indeed it does in 1 and 2 Samuel. We see him defeating Goliath, patient under Saul's persecution, abased, and finally exalted to the throne. The Psalms are filled with his expressions of faith in the Lord. With David God made "an everlasting covenant, ordered in all things and secure" (2 Sam. 23:5); a covenant that holds within itself the promise of the birth of the Messiah in his line (2 Sam. 7). Samuel was the prophet who anointed David (1 Sam. 16:13) and was the first in the line of the great succession of prophets that were to follow, hence the expression "Samuel and the prophets."

The writer goes on to mention those

> who through faith conquered kingdoms, enforced justice, obtained promises, stopped the mouths of lions, quenched the power of fire, escaped the edge of the sword, were made strong out of weakness, became mighty in war, put foreign armies to flight. (11:33–34)

Perhaps he still has in mind the period of the Judges and the faith of David and Samuel. David "enforced justice" (2 Sam. 8:15) after the character of God, and both Samson and David "stopped the mouths of lions" (Judg. 14:5–6; 1 Sam. 17:34–36). Or, probably, the writer has in mind Daniel in the Lion's Den (Dan. 6). The expression "quenched the power of fire" almost certainly refers to Shadrach, Meshach, and Abednego's escape from the fiery furnace by means of the pre-incarnate Christophany (Dan. 3:25). Those who "escaped the edge of the sword" might refer to many battles and victories or to specific deliverances (1 Kings 19:1–3; 2 Kings 6:31).

By faith God's people "were made strong out of weakness" which might be a general reference pointing to the method of grace which humbles before exalting. David before Goliath is an example of strength "out of weakness" as are the events in the lives of Daniel's three friends, and of Daniel himself, given their weakness before the power of the state. The battles were so frequent that it becomes difficult to think that the writer had specifics in mind when writing of those who "became mighty in war," and who "put foreign armies to flight" though some think that it references the Maccabees. The women of faith are singled out; "women received back their dead by resurrection." The woman of Zarephath and the Shunammite woman are examples of these women who received their dead sons back to life (1 Kings 17:17–24; 2 Kings 4:18–37).

By faith the people of God have also suffered. "Some were tortured, refusing to accept release, so that they might rise again to a better life. Others suffered mocking and flogging, and even chains and imprisonment" (11:35–36). Eleazar of the Maccabean period is often referenced by commentators at this point. Philip Hughes summarizes:

> The old scribe Eleazar "who, refusing release at the cost of compromising his profession, 'welcomed death with renown rather than life with pollution' and 'of his own accord advanced to the instrument of torture' (2 Macc. 6:18ff). The account of Eleazar's death is followed by that of the martyrdom of seven brothers and their mother. The brutal tortures they chose to endure rather than renounce the truth and defile themselves by eating swine's flesh in order to gain their release included tearing out the tongue, scalping, mutilation and frying over the flames (2 Macc. 7:4ff.), and the instruments used by their interrogators in the attempt to break the spirit of these and other indomitable martyrs were, the chronicler tells us, wheels, joint-dislocators, racks, bone-crushers, catapults, cauldrons, braziers, thumbscrews, iron claws, wedges, and branding irons (4 Macc. 7:12). Their expectation of a better resurrection was

expressed in the words uttered by one of the brothers: "The King of the universe will raise us up to an everlasting renewal of life, because we have died for his laws," and in the matter in which the mother exhorted her sons to suffer and die without flinching: "The Creator of the world, who shaped the beginning of man and devised the origin of all things, will in his mercy give life and breath back to you again" (2 Macc. 7:9, 23). So also the youngest brother, when his turn came to suffer and die, confidently testified to Antiochus the king that his brothers, now dead, "after enduring their brief pain, now drink of ever-flowing life, by virtue of God's covenant" (2 Macc. 7:36 JB).[5]

The author of Hebrews continues:

Others suffered mocking and flogging, and even chains and imprisonment. They were stoned, they were sawn in two, they were killed with the sword. They went about in skins of sheep and goats, destitute, afflicted, mistreated,—of whom the world was not worthy—wandering about in deserts and mountains, and in dens and caves of the earth. (11:36–38)

Mocking has been commonly endured by God's true people, especially the prophets (2 Kings 2:23) and so has scourging or *flogging* (Jer. 20:2). "Chains and imprisonment" have been and continue to be the lot of those who proclaim God's Word (Gen. 39:20; 1 Kings 22:27; Jer. 20:2). Zechariah, son of Johoiada, was *stoned* (2 Chron. 24:20–22). There is a tradition that Isaiah was "sawn in two," but nothing is recorded in Scripture about this or anyone who thus suffered. The divinely inspired writer was familiar with instances of which we are not aware.[6]

5. Philip E. Hughes, *Hebrews* (Grand Rapids: Eerdmans, 1990), 512–513.

6. A variant reading exists at this point *epeirasthēsan* "they were tempted." The term is very close in spelling and sound to the term for "sawn in two" (*epristhēsan*) leading some to think that it is an example of dittography, that is

Many were undoubtedly "killed with the sword" (1 Kings 19:10) and went about in makeshift clothing (2 Kings 1:8) because they were "destitute, afflicted, mistreated." Even though these servants of the Lord were often treated as the scum of the earth and the offscourings of the human race, they were those "of whom the world was not worthy." So great was God's grace in the lives of his saints! Calvin comments:

> Wherever God's servants come they bring His benediction with them like the fragrance of a sweet scent . . . Therefore whenever righteous men are taken away from us we should know that this presages evil for us since we are unworthy of their companionship and they are not to perish with us. At the same time the godly have ample ground for consolation if the world casts them off like refuse, when they see that the same thing happened to the prophets who found more mercy among wild beasts than among men themselves.[7]

The writer to the Hebrews goes on: "wandering about in deserts and mountains, and in dens and caves of the earth," thus again underscoring that the prophets were often completely destitute, as far as the goods of this world were concerned, and were unsafe in human terms, being hounded out of civilized locales to howling wildernesses where they were forced into subsistence living (1 Sam. 22:1–5; 1 Kings 18:4–13).

---

a copyist mistakenly repeating letters or sounds in the copying process. It may be genuine; the manuscript evidence is not uniform but it is missing from P46, the oldest papyrus manuscript for Hebrews. If genuine, the connection with the temptation of the Hebrew Christians being addressed, who are thinking of turning away, would be clear: "You are not the first to face this temptation and to overcome it."

7. Calvin, *Hebrews* (Grand Rapids: Eerdmans, 1979), 185.

Looking to Jesus, Part 3

Faith is Vindicated in the Coming of Christ

> And all these, though commended through their
> faith, did not receive what was promised, since God
> had provided something better for us, that apart
> from us they should not be made perfect (11:39–40).

The new covenant has come and the Old Testament saints
reach their goal only in our company. Here is incentive to persevere, drawn from the depths of God's plan in redemptive history, pushing us forward to consummation. God's better plan
brought with it a better hope through a better covenant, and the
Old Testament saints saved by sovereign free mercy are drawn
in our train, who have the privilege of living in the day of fulfillment of those promises to which they looked and for which
they longed. We are not victims, no matter how this world may
treat us; we are conquerors indeed and may well pity the world.
F. F. Bruce brings to our attention these lines from Charles Wesley: "E'en now by faith we join our hands/With those that went
before,/And greet the blood-besprinkled bands/On the eternal
shore." As we believe the promise, we too look forward to a fulfillment that waits for Christ's coming and the final consummation of all things.

It should be evident that the point of Hebrews 11 is not
simply a call that we be like the saints of old, but that we trust
the Lord and believe God's promise by faith, that same promise which is now being fulfilled in the splendid light of Christ's
coming. Through the historical events of God's deliverance of
his people in the progress of revelation, we see that God is true
to his promises. Faith must have an object, and that Object is
the Lord. This has ever been so and remains so; the Object of
our faith is Jesus. Salvation has ever been and continues to be
through grace by faith in Christ alone.

We must be careful not to turn the *roll* call of faith primarily into a *role* call of faith, as is often done. Indeed, there was much in the greatest believer mentioned in this chapter that we would not wish to emulate. To focus on the saints and to say, "This chapter is primarily here to help me be like Abraham and Samson," is to miss the point. The intent of the text is to ground us in the certainty of faith (11:1–2) and to direct out attention to the promise that has sustained God's covenant people throughout the centuries. The text is not preaching Abraham or Samson, but Christ. Moreover, as Calvin comments:

> A tiny spark of light led them to heaven, but now that the sun of righteousness shines on us, what excuse shall we offer if we still hold to the earth? This is the real meaning of the apostle. . . . Since the grace bestowed on us is more abundant it would be absurd for us to have less faith. He says, therefore, that those fathers who were endowed with such a little faith did not have such strong grounds for belief as we have. . . . We should know that we are ungrateful to God two or three times over if less faith appears in us under the reign of Christ than the fathers showed that they had under the Law by such outstanding examples of constancy. [8]

Looking Unto Jesus

The constant emphasis of the text is that faith must have an object, and the object of true faith is Christ. In the continuing conflict between truth and error, God's kingdom and Satan's kingdom, the writer exhorts us to keep our gaze on Christ.

> Therefore, since we are surrounded by so great a cloud of witnesses, let us also lay aside every weight, and sin which clings so closely, and let us run with

---

8 John Calvin, *Hebrews*, 186.

> endurance the race that is set before us, looking to
> Jesus, the found and perfecter of our faith. (12:1–2a)

The "great cloud of witnesses" with which we new covenant believers "are surrounded" comprises those who have borne witness to Christ before his incarnation, of whom we have read in chapter 11. Since "faith is the assurance of things hoped for, the conviction of things not seen" (11:1), this faith must be the motivating principle of Christian living. The same Christ (and promise) believed by the "great cloud of witnesses" of old beckons us on. This allows no syncretism or failure to acknowledge Christ's Lordship, but is a call to clear cut discipleship.

Therefore, "let us lay aside every weight [*ogkos* "weight," "burden"], and sin which clings so closely, and let us run with endurance the race that is set before us." Ultimately, the saints of old ran the race looking unto Jesus and so must we, removing in the process whatever would hinder our faithfulness to him, just as a runner eschews additional hindrances to running well. What might those things be in our lives that must be set aside to follow the Lord in the race before us?

When we look to Jesus, we see "the founder and perfecter of our faith, who for the joy that was set before him endured the cross, despising the shame, and is seated at the right hand of the throne of God" (12:2; compare 1:3 and 8:1). We see a remarkable Savior who as the "founder [*archēgon*] and "perfecter [or "completer," *teletōtēn*] of our faith" unflinchingly "endured the cross." The goal of his incarnation was "set before him" by the Father and with *joy* and delight, in obedience to the Father, Christ redeemed his rebellious people. The Lord Jesus did not turn aside from the future promised him (Phil. 2:1–11) but joyfully persevered through the anger and hatred of men, "despising the shame" and bearing the wrath of God as our substitute. The outcome of the cross was like a jewel "set before him" that beckoned him on; not because the cross was anything less than agony, but because the Father was glorified in the redemption of his people by Christ's once for all sacrifice so often expounded in Hebrews.

"For the sake of [preposition, *anti*] the joy that was set before him"—the complete and final redemption of sinners, the Lord endured our hell for us. Having accomplished this victory for us to the glory of God, our Lord Jesus now "is seated at the right hand of the throne of God," as we were told by the writer from the beginning (Hebrews 1:1–3). There our Lord Jesus sits regnant, as our great high priest, wielding his scepter as our King and bringing his Word to fruition as our glorious prophet.

On the basis of this wondrous accomplishment, the perseverance of our Lord Jesus for us, we too are now enabled to persevere toward our heavenly home. Erich Sauer tells of a visit to the Coliseum in Rome. There he took in the scene "where streams of martyr blood had flowed on this very spot in the two centuries from the time of the apostles." Yet, in the arena, in the center, he spied a plain, high cross. Its base bore the inscription: *Ave crux spec uinca,* "Hail to thee, O Cross, the only hope!"

> A cross in the Colosseum! Exactly where formerly believers on account of their testimony to the Crucified suffered a bloody death, exactly there a cross stands erect today, bearing this so simple but mighty inscription! The seats of the heathen mockers, the walls of the Colosseum itself, lie in ruins. On the place where God's witnesses died, in the middle of the arena, stands, like a sign of triumph, a victorious and lofty cross.

He beheld the market-place of ancient Rome in ruins, the street of processions and triumphs in ruins, the center of the world empire of Rome grown over with weeds, the temples of the heathen and ancient palaces all ruins, "sunk in dust; but the temple of the church remains. How is this?" Sauer answers:

> It is because Christ, the Crucified, is also the Risen
> One: because in His temple, the temple of the church,
> the true God dwells: because this house, though out-
> wardly plain, is the royal house of the Eternal!

He concludes, and it is a fitting conclusion to our discussion of this section of Hebrews: "Because Christ has triumphed, we also can conquer. His cross is at once the sign of victory, of duty, and of promise for all who believe on Him. Therefore faith in Him is both hope and assurance, and looking unto Him we can run with steadfastness the race with faith."[9] Amen, Amen.

---

9. Erich Sauer, *In the Arena of Faith* (Grand Rapids: Eerdmans, 1956), 47–48.

22

Our Father's
Loving Discipline

HEBREWS 12:3–17

Consider him who endured from sinners such hostility against himself, so that you may not grow weary or faint-hearted.

The writer of Hebrews addresses Christians enduring hardship; coming with that hardship was the temptation to turn back to the old from the new—to turn away from Christ and all his benefits. In hard times, we too may be tempted to turn away from the truth and even to question God's Fatherly goodness. "What is God doing?" we may ask. "Where is the kindness of God in this severe trial?" The antidote to that spiritual malady is given to us by the writer of Hebrews: consider Jesus. "Consider him who endured from sinners such hostility against himself, so that you may not grow weary or fainthearted" (12:3).

"Consider him." Look at Jesus from all angles, grow in grace by seeing the Lord Jesus from various perspectives and being captivated by the beauty and glory of his salvation. Remember particularly that he "endured from sinners such hostility against himself," that the memory of his sacrifice to save us will keep us so that we do "not grow weary or fainthearted."

When we are focused in this way on Christ's sacrifice and high priestly work for us, we will not know defeat in the hour of testing. Learning to keep our gaze on the Lord is not something automatic; we need to be exhorted to do so. Our heavenly Father trains us in these matters, takes us through circumstances while holding our hands in the dark, leads and guides us and disciplines us so that we may learn this essential trait of holiness—a focused, persevering, unwavering view of Christ.

Our Father's Loving Discipline

Verses 4–11 focus on the loving discipline of our heavenly Father, training us in righteousness so that we keep our gaze on Christ that we may "consider him who endured from sinners such hostility against himself, so that you may not grow weary or fainthearted" (v. 3). Let it not be forgotten for a moment, as the text will emphasize, that the discipline stressed here is that of our loving heavenly Father. It is love that moved the Father to send his Son, and it is love that moves him to discipline us so that we may never look away from Christ. In this the Father guarantees our perseverance. Let us then think through the components of the Father's loving discipline as found in this passage.

The Father's Discipline is Loving Care

> And have you forgotten the exhortation that addresses you as sons?

> > "My son, do not regard lightly
> > the discipline of the Lord,
> > nor be weary when reproved by him.
> > For the Lord disciplines the one he loves,
> > and chastises every son whom he receives"
> > (12:5–6).

Our Father's Loving Discipline

The writer cites Proverbs 3:11–12 in order to underscore this "exhortation" and to show that suffering in the course of Christian living must be viewed in the enveloping context of God's fatherly care for his family. Wicked men persecute in hatred of God and his people but God our Father accomplishes his gracious purpose even in that. When we "regard lightly the discipline of the Lord," we show that we do not understand the infinite love of God our Father in our circumstances, and we also fail to understand how God ministers to his children. God's discipline, his *paideia*, is comprehensive, including his teaching, direction, and more pointed chastisement for sin. Suffering is an appointed means of God for training in faith.

I have taken to heart many times Luther's dictum that three things make the theologian: prayer, study, and suffering. In communion with God our troubles are sanctified, yes even ordained, under his hand for our sanctification. "Nowhere, indeed, are our corruptions so manifest, or our graces so shining as under the rod," wrote Charles Bridges on the Proverbs passage cited here in Hebrews.

> We need it as much as our daily bread. Children of God are still children of Adam; with Adam's will, pride, independence and waywardness. And nothing more distinctly requires Divine teaching and grace, than how to preserve in our behavior the just mean between hardness and despondency; *neither despising the chastening of the Lord, nor being weary of his correction. . . .*
>
> After all we must add, that chastening is a trial to the flesh (Heb. xii.11); yet overruled by wonder-working wisdom and faithfulness to an end above and contrary to its nature. This very rod was sent in love to the soul. Perhaps we were living at ease, or in heartless backsliding. The awakening voice called us to our Bible and to prayer. Thus eyeing God in it,

we see it to be love, not wrath; receiving, not casting out. We might perhaps have wished it a little altered; that the weight had been shifted, and the cross a little smoothed, where it pressed upon the shoulder. But now that our views are cleared, we discern blessing enough to swallow up the most poignant smart. ...Faith understands the reasons of the discipline (I Pet. i. 6,7); acknowledges it as a part of his gracious providence (Deut. viii. 2, 15, 16), and the provision of his everlasting covenant (Ps. Lxxxix.30–32); waits to see the end of the Lord (Jam. v.11); and meanwhile draws its main support from the seal of adoption.

For indeed it is the declared test of our legitimacy. (Heb. xii. 7, 8. Rev. iii. 19). He *corrects whom he loves, the son in whom he delighteth.* His discipline is that of the family; not of the school; much less of the prison. He corrects his children, not as criminals, but as those whom he beholds without spot, "made accepted in the Beloved." (Eph. i.6.)

Bridges concludes: "What does it all mean, but the Lord holding to his determination to save us; all the thoughts of his heart, every exercise of his power, centering in this purpose of his sovereign mercy?"[1] This is correct and a profound observation upon which to meditate. We are tempted to faint, to give up, to turn back, to compromise, but God our Father in love disciplines us. This point that the Father's discipline is in love deserves a few additional lines so that we may stress this truth.

The Father's Discipline Shows that He Loves Us

Having stressed this truth, let us emphasize it again, for what but this grand reality will sustain us in trial? If our souls know the Lord's love for us what can we not endure for his sake? "For the Lord disciplines the one he loves, and chastises every son whom he receives" (12:6). It is necessary to underscore the Fa-

---

1. Charles Bridges, *Proverbs* (Edinburgh: Banner of Truth, 1998), 29–31.

Our Father's Loving Discipline

ther's love due to our tendency to question God's love when things seem to go against us. Rather than being against us, the text assures us that the Father shows love, the love of an infinite and caring Father, when disciplining us. Even the impeccable Son of God learned through suffering (Heb. 2:10); are we above this, who are adopted "sons whom he receives"? Since the discipline of the Lord is in love we may be assured that whatever befalls us is not by chance but by his fatherly design and is for our good. The providence of God is not simply mechanistic, that is, abstract and impersonal, but is in fact the sovereign direction of God for the good of his church. The beautiful words of the Heidelberg Catechism are once again applicable here.

> Q. 27: What dost thou mean by the providence of God?
>
> A. The almighty and everywhere present power of God; whereby, as it were by His hand, He upholds and governs heaven, and earth, and all creatures; so that herbs and grass, rain and drought, fruitful and barren years, meat and drink, health and sickness, riches and poverty, yea, and all things come, not by chance, but by His fatherly hand.
>
> Q. 28 What advantage is it to us to know that God has created and by His providence doth still uphold all things?
>
> A. That we may be patient in adversity; thankful in prosperity; and that in all things, which may hereafter befall us, we place our firm trust in our faithful God and Father, that nothing shall separate us from His love; since all creatures are so in His hand, that without His will they cannot so much as move.[2]

We must always remember that in our suffering the Lord is accomplishing his sovereign purpose; and that God's people

2. *The Heidelberg Catechism*, in *The Three Forms of Unity* (Birmingham, AL: Solid Ground, 2010), 76.

may be sure that his purpose for his people is loving and good. Herman Hoeksema correctly observed:

> Hence, the meaning of history is not that all things tend and make progress in the direction of the perfect world, as evolutionistic philosophy would have us believe. Nor is the end of God's providence the realization of the original creation ordinance, the full development of the original paradise, in spite of the opposition of Satan, and through a certain power of common grace. Again the meaning of history is not that this world develops in the direction of the kingdom of heaven, so that it will finally merge into the glorified creation. But it certainly is the proper stage that is set for the realization of God's purpose of predestination, election and reprobation, the revelation of the Son of God, the cross and resurrection, the cause of God's covenant, the bringing forth and the gathering of the Church, the wonder of grace; and that, too, in antithesis to sin and darkness, the devil and his host, the man of sin culminating in the antichrist of the latter days; and through it all the highest possible revelation of God's covenant friendship, the glory of the life of the Triune God.[3]

In the throes of trials, believers may not see these things. These truths may not be empirically obvious, but we should take this Scriptural truth to heart in every hard circumstance. We who know the Lord are a part of his kingdom. Our trials participate in something bigger than ourselves. Life should be lived in the realization of the cosmic sweep of things. The knowledge that God has planned in his sovereignty to show eternal love to his people and thus to glorify himself is actually being fulfilled in our lives.

---

3. Herman Hoeksema, *The Heidelberg Catechism (An Exposition)* (Grand Rapids: Eerdmans, 1944), 2.210–211.

Our Father's Loving Discipline

The Father's Discipline is for Spiritual Health and Development

This is an implication of verse 6 as well. The Lord "disciplines the one he loves, and chastises every son whom he receives." The Father's training is for correcting our hearts, growing us in grace, and forming our Christian characters. We cannot know the secret purposes of God in our chastisement, but we can know that his plan for his people is good, and his discipline and chastisement is in mercy. The purpose of this divine revelation is not to discourage us but is given to encourage us in the progress of Christian living. As those received in Christ's righteousness, we may know that the chastisements of the Lord are not condemnatory. In God's sovereign grace:

> suffering produces endurance, and endurance produces character, and character produces hope, and hope does not put us to shame, because God's love has been poured into our hearts through the Holy Spirit who has been given to us. (Rom. 5:3–5)

Suffering, discipline, chastisement—these things are intended for our spiritual health and development. Knowing these truths enables us to agree with the attitude of William Romaine: "Welcome every cross which brings me nearer to my Jesus, and makes me live in stricter fellowship with him."[4]

The Father's Discipline Demonstrates that We are Sons of God

The Lord "chastises every son whom he receives." This reality is stressed in verses 7 and 8:

> It is for discipline that you have to endure. God is treating you as sons. For what son is there whom his

---

4. Quoted in Tim Shenton, *'An Iron Pillar' The Life and Times of William Romaine* (Darlingon, England: Evangelical Press, 2004), 226.

father does not discipline? If you are left without discipline, in which all have participated, then you are illegitimate children and not sons.

The writer echoes Proverbs 3:11–12. Trials are a demonstration that the people addressed are actually sons. The goal in view is not condemnatory wrath but the demonstration of sonship and the growth of God's children. In the trials of life, coming as they do from God's fatherly hand, the goal is not wrath but love. God's goal for us is conformity to the image of God's Son (Rom. 8:28–29). What is our Father's goal in discipline? The Father's loving goal is to keep us from sin and to develop Christlikeness in the lives of his sons. He intends to develop within us hearts that more and more do not want to sin. This good and loving goal of God our Father is illustrated from the caring goals of a loving earthly father.

"God is treating you as sons. For what son is there whom his father does not discipline?" Every caring Father disciplines his children, and our heavenly Father who loves us with infinite love will do no less! A lack of discipline says something about a father and about a child: "If you are left without discipline, in which all have participated, then you are illegitimate children and not sons" (v. 8). Every well-disciplined child sees in time the wisdom of his father's discipline, even though he may question it while it is going on. And who has not seen the tragic results of an indulged and undisciplined child? We have no such Father; God loves and therefore disciplines his sons. All true children of God will be disciplined at one time or the other—if not, it would show that God is not our Father and that we are not his children. Indeed, as the Westminster Confession says so brilliantly in chapter XII on Adoption, the Lord's chastening takes place in a context of grace, love, and protection—with eternity as its ultimate goal:

Our Father's Loving Discipline

> All those that are justified, God vouchsafeth, in and for his only Son Jesus Christ, to make partakers of the grace of adoption: by which they are taken into the number, and enjoy the liberties and privileges of the children of God; have his name put upon them, receive the Spirit of adoption; have access to the throne of grace with boldness; are enabled to cry, Abba, Father; are pitied, protected, provided for, and chastened by him as a father; yet never cast off, but sealed to the day of redemption, and inherit the promises, as heirs of everlasting salvation.

Finally, the Father's Discipline has Holiness as Its Goal

In verses 9 and 10, the writer makes it plain that the goals of discipline are life and holiness:

> Besides this, we have had earthly fathers who disciplined us and we respect them. Shall we not much more be subject to the Father of spirits and live? For they disciplined us for a short time, but he disciplines us for our good, that we may share his holiness.

How the love of the Father is seen here most clearly! We should pause and consider the wonder of such love. Lost, fallen, undone, unholy from birth, with no free will, but a will bound by sin, without Christ, and without hope, we would have been lost forever had the Lord not intervened to save us. Yet our Father has loved us with an everlasting love. On the basis of the merit of Christ we are justified once for all as a judicial act.

Furthermore, since our hearts are now regenerated, but still sinful, the Lord has promised to purify and progressively sanctify his people. The Lord has promised to make us holy, and that is the goal of discipline. God always keeps his promises. To be "subject to the Father of Spirits" (i.e., the one who gives us spiritual life and heavenly love, as distinguished from earthly fathers) is to "live." The discipline of the Lord is the way of life, not of death. Conversely, to turn from his discipline is the way of death and not of life.

The writer argues "how much more." If our earthly fathers did us good by disciplining us, then will not our heavenly Father give life that leads to holiness by his caring and ever faithful discipline? If we benefited from the "short time" our fathers administered discipline during our maturing years, will we not know much greater benefit from the discipline the Lord administers to us? "For they disciplined us for a short time as it seemed best to them, but he disciplines us for our good, that we may share his holiness?" The Lord's discipline is perfect and is designed to develop holiness of life. This is the goal for all of God's people. J. C. Ryle reminds us:

> I fear that it is sometimes forgotten that God has married together justification and sanctification. They are distinct and different things, beyond question, but one is never found without the other. All justified people are sanctified, and all sanctified are justified. What God has joined together let no man dare to put asunder. Tell me not of your justification, unless you have also some marks of sanctification. Boast not of Christ's work *for you,* unless you can show us the Spirit's work *in you.* Think not that Christ and the Spirit can ever be divided.[5]

The holiness that is the goal of discipline is leading us on to entire sanctification known by believers only at death, but the process bringing us there is progressive throughout our sojourn on earth. Holiness comes in stages over time, not all at once, just as disciplined children grow in character over time. The

---

5. J. C. Ryle, *Holiness: Its Nature, Hindrances, Difficulties and Roots* (Peabody, MA: Hendrickson, 2007), 59.

goal is conformity to the image of God's Son (Rom. 8:28–29), "that we may share his holiness."

There are no spiritual gains without spiritual pains. "For the moment all discipline seems painful rather than pleasant, but later it yields the peaceable fruit of righteousness to those who have been trained by it" (12:11). Note the athletic metaphor; holiness of life requires that we be "trained." The trial will be difficult, the discipline may seem to us at times to be severe, but in the end all of this results in "the peaceable fruit of righteousness." The Psalmist teaches us this. "Before I was afflicted I went astray, but now I keep your word. . . . It is good for me that I was afflicted, that I might learn your statues" (Ps. 119:67, 71).

If we think that the cross of Christ accomplishes our justification and stops there, we dishonor the Lord and make Christ only half a Savior in our minds. The Lord Jesus went to the cross to deliver his people from the guilt of sin but also from its dominion. Christ "bore our sins in his body on the tree, that we might die to sin and live to righteousness" (1 Pet. 2:24). From this perspective we should see that the discipline of the Lord is the purchase of Christ for God's children. Those for whom Christ died will be inevitably disciplined of the Lord as the fruit of Christ's atonement. Holiness is the fruit of the cross.

Our Response to Our Father's Discipline

The Lord calls his people to holiness and disciplines us as a loving Father to train us in righteousness. How should sons of the Father respond to the discipline of the Lord?

Respond with Inner Resolve

We must respond to the discipline of the Lord with the inner resolve to profit from the Lord's loving care in the trial: "Therefore lift your drooping hands and strengthen your weak knees, and make straight paths for your feet, so that what is lame may not be put out of joint, but rather be healed" (vv. 12–13). The picture, appealing to Isaiah 35:3, is of slack hands and paralyzed knees due to the severity of the trial; the Christian may at times feel spiritually as if he is about to drop. However, the Lord's purpose in the trial is not to make us weak but to make us strong. "Therefore" points us back to the Lord's work and purpose in discipline, "lift your drooping hands and strengthen your weak knees, and make straight paths for your feet."

Here the writer alludes to Proverbs 4:26: "Ponder the ways of your feet; then all your ways will be sure." The Lord's goal is not to further paralyze us but to cure our limbs and make us move toward the goal of holiness: "so that what is lame may not be put out of joint, but rather be healed." The Lord would have us profit from his discipline. Spurgeon was right to comment: "It is a special proof of grace when nothing can drive truth from our thoughts, or holiness out of our lives."[6]

Respond with a Peaceful Heart that Pursues Holiness

Nothing so hinders growth in grace than does a trustless, agitated heart. The writer addresses our calling as tried and strained believers to "strive for peace with everyone, and for holiness without which no one will see the Lord." Believers must not let the relational stresses of life keep us from growth, but we should make every attempt to "strive for peace with everyone" evidently meaning persecutors *and* believers. The dual striving includes peace with men and holiness before the Lord, "holiness without which no one will see the Lord" (v. 14).

Why is this true? Why will "no one see the Lord" without holiness? Because the purpose for which Christ came is to make his people holy, and present holiness prepares us for heaven,

---

6. C. H. Spurgeon, *The Treasury of David* (Pasadena, TX: Pilgrim Publications, 1893 reprint), 6.245.

the full enjoyment of our holy God, and a completely holy life. Unbelievers could not enjoy heaven even if it were possible for them to go there, and believers are being prepared for the enjoyment of that world by being trained now as holy citizens of the world to come.

Our growth in holiness is but a foretaste of the time when we will be without temptation and sin. How our hearts should long for this and how that should motivate us as we now "strive for holiness" to attend in faith on the appointed means for our growth in grace, the preached Word and sacraments, and the prayers and fellowship of Christ's church.

There is a new principle at work in the Christian's heart; it is as yet an imperfect and incomplete work, but it is a real work. The Holy Spirit applies the gospel and yes, also the Father's discipline, to our hearts to wean us from the love of this world, so that we long for the next and reflect that longing in our character.

Respond with Opposition to Everything that Hinders Sanctification

The call to holiness is a call to careful Christian living and a call for us to be rid of all that opposes the holiness to which we are called. We should want to search God's Word with the purpose of removing from our lives all that the Holy Spirit shows us is contrary to God's Word. Hence these pastoral exhortations are designed to encourage holiness. "See to it that no one fails to obtain the grace of God; that no 'root of bitterness' springs up and causes trouble, and by it many become defiled" (12:15). The idea expressed here is that of apostasy, giving up on the race. The idiom *husterein apo* is to cut oneself from the contest.[7] Do not miss the goal, do not come in late; "see to it" (literally, *show oversight over*).

---

7. Philip E. Hughes, *Hebrews* (Grand Rapids: Eerdmans, 1977), 538.

While no true believer will apostatize, the writer by divine inspiration applies this warning consistently in Hebrews to spur on those who do know the Lord. Heeding our Father's warning is a part of being a faithful son. The writer carefully warns "that no 'root of bitterness' springs up and causes trouble, and by it many become defiled." Every pastor knows that bitterness can trouble and destroy a congregation. Especially when the church is in troubled times, such a temptation can emerge, and rarely are others unaffected by the bitterness of a church member; rather, "by it many become defiled" (v. 15).

> If some incipient sin manifests itself in their midst, it must be eradicated at once; if it is tolerated, this is a sure way of falling short of God's grace, for the whole community will then be contaminated. Such a sin is called a "root of bitterness," in language borrowed from Deut. 29:18, where Moses warns the Israelites against any inclination to fall into the idolatrous practices of Canaan, "lest there should be among you a root that beareth gall and wormwood" . . . Perhaps the best commentary on our author's words here is his earlier warning in Ch. 3:12: "Take heed, brethren, lest haply there shall be in any one of you an evil heart of unbelief, in falling away from the living God."[8]

Verses 16 and 17 continue the pastoral exhortation, calling believers to be rid of anything that conflicts with God's goal of sanctification. The writer wants to make sure that

> no one is sexually immoral or unholy like Esau, who sold his birthright for a single meal. For you know that afterward, when he desired to inherit the blessing, he was rejected, for he found no chance to repent, though he sought it with tears.

---

8. F. F. Bruce, *Hebrews* (Grand Rapids: Eerdmans, 1979), 365–366.

Profane Esau traded his birthright, wanting immediate gratification. Even though he regretted his decision, he could not alter the consequences. Esau's tears were totally in vain. He could not undo what he had done. Some decisions simply cannot be changed (4:1); actions have consequences. Sexual immorality in particular can bear bitter fruit in unchangeable ways despite the way such disobedience to God's law is glamorized by the culture in which we live.

Discipline and Holiness: Some Pastoral Implications

Among the many pastoral implications of this section of the book of Hebrews, these implications are certainly to be underscored. First, grace produces effort. Where the Word of God is applied to the heart by the Holy Spirit, the true believer will care about growth in grace and will actively pursue it. Believers will "lay aside every weight, and sin which clings so closely," and will "run with endurance the race that is set before us, looking to Jesus;" we will "consider him who endured," and struggle against sin, endure, lift drooping hands, strengthen weak knees, and strive for peace. Hebrews 12:1–17 is flush with the actions that God expects of his people in the sanctification of their souls.

By faith we are called to pursue holiness. J. C. Ryle warned in a tract, *The Great Battle*:

> I do fear much for many professing Christians: I see no sign of fighting in them, much less of victory; they never strike one stroke on the side of Christ. They are at peace with His enemies: they have no quarrel with sin. Reader, I warn you this is not Christianity: this is not the way to heaven.

Ryle writes in the pastoral tradition of the writer of Hebrews.

Second, to benefit from the discipline of the Lord as we should requires that we continually give attention to God's

Word. The Word preached, read, and meditated upon is the context that makes discipline a welcomed blessing. God's people must not neglect God's Word, but they must cherish this primary means of grace as the *sine qua non* of the Christian life. Why insist upon this? The answer is because we must be vitally concerned with what God says and his interpretation of the facts lest we become confused, cynical, or even unbelieving in the midst of trial. How subtle the temptation can be to follow our own devices and turn our minds to autonomous thinking.

I remember reading somewhere a story relating to Professor John Murray. A student failed a theology exam and came to Professor Murray to express his opinion. Professor Murray responded: "Mr. Neeham, I am not in the *least* bit interested in what you think, but I am keenly interested in finding out if you know what God thinks." Evidently the stunned student replied, "Thank you," and departed, but this forthright rebuke from his professor was a turning point in his life. In a far greater way, the fatherly discipline of the Lord is for the purpose of driving us to the Bible so that we may gain God's inerrant perspective on the matter of how to view life and serve him.

Third, we must live *Coram Deo*—"before the face of God." If we are to pursue holiness of life single heartedly we must do so with a view to pleasing God and not man. We must live like a musician who does not care if he pleases the audience, so long as he is sure his teacher would be pleased. The King is the teacher, and we must live to please him. Nothing will so derail us in the pursuit of holiness than caring what man thinks more than what God thinks. Let us bow before the Word.

> You must not search inside yourself for anything—
> whether it is under the name of reason or intelli-
> gence or feeling or conscience or some other lovely
> thing—that dominates or judges or controls the
> Word of God. It is not a matter of controlling it but

of being controlled by it. The greatest of all God's servants are those who bow before that Word. Saint Paul, David, Luther, and Calvin were jealous to humble themselves in the dust before it, and if possible would have gone still lower. . . . May it [God's Word] reign alone.[9]

---

9. Adolphe Monod, *Living in the Hope of Glory* (Phillipsburg, NJ: Presbyterian and Reformed, 2002), 35.

23

You Have Come to Mount Zion

HEBREWS 12:18–29

For you have not come to what may be touched, a blazing fire and darkness and gloom and a tempest and the sound of a trumpet and a voice whose words made the hearers beg that no further messages be spoken to them. For they could not endure the order that was given, "If even a beast touches the mountain, it shall be stoned." Indeed, so terrifying was the sight that Moses said, "I tremble with fear." But you have come to Mount Zion and to the city of the living God, the heavenly Jerusalem, and to innumerable angels in festal gathering, and to the assembly of the firstborn who are enrolled in heaven, and to God, the judge of all, and to the spirits of the righteous made perfect, and to Jesus, the mediator of a new covenant, and to the sprinkled blood that speaks a better word than the blood of Abel.

We often feel overwhelmed as the world changes around us, and as we experience change within ourselves. Health and sickness, cheefulness and sadness, a life-time that is a short time, good leaders and bad leaders, purpose and vanity, justice and injustice—all flesh is grass! Nothing seems fixed. In times such as these, God's people need to remember that we belong to an unchangeable God, who has an unchangeble purpose, who has brought us into an unshakable kingdom through Christ. It is that blessed truth we now turn to in this text.

We have seen that the book of Hebrews is characterized in part by warning passages. We have come to the fifth and final warning passage in Hebrews 12:18–29. It is also essential to note the contrast that continues between the old covenant and the new that forms the backbone of the epistle. The warning, in other words, comes in the context of showing once again the glory and immeasurable superiority of the new covenant. This helps the new covenant believer to appreciate the work of Christ and provides additional encouragement as new covenant believers persevere under adversity and persecution. The writer begins with the position of believers under the law in order to draw the contrast, thus demonstrating the glories of the new covenant fellowship *founded* on the sacrifice of Christ and *secured* by his intercession.

The Position of Believers under Law

God's Awesome Presence at Sinai

> For you have not come to what may be touched, a blazing fire and darkness and gloom and a tempest and the sound of a trumpet and a voice whose words made the hearers beg that no further messages be spoken to them. (12:18–19)

The contrast of positions for believers prior to and following the atonement and exaltation of Christ is first drawn out by the description offered of God's theophanic presence at Sinai (Exod. 19:10–25; 20:18–21; Deut. 4:10–24). In wondrous ways and with solemn majesty, the Lord showed his holy power and transcendent majesty when he gave the Law. The Mount was aflame, God's presence descended in fire, smoke and earthquake, darkness, gloom, and storm. The sound of the trumpet, perhaps sounded by angelic lips, became louder and louder, and the Word of the Lord given to Moses was so alarming that the Israelites begged Moses to act as God's spokesman, so that they could escape, if possible, his awesome presence.

God's Fearful Command

It was in the midst of flame and smoke that the Lord revealed the fearful command: "For they could not endure the order given that was given, 'If even a beast touches the mountain, it shall be stoned.'" The regulations given about how to approach the mountain of God's presence demonstrated the awful gulf that separates God from sinful man. "If even a beast touches the mountain, it shall be stoned"—so sinful man better beware!

The Terrifying Sight

Accompanying these regulations and the fearful presence of God in smoke and fire, noise, and earthquake, was the terrifying sight before the eyes of Moses, the man of God. "Indeed, so terrifying was the sight that Moses said, 'I tremble with fear.'" The senses of God's servant Moses were overwhelmed—hearing and smell, touch and sight.

Now the writer will contrast Sinai with the present position of believers in Christ. Here we see that the terror of the law has nothing to do with us; that is, for those in Christ for whom he died and for whom he intercedes, the blessing is great, and our acceptance clear and wonderful. However, does this mean that the new covenant believer has less awe in God's presence? Let us see.

Our Present Position as Believers

The City of the Living God, the Heavenly Jerusalem

In contrast to the old covenant believer, the writer says of us:

> But you have come to Mount Zion and to the city of the living God, the heavenly Jerusalem, and to innumerable angels in festal gathering, and to the assembly of the firstborn who are enrolled in heaven, and to God, the judge of all, and to the spirits of the righteous made perfect, and to Jesus, the mediator of a new covenant, and to the sprinkled blood that speaks a better word than the blood of Abel. (12:22–24)

Sinai points to *law*; Zion is the mount of *grace*. Zion is one of the hills upon which Jerusalem was built that became synonymous with God's purpose of grace and salvation, his presence with his people (Ps. 145:3). Here, in particular, it is a symbol of grace and of salvation, the ultimate fulfillment of God's presence of blessing in the new covenant era. *Zion* is synonymous with "the city of the living God, the heavenly Jerusalem." We have seen in 11:10, 16 that the patriarchs looked for the city whose builder and maker is God. There is a future aspect, a longing for, and a desiring to enter that city as we read in Revelation 21:2: "And I saw the holy city, New Jerusalem, coming down out of heaven from God, prepared as a bride adorned for her husband."

While on earth, we are already citizens of that city, and in that sense we already possess it. We are in principle already where we shall be forever, since we are in union with Christ in the heavenlies (Eph. 2:6). Indeed:

> Our citizenship is in heaven, and from it we await a Savior, the Lord Jesus Christ, who will transform our lowly body to be like his glorious body, by the power

that enables him even to subject all things to himself.
(Phil. 3:20)

This reminds us of Vos' beautiful description of the "shifting of the center of gravity from the lower to the highest sphere" due to the ascension of Christ. He adds:

> The bond between the believer and Christ is so close that, from Paul's point of view, a detachment of the Christian's *interest* not only, but even a severance of his *actual life* from the celestial Christ-centered sphere is unthinkable.[1]

Hence, our citizenship in the New Jerusalem determines the believers' affections, choices, and direction.[2]

Innumerable Angels in Festal Gathering

"But you have come to Mount Zion and to the city of the living God, the heavenly Jerusalem, and to innumerable angel's in festal gathering" (12:22). Reading this most impressive verse, one cannot help but think of the Revelation with its emphasis on heavenly worship. John writes:

> Then I looked, and I heard around the throne and the living creatures and the elders the voice of many angels, numbering myriads and thousands of thousands, saying with a loud voice, "Worthy is the Lamb who was slain, to receive power and wealth and wisdom and might and honor and glory and blessing!" (Rev. 5:11–12)

By divine inspiration, John reflected on the events following Jesus' return:

---

1. Geerhardus Vos, *The Pauline Eschatology* (Grand Rapids: Baker, 1979), 37.

2. Clearly we have in this text new covenant fulfillment of Isaiah 60:14 and Micah 4:1–2. For a discussion of how this relates to the discussion of the hermeneutics of dispensationalism, see Vern Poythress, *Understanding Dispensationalists* (Phillipsburg, New Jersey: Presbyterian and Reformed, 1994), 118–125.

> And after this I looked and behold, a great multitude
> that no one could number, from every nation, from
> all tribes and peoples and languages, standing before
> the throne and before the Lamb, clothed in white
> robes, with palm branches in their hands, and crying
> out with a loud voice, "Salvation belongs to our God
> who sits on the throne, and to the Lamb!" And all the
> angels were standing around the throne and around
> the elders and the four living creatures, and they fell
> on their faces before the throne and worshiped God,
> saying, "Amen! Blessing and glory and wisdom and
> thanksgiving and honor and power and might be to
> our God forever and ever! Amen." (Rev. 7:9–12)

Myriads, ten thousand times ten thousand, of those "ministering spirits sent out to serve for the sake of those who are to inherit salvation" (Heb. 1:14) will on that Day (and do now) worship the Lamb upon his throne. New covenant believer, "you have come to . . . innumerable angels in festal gathering" (12:22). How this should inform our worship on the Lord's Day; how this should spur us on to faithfulness in daily living!

The Assembly of the First-Born Who are Enrolled in Heaven

You have also in Christ come "to the assembly of the first-born who are enrolled in heaven" (12:23). While yet on earth, you are a part of that total assembly of God's people (the *qahal*, "assembly" of the Old Testament, now applied to the New Testament believers), who now by faith belong to God's kingdom as those who are "the first-born." The "first-born" was the one who inherited, and we are the heirs of all things being conformed to Christ the first-born (Rom. 8:17, 28–29; Col. 1:15).

As such you are one with them who are "enrolled in heaven." Moses enrolled all the first-born males in ancient Israel and Paul refers to his co-workers as those "whose names are in the book of life" (Phil. 4:3). This assembly includes the Old Testament believers who had not received the fulfillment of the promises, and you who now believe. Both belong to this reality in which the center is the throne of the Lamb.

A Judge Who is the God of All

As we strive in the persevering grace that God supplies, we have also come to "God, the judge of all" (12:23). This is both solemn and reassuring. Through Christ we have been reconciled to the Judge. His throne is not one of condemnation but of grace. Christians are called upon now to "draw near with a true heart in full assurance of faith, with our hearts sprinkled clean from an evil conscience and our bodies washed with pure water" (Heb. 10:20). Our "confidence to enter the holy places" is solely "the blood of Jesus" (Heb. 10:19). Remarkably, because of the sacrifice of Jesus, who loved us and whom we now love in return, "we may have confidence for the day of judgment" (1 John 4:17). It is that confidence to which we have now come. The confidence of the believer is that that the Judge will bring the enemies of his people to the bar; it is the confidence that the Judge who poured out the due deserts of our sin upon Christ receives us totally.

The Spirits of Righteous Men Made Perfect

Moreover, we have come "to the spirits of the righteous made perfect" (Heb. 12:23). Here is justification for that line in the grand hymn, "The Church's One Foundation":

> Yet she on earth hath union
> with God the Three in One,
> and mystic sweet communion
> with those whose rest is won:
>
> O happy ones and holy!
> Lord, give us grace that we,

like them, the meek and lowly,
on high may dwell with thee.[3]

The hymn does not imply "communion with the dead" in the sense of occultism; rather, it implies that God's people have a common Lord, that we are in union with Christ, and therefore are a part of one worshiping people of God; though for now upon different shores.

"Blessed are the dead who die in the Lord" (Rev. 14:13), because Christ has tasted death for us, and we are one with Christ in the perfection of his resurrection and ascended life. We who yet remain have come "to the spirits of the righteous made perfect" as we await the perfection that is promised us at death. Indeed, we join with that innumerable company worshiping the Lamb even now through the Lord with whom we are in union. The ultimate issue is that we have come "to Jesus, the mediator of a new covenant" (12:24).

Jesus, the Mediator of the New Covenant

Jesus is the "mediator of the new covenant," to whom we have come by faith as the Father effectually drew us. From Mount Calvary, where our Lord shed his precious blood, the Lord has brought us to Mount Zion and has given us all of the precious promises of our undefiled inheritance. He has done away with all of the legal demands of Mount Sinai through his death on the cross. Since our Savior is the Mediator, as Newton has it in the hymn, "He has hushed the law's loud thunder, he has quenched Mount Sinai's flame."[4]

The writer alludes to the pervasive theme of Hebrews—Jesus our high priest, our surety, who bore our legal obligations for us and secured our eternal redemption through his sacrifice

3. Samuel J. Stone, "The Church's One Foundation," from *Trinity Hymnal*, rev. ed., (Suwanee, GA: Great Commission Publications, 1990), selection 347.

4. John Newton, "Let Us Love and Sing and Wonder," from *Trinity Hymnal*, rev. ed., (Suwanee, GA: Great Commission Publications, 1990), selection 172.

(8:6; 9:14–15; 12:24). The thrill of this announcement is seen in the order of words in the sentence, literally: "to the mediator of the new covenant, that is, Jesus." We are now come to the heavenly Jerusalem and are now come to the mediator that makes access to God possible. We do not push off these realities to some future millennial reign, and we do not sever the connection of Christ's mediatorial session at God's right hand from the present reality of believer's lives. To these realities, we have come. Through Jesus the mediator, we have also come to "the sprinkled blood."

The Sprinkled Blood

God's people have come by the guiding hand of grace "to the sprinkled blood that speaks a better word than the blood of Abel" (12:24). Let us extol Jesus' blood. The blood of Jesus validates and secures the new covenant. We have already been told that "Christ has obtained a ministry that is as much more excellent than the old as the covenant he mediates is better since it is enacted on better promises" (8:6; see also 9:15). Because of this saving reality, we are to obey the exhortation to "draw near with a true heart in full assurance of faith, with our hearts sprinkled clean from an evil conscience and our bodies washed with pure water" (10:22).

Moses mediated the old with blood, but the new covenant is confirmed through Jesus' blood. His blood is the blood of the covenant of grace. The sprinkled blood of Christ "speaks a better word than the blood of Abel." Abel's blood speaks (11:4). His death called for God's vengeance (Gen. 4:10), but the blood of Christ was shed to remove God's just vengeance, bringing forgiveness and life to us, his people. Indeed, how much better is the blood of Christ! His blood was shed for:[5]

- Eternal redemption from sin (Heb. 9:12)

---

5. Some of these Scripture passages are pointed out and commented on by Philip E. Hughes.

- The putting away of our sins (Heb. 9:26)

- The purging of an evil conscience (Heb. 10:22)

- The perfection and sanctification of God's people (Heb. 10:10, 14)

- Our acceptance with God providing confidence to enter his throne room (Heb. 10:19)

- Our participation in the heavenly Jerusalem (Heb. 12:24)

The citizen of the heavenly Kingdom has come to Jesus' blood; the accusing voice of sin and the law is silenced. We are forgiven of our sins and have the right to all of the privileges of Jesus' purchase. The blood of Abel could merely point forward in a shadowy type to the infinitely greater and more wondrous sacrifice of Jesus for our sins.

Hearing God's Voice in Awesome Reverence

Having come to the heavenly Jerusalem through the mediation of Christ, our privileges and responsibilities are more awesome than those imposed by Sinai. It is important to note and keep in mind, as we proceed to these next verses, that having contrasted Sinai with the solemn wonder of Calvary, the writer does not conclude that our sense of awe and reverence is *less* than was the case with Sinai, but *more*. Our privileges have increased, and our sense of reverence and awe should also increase.

Having come to "the sprinkled blood that speaks a better word than the blood of Abel," we have a greater obligation to hear him whose blood speaks out before the Father for our redemption. Through his Son, God speaks privilege and duty, blessing and warning.

You Have Come to Mount Zion

God Speaks in His Son

> See that you do not refuse him who his speaking. For if they did not escape when they refused him who warned them on earth, much less will we escape if we reject him who warns from heaven. (Heb. 12:25)

God descended in perceptible awe at Sinai to speak his law to sinners. He then descended in Christ to speak the good news of salvation in his name. The writer's point is to help these Hebrew Christians, who are tempted to return to the law, to pause and ask this question: "Which requires the greater obligation to hear?" Christianity is the revelation of the will of God to sinners in finality:

> Long ago, at many times and in many ways, God spoke to our fathers by the prophets, but in these last days he has spoken to us by his Son, whom he appointed the heir of all things, through whom also he created the world. (Heb. 1:1–2)

God has spoken in his Son, and we must hearken. But God continues to speak as well, not by means of additional revelation, but through the proclamation of his Word. Every time the Word is preached, God personally addresses his people through the faithful exposition of his will. Life without the Word of God read and preached is absurd; but, this is the temptation pulling these tempted Christians. They would set aside God's clear and final revelation in his Son and turn back to the types and shadows. Hear the Son, "for if they did not escape when they refused him who warned them on earth, much less will we escape if we reject him who warns from heaven" (12:25).

A Shaking is Coming

The writer reminds these tempted Christians that God's voice shook the earth at Sinai:

> At that time his voice shook the earth, but now he has promised, "Yet once more I will shake not only the earth but also the heavens." This phrase, "Yet once more," indicates the removal of things that are shaken—that is, things that have been made—in order that the things that cannot be shaken may remain. (Heb. 12:26–27)

A greater shaking than that of Sinai is yet to come (Hagg. 2:6). Here the writer pushes us forward to the great theme of the return of Christ. This shaking will be the final shaking of heaven and earth. The whole created order will shake and tremble at the Lord's terrible voice. All that is insecure will be shaken apart and driven away. All that the Lord himself has established, and that alone, will remain.

An Unshakable Kingdom

The sovereign Lord will establish his unshakeable kingdom. "Therefore let us be grateful for receiving a kingdom that cannot be shaken, and thus let us offer to God acceptable worship, with reverence and awe, for our God is a consuming fire" (12:29–30). What can possibly survive the shaking that is coming when the Lord comes "in flaming fire taking vengeance on them that know not God, and that obey not the gospel of our Lord Jesus Christ: who shall be punished with everlasting destruction from the presence of the Lord, and from the glory of his power" (2 Thess. 1:8–9, AV). But look! Even though the kingdom waits to be established in its consummated state by Jesus' second coming, we are already by faith its citizens, and his city is our deepest reality: "Therefore let us be grateful for receiving a kingdom that cannot be shaken" (12:27a).

Have you ever stopped to think that the only people who actually possess anything, that is, possess anything *with permanence*, are Christians? The promise of God to his people is unshakable, unchanged and will remain unshaken at the judgment.

> Lift up your eyes to the heavens, and look upon the
> earth beneath: for the heavens shall vanish away like
> smoke, and the earth shall wax old like a garment,
> and they that dwell therein shall die in like manner:
> but my salvation shall be forever, and my righteous-
> ness shall not be abolished. (Isa. 51:6, AV)

Gratitude

"Therefore let us be grateful for receiving a kingdom that cannot be shaken" (12:28). Here, on the basis of the promise of the
permanent in our immutable salvation, is the exhortation to
gratitude. Our hearts should break with joy at the thought that
when the earth shall melt with fervent heat (2 Pet. 3:1–18), we
shall stand. Like Peter, the writer of Hebrews exhorts to gratitude and holy living in view of the coming of the Lord: "Since all
these things are thus to be dissolved, what sort of people ought
you to be in lives of holiness and godliness" (2 Pet. 3:11).

The proper response to grace is gratitude. When we consider that we belong to an unshakeable kingdom, we marvel to
remember that we will be spared when the world goes up in fire.
We have a part in the new heavens and earth, and we are amazed
that "since the beginning of the world men have not heard, nor
perceived by ear, neither hath the eye seen, O God, beside thee,
what he hath prepared for him that waiteth for him" (Isa. 51:6,
AV). We can be grateful that we belong to an unshakeable kingdom because our Lord Jesus is the immutable God:

> You, Lord, laid the foundation of the earth in the be-
> ginning, and the heavens are the work of your hands;
> they will perish, but you remain; they will wear out
> like a garment, like a robe you will roll them up, like a
> garment they will be changed. But you are the same,
> and your years will have no end. (Heb. 1:10–12)

Our gratitude and all that is written here produces a worshipful attitude: "and thus let us offer to God acceptable worship, with reverence and awe, for our God is a consuming fire" (Heb. 12:28–29). Since these awesome realities are revealed, let us worship God in that way which is *acceptable*, that is, through God's Son our High Priest, and in that way prescribed in the Holy Scriptures. The attitude and the ethos of worship are also addressed. We are to worship God "with reverence and awe, for our God is a consuming fire."

This needs underscoring in our day perhaps more than ever. The church has brought pop culture into her worship. This is clearly wrong. Pop culture does not focus on the timeless and permanent and is consistent with the relativism of our society. The Christian faith is no new thing; it is old and cannot be properly expressed by "pop" culture. We should not think we can impose a form on Reformed worship that is foreign to its theology without ill effects, in time, on our doctrine and life. Our forms should reflect the weight and significance of the worship to which we are called, and pop culture cannot do that because it is wedded to triviality. A "worship" driven by the present hour simply cannot lift us up in mind and heart to the Holy God, before whom we are called to bow.

One of the distressing things about the changes that have been made in Presbyterian worship is that those who have made the changes have done so with little theological reflection, with little or no concern for the past, and no consideration for where it might lead. As a friend said to me, it is like a golfer who goes to tee off and sets the driver head just slightly off kilter; it *will* have an effect! But many of us have intentionally reset the driver head with no thought to where it will lead long term.

In applying this command to worship "with reverence and awe," it seems that many in today's church have forgotten that worship is not for unbelievers. I am not saying that unbelievers should be ignored in worship, nor am I saying that the worship of believers has no evangelistic impact. Paul tells us in 1 Corinthians 14 that an unbeliever in the midst of God's worshiping people might well be converted; but, he does not suggest that the service be determined by the presence of unbelievers among us.

This is basic Pauline theology; men dead in trespasses and sins cannot worship God. Linguistic intelligibility aside, the vocabulary and grammar of the Christian religion is incomprehensible to the unconverted. Instead of removing the difficulties, we should see this principle as an opportunity to highlight the antithesis between the Church and the world and explain the gospel in its own terms. Comprehension of worship requires the work of the Holy Spirit and long exposure. "Reverence and awe"; here we have the missing note in worship today. Reverence and awe are not principles that come and go in worship. We are commanded in the Bible to express reverence and awe at every single point.

This is the note that has, in large measure, defined Reformed worship in the past, though it is very much neglected or intentionally set aside today. Since our worship is offered with reverence and awe because of the nature of our God as "consuming fire," the point is simply that God's holiness determines our worship. At any point that this is set aside, worship has gone astray. This is another reason that worship cannot be offered by unbelievers and further evidence that worship must not be determined by the tastes and trends of unbelievers. Worship must be congruent with God's holiness. Reverence and awe must pervade every aspect of worship just as God's holiness is true of all of God's attributes. Indeed, the conclusions concerning worship drawn from this chapter confirm what John Owen somewhere said: "[Worship] is performed in heaven. Though they who perform it are on earth, yet they do it, by faith, in heaven."[6]

One implication of all of this is that when an unbeliever walks into a worship service, he should sense that he has walked into a different universe, because that is what is happening. It should be disconcerting and uncomfortable to him. Worship should not resemble what can be received from other sources, such as television, clips from movies, etc. There should be no gimmicks in worship. Moreover, God's people are refreshed when the worship context is different from what they have experienced through the week.

Final Applications

Hebrews 12:26–27 should remind us that believers in Christ are the only ones who really possess anything. A Christian may have little in this life, he may be in prison and his ankles in shackles, but he has Christ, everlasting life, and the promise of "an inheritance that is imperishable, undefiled, and unfading" (1 Pet. 1:4). An unbeliever, by contrast, may have mansions and mountains of gold in this life, but he can take none of it with him to hell. A shaking is coming and those who do not belong to God's kingdom will be shaken with the convulsions that overtake the world when Christ returns in glory. The shaking spoken of in Hebrews 12 is referenced by Peter as the conflagration of the universe (2 Pet. 3:7, 10). Samuel Davies, the eighteenth century father of Southern Presbyterianism in America, spoke movingly to unbelievers about that day:

> Let us now enter upon the majestic scene. But alas! what images shall I use to represent it? Nothing that we have ever seen, nothing that we have ever heard, nothing that has ever happened on the stage of time,

---

6. From the sermon, "The Nature and Beauty of Gospel Worship," by John Owen.

can furnish us with proper illustrations. All is low and groveling, all is faint and obscure that ever the sun shone upon, when compared with the grand phenomena of that day; and we are so accustomed to low and little objects, that it is impossible we should ever raise our thoughts to a suitable pitch of elevation. Ere long, we shall be amazed spectators of these majestic wonders, and our eyes and our ears will be our instructors. But now it is necessary we should have such ideas of them as may affect our hearts, and prepare us for them. Let us therefore present to our view, those representations which divine revelation, our only guide in this case, gives us of the person of the Judge, and the manner of His appearance; of the resurrection of the dead, and the transformation of the living; of the universal convention of all the sons of men before the supreme tribunal; of their separation to the right and left hand of the Judge, according to their characters; of the judicial process itself; of the decisive sentence; of its execution, and of the conflagration of the world.[7]

Can anything more evince the rebellion and inability of fallen humanity than that we can hear this and remain unmoved and unsaved? Apart from the regeneration of the Holy Spirit, we will continue in sin rather than bow before the judgment of God. By contrast, the citizen of the heavenly kingdom has come to Jesus' blood. The accusing voice of sin and the law has been silenced. We are forgiven of our sins, and when the conflagration of the world comes, those under the value of Jesus' blood will not perish and will not be shaken.

Let us therefore hear him who speaks (12:25) and live with gratitude for this marvel of belonging to a kingdom that cannot be shaken.

---

7. Samuel Davies, "The Universal Judgment," in *Substance of Sermons* (New York: M. W. Dodd, 1851), 144.

> Everything in the new dispensation is solid. We have
> not the emblem of Divinity, but God Himself; not a
> typical expiation, but a real atonement; not bodily
> purifications, but spiritual holiness: all is spiritual, all
> is real, all is permanent. How happy is the individual
> who is interested in this new and better economy.[8]

These things being revealed, let us be loose in our hearts
from shaking things, loose from the temporary, from those
things that pass away. Let us live life in the reality of the coming
of Christ, the conflagration of the universe, and in the knowledge that the shaking of heaven and earth will come with fervent heat. "Since these things are thus to be dissolved, what sort
of people ought you to be in lives of holiness and godliness" (2
Pet. 3:11). That means when shaking things come now, those
things that shake the world before the return of Christ, king-
doms tottering, political upheaval, and personal tragedy, let us
see these things as adumbrations of the great shaking that is to
come and live faithfully in the present. Contrast how a believer
and unbeliever might face such times. When the stock market
crashed in 1929 many people took their own lives because they
lost everything—again the believer is the only one who really
possesses anything! By contrast the example of Dutch theologian G. H. Kersten is instructive as his world convulsed under
the bombs of Nazi aircraft. In the afternoon of May 14, 1940
the pastor's hometown of Rotterdam was bombed by the Nazis.
Here is what Kersten wrote:

> When the streets in the vicinity of our home were
> set aflame, even hospitals were destroyed, and our
> home shook on its foundations and the floor heaved
> under our feet, I was privileged to bow under God's
> justice and to worship His majesty in the midst of
> judgment. I do not write this to exalt myself. By na-

---

8. John Brown, *Hebrews* (Edinburgh: Banner of Truth, 1983), 664.

ture we are all rebels against God; however, God's grace humbles, and that humility gave me peace and helped me to calm my family. This has compelled me to admonish the people in both writing and preaching to bow before God and acknowledge that He has not dealt with us according to our sins.[9]

How true, as Jeremiah Burroughs put it:

> True fear and trembling at the Word is that which will settle the heart and strengthen the heart against all other fears. . . . The more fear there is of God's Word, the less fear there will be of any creature in the world. It is the only way to free you from all fears whatsoever.[10]

These truths encourage us now and give confidence for the future. As Palmer Robertson has wisely noted:

> Hebrews speaks directly against harmful self-understandings of the people of God today. The church is not an established institution that draws its strength by connections with political, social, financial, cultural or educational establishments. Instead, God's people of the wilderness transcend all these temporal organizations as a community that is in the world but not of this world. Whenever and wherever these other institutions crumble, their fall will never function as a harbinger of the fate of the church.[11]

This applies as well to the end of all things. When the Lord Jesus returns and plays the organ of the Last Day and pulls out the

---

9. M. Golverdingen, *Rev. G. H. Kersten: Facets of His Life and Work,* translator Bartel Elshout (Grand Rapids: Netherlands Reformed Publishing, 2008), 202.

10. Jeremiah Burroughs, *Gospel Fear* (Orlando, FL, Soli Deo Gloria, 1991), 36.

11. O. Palmer Robertson, *God's People in the Wilderness* (Ross-shire, Scotland: Christian Focus, 2009), 145–146.

stops,[12] shaking the earth and heavens, the Christian will stand when the world will not.

Listen! God's Word to Moses was so alarming that the people begged Moses to be their mediator. God's Word has come to us from heaven and we turn—not to Moses—but to Jesus as Mediator of the New Covenant who secures true believers in his loving, yet awe-filled promise of redemption! Do you know the Lord Jesus? Can you say with the hymn writer, "When all around my hope gives way, He then is all my hope and stay; On Christ the solid rock I stand, all other ground is sinking sand"? When the conflagration of the world takes place at the coming of Christ, and all shakes to pieces, the people of God will sing: "Built on the Rock, the church doth stand."

---

12. An image suggested to me while reading Klaas Schilder.

24

Pastoral Exhortations

HEBREWS 13:1–25

Let brotherly love continue.

I will never forget the power of the exhortation delivered by my friend Roland Barnes when he charged me before Presbytery as a part of my licensure to preach the gospel. "David," he said, "You must love the church of Christ no matter how spotted or blemished she may be for she is purchased with his own blood." Through thick and thin in gospel ministry, Roland's simple, profound exhortation has come to me again and again. When I have felt like giving up, when mistreated or misunderstood, when overwhelmed by duties, and when I have felt discouraged by lack of progress, I have remembered my friend's exhortation. Exhortation can be a powerful thing in a believer's life. Therefore it should not surprise us that, as the author of Hebrews comes to the end of his sermon-epistle, he concludes with a number of pastoral exhortations.

Having dwelt upon what may be viewed as the high point of the epistle and final warning, with reminders of our privileges and obligations that call us to "see that you refuse not him who is speaking" and to "offer to God acceptable worship, with reverence and awe, for our God is a consuming fire" (12:25,

28–29)—the following exhortations might appear to be abrupt. This would be a mistake, however. The writer is underscoring the reality of doctrine deep down in the heart; that is, a right understanding of these truths will have an impact on how the Christian lives. Essentially the writer is saying, "If you understand the message, this is how it will look in your life."

To use the words of the Westminster Confession, the preacher of Hebrews wants the readers to understand the "communion of the saints," that those who are "united to one another in love, . . . have communion in each other's gifts and graces; and are obliged to the performance of such duties, publick and private, as do conduce to their mutual good, both in the inward and outward man" (XXVI.I). The author's pastoral heart has shown through continually, and here he wants his readers to know that believing the message that he proclaims will result inevitably in changed lives.

Pastoral Exhortations

Love One Another

The first three verses are a call to love one another within the church. The writer begins this section with the general exhortation: "Let brotherly love continue" (13:1). Even though this exhortation is of perennial concern in the church, the need for such exhortation can become acute in times of persecution. Some of the audience of Hebrews may have been tempted to withdraw from persecuted brothers in order to avoid persecution themselves. This would have been especially tempting when so many were already harboring thoughts of returning to Judaism due to its protected status in the empire. Hence the writer calls them to continue their prior example of brotherly love (*philadelphia*). This brotherly love, with its sympathetic kindness and helpfulness is a consistent theme in the New Testament epistles (Rom. 12:10; 1 Thess. 4:9; 1 Pet. 1:22; 2 Pet. 1:7; 1 John 3:16ff). Christ has died for us and shown everlasting love; let us then, even and especially in times of trial, show love one for another.

Friendliness to Strangers

"Do not neglect to show hospitality to strangers, for thereby some have entertained angels unawares" (13:2). This is, it seems, an exhortation to care for Christians who may travel. Perhaps some are traveling on business, or are ministers preaching the gospel (3 John 5), while others are possibly displaced because of persecution. Ancient accommodations were often unsafe and morally decadent, presenting dangers for traveling Christians.

Moreover, to share a meal was an extension of friendship in the ancient east. In the history of God's people, some have entertained angels without knowing it—such as Abraham (Gen. 18:1–3), Lot (Gen. 19:1–2), Gideon (Judg. 6:11ff), and Monoah (Judg. 13:6–20). The writer does not seem to suggest that we may also be entertaining angels when hosting strangers, but that the Lord is honored when his servants show such hospitality.

Concern for the Prisoner

The hospitable heart of the people of God is shown also in the loving care of prisoners who suffer for the faith. "Remember those who are in prison, as though in prison with them, and those who are mistreated, since you also are in the body." Did not our Lord make this very point in Matthew 25?

> For I was hungry and you gave me food, I was thirsty and you gave me drink, I was a stranger and you welcomed me, I was naked and you clothed me, I was sick and you visited me, I was in prison and you came to me . . . Truly, I say to you, as you did it to one of the least of these my brothers, you did it to me. (Matt. 25:35–36, 40)

If one suffers, we all suffer (1 Cor. 12:26). We are called to "rejoice with those who rejoice" as well as to "weep with those who weep" (Rom. 12:15). It is understandable that in times of persecution a Christian might become cautious and even be tempted to become obsequious; but, the temptation to stay away from brothers in prison out of fear must be resisted. When possible, persecuted prisoners should be visited and their needs met.

To "remember those who are in prison" must include as much relief of their dire circumstances as may be possible. When the State does not allow us to care for fellow believers in prison, the church has recourse always to the throne of grace. An example of this is the bold prayer of God's people in Acts when Peter and John were imprisoned before the counsel (Acts 4:23–31).

Those "in prison, and those who are mistreated" must be remembered "since you also are in the body." This is not a reference to the body of Christ but to the physical body; there but by the grace of God go I! Indeed, we are one in Christ with our persecuted brothers, and so we suffer "as though in prison with them." The writer has already had occasion to remind the believers of their faithfulness, which included a display of "compassion on those in prison" during persecution (10:32–39). So now, he calls them to persevere and bind together in persecuting times.

Faithfulness in Marriage

The writer next calls upon believers to be faithful in the marriage covenant. "Let marriage be held in honor among all, and let the marriage bed be undefiled, for God will judge the sexually immoral and adulterous" (13:4). That the writer stresses this should be no surprise. Living, as the early church did, in the midst of paganism, sexual temptation was great and called for careful and deliberate Christian commitment. The writer exhorts believers to regard marriage as an honorable estate and calls them to sexual fidelity in view of the judgment of God upon the "sexually immoral and adulterous."

It is not only overt persecution that can pull one away from his profession; the stresses of cultural expectations, and the disdain for morality can "wear down" the Christian who is not vigilant. The Lord God is judge; God "will judge the sexually immoral and adulterous." Christians must live life in view of the coming of Christ and the judgment of the last day. Our choices and actions must be determined by the past—what Christ has done for us—and by the future—God's promise to judge the world and usher us into the new heavens and new earth. We do not live for the present but for Christ, who has purchased a bright future for us, no matter our lot in this world. "Since all these things are thus to be dissolved, what sort of people ought you to be in lives of holiness and godliness" (2 Pet. 3:11).

This passage and others like it are pertinent to the cultural paganism that has engulfed the Western world. People are terribly confused about marriage and sexuality. This is to be expected from the world, but sadly much of the professing church shares this confusion. What can we expect when we forsake the Word of God as our sole authority of faith and practice? For many today, the whole concept of marriage is no longer acceptable; portions of the marriage vows seem archaic and are replaced by sentimental exchanges of good wishes. The idea of male headship and of the wife's submission is considered nonsense. The truth revealed in God's Word that marriage is between one man and one woman is considered bigoted.

But God has spoken; and we go back to the beginning in which God has, right from the first, shown the way (Gen. 2:15–25). The world is indeed confused, but there is no excuse for the church to share that confusion. The church must bow before King Jesus who in royal authority has revealed his will in inscripturated revelation. The Westminster Confession clearly summarizes what the Bible teaches about marriage, reflecting the language of the *Book of Common Prayer*: "Marriage was ordained for the mutual help of husband and wife; for the increase of mankind with a legitimate issue, and of the church with an holy seed and for the prevention of uncleanness" (XXIV.II). Oh, for a return to the biblical reality of what marriage truly is and to the preaching of the judgment upon those who disregard it. Indeed, that this follows the exhortation to brotherly love reminds us that being faithful to one's wife not only honors the Lord, but also serves our spouse and others around us.

Contentment

Living for Christ in persecuting times can bring in its wake the peculiar temptation to be discontented with our lot in life. Hence the exhortation:

> Keep your life free from love of money, and be content with what you have, for he has said, "I will never leave you nor forsake you." So we can confidently say,
>
> > "The Lord is my helper;
> > I will not fear;
> > what can man do to me?" (13:5–6)

Perhaps loss of property tempted some to hold to possessions inordinately (10:34). The preacher warns his hearers against a life dominated by "love of money" (*aphilaguros*) for, as Paul wrote, "the love of money is a root of all kinds of evils" (1 Tim. 6:10). Further, "now there is great gain in godliness with contentment, for we brought nothing into the world, and we cannot take anything out of the world" (1 Tim. 6:6–7).

The writer would have his hearers be free from the worries and anxieties that can accompany the spoiling of our possessions in persecution. He does not suggest that money and material goods are unimportant, but would have these believers put it all into perspective: to love the Lord, not money; to trust in Christ, not material things. This is why the writer focuses on two Old Testament passages in order to promote contentment of heart. The promise of the Lord to Joshua in Joshua 1:5 is a promise to us, "I will never leave you nor forsake you." With confidence, the believer can recite with the Psalmist: "The Lord is my helper; I will not fear; what can man do to me?" (Ps. 118:6). The believer has all things in Christ and should be content in that knowledge.

Remembering Former Leaders

The mature Christian will gather up the fragments of past experience and learn from the former stresses, strains, and instructions of the past. Especially when persecuted or threatened by the state or other hostile forces, the believer is wise to apply former lessons that the Lord has taught in our Christian experience. Therefore, the writer exhorts his readers to "remember your leaders, those who spoke to you the word of God. Consider the outcome of their way of life, and imitate their faith" (v. 7). Here the minister of the Word has an immediate justification to immerse himself in ministerial biography! Those of us who are motivated to read about the Reformed fathers of the past most often do so from this very motive in the text before us. How we learn and are inspired to push on as we read of Calvin, Edwards, or Davies. This is but one of many applications of the exhortation.

From observing the work of God in the lives of former godly leaders, we take to heart experientially in the reality that "Jesus Christ is the same yesterday and today and forever" (v. 8). We follow our former leaders in the faith by relying as they did upon the immutability of Christ's love, grace, and promise. Every generation of believers has proven Christ's commitment to his people in the covenant of grace.

There also seems to be some connection of thought between the exhortation to "remember your leaders" and the command "do not be led away by diverse and strange teachings, for it is good for the heart to be strengthened by grace, not by foods, which have not benefited those devoted to them" (13:9). Believers must be sound in the faith passed down, holding on to the truth tenaciously, refusing to be led astray. Rather than having a heart that can be led away from truth, the writer would see in his readers "the heart . . . strengthened by grace." They must resist the temptation to return to Jewish rites and rituals, to "foods, which have not benefited those devoted to them."

Bruce adds that the language should not be limited to Jewish dietary law:

> The language here suggests something more than a relapsing into orthodox Judaism; it reminds us of Paul's appeal to the Colossian Christians not to let any one sit in judgment on them in respect to food or drink, because things like these disappeared in the very act of being used; regulations and prohibitions regarding such evanescent things provided no spiritual support or defence (Col. 2:16, 21ff; 1 Cor. 8:8).

Indeed, "rules about food, imposed by external authority, have never helped people to maintain a closer walk with God."[1] Rather than dependence upon those things that pass—spider webs that can hold no weight—the writer encourages these Jewish Christians to become firmer and more committed to the One who never passes away, never changes, and never needs replacement.

Separation to Christ

The ultimate typology of atonement points to the fact that attributing salvific significance to food and dietary regulations is contrary to the point of Christ's sacrifice for us. "We have an

---

1. F. F. Bruce, *Hebrews* (Grand Rapids: Eerdmans, 1979), 397–398.

altar from which those who serve the tent have no right to eat. For the bodies of those animals whose blood is brought into the holy places by the high priest as a sacrifice for sin are burned outside the camp" (13:10–11). On the Day of Atonement, the sacrifices were not eaten but burned outside the camp.

> And the bull for the sin offering and the goat for the sin offering, whose blood was brought in to make atonement in the Holy Place, shall be carried outside the camp. Their skin and their flesh and their dung shall be burned with fire. (Lev. 16:27)

The Priests had no right to eat of the sacrifices offered on that Day. Christ, once offered for our sins, is the nourishment of his redeemed people; Jesus, not food and dietary laws, provides our spiritual refreshment. The *altar* that we now have, then, is "a metonym for the sacrificial death of Jesus."[2]

The sin offering was taken outside the camp. "So Jesus also suffered outside the gate in order to sanctify the people through his own blood" (13:12). The removal of the sin offering outside the camp of Israel was intended to stress the removal of sin, and the shame associated with sin, from Israel. In like manner, Jesus our sacrifice redeemed us from sin and shame. His purpose was to sanctify us, removing our guilt, and to give us free access to God by his blood. Christ's death outside the camp on a by-way outside Jerusalem was the death of a common criminal. We who are Christ's are committed to following him and bearing his reproach.

"Therefore let us go to him outside the camp and bear the reproach he endured" (13:13). Moses also had born this reproach. "He considered the reproach of Christ greater wealth than the treasures of Egypt, for he was looking to the reward" (11:26). For the Jewish believer to bear Christ's reproach meant that Ju-

---

2. Marie E. Issacs, "Hebrews 13:9–16 Revisited," *New Testament Studies* 43 (1997): 268–284.

daistic family members might reject them, that social and political pressures would be weighty, and that the state might persecute them. This remains the calling of every believer in Christ until the Lord Jesus returns. Along with Moses, we must see the reproach of Christ as "greater wealth" than the passing wealth that is offered by the world through compromise.

What is the greater wealth? Once again, reflecting what the writer has already taught in chapter 11, it is the inheritance that awaits us. Always the writer pushes us forward to perseverance in view of the great blessings that await the believer purchased for us by Christ. "For here we have no lasting city, but we seek the city that is to come" (13:14 with 11:10, 16; 12:28). We are strangers and aliens, just as surely as were the patriarchs.

Are we wholehearted in our identity with the Lord Jesus, ready to bear his reproach, and longing for the city to come? Is our gaze fixed ahead on that promised inheritance so that, come what may, we persevere with that promise galvanizing our hearts and determining our actions? "Let us go to him outside the camp."

It should not be lost on us that those who murdered the Savior included the religious establishment of his day, the official Jewish establishment. While we should always encourage a strong doctrine of the church and call every Christian convert to associate himself with a true expression of the church locally, let us remember that much that calls itself Christian today is false to Christ and denies the faith once delivered to the saints. In many instances, going outside the camp may be a call to separate from false religious establishments that call themselves Christian while bearing the reproach of association with a church that is faithful to the Word of God.

Examples of this abound. J. Gresham Machen bore the reproach of Christ "outside the camp" when liberalism gained the upper hand in the Presbyterian Church, U.S.A. Before him,

Pastoral Exhortations

Charles Spurgeon left the Baptist Union due to its unbelief. Even in the professing church (as distinguished from faithful expressions of the church), we have abundant evidence of the fact that we are strangers and aliens and have no abiding city here.

Spiritual Offerings

Oh, how beautifully the writer of Hebrews has extolled the once for all and sufficient sacrifice of Christ! Is there no sacrifice that remains for us? Only this, the sacrifices of praise and service offered through our great high priest. Only Christ can atone for sin; we who trust in him offer our hearts in praise. "Through him let us continually offer up a sacrifice of praise to God, that is, the fruit of lips that acknowledge his name" (13:15). In addition to the paean of praise offered from the lips we are called upon to serve others to the praise of God's name. "Do not neglect to do good and to share what you have, for such sacrifices are pleasing to God" (13:16). Having pointed to 1 Peter 2:5 and Romans 12:1, F. F. Bruce wisely adds:

> Christianity is sacrificial through and through; it is founded on the one self-offering of Christ, and of the offering of His people's praise and property, of their service and their lives, is caught up into the perfection of His acceptable sacrifice, and is accepted in Him.[3]

The sacrifice of praise is costly, but what of it? The Lord Jesus has paid the price for our sins and his once for all and sufficient sacrifice *for us* calls *from us* lives that live for his glory. Pastor Richard Wurmbrand, who suffered great persecution for his faith at the hands of atheistic communists, once told of an unusual trip he took with the communicants class of his church. He took them to the zoo and held services outside the lion's den in Bucharest to prepare them to stand for Christ against the

---

3 F. F. Bruce, *Hebrews*, 407.

roaring lion that "walketh about, seeking whom he may devour" (1 Pet. 5:8).

Yes, the sacrifice of praise and of service will be offered amidst the demands of living for Christ in a fallen world with joy in the knowledge of the victorious conquest of sin and guilt accomplished by Christ our penal substitute. How can we fail, whatever the circumstance, to offer praise to our King? We Christians are loved, loved eternally, loved incredibly, loved magnificently, forgiven of infinite debt, we commune with our covenant Lord, we are children of the King, we are upon his heart, and the intercessions of Christ our Priest secures our perseverance to the end: how can we do other than offer a sacrifice of praise?

Obey and Encourage Your Leaders from the Heart

A sacrificial heart keeps us from carping and is inconsistent with a spirit of idle criticism.

> Obey your leaders and submit to them, for they are keeping watch over your souls, as those who will have to give an account. Let them do this with joy and not with groaning, for that would be of no advantage to you.

The elders of the church carry a heavy load watching our souls and will give an account for it. While the God gives serious directives to leaders about their duties, he also, as we find here, instructs congregants to walk with care, *encouraging* their leaders rather than dragging them down in spirit and burdening them with rebellious behavior. The leaders "will have to give an account." Let this inform the minster and elders at every turn.

The watchfulness of the Teaching and Ruling Elders is a solemn reality. "Keeping watch" is from the same verb found in Ephesians 6:18, in which believers are called to be alert in prayer in our battle with cosmic darkness. Leaders are constantly called to watch over the flock (2 Cor. 11:28; 1 Pet. 5:2; Acts 20:28). To keep watch over *souls* reminds the reader of the leaders' deep and serious responsibility in light of a solemn eternity. Charles Simeon preached a sermon that should remind church leaders of the depth of seriousness in their call. A hearer recalls:

> I remember well his preaching a most striking sermon on ministerial duties and faithfulness, in which he introduced, with a view to illustration, the keeper of the lighthouse on Inch-keith, the island situated in the middle of the Firth of Forth. He supposed the keeper to have let the light go out, and that in consequence the coast was strewed with wrecks and with dead and mangled bodies; and that the wailings of widows and orphans were everywhere heard. He supposed the delinquent brought out for examination before the full court and an assembled people; and at the last the answer to be given by him, that he was "asleep."—"Asleep!" The way in which he made "asleep!" burst on the ears of his audience, who were hanging in perfect stillness on his lips, contrasting the cause with the effects, I remember to this day.[4]

Oh! What a calling is that of the shepherd of a flock! How serious is his responsibility.

Even the most conscientious leaders are flawed and faulty, however. Ryle reminds us, as Whitby rightly wrote: "The best of overseers do sometimes make oversights." Ryle adds:

> Fault-finding is the easiest of all tasks. There never was a system upon earth, in which man had anything to do, in which faults, and many faults too, might not soon be found. We must expect to find imperfections in every visible Church upon earth. There always were such in the New Testament Churches. There always will be such now. There is only one

4 Handley C. G. Moule, *Charles Simeon* (London: Inter-Varsity,1948), 74.

Church without spot or blemish. That is the one true
Church, the body of Christ, which Christ shall present to His Father in the last great day.[5]

It should be the believers' design to help the leaders in their
calling, "to let them do this with joy and not with groaning, for
that would be of no advantage to you" (13:17). The church is
therefore to *obey* and to *submit* to the leadership. This does not
mean that the church is to overlook unbiblical doctrine or behavior on the part of her leaders; such an assumption would
be far removed from the concerns of the author. It does mean,
however, that the people of God must have a good doctrine of
the church, and that the flock must realize that obedience to officers facilitates the communion of the saints.

Pray for Church Leadership

The writer, as a leader himself, notes one major way in which
congregants can assist their leaders: "Pray for us, for we are sure
that we have a clear conscience, desiring to act honorably in
all things" (v. 18). Since the faithful leaders of the church are
used of the Lord for the extension of Christ's name and kingdom, they have a "bull's eye" painted on them. Faithful men are
Satan's targets and can know peculiarly strong temptations and
stresses. The faithful minister and elder will function with "a
clear conscience" and will "desire to act honorably in all things."
Universal obedience is the aim, and integrity in both the inner
man and outward acts. No wonder the writer says "pray for us."
That prayer, in this case, included the specific request of personal restoration to these Christians he loves so much. "I urge
you the more earnestly to do this in order that I may be restored
to you the sooner" (13:19).

Ask yourself: "Do I love the church as these exhortations
call me to? Do I pray for the minister as he studies, for the wor-

---

5 J. C. Ryle, *Knots Untied* (London: William Hunt, 1879), 286.

ship services before we meet, for the preaching of the Word to bless our hearts? Do I pray for the elders in their heavy responsibilities, and the deacons as they assist the elders in innumerable tasks? Do I love the church of Christ no matter how spotted and blemished she may be?"

25

Benediction

HEBREWS 13:20–25

Now may the God of peace who brought again from the dead our Lord Jesus, the great shepherd of the sheep, by the blood of the eternal covenant, equip you with everything good that you may do his will, working in us that which is pleasing in his sight, through Jesus Christ, to whom be glory forever and ever. Amen.

For many Christians, the benediction is among the most glorious moments in worship. With raised hands, the minister pronounces a biblical blessing on the congregation. The benediction is at once a naming ceremony, in which God's people are reminded of who they are, and a prayer for blessing. Believers walk out of the service refreshed in his Word, having offered praise to the Lord and with the blessing of the Triune God ringing in their ears. This portion of Hebrews contains such a benediction.

The glorious benediction of 13:20–21 is climactic, wondrous, and filled with encouragement. The benediction in many ways summarizes the epistle-sermon's stress on assurance of faith on the basis of Christ's finished work.

Remember, the letter was written to Christians suffering trials leading to exhaustion. They found it difficult to reconcile the fact that Jesus has come with the ongoing trials of the Christian life. How could the kingdom have come in Christ while such suffering seems normative in the Christian life? As a capstone to the encouragement that permeates Hebrews to live in the reality of the priestly work of Christ, the writer now pronounces this profound benediction. The benediction is also a prayer.

Our Ground of Confidence

The readers are directed away from their consternation to "the God of peace." God in all of the fullness of his character and attributes is the font of our peace. *Peace* means far more than tranquility. The *shalom* of the Old Testament brings with it the sense of complete well being; in a word, salvation. Our God is the source of our salvation. He is ready, willing, and able to save. How necessary to dwell on this theme in light of modern substitutes for the biblical doctrine of God. The God of modern theology is not able to intervene. He is an abstract idea—not the personal God of the Bible. The God of Scripture is the living God who has come in mercy to save us! How has he done this?

God's Mighty Act of Redemption

In Christ's Crucifixion

The Lord is the source of his people's peace by the mighty redemption he has brought to them through Christ crucified. There are two wondrous and inseparable acts mentioned here that form one complex of redeeming love and intervention into our fallen state. The first is found in the expression "who through the blood of the eternal covenant." The ground of our peace could be nothing other than redemption through the cross. This means that the cross has met our need in all of the possible relations in which it was necessary. Our need of reconciliation by the removal of God's wrath, the removal of guilt, the imputation of righteousness, are all accomplished through Jesus' shed blood.

The preacher's reference to "the blood of the eternal covenant" brings Exodus 24 to mind. There, as the covenant was confirmed, we read:

> And Moses took half of the blood and put it in basins, and half of the blood he threw against the altar. Then he took the Book of the Covenant and read it in the hearing of the people. And they said, "All that the LORD has spoken we will do, and we will be obedient." And Moses took the blood and threw it on the people and said, "Behold the blood of the covenant that the LORD has made with you in accordance with all these words. (Exod. 24:6–8)

This confirmation of the covenant pointed ahead to the accomplishment of atonement through the blood of Christ the King, predicted by Zechariah, who says "As for you also, because of the blood of the covenant with you, I will set your prisoners free from the waterless pit" (Zech. 9:11). The new covenant established in Christ's blood (Jer. 31:31; Mark14:24) is the ground of our peace.

This covenant is *eternal* because there is nothing provisional about the sacrifice of Christ. His blood poured out particularly for his people secured for them an everlasting relationship with God. The cup of God's judgment has not merely been sipped by our Lord; the cup has been drained. Through Christ's shed blood, the Lord proclaims that he will remember our sins no more forever. Our sins judicially were laid upon Christ; the guilt of our sin was borne by our substitute. Therefore, he has secured for us an everlasting relationship with God. As Calvin puts it, Christ's shed blood "brings forth its fruit as though it were always flowing."[1] Calvin rightly associates this thought with the resurrection, the second act of salvation rehearsed in our text.

Here is covenant theology indeed, rich and filled with comfort! Charles Spurgeon wrote words that should thrill the heart of any believer:

> Covenant theology glorifies God alone. There are other theologies abroad which magnify men; they give him a finger in his own salvation, and so leave him a reason for throwing up his cap and saying, "Well done I;" but covenant theology puts man aside, and makes him a debtor and a receiver. It does, as it were, plunge him into the sea of infinite grace and unmerited favour, and it makes him give up all boasting, stopping the mouth that could have boasted by filling it with floods of love, so that it cannot utter a vainglorious word. A man saved by the covenant must give all the glory to God's holy name, for to God all the glory belongs. In salvation wrought by the covenant the Lord has exclusive glory.[2]

In Christ's Resurrection from the Dead

"Now may the God of peace who brought again from the dead our Lord Jesus"; the Lord who died is the Lord who was raised from the tomb. The resurrection is the resurrection of the crucified Lord. The language reflects Isaiah 63:11 (LXX). In that passage, Moses the shepherd of Israel, is delivered with God's flock from Egyptian bondage. This prefigures God's deliverance of Jesus from the dead who is the shepherd of his flock. That flock consists of the many sons whom he brings to glory. One who is greater than Moses has come.

---

1. John Calvin, *Hebrews* (Grand Rapids: Eerdmans, 1979), 215.

2. Charles H. Spurgeon, *The Blood of The Covenant* in *Metropolitan Tabernacle Pulpit* (Pasadena, TX: Pilgrim Publications, 2002), 20.443.

Benediction

This comparison between the Exodus (Moses) and the resurrection of Jesus underscores the historical nature of the resurrection. Jesus' resurrection was a real resurrection, a bodily resurrection from the tomb. We confess "the third day he rose again from the dead." This is the great, grand, and indispensable message that the world needs to hear. It is also the antidote to lazy, unbelieving, careless Christian living. Because God has intervened decisively in time and space, in history, the prayer of this text can be answered in our lives.[3]

The Aim of the Petition

The benediction is also a prayer, and the aim of the petition is the sanctification of God's people. The desire of the writer is that God may "equip you with everything good that you may do his will, working in us that which is pleasing in his sight." The aim of the petition is obedience. The law of God written on the heart takes on new and deeper significance since, in the new covenant, the law is written on the heart. The writer does not envision our attempting to do God's will, to love God and our neighbor, on our own, powerless and without strength; rather, the prayer is answered in the power of a crucified and risen Christ. He will *equip* and is the one "working in us that which is pleasing in his sight." We no longer need be curved in upon ourselves but now are enamored of God's being and revelation, having regenerate hearts that long to do God's will.

The text is implicitly Trinitarian. The Holy Spirit is operative "working in us that which is pleasing in his sight." The Holy Spirit enables us to respond to the work of Christ and to look to our high priest for sustenance. The work of the Holy Spirit can never be severed from the work of our high priest, the ascended and regnant Lord. Because Jesus died, rose from the dead, and

---

3. For this thought, I am indebted to C. E. B. Cranfield, *Hebrews 13:20–21*, in *The Bible and Christian Life* (Edinburgh: T&T Clark, 1985), 146.

intercedes, we who believe must receive saving grace and our hearts must be transformed. His intercession is continually effective because his once for all offering never loses its power. In the language of Cowper: "Dear dying Lamb, thy precious blood shall never lose its power, Till all the ransomed Church of God be saved to sin no more." Since Christ has purchased his people, we are being transformed. This is accomplished "in his sight," under the watchful eye of "the God of peace, through"—that is on the basis of the mediation of—"Jesus Christ."

Doxology

No wonder the benediction ends in doxology, praise to our Savior: "to whom be glory forever and ever. Amen." This work of our High Priest in redeeming and transforming us by his grace leads to doxology. There is no sacrifice for sins left to offer for our redemption; the only sacrifice remaining is that of a life of praise (13:15). The moralist will never understand this. Obedience is always drudgery for that person whose heart knows nothing of redemption and nothing of a life of praise. Someone entering the rooms of that eminent preacher Charles Simeon found him

> so absorbed in the contemplation of the Son of God, and so overwhelmed with a display of His mercy to his soul, that he was incapable of pronouncing a single word, till at length, after an interval, in a tone of strange significance, he exclaimed "Glory, glory."[4]

Would that our lives were filled more with such doxology!

Final Greetings

In his postscript, the writer of Hebrews presses his readers one final time to take heed to all that he has written for the good of

---

4. Handley C. G. Moule, *Charles Simeon* (London: Inter-Varsity, 1948), 135.

their souls. Like the preacher finishing his sermon, he presses the essential importance of the unified design of his sermon: "I appeal to you, brothers, bear with my word of exhortation, for I have written to you briefly." The entire book of Hebrews is "a word of exhortation" which, when combined with 8:1, reminds us that the point of the book is the heavenly high priestly work of Christ. His entire book is a warm, pastoral exhortation and encouragement not to turn back but to realize the Christian life in view of the accomplishment of Christ and his ongoing ministry as high priest of his people. The book may not seem brief to us, but remember that there is much about which the author could have expounded that he did not (cp. Heb. 9:5).

We cannot know precisely the details surrounding the reference to Timothy. "You should know that our brother Timothy has been released, with whom I shall see you if he comes soon" (v. 23). Timothy is the only Christian named in Hebrews. He was known to those reading the epistle, the readers were obviously eager for news concerning him, and Timothy had evidently been confined or imprisoned though he, then, was free. In the same way, we cannot draw great conclusions from his parting greetings: "Greet all your leaders and all the saints. Those who come from Italy send you greetings."

The author concludes with the simple benediction, "Grace be with all of you" (cp. Titus 3:15). He wishes *grace* for these beloved believers, the free favor of God sovereignly extended to ill-deserving sinners. This grace finds its source in God's own will and plan. Its origin is in eternity past, its movement toward chosen sinners for whom Christ died, its promise of final perseverance, and its channel of reception is faith. For every believer, that grace remains ever available, even in the midst of temptation to turn back. "Let us then with confidence draw near to the throne of grace, that we may receive mercy and find grace to help in time of need" (Heb. 4:16). G. C. Berkouwer observed:

> In the very midst of the admonitions of Hebrews 13 comes the assurance that Jesus Christ is always the same (Heb. 13:8), and that it is good for the heart to be established by grace (Heb. 13:9). The redemptive work of Jesus Christ of which the epistle is full is never out of sight: amidst the exhortations is an altar and the Man of Sorrows suffering without the gate (Heb. 13:12), "that he might sanctify his people." All the admonitions about brotherly love and hospitality, about concern for prisoners and the purity of married life, find their point of gravity in the continual sacrifice of praise to God and in confessing his Name (Heb. 13:15). The golden ring which encloses all of sanctification is shut with the words: "Grace be with you all." (Heb. 13:25)

To which Berkouwer adds: "It cannot be denied that grace is the dominant motif in all admonition."[5]

As we conclude our study of Hebrews, we may wonder: Was the writer of Hebrews successful in his pastoral effort to keep this church in the way and to bring back some from the brink? Barnabas Lindars suggests that "the fact that Hebrews has survived for posterity perhaps permits the conclusion that this passionate appeal did not fail in its effect."[6] I think he may well be right. One thing is sure: you and I have Hebrews to read and love and are called to receive its message and to trust for persevering grace on the basis of the once-for-all sacrifice and high priestly intercession of Jesus Christ, who "is the same yesterday and today and forever" (13:8).

Soli Deo Gloria

---

5. G. C. Berkower, *Faith and Sanctification* (Grand Rapids: Eerdmans, 1952), 109.

6. Barnabas Lindars, "The Rhetorical Structure of Hebrews," *New Testament Studies* 35 (1989), 382–406.

AUTHOR

DAVID B. MCWILLIAMS (Ph.D. University of Wales) has been Senior Minister of Covenant Presbyterian Church in Lakeland, Florida, for twenty-five years. A former Associate Professor of Systematic Theology on the faculty of Westminster Theological Seminary (Dallas), he continues to teach Systematic Theology at Redeemer Theological Seminary. The author of numerous articles, he has also published, *Galatians, A Mentor Commentary.*

SERIES EDITOR

JON D. PAYNE (M.Th. New College, University of Edinburgh; D.Min., Reformed Theological Seminary) is pastor of Christ Church Presbyterian (PCA) in Charleston, South Carolina, and Visiting Lecturer in Practical Theology/Homiletics at Reformed Theological Seminary, Atlanta. He is the author of *In the Splendor of Holiness* and *John Owen on the Lord's Supper.*